AF714687

State of Data

State of Data

National Power in an Age of Infinite Memory

By

Kiran Solvay

Vij Books

New Delhi (India)

Published by

Vij Books
(Publishers, Distributors & Importers)
4836/24, 3rd Floor, Ansari Road
Delhi – 110 002
Phone: 91-11-43596460
Mobile: 98110 94883
e-mail: contact@vijpublishing.com
www.vijbooks.in

Copyright © 2026

ISBN: 978-93-7794-230-4 (PB)

All rights reserved.

No part of this publication may be reproduced, distributed, or transmitted in any form or by any means — including photocopying, recording, or other electronic or mechanical methods — without the prior written permission of the publisher, except in the case of brief quotations used in reviews or permitted by applicable copyright law.

This book was developed using advanced writing tools to support the drafting and ideation process. All content has been thoughtfully curated, refined, and reviewed to ensure quality and relevance.

Contents

Introduction

On 12 May 2017, in hospitals across England, the screens changed first. At Barts Health NHS Trust in London, staff who had begun an ordinary Friday found terminals frozen by the WannaCry ransomware attack, red warning windows replacing patient charts and appointment schedules, the antiseptic smell of wards meeting the harsh electronic ping of machines that could no longer be trusted. Ambulances were diverted. Operations were delayed. Nearly 19,000 appointments were cancelled, according to the UK National Audit Office in 2018. The immediate drama was visible enough. Less visible was the deeper fact it exposed: a modern state can be surrounded by data and still be rendered clumsy, blind, and dependent when the systems that order that data falter. The ledger was already there.

That moment was not merely a cyber incident, nor simply a story about neglected software patches. It was a glimpse of a wider condition. States now remember through sprawling technical arrangements: hospital systems, tax files, mobile networks, cloud contracts, biometric registers, intelligence databases, customs platforms, benefits software, certificate authorities, routing tables. These do not merely store facts. They organise what officials can see, what firms can infer, what police can request, what courts can verify, and what citizens are asked to accept as reasonable. Data has become less like an archive at the edge of administration and more like the operating medium of public authority itself. Memory had acquired infrastructure.

This shift is often described badly. One cliché treats data as the new oil, as if accumulation alone produced power. Another treats digital capability as a smooth escalator to efficiency, security, and growth. Both mistakes flatter quantity and neglect control. Raw records are not knowledge; knowledge is not judgment; judgment is not capacity. A state may collect immense volumes and still fail to compare, authenticate, protect, or lawfully use what it holds. It may outsource the most consequential parts of its memory to foreign suppliers while insisting on sovereignty. It may build powerful systems of monitoring while draining the trust needed to govern effectively in a crisis. The issue is not abundance. It is command over the pipelines through which records become action.

That distinction matters because the same data can animate several forms of national strength at once. A tax database, properly maintained, helps a treasury collect revenue, a fraud unit detect abuse, an anti-corruption body compare disclosures, and a government justify claims of fairness. A mobile location dataset can help trace a hostile network, optimise urban transport, or price insurance more precisely. A digital identity system can widen access to services, cut administrative error, and reduce impersonation; it can also exclude, misclassify, or centralise failure. Here lies the central tension of contemporary statecraft: the mechanisms that make a society more legible to institutions can also make citizens more exposed to institutions, markets, and adversaries. Efficiency leaves fingerprints.

India offers one of the clearest examples of this double movement. Aadhaar, launched nationally after 2009 and administered by the Unique Identification Authority of India, became the world's largest biometric identification system, with more than a billion enrolments. In New Delhi, policy ambition was easy to state: reduce leakages, simplify verification, widen access to welfare and banking, and give residents a portable means of proving identity in a fragmented administrative landscape. The concept has a name—bureaucratic legibility—and its appeal is obvious in a country of continental scale. When subsidies, pensions, and rations pass through intermediaries, any system that can compare identities at speed promises cleaner delivery and fewer ghosts in the books. Yet legibility does not arrive alone. Reports of exclusion, authentication failures, and function creep raised harder questions about who bears the cost when a grand instrument meets imperfect records, patchy connectivity, or institutional haste. In September 2018, India's Supreme Court upheld Aadhaar's constitutionality in substantial part while placing limits on some uses, notably restricting private companies' mandatory reliance on the identifier. The ruling mattered less as a tidy settlement than as a signal of the real terrain: not whether data systems are useful, but under what boundaries, with what remedies, and on whose terms.

That is why the politics of data cannot be confined to privacy debates in the narrow sense, important though those are. The stakes run through security doctrine, industrial structure, public administration, and democratic legitimacy. Consider what happened when the US Office of Personnel Management disclosed in June 2015 that sensitive background investigation records had been compromised. The agency later said 21.5 million individuals were affected, including current, former, and prospective federal employees and contractors. This was not only a theft of names and numbers. It was a penetration of trust anchored in the state's own personnel apparatus: security clearance forms, fingerprints, family histories, financial disclosures, foreign contacts, vulnerabilities. A personnel system had become an intelligence asset for someone else. The concept here is not merely confidentiality loss but strategic inference. When enough fragments are linked, a record ceases to be administrative and becomes operational. It can reveal who matters, who may be pressured, where institutional seams lie, and how future access might be cultivated. Data power emerges not from any single file but from the capacity to combine, compare, and act.

Such episodes are often narrated as cautionary tales about technology moving too quickly for law. The truth is less flattering and more interesting. The deeper contest is over control points. Undersea cables and landing stations determine routes that most users never see. Cloud contracts define who can access logs, who can isolate workloads, and who answers first when a system fails at 3 a.m. Domain name systems and certificate trust stores sit quietly beneath commerce and government, rarely noticed until a dispute or compromise turns them into matters of state. Procurement frameworks, audit standards, export controls, telecom licensing, disclosure laws, cross-border transfer rules, intelligence sharing arrangements, and incident reporting duties all help decide who can compel data, purchase it, infer it, protect it, or deny it to rivals. By the time a political scandal breaks into view, the decisive choices were often made years earlier in standards bodies, cabinet offices, infrastructure ministries, courts, and contracting teams.

The materiality of these arrangements is easy to forget because the language of "the cloud" encourages amnesia. Data sounds weightless until one asks where the server hall stands, who controls the fibre, which grid supplies the electricity, where the backup resides, how recovery is tested, and whether the administrators with the highest privileges answer to domestic law, foreign law, corporate policy, or some unstable mix of all three. The geography never vanished. It merely withdrew behind interfaces. A country may speak grandly of digital transformation while depending on a narrow set of data centres exposed to the same floodplain, the same energy market, the same vendor stack, or the same legal chokepoints. A ministry may celebrate a migration that cuts costs and improves baseline security while quietly concentrating national risk in a handful of contracts that few legislators could describe and fewer civil servants could truly audit. Convenience has architecture.

And yet concentration is not always folly. Some centralisation can improve security, cut duplication, and raise professional standards that fragmented public systems fail to meet. Here a credible counter-example matters. Estonia, especially after the cyber attacks of 2007, became an emblem of digitally capable government not because it rejected integration, but because it paired integration with institutional design. Its X-Road data exchange layer, distributed registries, strong digital identity, and insistence on logging access created a model in which reuse of data could coexist with visible audit trails and a public narrative of state competence. No serious observer should romanticise the system. Estonia's scale is unusual; its history, administrative culture, and threat environment are specific; even there, disputes over security, exclusion, and dependence have never disappeared. Still, the case punctures a lazy determinism. High-capacity data governance need not mean indiscriminate surveillance or reckless centralisation. Under certain conditions, technical design and institutional trust can reinforce one another rather than cancel each other out.

Still, scale changes the argument. What works in a small, coherent administrative setting may fray in a continental market, a polarised democracy, or a state with weak procurement and uneven local capacity. A digital identity credential that eases access in one setting may become a point of friction in another. A cross-agency sharing arrangement that reduces fraud may also multiply error when records are messy and appeals are slow. A lawful interception framework that appears tightly drawn in statute may drift once commercial data brokers, advertising identifiers, and location datasets offer new routes around older oversight. In the United States, reporting during the 2020s about government agencies purchasing commercially available data rather than seeking it through more traditional processes sharpened an uncomfortable point: markets can become shadow extensions of state capability. The concept is boundary failure. When commercial collection and public power mesh too neatly, old lines between purchase, compulsion, and surveillance begin to blur.

This blurring is one reason legitimacy belongs at the centre of national capability rather than at its ethical margins. A state that can extract, link, and analyse more data than ever before may appear stronger on paper. But paper is not compliance, and compliance is not consent. Trust becomes visible in conduct: whether citizens register willingly, whether firms report breaches promptly, whether hospitals share data during an emergency without paralysing fear of blame, whether courts and regulators are believed when they claim safeguards exist, whether the public accepts temporary exceptional measures as necessary rather than opportunistic. These are not sentimental questions. They are operational ones. During a crisis, governments need populations to do ordinary but decisive things—update details, answer messages, install patches, attend appointments, accept revised procedures, believe official corrections. Where data governance has become synonymous with opacity, mission creep, or administrative harm, those behaviours become harder to secure.

The same is true in markets. Discussions of competition often treat data concentration as if it were simply an antitrust puzzle: market shares, switching costs, mergers, barriers to entry. Those matter. But data concentration also shapes what kinds of firms can emerge, which standards become default, whose compliance practices define the field, and whether public institutions retain bargaining power. A state seeking domestic capability cannot merely exhort innovation or subsidise fashionable firms. It must ask dull, strategic questions about public procurement, interoperability mandates, audit rights, skilled staffing, and whether its own agencies create demand for dependable services rather than merely chase the lowest headline price. Industrial policy becomes real when it reaches the contract, the test environment, the retention pathway, the incident report, the civil-service pay scale. Otherwise it remains rhetoric wearing technical clothes.

Near-permanent memory sharpens every one of these tensions. Cheap storage and ubiquitous copying mean that forgetting is no longer the default outcome of time. Deletion must be designed, supervised, and verified. Archiving must preserve provenance, not merely content. An official record without trustworthy metadata can collapse in court or inquiry; a retained dataset without clear purpose can become a source of quiet mission creep; a backup kept for resilience can become a liability if nobody can say who is responsible for it or how it will be restored under pressure. Here the old state ambition to remember collides with an older liberal intuition that some forms of forgetting are not failures but safeguards. A society that never forgets administratively may become one that never fully forgives politically. The ledger returns.

Seen this way, the conventional separation between national security, economic governance, and democratic legitimacy begins to look artificial. Cyber operations aimed at integrity can damage public confidence as surely as they damage systems. Privacy regulation can become a tool of market ordering and diplomatic influence, not simply a set of moral prohibitions. Data localisation may answer a genuine concern about jurisdiction or resilience while also serving as industrial policy or political theatre. Intelligence sharing can raise collective security while entrenching asymmetries among partners. Cloud dependence may strengthen operational security for weak agencies yet deepen strategic dependence on external providers. None of these arrangements is reducible to a slogan. Each requires a more demanding diagnostic: who controls the infrastructure, who sets the standard, who can lawfully compel access, who can verify compliance, who bears the cost of failure, and who remains credible after the failure becomes public.

Those questions matter because the future of state power is unlikely to be settled by whichever country gathers the most information. States can collect themselves into fragility. They can mistake visibility for understanding, acquisition for capability, technical possibility for political sustainability. They can also, with more difficulty, build arrangements in which memory serves judgment rather than replacing it. That demands attention to mundane matters usually pushed below the horizon of grand strategy: legacy public-sector networks, identity proofing standards, procurement design, incident response chains, certificate disputes, skills retention, archival integrity, judicial remedies, reporting thresholds, and the social conditions under which citizens believe that what is collected about them will not simply be turned against them later. Grand ideas rise or fall on such details.

A serious account of data power therefore begins from an unglamorous premise. Power lies neither in databases alone nor in declarations of sovereignty. It lies in the fit between infrastructure, institutions, and incentives; in whether a state can secure and use what matters without becoming captive to its own systems or to the firms and foreign jurisdictions on which those systems depend. The strongest arrangements are not those that maximise extraction at every turn, but those that keep capability, restraint, and public trust in workable alignment. That alignment is difficult, contingent, and always vulnerable to decay. It can be weakened by scandal, hardened by overreaction, or quietly hollowed out by outsourcing and neglect. No dashboard captures it fully.

The pressing question, then, is not whether data will shape national power. It already does. The harder question is what kind of state is being built when memory becomes continuous, infrastructure becomes a political instrument, and legitimacy becomes inseparable from the management of records. Some states will answer by centralising faster, some by regulating harder, some by retreating into localisation, some by leaning on alliances and firms they do not fully control. Each path trades one dependency for another. Each makes a wager about security, prosperity, and social consent. The real test is whether those wagers remain governable when the next breach, outage, leak, procurement failure, or scandal arrives—not in theory, but in the thick of events, when the screens change, the phones ring, and the public asks who holds the ledger, and for whose benefit.

Chapter 1

Data Power and the State

What does it mean for a state to possess more information than any ruler in earlier centuries could have imagined, yet remain unsure of what it can truly know, what it may rightly do, and where its own authority begins to thin? The question matters because modern government no longer meets data at the margins of administration. It meets data at the point of action: when a border system flags a traveller, when a tax authority matches records, when a hospital verifies identity, when an intelligence service decides whether a pattern is meaningful or merely noise. The file is never just a file. It is a claim about reality, a prompt to intervene, and sometimes a quiet invitation to overreach.

The paradox grows sharper the closer one looks. States often speak as though possession were the same thing as power, as though the mere accumulation of records conferred strategic advantage. Yet records left unverified mislead. Records trapped in incompatible systems sit idle. Records acquired without lawful authority can poison the legitimacy of the very institutions that sought them. A government may hold vast quantities of information and still fail at tasks that appear almost mundane: identifying the right person, tracing the right payment, detecting the right threat, or correcting the wrong decision before damage hardens into grievance. More memory does not automatically produce more control. It can produce confusion, dependence, and false confidence.

This is where the central tension comes into view. Data strengthens the state only when it travels through institutions capable of judging, securing, and using it within boundaries that others recognise as valid. That is a technical matter, but never only a technical one. It reaches into law, procurement, public trust, and the structure of markets on which governments increasingly depend. A state may improve its reach while weakening its standing. It may become faster while growing more brittle.

It may widen surveillance without improving understanding. The friction sits not between the digital and the political, but inside their entanglement.

That entanglement deserves careful treatment because the language surrounding data power is unusually prone to exaggeration. Some accounts flatten the subject into a race for scale, as though larger databases and denser collection necessarily translate into national advantage. Others recoil in the opposite direction and treat data systems chiefly as instruments of domination, with little regard for the ordinary administrative tasks that keep a state solvent, services functioning, and obligations enforceable. Both views miss the practical character of the problem. Governments collect and use data not in the abstract, but through tax systems, welfare platforms, customs procedures, policing tools, procurement contracts, licensing schemes, and security arrangements. The serious question is not whether data matters. It is how value is made from it, who controls the terms of use, and what kinds of power are created in the process.

The stakes extend far beyond technical efficiency. Security depends on the ability to distinguish signal from distraction, to authenticate records, and to protect critical systems against theft, manipulation, or paralysis. Economic strength depends on standards, interoperability, and the market conditions that shape who can build, access, and profit from data-intensive services. Political legitimacy depends on whether public authority appears competent, proportionate, and subject to restraint. These are not separate worlds. They overlap constantly. A dataset assembled for one purpose can migrate into another. A tool procured for convenience can alter the balance between state capacity and private dependence. A system designed to reduce fraud can also widen suspicion, harden exclusion, or invite mission creep. Small design choices carry constitutional weight.

The harder truth is that states rarely confront these questions on a blank page. They inherit legacy systems, fragmented legal authorities, patchy oversight, uneven administrative talent, and supplier relationships that narrow what can be changed without disruption. Power, therefore, accumulates through pipelines rather than vaults. What matters is not merely whether data exists, but whether it can be cleaned, linked, interpreted, challenged, secured, and acted upon without corroding the institutional trust on which further action depends. A filing cabinet can be messy. So can a cloud tenancy. The difference is scale, speed, and consequence.

A more precise way of thinking begins by separating what public debate often compresses into a single word. Raw records are not the same as knowledge. Knowledge is not the same as operational capacity. Capacity is not the same as legitimate authority. Confusing these layers leads to bad analysis and worse policy. It encourages governments to mistake collection for competence, and critics to denounce capability without asking which capabilities are necessary to govern at all. The issue is not whether states should know things. Any functioning state must know certain things. The issue is what kind of apparatus turns records into decisions, what constraints keep that apparatus answerable, and what incentives push it towards prudence or excess.

From there, the path of inquiry tightens. The opening movement establishes why data becomes strategically valuable only when collection, curation, linkage, and use are organised into something more than storage. Attention then shifts to the three fields in which that value most clearly appears: security, economic competition, and legitimacy, each drawing on the same underlying systems while pulling them towards different ends. The argument then narrows again, pressing against the easy myths that distort judgment, before arriving at a comparative lens grounded in infrastructure, institutions, and incentives, where slogans about sovereignty or innovation begin to lose their magic.

What follows, therefore, asks for a more disciplined habit of assessment. Not who has the most data, but who can compel it, purchase it, verify it, combine it, protect it, and use it without setting off political damage that outweighs the gain. Not which state sounds most ambitious, but which one has built arrangements that can survive scrutiny, failure, and adaptation. The file still sits on the desk, whether as paper, screen, or distributed record. The real question is simpler, and harsher: when it arrives, who can do something valid with it?

Data as a strategic resource

In June 2015, the United States Office of Personnel Management disclosed that sensitive records tied to federal background investigations had been compromised in Washington, DC. The breach reached far beyond a few stray files. It exposed forms, fingerprints, security-clearance data, family links, financial histories, and personal vulnerabilities tied to millions of current, former, and prospective officials and contractors. The immediate outcome was administrative alarm and a long repair effort. The deeper outcome was conceptual. A personnel archive, once treated as an internal bureaucratic storehouse, suddenly appeared in plain view as a strategic asset: a reservoir of information that could help identify, map, pressure, or assess people connected to the machinery of state. The file had changed its meaning.

That change did not occur because the records themselves were new. Most were ordinary in origin. Governments have always gathered names, addresses, tax declarations, land titles, service histories, and travel records. What made the OPM breach strategically significant was the combination of sensitivity, linkage, and potential use. Data became valuable not when it sat still, but when it could be joined, searched, compared, and acted upon. That is the decisive shift. A record in isolation may tell very little. A record placed in relation to other records can alter choices, expose dependencies, and reshape the balance between knowledge and vulnerability. Storage matters. Movement matters more.

This is the first discipline required for serious thinking about data power: distinguishing raw records from actionable knowledge, and both from the institutional capacity to do something lawful, timely, and competent with that knowledge. These are often collapsed into one another in public debate, usually for rhetorical convenience. The result is confusion. A ministry may hold extensive records and still fail to detect a fraud pattern because fields were entered inconsistently, identifiers do not match across systems, or no team has the authority to compare datasets. An intelligence service may intercept large volumes of communications and still miss what matters because the material cannot be processed, translated, authenticated, or contextualised quickly enough. A regulator may know that harm exists and yet remain unable to intervene because the law is vague, procurement is weak, the evidence chain is contested, or the relevant expertise has been outsourced. Information alone does not govern. Institutions do.

The difference can be put plainly. Data is not oil. The comparison survives because it flatters scale and sounds modern, not because it explains anything important. Oil becomes useful when refined, but its underlying value is relatively stable once quality is known. Data does not behave like that. Its value depends on purpose, timing, format, legal authority, and the possibility of combination. A tax record that matters deeply to a revenue agency may mean little to an emergency physician. A mobile location trail that is highly valuable for traffic planning may be legally unusable for criminal prosecution. A biometric identifier may help prevent duplicate claims in one setting and create exclusion in another. Data acquires strategic force only within a pipeline: collected for some reason, curated into usable form, linked to other information, interpreted by institutions, and converted into decisions. Break the chain at any point and the apparent asset can turn inert or dangerous.

The word *curation* can sound genteel for a hard administrative task. In practice it means deciding what counts, what matches, what is missing, what can be trusted, and what should be discarded. That labour rarely attracts political glory. It should. A badly labelled dataset can distort an entire programme. A weak identifier can produce duplicate people on paper and invisible people in life. A mismatch in date formats or address fields can block cross-agency comparison that officials assumed would be simple. Much of state capacity depends on work that looks almost mundane from the outside: deduplicating records, verifying provenance, defining standards, testing assumptions, correcting errors, and documenting access. The file does not become useful by magic. It becomes useful by administration.

This is why collection alone is such a poor measure of power. Large states, and large firms, often mistake volume for advantage because quantity is easy to report. It produces impressive headlines, colourful charts, and a sense of momentum. But unstructured accumulation can create costs that compound faster than benefits. More records require more security, more permissions management, more audit trails, more retention decisions, more opportunities for error, and more avenues for misuse. They also create a familiar temptation: because information is available, institutions begin to imagine that it ought to be used. Technical possibility quietly expands practical appetite. Strategic resources invite strategy; they also invite overreach.

A more revealing example lies in the administrative success and controversy surrounding digital identity. In India, Aadhaar was rolled out from 2009 onward through the Unique Identification Authority of India as a biometric identity infrastructure intended to simplify verification, reduce duplication, and improve access across a fragmented administrative landscape. The strategic value here did not rest in the bare existence of numbers or fingerprints. It lay in the ability to authenticate an identity across transactions, connect welfare delivery to a portable credential, and lower the friction of proving personhood in dealings with the state and parts of the market. Those capacities can change the reach of government. They can speed service delivery, tighten control over payments, and reduce certain forms of impersonation. Yet the same case also makes the larger point unavoidable: data only becomes an asset within a system of governance. Questions about consent, exclusion, error correction, legal scope, and institutional oversight were not side issues added later by critics. They were central to the value of the system itself, because a database that people cannot contest, or that officials cannot bound, alters the relationship between state and citizen in ways that feed back into legitimacy and compliance.

That feedback loop matters. A strategic resource is not simply something useful. It is something that changes the terms on which decisions are made. When governments can identify individuals more reliably, they can target benefits, sanctions, and scrutiny more precisely. When customs authorities can compare manifests, ownership records, and shipping data at speed, they can detect anomalies that once passed unnoticed. When health systems can link prescribing data to outcomes, they can spot patterns that improve safety or expose abuse. But each gain depends on a chain of institutional judgements: who may access the data, for what purpose, under what safeguards, with what remedy when the system errs. Remove those judgements and value can invert into liability. Precision can become discrimination. Efficiency can become opacity. Knowledge can become a pretext for action unsupported by due process.

Strategic resources also derive value from timing. Information that arrives too late often loses its strategic content. This seems obvious, yet states repeatedly design systems that privilege accumulation over responsiveness. A record may be accurate and still useless if it cannot be retrieved in the moment a decision is required. Border control, sanctions enforcement, epidemic response, disaster relief, and cyber defence all depend on whether relevant information can be accessed, interpreted, and acted upon under pressure. Delay matters. So does sequence. A state that collects everything but cannot establish what happened first, which source is more reliable, or whether a record has been altered may drown in its own archive. Provenance is strategic because decisions rely on confidence in origin and integrity, not on presence alone.

The military and intelligence worlds have long understood this distinction, even if public commentary often does not. Signals intelligence became strategically potent not because states intercepted communications in the abstract, but because they built systems for filtering, classifying, translating, and integrating what they collected into operational judgement. The lesson generalises. Raw intercepts are like unprocessed administrative records: potentially valuable, but mostly inert until organised through labour, tools, and authority. The same holds in civilian government. A land registry gains strategic value when it can support taxation, adjudicate ownership, reduce disputes, and connect reliably to planning and credit systems. A company register matters more when beneficial ownership can be tested rather than merely declared. A public health dataset matters when it can guide interventions without collapsing confidentiality or public trust. Records are inputs. Capability is the achievement.

This is also why access deserves more attention than storage. Access sounds procedural, almost secondary, yet it determines whether the asset exists in any meaningful sense. Who can query the system? Who can export results? Who can compare one dataset with another? Who can compel disclosure from a private intermediary? Who can audit prior access? Who can challenge a false match or unlawful request? Strategic advantage often turns on these apparently technical permissions. A state may not physically hold a dataset and still wield power over it through legal compulsion, contractual rights, procurement conditions, or partnership. Conversely, a state may physically possess an immense archive and still lack meaningful control because the tools for analysis sit with external vendors, the schema is poorly documented, or the law blocks use for the purpose now deemed urgent. The decisive question is not always ownership. It is governable access.

A credible limitation should be admitted here. Not all strategic value depends on extensive pipelines or tightly integrated systems. Sometimes smaller, well-defined datasets outperform grand architectures because they are cleaner, narrower in purpose, and easier to secure. A targeted sanctions list, a carefully maintained watchlist, or a specialist epidemiological register may deliver more practical value than a sprawling central repository assembled without clear boundaries. The lesson is not that large systems are futile. It is that scope without discipline degrades usefulness. Narrowness can be a strength when precision, accountability, and speed matter more than breadth. This limitation does not weaken the broader argument. It sharpens it. The point is not that more linkage always helps, but that value arises from a fit between purpose, design, and authority.

Private firms illustrate the same truth from another angle. A platform company may appear powerful because it captures vast behavioural traces, yet those traces only become commercially decisive when they can be standardised, modelled, and converted into pricing, ranking, advertising, logistics, or product design. Firms invest heavily in the invisible middle of the pipeline for this reason. They clean inputs, test outputs, manage permissions, and engineer defaults that keep data flowing across products. States increasingly confront private actors not merely as holders of information but as competitors in the organisation of information. The contest is therefore not only over possession, but over analytical speed, technical standards, legal reach, and the capacity to make one dataset speak to another. A government that cannot evaluate the systems on which it depends will often discover too late that its formal authority outruns its practical command.

The strategic quality of data, then, lies in conversion. Can a record be turned into a defensible decision? Can a pattern be distinguished from a coincidence? Can a flag be reviewed before harm hardens? Can a dataset be shared without losing control, or sealed without losing utility? These are questions about governance as much as computation. They direct attention to standards, oversight, procurement, training, audit, and institutional memory. They also expose a deeper political fact. When data becomes central to the conduct of security, markets, and public administration, the strongest actors are rarely those with the biggest warehouses. They are those that know what to collect, what to connect, what to ignore, and what to forbid.

The file remains a useful image because it reminds us what strategy often tries to hide. Every data system, however sophisticated, still asks versions of old questions. What do we know? How do we know it? Who may see it? Who may contest it? What follows from it? Modern states can store more than any predecessors, and yet strategic advantage still depends on restraint as much as reach. An archive without judgment becomes clutter. A pipeline without oversight becomes hazard. The harder test lies ahead: when the record is available and the pressure to act is real, which institutions can turn data into capability without turning capability into abuse?

Three arenas of national advantage

On 15 April 2013, as smoke spread along Boylston Street in Boston after the marathon bombing, investigators moved quickly through a city already saturated with records. CCTV footage, mobile phone data, licence plate readers, digital photographs from spectators, payment trails, travel records, and fragments of online activity did not remain in their original compartments for long. They were pulled into relation. Faces were compared. Timelines were assembled. Movements were inferred. The immediate purpose was security: identify suspects, prevent further violence, restore control. Yet the same episode also revealed something wider about modern state capacity. Data collected for traffic management, private commerce, or routine administration could be drawn into a security response within hours. The file changed hands.

That transfer of meaning matters. A record rarely belongs to one arena alone. It may begin as a commercial transaction, an administrative declaration, or a technical log, then become evidence, a source of revenue assurance, an index of public behaviour, or a test of state competence. This is why data cannot be understood as a single-purpose asset. Its strategic value often lies precisely in its portability across functions. A tax database can support revenue collection, detect fraud, inform industrial policy, and signal whether a government treats like cases alike. A health register can guide treatment, monitor procurement, and show whether public authorities can be trusted with sensitive information. The same system can produce reassurance in one setting and fear in another. The ledger has several readers.

National advantage built from data therefore emerges in at least three closely related arenas: security, economic competitiveness, and governance legitimacy. Each gives the state a different reason to collect, compare, and use information. Each also imposes a different discipline on how that information should be handled. Security prizes speed, relevance, and the ability to distinguish signal from noise under pressure. Economic competitiveness prizes coordination, predictability, and the conditions under which firms can innovate, comply, and scale. Governance legitimacy prizes fairness, restraint, and visible accountability, because citizens judge systems not only by whether they function, but by whether they function on terms that feel lawful and proportionate. These arenas overlap constantly. That overlap is not a minor complication. It is the real political problem.

Security offers the most intuitive starting point because the stakes are immediate and often dramatic. Border control, intelligence analysis, sanctions enforcement, cyber defence, and counter-fraud operations all depend on linking records that were not originally created together. A passenger name record may become relevant when compared with visa data, payment details, known associations, or travel anomalies. A suspicious payment may matter because it fits a pattern established elsewhere. A procurement irregularity may point not merely to waste, but to infiltration or coercion. In each case, data contributes to national advantage by reducing uncertainty about action: who to stop, what to inspect, where to allocate scarce attention, when to intervene. Security is never simply about possession. It is about prioritisation under constraint.

That is why poor information can be more dangerous than sparse information. A state that collects widely but matches badly may overwhelm analysts, misidentify targets, or harden false suspicion into official judgment. A weakly governed system can produce a kind of confident error: the screen shows a pattern, the officer acts, the institution later discovers that the pattern was an artefact of inconsistent identifiers, stale records, or untested assumptions. Visible behaviour matters here. Does an analyst trust a match enough to escalate it? Does a border official detain a traveller because a database flag is opaque and difficult to challenge? Does a cyber responder isolate a system because telemetry appears compromised? Security advantage rests not on abstract access to information, but on whether the people using systems can distinguish reliable signals from seductive rubbish.

Economic competitiveness looks calmer, but the logic is equally sharp. States that can organise data well tend to lower friction across markets. They make identity verification cheaper, customs processing faster, logistics more predictable, payments more secure, and compliance less arbitrary. Firms notice the difference in concrete decisions: whether to enter a market, how much paperwork to tolerate, how quickly to ship, whether to build local capacity, whether to trust a public register, whether to spend resources on productive work or defensive administration. Data helps markets function when it reduces uncertainty without multiplying hidden obligations. Good company registers, land records, standards regimes, and digital identity systems do not merely tidy bureaucracy. They help determine whether contracts can be enforced, ownership can be verified, and transactions can proceed without endless rechecking.

The economic arena also includes competition over who captures value from data-intensive activity. A country that relies entirely on foreign platforms, foreign cloud services, foreign identity tools, or foreign analytics vendors may enjoy convenience while surrendering bargaining power. Market advantage does not require autarky, which is usually neither feasible nor desirable. It does require enough domestic capability, legal clarity, and procurement intelligence to avoid becoming a price-taker in matters that affect public administration and national resilience. The visible signs are practical. Can local firms compete for public contracts without impossible compliance burdens? Can regulators understand the systems they supervise? Can public agencies audit what suppliers actually do with sensitive workloads? Does a start-up confront a market structured by open standards or by closed dependencies that only incumbents can navigate? Competitiveness, in this sense, is not only about innovation. It is about the terms of participation.

Estonia offers a useful example because it connects economic and administrative value without dissolving either into rhetoric. Its digital state architecture, developed over many years and closely associated with institutions in Tallinn, has often been praised for enabling online public services, efficient identity verification, and relatively seamless interactions between citizens, firms, and government. The strategic point is not that Estonia became powerful by storing more than larger states. It is that it built data flows and access controls that reduced administrative friction while sustaining a public story of competence. A business registration completed quickly, a prescription retrieved without repeated paperwork, or a tax filing handled with limited hassle all become visible evidence that state systems can serve economic life rather than obstruct it. Efficiency becomes a civic experience. That matters for competitiveness because predictable administration lowers the cost of operating within the state's legal order.

Yet efficiency alone does not secure the third arena, legitimacy. A system may work smoothly and still lose public consent if citizens believe it watches too much, shares too widely, corrects errors too slowly, or punishes those least able to contest it. Governance legitimacy is often discussed in broad moral language, but it shows up in concrete behaviours. People comply more readily when procedures appear fair. Firms cooperate more fully when rules are legible. Public servants trust systems more when audit trails are clear and responsibilities are not blurred across contractors, ministries, and databases. Courts command more authority when records can be verified and challenged. Legitimacy, then, is not a vague halo around policy. It is the condition under which data-driven governance remains politically durable.

Few examples show this more clearly than the United Kingdom's Windrush scandal, which became a major public controversy in 2018. Long-term Commonwealth residents, many of whom had arrived lawfully decades earlier, were wrongly classified by the Home Office as lacking legal status because of gaps in documentation and hostile administrative practices. People lost jobs, housing, healthcare access, and security. The records were incomplete, the demands for proof were rigid, and the burden of correction fell on those least well placed to bear it. This was not a simple case of insufficient data, nor merely of bureaucratic error. It showed how administrative data, when fused with enforcement logic and narrow procedural assumptions, can damage the credibility of the state itself. A government trying to demonstrate control over borders instead demonstrated something else: that institutional misuse of records can produce injustice visible enough to become a national political wound.

The same database can therefore operate in all three arenas at once. Consider tax administration. For security services and financial intelligence units, tax records can illuminate suspicious networks, shell entities, or unexplained flows when linked lawfully with other data. For economic governance, they support revenue collection, shape investor expectations about state competence, and reveal patterns relevant to policy design. For legitimacy, they matter because citizens watch whether enforcement appears even-handed, whether elites escape scrutiny, and whether errors can be corrected before livelihoods are damaged. One dataset, several functions. That versatility explains why tax authorities, customs agencies, and company registries often sit closer to strategic power than public debate assumes. They are not glamorous institutions. They are decisive ones.

Trade-offs follow from that versatility. A tax authority may wish to share more data with security agencies to detect sanctions evasion or organised crime. That may be justified under tightly drawn conditions. But every extension of access changes the character of the institution in the public mind. It can alter what firms disclose, what advisers assume, what citizens fear, and how courts interpret the boundary between fiscal administration and broader surveillance. Similarly, a digital identity system that reduces fraud and speeds service delivery may also tempt governments to centralise authentication across unrelated domains, turning convenience into a universal key. The strategic challenge is not to deny cross-use altogether. It is to decide which cross-uses strengthen the state's overall position and which quietly corrode the consent on which future use depends.

A credible limitation should be faced directly. States do not always need integrated, multipurpose datasets to gain advantage in these arenas. Sometimes separation protects value. Compartmentalisation can prevent abuse, reduce breach impact, and preserve trust by ensuring that a system built for one purpose cannot simply be repurposed for another. Electoral registers, health records, and intelligence holdings often require different handling precisely because institutional legitimacy depends on those differences being real rather than rhetorical. The desire to join everything to everything else can reflect administrative impatience more than strategic wisdom. Reconciliation lies in recognising that advantage does not always come from maximum integration. It comes from controlled integration:

enough connection to act, enough separation to remain lawful, credible, and correctable.

This matters because governments often experience pressure in one arena and answer by weakening another. After a security shock, demands for wider access can expand before safeguards are tested. During fiscal strain, efficiency drives can lead agencies to merge systems or outsource functions without understanding the long-term implications for oversight and dependence. In periods of political distrust, leaders may promise transparency while building monitoring tools that citizens read as extraction rather than accountability. The visible consequences arrive later. Complaint volumes rise. Courts intervene. Vendors gain quiet influence over public choices. Officials stop sharing information for fear of blame. Citizens comply formally while trust drains away underneath. A state can win speed and lose standing.

The deeper lesson is that data does not confer one kind of advantage at a time. It rearranges the balance among several kinds at once. Security measures can increase economic certainty or spook investment. Pro-competition rules can widen access while increasing privacy and integrity risks if systems are poorly specified. Legitimacy-enhancing safeguards can slow immediate action yet strengthen resilience over time because citizens and firms remain willing to cooperate. None of these outcomes is automatic. Institutions mediate them through law, procurement, standards, training, and the habits of officials making ordinary decisions in offices, checkpoints, control rooms, and courts. Strategy begins there.

The recurring image of the ledger matters because it captures this multiplicity without romanticising it. A ledger records, compares, and judges. It supports payment, sanction, proof, and memory. But its authority depends on who writes in it, who reads from it, who may challenge an entry, and what happens when a line is wrong. The same is true of modern data systems. They are not merely repositories. They are instruments through which the state secures itself, organises markets, and asks to be believed. The hard question is not whether one arena should dominate the others. It is whether institutions can use the same records for security, prosperity, and public authority without allowing one purpose to consume the rest. When a dataset proves most useful, that is exactly when the boundary test begins.

Metrics, myths, and mismeasurement

On 6 January 2021, as the assault on the United States Capitol unfolded in Washington, DC, one fact stood out with unusual force: this was not an event hidden from the sensors of a modern society. Images spread in real time. Posts circulated openly. Law enforcement agencies possessed extensive technical means, broad data access, and years of prior discussion about online extremism. Yet visibility did not yield prevention. The problem was not simple blindness. It was mismeasurement. Institutions had signals, but they struggled to rank them, combine them, interpret them, and act on them with sufficient clarity. The screen was full. Judgment lagged.

That distinction matters because public argument about data power still leans on crude proxies. Bigger databases, larger populations, more sensors, more clicks, more storage, more users: these are treated as if they were straightforward measures of national advantage. They are not. They may indicate potential. They may also conceal disorder. A state can collect enormous quantities of records and remain weak at the points that matter most: authenticating identity, linking systems, enforcing standards, lawfully compelling access, or translating fragments into defensible decisions. The dashboard can impress. The pipeline can fail.

The appeal of bad metrics is easy to understand. Quantity is visible. It can be counted, compared, and placed on a slide. Quality is slower, more awkward, and often embarrassing. Interoperability requires a patient look at schemas, identifiers, permissions, and legacy constraints. Legal usability demands attention to warrants, procurement terms, evidentiary rules, jurisdiction, and administrative authority. Organisational readiness forces harder questions still: who has clearance, who has training, who has time, who bears liability for a false match, who may challenge a result, who signs the order when the system produces an ambiguous answer? These are less glamorous forms of power. They are usually the decisive ones.

Mismeasurement begins when analysts confuse what can be stored with what can be used. A national archive of records, however immense, does not automatically help an investigator, regulator, tax authority, or emergency responder. Records must be collected in forms that allow comparison. They must be curated so that duplicates, gaps, and contradictions are visible rather than buried. They must be linked through identifiers that are accurate enough for the purpose at hand. They must be legally accessible at the relevant moment. They must also be trusted by the people who rely on them, which means more than technical integrity. It means visible procedures: audit trails, access controls, correction mechanisms, and institutional habits that keep convenience from replacing judgment.

That is why the slogan "more data equals more power" survives mostly because it flatters the collector. It mistakes abundance for capability. In practice, additional data often imposes additional burdens. It widens the attack surface. It increases retention risk. It complicates compliance. It raises the cost of permissions management and the difficulty of reviewing access. It also encourages a familiar institutional vice: once information exists, someone will argue that it ought to be used. That pressure can stretch systems beyond their lawful purpose or analytical reliability. A large archive may therefore generate not strength but drag. More is not always better. Sometimes it is merely more.

The sharper metric is not volume but fitness for purpose. Can a customs authority compare shipping records quickly enough to detect a suspicious pattern before goods move? Can a hospital system match the right patient to the right medication record without dangerous ambiguity? Can a sanctions team trace beneficial ownership through corporate layers without relying on stale declarations? Can a court or tribunal accept a digital record as reliable because provenance and chain of custody are clear? Each question concerns usefulness under pressure, not possession in the abstract. The records that matter are the ones that survive contact with action.

A useful example sits in Estonia, where state digital systems have often been treated as proof that small countries can outperform larger ones in administrative data use. The relevant lesson is not that Estonia accumulated more data than its peers. It did not need to. Its advantage came from coherent identity infrastructure, standardised exchange mechanisms, and a political commitment to making government records retrievable, reusable, and auditable across institutions. The visible behaviour is ordinary but telling: a citizen accesses a service without repeated form-filling; an official retrieves a needed record without sending the same request to several agencies; system logs show who looked at what and when. That is interoperability made concrete. The power lies not in the warehouse, but in the connection and the rule that governs it.

The counterpoint is just as instructive. Large organisations often possess data riches that prove operationally disappointing because systems do not speak to each other. A police force may hold case records, call logs, custody data, and intelligence notes across incompatible platforms. A ministry may commission repeated "single customer view" projects that never quite settle the problem of matching identities across legacy estates. A health authority may digitise vast numbers of files only to discover that different hospitals code the same condition differently, that permissions vary by region, or that contractors maintain key interfaces under terms that frustrate scrutiny. In such settings, scale becomes a trap. The institution owns the records but not the coherence required to use them well.

The myth of scale also obscures legal usability. A dataset can be technically available and strategically weak if it cannot be used lawfully for the task at hand. This point is often missed by commentators who imagine that states either possess information or do not. In reality, the crucial question is narrower and more demanding: under what authority, for what purpose, with what evidentiary status, and under which safeguards may a record be used? A commercial location dataset may be rich, timely, and tempting. That does not settle whether it can support a prosecution, justify an administrative sanction, or survive judicial scrutiny. A platform may hold valuable behavioural data. That does not mean a government can compel access without political, diplomatic, or legal cost. Access is stratified. So is power.

One of the clearest demonstrations came from the Cambridge Analytica affair, which became a global political scandal in 2018 after reporting on how Facebook user data had been harvested and used for political profiling. The lesson was not merely that large datasets can be misused, though they can. It was that inference can matter more than ownership. Actors did not need to know everything about everyone to claim influence. They needed enough data, combined in plausible ways, to classify, segment, target, and test messages against behaviour. What looked like a contest over possession was equally a contest over the ability to infer meaningful traits from partial records. The strategic implication reaches beyond electoral politics. States, firms, and intermediaries often derive value less from direct access to sensitive facts than from the power to infer them from proxies.

This is why any serious assessment of data power needs a better diagnostic. Not how much data exists, but who can compel it, who can purchase it, and who can infer it. Compulsion points to legal authority. Can a state require disclosure from telecom providers, banks, cloud companies, or data brokers? Can it do so quickly? Under what oversight? Purchase points to market structure. If data can be bought lawfully from commercial intermediaries, the formal boundaries around public access may become less decisive than many assume. Inference points to analytical capacity. If a state, or a firm acting within its orbit, can derive sensitive conclusions from ordinary transactional exhaust, then apparent restrictions on direct collection may offer less protection than they promise. This three-part question cuts through many comforting illusions.

Compulsion is often overestimated in theory and underestimated in practice. Strong laws on paper do not guarantee usable access. Providers may store data in fragmented ways, contest requests, or hold key records outside the jurisdiction asserting authority. Technical changes can reduce what is retained. Encryption can narrow what is intelligible even where collection remains possible. Administrative weakness can slow the process until the opportunity has passed. A government may therefore possess formal powers that look formidable in statute and feeble in use. The reverse can also occur. A state with more limited formal authority may obtain considerable access through partnerships, licensing conditions, procurement design, or the simple fact that major firms need to remain in good standing with domestic regulators. Legal power is not binary. It operates through institutional relationships as much as through headline law.

Purchase, by contrast, often hides in plain sight. Data brokerage markets allow location traces, advertising identifiers, consumer profiles, and other behavioural fragments to circulate in forms that can be bought, licensed, and recombined. The boundary between public and private access starts to blur. A government that could not easily collect certain data directly may encounter a route through commercial acquisition or contractor relationships. That route may be lawful, contested, or poorly understood depending on the jurisdiction and the type of data involved. Either way, the strategic point stands. Market access can alter the real distribution of information power without any dramatic legislative expansion. What matters is not only what the state can seize, but what it can buy.

Inference is the least visible and, in some respects, the most consequential. Many institutions still speak as though sensitive data were a fixed category defined by the content of a record. Yet modern analytics often work through accumulation of apparently mundane details: purchase times, travel patterns, device links, frequency of contact, browsing rhythms, transaction anomalies. No single piece tells the full story. Together they can classify households, identify networks, estimate income, predict vulnerability, or flag behaviour for scrutiny. The methodological point is familiar in statistics and machine learning. The political point is often neglected. Restrictions aimed at one category of data may not prevent powerful inferences drawn from another. A regime that celebrates minimisation while tolerating dense proxy collection may be measuring the wrong thing.

A credible limitation should be acknowledged. Quantity sometimes does matter. Large datasets can improve pattern recognition, strengthen model performance, widen the sample for anomaly detection, and support national-scale planning that smaller collections simply cannot. Public health surveillance, weather forecasting, transport management, and certain fraud detection tasks benefit from breadth. The correction is not to dismiss scale, but to place it in order. Size helps when collection is relevant, labels are meaningful, infrastructure is dependable, and legal and institutional arrangements allow appropriate use. Scale without these conditions becomes clutter, cost, or risk. Scale with them can be powerful. The error lies in treating the largest pile as the strongest system.

Bad metrics do more than distort analysis. They distort policy. Governments seduced by volume may fund collection before they fund standards, retention rules, audit capability, or correction processes. They may prize headline procurements over the slow work of integration. They may compare themselves to rivals by counting users, sensors, or terabytes rather than by asking whether crucial systems can authenticate, exchange, and defend the records on which decisions rely. This kind of mismeasurement creates a peculiar brittleness. Institutions look ambitious from a distance and improvisational at the moment of strain. The outward sign is familiar: a breach occurs, a scandal erupts, or a crisis demands coordination, and officials discover that the impressive dashboard never told them whether the pipes beneath it actually joined.

The most reliable indicators of data power therefore tend to be humble. Can records from one agency be matched to another without manual workarounds that invite error? Can a regulator inspect logs and understand what access took place? Can a court receive a digital record and trust its provenance? Can a government replace a supplier without losing visibility into its own systems? Can a public body explain why it holds a dataset, when it will delete it, and who may query it? Can those affected challenge a false or unlawful use in a way that changes outcomes rather than merely producing paperwork? These questions lack the glamour of scale. They are closer to the truth.

The recurring image is the gauge. A bad gauge does not merely misdescribe reality; it invites bad driving. States use proxies because governing complex systems requires simplification. That is unavoidable. The danger begins when proxies harden into myths. More storage, more cameras, more feeds, more identifiers, more vendors, more dashboards: these can look like evidence of strategic progress while quietly masking fragmentation, legal weakness, vendor dependence, or analytical confusion. The state then mistakes the fullness of the instrument panel for control of the road.

A more serious approach starts with the question that will recur throughout this book: who can compel, purchase, or infer the data that matters? It is a deliberately awkward question, because it forces attention away from sheer quantity and towards the means by which information becomes actionable. It also refuses the fantasy that power sits neatly inside government databases. Often it sits at the boundary between public authority and private infrastructure, between formal law and commercial availability, between declared collection and derived inference. The systems that matter most may not be the biggest. They may be the ones whose records can travel, whose permissions can be enforced, whose outputs can withstand challenge, and whose owners can be made to answer. When analysts stop counting piles and start tracing those pathways, a different map of national power begins to appear.

A framework for comparative assessment

In July 2024, a software update from CrowdStrike triggered widespread disruptions across airports, hospitals, broadcasters, banks, and government services in multiple countries. In London, check-in lines stalled. In the United States, flights were grounded. Screens went blue. The immediate cause sat in a technical chain, but the strategic lesson was larger and harder to ignore. States that differed sharply in wealth, regime type, and policy style all discovered a common vulnerability: critical functions had come to depend on tightly coupled digital infrastructure that many public officials did not directly control. The outage was not a cyber attack in the conventional sense. It still behaved like a national test. A single fault travelled across sectors and borders because systems had been standardised, centralised, and embedded so deeply that failure became social before it was fully understood. One broken link mattered.

That is why headline narratives about data power so often mislead. They encourage comparisons built on size, rhetoric, or prestige: which country has the largest population, the biggest platform companies, the most advanced artificial intelligence, the strictest laws, the most ambitious sovereignty language, the boldest industrial policy. Such comparisons are tempting because they are legible at a distance. They are also unreliable. A state may appear digitally formidable while depending on fragile suppliers, permissive procurement, weak oversight, or low public trust. Another may look modest by conventional measures yet perform better because its systems are interoperable, its institutions are disciplined, and its political incentives reward correction rather than concealment. The serious question is not who talks most grandly about data. It is who can sustain control, continuity, and legitimacy when systems are actually used.

A better comparative framework begins from a blunt premise: data power rests on an alignment among infrastructure, institutions, and incentives. These are distinct but inseparable. Infrastructure concerns the physical and technical arrangements that allow data to move, be stored, be processed, be authenticated, and be recovered. Institutions concern the formal and informal bodies that decide what may be collected, shared, purchased, compelled, secured, audited, and challenged. Incentives concern the market structures and political pressures that shape how actors behave when no one is making speeches: whether firms invest, whether agencies cooperate, whether officials disclose failure, whether citizens tolerate data collection, whether courts command obedience, whether suppliers gain quiet leverage over public choices. Comparative assessment becomes useful only when these three layers are examined together. Pull one away and the picture distorts.

Infrastructure comes first not because it is most important in a moral sense, but because it often sets the hard limits within which everything else must operate. Networks determine speed, reach, and chokepoints. Compute capacity shapes what can be processed in time. Storage systems define retention, recovery, and the costs of keeping or deleting records. Identity systems determine whether records can be joined to persons, organisations, or devices with sufficient confidence for the relevant purpose. These are not neutral utilities. They govern what kinds of state action are even possible. A government that lacks trusted identity infrastructure will struggle with benefits administration, border control, electoral integrity, procurement vetting, and tax enforcement in ways that no amount of high-level strategy can simply wish away. A state dependent on a narrow band of data centres, routes, or vendors may discover that efficiency and fragility grew together.

The visible signs of infrastructural strength are usually practical rather than theatrical. Can agencies exchange records without manual re-entry that invites error? Can systems recover after an outage without days of improvisation? Can logs be inspected when something goes wrong? Can a government migrate workloads without losing continuity or oversight?

Can a hospital verify identity and retrieve a patient record quickly enough to matter? Can a customs authority compare manifests and sanctions lists before goods clear the port? Infrastructure should be judged by what it permits under stress, not by how modern it sounds in procurement language. Reliability is strategic. So is recoverability.

Estonia offers a high-confidence example of how infrastructure can amplify state capability when it is tied to disciplined design. Its digital identity system and X-Road data exchange architecture, developed over many years and centred in Tallinn, have often been cited for enabling relatively seamless movement between public services while maintaining a strong emphasis on authentication and logging. The point is not that Estonia solved every problem or built a universally exportable model. The point is that infrastructure was treated as a governance backbone rather than a collection of isolated applications. A citizen logging in, a doctor retrieving a record, a business filing data, or an official checking access logs are all performing the state at the level that matters most: routine use. Comparative assessment should start there, at the point where a design choice becomes an ordinary action.

Yet infrastructure alone explains less than enthusiasts and critics alike often assume. Institutions decide whether technical possibilities become lawful practices, restrained capabilities, or public liabilities. Law matters here, but not only in the declaratory sense. The relevant issue is not whether a state has enacted impressive legislation. It is whether laws can be interpreted consistently, enforced credibly, and adapted without collapsing into either paralysis or abuse. Oversight bodies matter for similar reasons. Their existence on paper tells us little. The sharper questions concern staffing, jurisdiction, technical literacy, independence, audit access, and the political consequences of their findings. Procurement matters because states increasingly govern through purchased systems, managed services, and contractual dependencies that quietly shape what public authority can see and do. Security organisations matter because they often possess the strongest technical capabilities in government, and their relationships with civil agencies can either raise standards or distort priorities.

This institutional layer becomes visible in moments of failure. When the United Kingdom's Windrush scandal became a major political crisis in 2018, the damage did not arise from a shortage of data. It arose from institutional use of records under hostile administrative assumptions, rigid evidentiary demands, and weak corrective pathways. People who had every reason to be secure in their status were asked to prove what the state itself had failed to preserve adequately. That was not simply a legal failure, nor simply a data-management failure. It was an institutional failure in the deepest sense: the rules, habits, and review mechanisms around data use could not prevent administrative harm from becoming politically explosive. Comparative assessment should treat such episodes as diagnostic. They reveal whether institutions can correct themselves before injustice hardens into scandal.

The same logic applies to procurement, though the consequences often surface more quietly. A ministry may sign contracts that appear to modernise services at speed, only to discover later that audit rights are narrow, exit costs are punishing, interfaces are opaque, and core knowledge now sits with vendors rather than officials. Formal sovereignty remains intact; practical discretion narrows. That narrowing matters. A state that cannot inspect its own systems, challenge supplier claims, or retain enough internal skill to act as an intelligent customer is not simply outsourcing convenience. It is redistributing authority. Institutions worthy of comparison are those that can buy capability without dissolving their own capacity to govern it.

Then come incentives, the layer most often neglected because it resists clean diagrams. Markets generate incentives through concentration, switching costs, standards, investor expectations, and the distribution of technical talent. Political systems generate incentives through elections, media scrutiny, judicial intervention, bureaucratic career paths, and the public memory of past scandals. These forces shape behaviour long before formal policy does. A regulator with broad powers but little appetite for confrontation may produce weaker outcomes than a narrower body whose decisions firms take seriously. A government that loudly praises innovation may still smother domestic capability through procurement rules that only large incumbents can satisfy. An administration that demands aggressive data sharing may find agencies quietly hoarding records if blame for misuse falls faster than credit for cooperation. Incentives are where declared goals meet lived behaviour.

This is also where legitimacy enters comparative assessment as a strategic variable rather than an ethical ornament. Public trust sounds abstract until it appears in decisions. Do citizens enrol in a digital identity system without fear that routine verification will become broad surveillance? Do firms disclose incidents promptly because they believe regulators will distinguish good-faith reporting from negligence? Do judges accept digital evidence because provenance is clear and challenge remains possible? Do civil servants share data across departments because the legal basis is workable and the reputational risk of prudent action is not ruinous? These are visible tests. They shape whether data systems deepen state capacity or remain resented, avoided, or quietly subverted.

A useful counter-example sharpens the framework. China is often described as a data superpower because of its scale, platform reach, state capacity for compulsion, and extensive digital infrastructure. Some of that description is justified. It would be foolish to deny the significance of its payment systems, platform integration, industrial depth, and state access to data within its jurisdiction. Yet scale alone does not complete the assessment. Comparative analysis must also account for dependence on political command, uneven local implementation, tensions between innovation and control, and the costs imposed by distrust, censorship, or abrupt regulatory shifts. The limitation here is important. A state can score highly on some dimensions of infrastructure and compulsion while generating different weaknesses in institutional adaptability or incentive quality. This does not refute the framework. It proves why the framework must remain multidimensional.

The same multidimensional discipline helps prevent another common mistake: assuming that the best model in one sector or country can simply be transferred to another. A secure digital identity regime that functions well in a small, administratively coherent state may behave differently in a federal system with fragmented authority and strong political distrust. A cloud strategy that improves resilience for one set of public workloads may create concentration risks for another. A privacy regime that disciplines firms effectively may impede information sharing in health or security unless exemptions are drawn and supervised with unusual care. Comparison becomes serious only when it resists slogans like open versus closed, sovereign versus dependent, innovative versus regulated. Those oppositions conceal more than they reveal.

The framework therefore asks a set of recurring questions rather than offering a single ranking. On infrastructure: where are the chokepoints, who controls them, how are they audited, and what happens when they fail? On institutions: who may compel access, who interprets the rules, who reviews misuse, who buys systems, who holds technical knowledge, who can force a correction? On incentives: who profits from concentration, who bears the cost of outages or breaches, what behaviours are rewarded inside agencies, what forms of public doubt can a government survive, and which cannot it? These questions are intentionally pedestrian. Grand strategy often turns on such things.

One broken link can reveal the whole chain. That is the quiet motif worth keeping in view, because failures in data systems rarely remain where they begin. A routing fault becomes a payment problem. A procurement shortcut becomes a sovereignty problem. A weak audit trail becomes a courtroom problem. A disputed identity match becomes a legitimacy problem. Comparative assessment should therefore resist static measurement. States are not to be judged only by what they possess, but by how their arrangements behave under strain, across sectors, and over time. What looks like strength in peacetime administration may turn brittle in crisis. What looks cumbersome in ordinary politics may prove valuable when scandal demands credible correction.

A durable framework must also make room for asymmetry. States rarely achieve even performance across all three layers. Some have impressive infrastructure and thin institutions. Others have capable institutions but weak market incentives that drive dependence on foreign suppliers. Some maintain public trust in specific domains, such as taxation or health, while facing deep suspicion in policing or immigration. Sectoral variation matters. A country may run an excellent payments system and a poor welfare data architecture; a strong national identity regime and a weak cyber incident response structure; credible privacy supervision and feeble procurement discipline. Assessment that collapses these differences into a single national label is usually a form of impatience dressed as insight.

That is why the framework should be used less as a scoreboard than as a method of disciplined comparison. It helps explain why countries with similar levels of wealth can diverge sharply in digital resilience, why states with ambitious sovereignty rhetoric may remain deeply dependent, why platform-rich economies may still struggle with public-sector integration, and why legality without operational capacity can produce false reassurance. It also guards against the seductions of novelty. New tools matter, but they enter older arrangements of law, bureaucracy, contracting, and political belief. The question is never only what the technology can do. The harder question is what kind of order it enters.

The point, then, is not to flatten national cases into a universal template. It is to compare them without falling for their self-descriptions. Infrastructure shows where control is materially possible. Institutions show whether control is governable. Incentives show whether the system will actually behave as designed when pressure arrives. When those three layers pull in the same direction, data power becomes more durable, more intelligible, and less reliant on improvisation. When they pull apart, states may still look strong until an outage, a scandal, a vendor dispute, or a jurisdictional conflict exposes the gap.

The forward test is severe but simple. Faced with a concrete system in a concrete country, what matters more: the size of the database, the elegance of the law, or the market confidence of the vendor? The safest answer is none of them alone. The real measure lies in the chain between them, and in whether that chain holds when a record must be trusted, a supplier must be challenged, a misuse must be corrected, or a public asked to believe that the system works for more than those who built it.

Chapter 2

From Records to Digital Memory

In 1791, revolutionary France ordered the standardisation of civil registers, binding births, marriages, and deaths more tightly to the authority of the state. On paper, the task looked administrative. In practice, it altered power. A name entered in a register could now travel further than the local priest, the village memory, or the family Bible. It could be counted, compared, taxed, conscripted, inherited through, and disputed before officials who would never meet the person concerned. The page mattered.

That page did more than record a life event. It helped turn scattered populations into governable subjects. The state could see more clearly, but only by insisting that society speak in forms it recognised: categories, maps, tables, property lines, household counts, standard spellings, fixed addresses. Every such gain in clarity carried a cost. Records simplified reality to administer it, and people pushed back when the simplification injured custom, obscured local knowledge, or widened official reach. The politics of data did not begin with servers or software. They began when rulers learned that a ledger could travel further than a soldier.

This older history matters because digital memory often arrives wrapped in the language of rupture, as though computers created an entirely new condition of state power. They did not. They accelerated, thickened, and redistributed an older ambition: to make people, resources, and risks legible enough for action. What changed was not the basic desire to record, classify, and compare. What changed was the speed of capture, the density of linkage, and the number of institutions that could claim a right to look. The filing cabinet did not disappear. It multiplied, networked itself, and slipped behind screens.

The central tension follows from that continuity. Records promise order. They also produce exposure. A state that cannot identify, count, and trace will struggle to tax fairly, police consistently, protect borders, manage welfare, or plan infrastructure. Yet every expansion of legibility also expands the chance of error, coercion, and political resentment. Classification can stabilise authority, but it can also flatten lives into categories that administrators trust too much. Secrecy can protect genuine security interests, but it can also become a habit of insulation. Continuous collection can make systems more responsive, yet it can also shift practical power towards the firms that mediate everyday digital life. The archive grows, and so does the argument over who controls it.

That argument now reaches far beyond archives in the narrow sense. It touches the terms on which states claim knowledge, the methods by which security agencies justify intervention, and the reasons private firms have become indispensable intermediaries in national information systems. A birth record once sat in a drawer until needed. A mobile device now emits a steady trail of location, contact, payment, and behavioural traces without any ceremonial moment of registration at all. The difference is not merely technical. It changes what counts as a record, when collection begins, and whether the subject even recognises that memory is being made. Administrative visibility once arrived in episodes. It now often arrives as background condition.

The stakes are therefore historical and immediate at once. Historical, because many disputes that appear novel are recognisable versions of older conflicts over registration, counting, secrecy, and official discretion. Immediate, because the scale and intimacy of current systems alter the consequences of each design choice. When records were sparse and retrieval was slow, forgetting often occurred by default. When records are copied endlessly and joined across systems, forgetting requires deliberate policy, technical discipline, and institutional restraint. When collection depended mainly on direct contact with the state, public resistance could often identify the collector. When collection is embedded in platforms, sensors, and services people use for ordinary life, the boundaries between public and private power become harder to see and easier to exploit.

Another stake lies in doctrine. National security institutions did not simply inherit digital tools; they helped shape the intellectual habits through which information came to be treated as an operational domain. Classification systems, signals intelligence, cryptographic practice, and early computing taught governments to regard information not as passive background but as terrain to be controlled, denied, protected, and acted upon. That habit migrated outward. Civil administration, policing, infrastructure management, and market regulation now operate in a world partly organised by concepts first sharpened under conditions of strategic rivalry. The language changes. The underlying impulse endures.

The path ahead follows that long arc. It begins with the administrative need to standardise people and territory into records that states could read, then moves into the security institutions that made information handling central to doctrine and organisation, before arriving at a condition in which memory no longer depends on deliberate filing alone but on continuous extraction from devices, platforms, and networks. The movement is not from primitive past to advanced present. It is from episodic inscription to persistent capture, from paper bottlenecks to distributed dependence, from state-centred recordkeeping to a world in which public authority must bargain with private infrastructures to know what it once recorded itself.

A useful way to hold the chapter together is to keep the page in view. A page can register a birth, conceal a programme, classify a secret, or become a data point inside a platform log. Its material form changes, yet the same struggle persists: who gets to write the record, who may read it, who may correct it, and what forms of power become possible once the record can travel. Some states built legitimacy through visible procedure around those questions. Others built fear. Most built mixtures of both.

What demands attention, then, is not whether digital memory is unprecedented in every respect. Parts of it plainly are. The deeper question is what remained constant beneath the novelty: the drive to render society intelligible, the institutional temptation to expand use once a record exists, and the political resistance that follows when memory ceases to look like service and becomes permanent supervision. Before asking what contemporary systems can do, it helps to ask what older record regimes were trying to achieve, what they broke in the process, and why the page still casts such a long shadow.

Bureaucratic legibility and early data regimes

In 1086, scribes working for William I completed what later generations called the Domesday Book, an extraordinary survey of landholding and productive capacity across much of England. The immediate purpose was practical and hard-edged: taxation, obligation, command. Villages, ploughlands, tenants, mills, woodland, livestock, dues - all were pressed into a written form that the Crown could read at a distance from the lives it described. The parchment mattered. A king who could not stand in every field could still claim to know what that field yielded, who held it, and what might be demanded from it.

Domesday did not invent state recordkeeping, but it crystallised something essential about political power: rulers govern better when reality arrives in standardised fragments they can compare. This was legible in an early form. The raw materials of social life - land, labour, lineage, custom, obligation - were translated into entries that could travel upwards through administrative layers. Local complexity did not disappear. It was compressed. That compression made the rule more portable, more durable, and more extractive. The page could move further than the official.

The lesson reaches far beyond medieval England. Modern administration did not simply grow larger; it grew more dependent on records that turned people and economies into objects of comparison. Registration, mapping, and statistics became instruments through which states learned to see populations not only as subjects of loyalty or force, but as countable units, taxable resources, military manpower, disease vectors, property holders, debtors, workers, migrants, and risks. The concept often called bureaucratic legibility names this transformation, but the phrase can sound too tidy. In practice, legibility was built through patient, coercive, and often contested acts of simplification. Names were fixed. Borders were drawn. Houses were numbered. Occupations were classified. Fields were measured. Categories hardened. The ledger closed around daily life.

That work always had a double character. It enabled coordination that looser political orders struggled to achieve. A state that can register births and deaths can plan schools, probate estates, and trace inheritance. A state that can map land can tax it more evenly, adjudicate disputes more consistently, and build roads or canals with greater confidence. A state that can count population by age, place, and occupation can mobilise armies, administer relief, and respond more coherently to epidemic disease. These were not trivial gains. They often served public goods as well as state interests. Better records could reduce arbitrary treatment. They could stabilise title. They could make obligations clearer. Administrative vision, at its best, did not merely extract; it also regularised.

Yet regularisation carried a cost. Standardised records flatten what they describe. The village with overlapping customary rights becomes a parcel with a taxable owner. The household with fluid kin arrangements becomes a census unit. The forest, used seasonally by different communities, becomes mapped as property. Once entered into official categories, local knowledge loses some of its authority. That is the deeper politics of early data regimes. States expanded their reach not only by force, but by persuading or compelling society to render itself in terms the centre could read. Legibility was therefore never a neutral administrative improvement. It was a transfer of interpretive power.

One can see this clearly in cadastral surveys. Napoleonic administration relied heavily on standardised land measurement and registration, and the cadastre became one of the defining tools of modern fiscal rule in parts of Europe. Measured fields, recorded ownership, and systematic maps made assessment more regular and, in principle, more equal. This was the language of fairness. It was also the language of penetration. Once landholding became visible in a more uniform way, taxation could bite more predictably, conscription could draw from better lists, and legal disputes could be settled with increasing reference to central records rather than purely local memory. The map did not simply describe territory. It reorganised authority over it.

The same pattern appeared in population statistics. The nineteenth-century census, taken in various forms across Europe and North America, did more than count heads. It trained states to think in aggregates. Population ceased to be only a collection of communities and became something that could be tabulated by age, sex, occupation, disease, literacy, housing, and movement. Public health, labour policy, urban planning, policing, and social insurance all benefited from this widening field of vision. But aggregation also encouraged a new confidence in categories that were often provisional, political, or blunt. Once a category entered official use, it could acquire a life of its own. People learned to live under it, evade it, exploit it, or resist it. Statistics did not merely reflect society. They helped to organise it.

Resistance, then, was not an accidental accompaniment to bureaucratic growth. It was built into the process. People resisted registration because records invite claims: taxes, military service, eviction, debt recovery, surveillance, religious interference, and loss of customary privilege. House numbering, passport systems, civil registration, and mandatory surnames often met opposition not because populations were irrationally hostile to order, but because they recognised what orderly knowledge could do in the hands of distant authority. Refusal sometimes took a dramatic form. More often, it took quieter forms: under-reporting, evasive mobility, false declarations, delayed registration, duplicate identities, informal transactions, reliance on community witnesses over documents, or selective compliance shaped by season and circumstance. Every early data regime produced its own shadow archive of avoidance.

A powerful example lies in civil registration. When states began to centralise the recording of births, marriages, and deaths, they did more than improve administrative neatness. They displaced older custodians of social fact, especially churches and local communities, and redefined which events counted as legally visible. A birth unregistered could complicate inheritance, military obligation, schooling, marriage, and poor relief. A death improperly recorded could distort property transfer or official demography. Civil registration created a more stable documentary foundation for modern government, yet it also inserted the state more deeply into intimate life. Parents, clergy, local notables, midwives, and household heads no longer stood alone as witnesses. The record now travelled upward. Families learned quickly that visibility could protect, but also bind.

The Prussian example in the nineteenth century is instructive because it shows how recordkeeping, statistics, and military administration could reinforce one another. Prussian governance acquired a reputation for disciplined record use, linking population knowledge to taxation, education, and conscription in ways that strengthened central control. Here the concept is not efficiency in the modern managerial sense, but administrative coherence. Lists matched obligations. Districts reported in regular form. Officials compared households against expected duties. The implication was political as much as technical. When records line up across domains, the state becomes harder to fool and easier to obey, whether citizens welcome that condition or not.

Still, legibility was never complete, and its incompleteness matters. Mountains, borderlands, informal settlements, nomadic groups, seasonal labour, illicit trade, and local patronage networks often exceeded or distorted what states believed they knew. Even strong administrative systems depended on intermediaries whose interests did not always align with the centre. Clerks copied badly. Surveyors cut corners. Local elites manipulated categories. Households adapted to the record. A tax roll might look authoritative while resting on stale assumptions or negotiated fictions. This is a useful limitation because it tempers any triumphalist account of early data regimes. States did not simply see more and therefore rule better. They saw selectively, through instruments that both clarified and deceived.

That limitation does not weaken the central claim. It sharpens it. The importance of early data regimes lies precisely in the fact that imperfect records still transformed political possibility. A flawed census can still enable conscription better than no census at all. A rough cadastral map can still widen taxation. A patchy civil register can still shift the burden of proof onto the individual who lacks documents. Administrative vision need not be total to be consequential. Partial legibility is often enough to alter the balance between ruler and ruled. The archive need not be complete to matter.

The colonial setting makes this even clearer. Imperial administrations used mapping, ethnographic classification, land surveys, and census categories to make distant populations governable with limited personnel. British India offers many examples, from revenue surveys to census practices that classified caste, tribe, religion, and occupation in increasingly formal ways. These exercises often presented themselves as descriptive and scientific. They were also political acts. Categories became administrative facts, and administrative facts shaped access to land, employment, law, and representation. The census table and the district map did not merely mirror society; they intervened in it. Resistance followed, sometimes through protest, sometimes through strategic self-description, sometimes through the stubborn refusal of lived identities to sit neatly inside official boxes.

The motif of the page helps here because it keeps the argument grounded. A page records, but it also excludes. To fit a life onto a form requires choices about what counts and what does not. Those choices accumulate into regimes of visibility. A pastoral route invisible to the cadastre may later appear as trespass. A customary marriage invisible to civil registration may later appear invalid. A local title invisible to the land office may later appear nonexistent. Bureaucratic legibility therefore creates not only knowledge, but vulnerability. People become governable through the same process that makes them contestable.

This is why trust cannot be separated from early data regimes. Trust sounds abstract until one asks what people actually do when officials arrive with forms, maps, and measuring chains. Do they disclose accurately? Do they hide assets? Do they contest classifications? Do they treat the register as protection or threat? Administrative knowledge grows faster where records carry reciprocal value, where the state not only extracts but can credibly secure rights, settle disputes, and constrain predation. Where records mainly serve taxation, conscription, or policing, compliance becomes thinner and more strategic. The visible behaviour is telling. A community that lines up to register land without fear is politically different from one that treats every form as a trap.

A second named example brings the point into sharper focus. The General Register Office in England and Wales, established in the nineteenth century, helped institutionalise civil registration and official statistics as routine foundations of governance. The achievement was not dramatic in the way battles or treaties are dramatic. It was administrative, and therefore durable. Births, marriages, deaths, causes of death, districts, occupations, and family events entered a more regular documentary order. That order strengthened public health analysis, inheritance procedures, and later welfare administration. But it also widened the state's claim to know society through forms that it designed. Standardisation brought protection and exposure together. The same certificate that enabled a claim could also become a gate through which the undocumented could not pass.

From the vantage point of the present, it is tempting to treat all this as prehistory - a slow paper world superseded by databases, networks, and sensors. That is a mistake. The central political logic remains strikingly familiar. Modern states still seek to turn complex lives into administrative categories that can circulate across institutions. They still rely on identifiers, maps, registers, and statistical abstractions. They still face resistance when records appear to exceed their declared purpose or when categories produce visible harm. The great change is not the birth of data politics, but the collapse of older frictions. Copying became easier. Linking accelerated. Retrieval quickened. Categories travelled further and faster. The page multiplied without disappearing.

Early data regimes therefore deserve attention not as quaint antecedents, but as the formative layer of modern information power. They established habits that still govern contemporary debates: the belief that better records yield better rule, the temptation to mistake classification for understanding, the administrative urge to reuse records for adjacent purposes, the resentment that grows when official vision outruns official restraint. Registration, mapping, and statistics taught states how to see populations in standardised form. They also taught populations that being seen can protect, discipline, burden, or erase.

The unresolved question is the one that will follow us forward. At what point does legibility cease to be the condition of fair administration and become a method of domination too deeply embedded to resist? Early states rarely answered that question cleanly. They proceeded by extending the register, refining the map, improving the count, and dealing with resistance as it appeared. Modern systems inherit the same impulse with far greater reach. Before turning to secrecy, intelligence, and the operational treatment of information, it is worth pausing over the old page and asking what kind of state first learned to trust it more than the people it described.

Cold War information systems and security doctrine

On 4 November 1952, the United States National Security Agency was established in Washington, inheriting and consolidating signals intelligence functions that had expanded rapidly after the Second World War. The bureaucratic act looked dry enough: a new agency, a new mandate, a new place in the machinery of government. The deeper change was harder to see at once. Information had ceased to be merely something governments possessed. It had become something they would fight over, shield, sort, intercept, classify, and operationalise as a distinct domain of statecraft. The message mattered.

That shift did not begin from nowhere. Wartime cryptanalysis, secure communications, and traffic analysis had already shown that intercepted signals could alter campaigns, expose intentions, and shape command. The Cold War hardened those lessons into doctrine. Rival blocs faced one another across military frontiers, diplomatic crises, ideological struggle, and nuclear risk. Under those conditions, information could no longer be treated as a passive record left behind by politics. It became part of politics itself: a field of contest in which advantage depended on who could collect, decrypt, conceal, authenticate, and act faster than an adversary. The file cabinet remained. The listening post joined it.

This was a decisive turn because it changed how states imagined the relationship between knowledge and power. Earlier administrative regimes sought legibility mainly to tax, conscript, regulate, and govern territory. Cold War institutions retained those habits but added a harsher premise: uncertainty itself could be lethal. A missile capability misunderstood, a troop movement missed, a cipher broken too late, a diplomatic signal misread, a source exposed by poor handling - each could carry strategic consequences well beyond the immediate document or transmission concerned. The result was a new kind of bureaucratic seriousness around information. Classification systems thickened. Clearance procedures grew more elaborate. Secure compartments multiplied. Communications security moved from technical speciality to institutional obsession. Information was no longer just evidence. It was terrain.

Signals intelligence showed the logic most clearly. A radio transmission intercepted at distance could reveal disposition, readiness, location, hierarchy, even when the text itself remained unreadable. This is the importance of traffic analysis, often underrated because it lacks the glamour of codebreaking. Who is communicating, how often, from where, in what pattern, with what interruptions - these questions turned emissions into operational clues. The concept matters because it reveals continuity with later digital systems. Valuable intelligence often lies not only in content but in relation, frequency, and timing. Cold War services learned to treat metadata, though they did not yet use that now familiar term, as a strategic asset. The implication was lasting: one need not know everything said to know something consequential.

Cryptography then sharpened the contest. Encryption promised secrecy, but secrecy itself became a competitive system rather than a fixed condition. Ciphers had to be designed, distributed, updated, protected, and used correctly by fallible humans. Key management mattered. Physical security mattered. Training mattered. A government could possess technically sound encryption and still fail because operators reused key material, mishandled devices, or sent sensitive traffic over insecure channels under pressure. Here again, the lesson reached beyond intelligence agencies. Information security did not rest in the elegance of the algorithm alone. It depended on organisations, procedures, and discipline. Doctrine followed practice: treat communications security as a matter of command responsibility, not merely engineering.

A named example makes the point. During the Cuban Missile Crisis of October 1962, signals intelligence, aerial reconnaissance, and analytical integration became central to decision-making in Washington. U-2 imagery provided visual confirmation of Soviet missile sites in Cuba, but that intelligence did not stand alone. It entered a system already shaped by interception, classification, compartmentation, and controlled dissemination. Information had to move fast enough to matter, yet narrowly enough to protect sources and methods. The visible behaviour was institutional: briefings structured around selected material, circulation restricted to cleared officials, decisions conditioned by what could be shown, inferred, or withheld. This was information treated as an operational domain under conditions of acute risk. The implication remains important. When stakes rise, the question is not simply what a state knows, but how it organises what it knows without either paralysing decision or compromising the means by which it came to know it.

Early computing expanded that organisational challenge. Machines entered intelligence and defence bureaucracies not as abstract symbols of modernity, but as tools for sorting, storing, comparing, and retrieving volumes of data that paper alone could no longer handle efficiently. Computing promised speed. It also imposed structure. Information had to be standardised enough for machine processing. Fields had to match. Categories had to be defined. Inputs had to be rendered legible to systems before systems could assist human analysis. That administrative demand linked Cold War security doctrine to older regimes of registration and tabulation. The computer did not abolish classification. It intensified the need for it. A badly ordered archive had once frustrated clerks; now it could degrade national-security analysis at scale.

This is why one should resist treating Cold War information systems as merely secret versions of civilian administration. They were secret, certainly, but they also developed distinctive assumptions that later spread outward. One assumption was that collection should be persistent, not merely episodic. Another was that retention might create future value even where current meaning was unclear. A third was that compartments could protect sensitivity while still allowing highly selective sharing. A fourth was that information flows could be engineered, audited, and prioritised as part of operational design. None of these ideas vanished when the Cold War ended. They migrated into cybersecurity, counter-terrorism, border control, platform governance, financial surveillance, and public-sector data infrastructures more broadly. The sealed envelope became a system.

The intelligence alliance often referred to as the Five Eyes illustrates this migration from national capability to networked information doctrine. The UKUSA Agreement, concluded in the early Cold War and shaping cooperation among the United States, the United Kingdom, Canada, Australia, and New Zealand, helped institutionalise a model in which interception, analysis, and dissemination could be distributed across trusted partners. The practical outcome was not simply more collection. It was a doctrine of shared access under controlled conditions, supported by common security understandings and reciprocal dependence. The concept here is asymmetrical cooperation. Intelligence sharing can enlarge capability, but it also redistributes authority over what is seen, what is withheld, and whose standards govern use. That pattern, too, survives. Contemporary states still enter data arrangements that promise collective security while quietly creating long-term dependencies.

Classification systems deserve special attention because they are often dismissed as bureaucratic routine when they are in fact constitutional mechanisms in disguise. To classify is to decide who may know, when they may know, and under what consequences disclosure becomes punishable. Cold War states built elaborate hierarchies of secrecy not simply to hide embarrassing facts, but to manage the operational value of information. A source protected could yield more. A method concealed could be reused. A channel preserved could sustain warning. Yet classification also created its own pathologies. Material could be overclassified out of caution, habit, or institutional self-protection. Relevant knowledge could remain trapped in compartments. Civilian oversight could weaken because those outside the system lacked access to challenge its claims. The visible behaviour tells the story: memos distributed only to narrow circles, committees briefed selectively, archives withheld for decades, officials learning to equate secrecy with responsibility itself.

A second named example reveals both the power and the limits of that approach. Venona, the United States project that decrypted portions of Soviet intelligence communications, began during the Second World War and continued into the early Cold War, with work centred in Arlington Hall, Virginia. The decrypts provided valuable insights into Soviet espionage, but their use was constrained precisely because revealing them too openly would expose the cryptanalytic achievement. Here secrecy protected capability. It also complicated public accountability and legal action. Evidence known inside the state could not always be deployed openly outside it. The lesson is enduring. Information power often produces a gap between what institutions know and what they can publicly justify. That gap may be strategically necessary. It can also corrode trust when citizens or courts encounter decisions without seeing the evidentiary scaffolding beneath them.

This is where continuity with the paper era becomes clearest. Earlier administrations used files, registries, and sealed memoranda to manage access and preserve authority. Cold War systems did not abandon these habits; they layered new technical means on top of them. Paper circulation lists, vaults, burn bags, codebooks, courier systems, and compartmented archives remained central even as computing and interception expanded the volume and speed of what could be handled. The old grammar of control persisted: mark, file, restrict, need-to-know, retain, destroy. Digital-era practices would later inherit the same grammar in altered form: access permissions, audit logs, segmentation, retention policies, and privileged users. The medium changed. The governing instinct did not.

Still, one should not exaggerate coherence. Cold War information systems were powerful, but they were often fragmented, duplicative, and vulnerable to the very bureaucratic failings they were built to contain. Rival agencies guarded holdings. Analysts drowned in reporting. Technical collection outpaced interpretive capacity. Classification obstructed coordination. False confidence sometimes attached itself to intercepted or processed material simply because it arrived through secret channels. This is the credible limitation any mature account must acknowledge. States did not master information merely by building larger secrecy machines. They also produced blind spots, delays, and internal barriers that could distort judgment as much as sharpen it.

The limitation does not undercut the broader argument. It refines it. What mattered in the Cold War was not flawless control, but the institutionalisation of information as an operational problem. National-security bureaucracies learned to ask recurring questions that now sit at the heart of data politics more generally. What should be collected? What should be retained? Who should have access? How should sensitive information be segmented? When does sharing increase capability, and when does it widen exposure? What forms of oversight are compatible with secrecy? What counts as operational necessity, and who gets to decide? These are not relic questions. They were sharpened in the Cold War and remain with us because modern states still struggle to balance capability, control, and legitimacy.

The private sector also entered the story earlier than nostalgia allows. Communications infrastructure, computing hardware, cryptographic equipment, and later software systems depended heavily on corporate research, manufacturing, and service provision. Even at the height of state secrecy, governments did not operate in total administrative isolation. They relied on contractors, laboratories, telecommunications providers, and industrial supply chains. The strategic implication is familiar by now. Information power has long depended on arrangements that blur the boundary between sovereign authority and private capability. Later chapters will show how that blur widened dramatically with platforms and cloud services, but its roots lie deeper. The state learned to operationalise information through systems it did not always fully own.

The motif of the message helps hold the argument together. A message can be intercepted, encrypted, routed, delayed, stored, classified, misread, or withheld. It can reveal content or only pattern. It can travel as paper, radio signal, cable traffic, machine-readable input, or database entry. Across those forms, the same political question recurs: who controls its movement and meaning? Cold War doctrine answered by building institutions that treated informational control as central to security itself. That answer was historically specific, born of nuclear rivalry and ideological confrontation, yet it also prepared the mental world of the present. Contemporary debates over data access, lawful interception, platform cooperation, metadata, retention, and oversight all carry traces of that earlier settlement.

What remains unresolved is whether the Cold War inheritance can be adapted without being simply reproduced at larger scale. Security institutions learned, with good reason, to prize collection, secrecy, and compartmented control. But when those habits migrate into wider administrative and commercial systems, the old logic can expand beyond its proper theatre. The question is no longer only how to protect a source or decode a transmission. It is when the treatment of information as an operational domain begins to reorganise ordinary governance in its image. That boundary matters, and it is not self-enforcing.

The turn to platforms and continuous collection

In June 2013, reporting based on documents disclosed by Edward Snowden revealed that the United States National Security Agency had obtained access to large volumes of communications data through a range of legal authorities and corporate relationships. The disclosures reached readers first through newspapers, but their force came from a more unsettling recognition: modern states no longer needed to build every channel of observation themselves. In Silicon Valley and far beyond it, private platforms had already built the habits, devices, and services through which people communicated, searched, travelled, purchased, watched, and worked. The state had not vanished from the picture. It had moved to the side of it, seeking access to systems that others had made indispensable. The tap had changed hands.

That moment mattered because it exposed a shift deeper than surveillance controversy alone. Earlier record regimes were often episodic. A person registered a birth, filed a tax return, crossed a border, applied for a licence, purchased land, or appeared in court. Information entered the record at recognisable moments. By the early twenty-first century, much of social and economic life was generating records continuously. Smartphones emitted location trails. Search engines logged queries. Payment systems captured transactions. Connected vehicles registered movement. Online platforms stored clicks, pauses, contacts, interests, and patterns of attention. Sensors in workplaces, cities, homes, and supply chains added further layers. Recording no longer depended chiefly on deliberate encounter with an official or institution. It became a background condition of ordinary life.

This change altered the strategic meaning of data in three ways at once. It multiplied volume, certainly, but volume is the least interesting feature. More important was the collapse of temporal distance between action and recording. Events no longer waited to be written down later. They were captured as they occurred, or close enough to it that reconstruction became routine. More important still was the expansion of *exhaust data*: records produced not because someone set out to describe a particular fact, but because digital systems leave traces as they function. Location histories, device identifiers, timestamps, browsing sequences, ad clicks, battery states, contact graphs, ride requests, failed logins, delivery scans, watch histories, and behavioural metadata often arise as by-products rather than formal declarations. These traces can look trivial in isolation. Joined together, they become unusually revealing.

Exhaust data differs from classical administrative records in both origin and political character. A census asks questions. A land register formalises title. A civil register records defined events. Exhaust data accumulates through use. The system does not wait to be told. It watches itself operate and stores the residue. That residue has strategic value precisely because it is plentiful, granular, and often difficult for the subject to perceive in full. A map application does not merely help someone navigate. It may also log routes, dwell times, destinations, device characteristics, and patterns of repetition. A social platform does not merely host speech. It can compare networks, infer affinities, track engagement rhythms, and detect changes in behaviour that users themselves barely notice. A food delivery service does not merely mediate a purchase. It generates data about household routine, address stability, timing, movement, and the reliability of local logistics. The record comes attached to the service.

This is the essence of the turn to platforms. Platforms do not simply store information. They organise repeated interactions among users, devices, advertisers, merchants, and infrastructures in ways that make continuous collection economically useful and technically normal. Their power comes from intermediation. They sit between parties, define the interface, set the defaults, and harvest the by-products. The strategic implication is profound. When the most consequential records of communication, mobility, consumption, and association are produced inside privately operated systems, states face a new condition of dependence. They may regulate, subpoena, license, procure, pressure, or partner, but they do not begin from ownership. Public authority meets a privately managed memory.

A good example lies in the smartphone. When Apple introduced the iPhone in 2007, and when Android rapidly followed, the mobile handset ceased to be merely a communication device and became a constant sensor bundle carried voluntarily through everyday life. GPS, accelerometers, cameras, microphones, Bluetooth radios, app permissions, browser histories, contact lists, messaging logs, and payment functions converged inside a device people kept close to the body. The strategic importance of the smartphone does not rest only in what it can explicitly reveal, such as a message or a call log. It rests in the dense trail of behavioural exhaust produced by routine use. A phone can show not just who someone spoke to, but whether they tend to move at regular hours, visit the same clinic, travel with another device, sleep in a stable location, linger at protest sites, commute across jurisdictions, or deviate from past patterns in ways that attract attention. This is not a ledger filled in after the fact. It is a trail continuously shed.

The commercial logic behind this arrangement matters as much as the technical one. Platforms collect exhaust data because it improves ranking, targeting, fraud detection, recommendation, logistics, pricing, retention, and product design. The state benefits indirectly from those investments even when they were not made for public purposes. A law-enforcement agency may request account data from a platform because the platform has already standardised, retained, and indexed it for its own reasons. A transport regulator may rely on ride-hailing records because a company has already built an operational view of mobility. A public-health authority may seek mobility or search data because private services captured behavioural changes faster than official statistics. States increasingly draw from wells they did not dig.

This explains why access has become more politically charged than collection in the older sense. During the paper era, states often controlled the institutions where records were created. In the platform era, the question is frequently whether and how public bodies can reach records generated elsewhere. Three broad routes recur. The first is compulsion: warrants, subpoenas, production orders, lawful access frameworks, or national-security authorities that require firms to disclose data. The second is partnership: voluntary information sharing, emergency coordination, research agreements, content moderation cooperation, procurement relationships, or public-private analytic arrangements. The third is market acquisition: data bought from brokers, vendors, or intermediaries that package behavioural traces into usable products. Each route distributes power differently. Each also alters the boundary between public authority and private information control.

The COVID-19 pandemic made this boundary unusually visible. In 2020, governments around the world sought faster ways to understand movement, contact, exposure, and compliance. In some places, public-health authorities turned to telecommunications providers and platform companies for mobility data or technical support. Apple and Google collaborated on exposure notification protocols built into mobile operating systems, effectively shaping the design space within which many national contact-tracing apps had to operate. This was an extraordinary display of private infrastructural power. States retained legal authority over public health policy, yet two technology firms could define what forms of proximity sensing were technically feasible, privacy-preserving, scalable, or politically acceptable across millions of devices. The visible decision was architectural: whether an exposure system would store data centrally or in a more decentralised way, whether identifiers would rotate, whether operating systems would permit certain background functions. The strategic lesson was unmistakable. Sometimes sovereignty encounters an application programming interface.

This platform dominance carries obvious benefits. Private firms often move faster than public agencies, attract stronger engineering talent, invest more consistently in usable interfaces, and maintain global infrastructures at scales many governments cannot match. Their systems can improve fraud detection, resilience, translation, routing, payments, cloud storage, and identity management. They can produce records of extraordinary richness. A state that refused all engagement with private platforms would often cripple its own ability to respond to cyber incidents, investigate crime, understand digital markets, or deliver services through channels people actually use. Dependence is real. So is utility.

Still, dependence is not a synonym for partnership, and utility is not the same as control. When states rely on private platforms for access to socially vital data, several tensions emerge at once. One concerns retention. Firms keep data for reasons shaped by business models, legal risk, storage cost, and public relations, not by the ideal needs of democratic accountability or national security. Another concerns format. Data may exist but remain difficult to export, interpret, or compare outside the systems that produced it. A third concerns jurisdiction. A platform may operate globally while storing data across regions, using affiliates, contractors, and legal entities that complicate straightforward access. A fourth concerns legitimacy. Citizens may accept data use for service improvement and reject the same data being repurposed for intelligence or enforcement. The trace exists. Its authorised uses do not settle themselves.

The market for data brokerage makes the situation still more complex. Commercial actors package location data, advertising identifiers, consumer attributes, and behavioural signals gathered from apps, websites, loyalty schemes, and other services. Some of these data products are highly aggregated. Others can be far more detailed. For states, this creates a tempting route around older assumptions about direct collection. A government agency may not need to compel data if similar material can be purchased. The legal and ethical status of such practices varies by jurisdiction and dataset, but the strategic point is broader than any one controversy. Public authority increasingly operates in an informational marketplace where the difference between what is possessed, what is bought, and what is inferred can be politically decisive.

Inference deserves special emphasis because platforms do not only capture what users explicitly disclose. They classify from patterns. A platform can infer likely home and work locations from repeated movement, estimate interests from browsing and viewing behaviour, identify clusters from social ties, detect mood shifts from interaction patterns, and model future choices from past routines. States benefit from this inferential turn when they access platform data directly, receive analytic products, or imitate commercial techniques in their own systems. Yet inference also complicates oversight. Rules written to govern specific categories of collected data may fail to address what can be derived from apparently mundane traces. A user may never disclose a sensitive trait in plain terms, while the system predicts it with troubling confidence from exhaust. The raw trace may look harmless. The model's output may not.

A credible limitation should be admitted here. Continuous collection is not universal, and platform power is not absolute. Many states still rely heavily on older administrative records. Large parts of daily life remain off-platform, informal, or only lightly digitised. Strong encryption, local processing, data minimisation, legal protections, and user choices can narrow what firms hold and what states can obtain. Some services retain less than outsiders assume. Some data are too noisy, too fragmented, or too legally restricted to yield much practical value. It would be foolish to imagine seamless omniscience. The modern record remains uneven. That limitation matters because it blocks a slide into technological fatalism.

Yet the limitation does not erase the structural change. Even imperfect continuous collection transforms the political economy of knowledge. States increasingly govern in a world where some of the most actionable records are generated outside traditional administrative channels, by firms whose incentives only partly align with public purposes. This changes how law is written, how investigations proceed, how emergency response is organised, and how sovereignty is understood. A ministry drafting lawful access rules must now think about encrypted messaging services and multinational cloud providers. A competition authority must consider whether market dominance over data-rich platforms distorts not only prices but state dependence. A privacy regulator must ask whether consent frameworks make sense when exhaust data are generated by routine system operation rather than conscious disclosure. An intelligence service must decide when partnership with platforms strengthens capability and when it creates political liabilities that outlast the immediate gain.

The older language of records also starts to fray under these conditions. A record once suggested a bounded document: a certificate, a file, a form, a ledger entry. Platform-era memory looks more like a stream. It is updated, versioned, copied, enriched, scored, and recombined across services. A person's digital presence may exist not as one stable dossier but as a shifting set of traces held in many places under many contractual terms. This makes both governance and resistance harder. Officials struggle to define the object they seek access to. Individuals struggle to know what exists, where it sits, and how one trace feeds another. Even deletion becomes ambiguous when backups, derived features, models, and partner systems remain in play. The tap never quite turns off.

The quiet motif of the trail helps keep the change in view. Earlier states built archives from deliberate encounters. Platform societies generate trails through movement itself. The trail is economically valuable, legally contested, and politically unstable. It can support fraud detection, public health, logistics, emergency response, and national security. It can also support manipulation, mission creep, discrimination, and a form of low-visibility dependence in which public authority leans ever more heavily on infrastructures it neither built nor fully governs. The same trace can reassure, expose, enrich, or accuse depending on who holds it and under what rules they act.

That is why the turn to platforms should not be described merely as a story of technological convenience or corporate success. It marks a reallocation of informational power. The state no longer stands only as collector and classifier. It increasingly appears as requester, negotiator, customer, regulator, litigant, and sometimes supplicant before private systems that mediate ordinary life. Some governments answer by expanding compulsion. Some cultivate partnerships. Some push for localisation, sovereign alternatives, or stricter retention duties. Some try to do all three. None escapes the basic fact that continuous collection has altered the location of strategic knowledge.

The hard question now presses forward. When the most valuable records are not those deliberately filed with the state but those continuously generated within private platforms, what counts as effective public control: the power to compel access after the fact, the capacity to shape platform design in advance, or the discipline to refuse certain kinds of access even when they are technically and commercially available? The answer will determine not only how states know, but what sort of authority they become in the act of knowing.

Chapter 3

National Data Infrastructure Dependencies

What does sovereignty mean when a government can issue orders within its territory but cannot easily trace the routes by which its most important data travels, where it rests, whose software governs it, or which supplier failure would force public services to a halt? The question sounds technical until a port stops clearing cargo, a ministry loses access to email, a hospital cannot verify records, or a certificate failure turns routine transactions into visible paralysis. Power begins to look less like command and more like maintenance.

The difficulty is that digital life invites a dangerous optical illusion. It appears weightless. Messages cross oceans without visible ships, services scale without new public buildings, identity checks happen with a click, and critical databases seem to reside nowhere in particular. Yet every act of apparent abstraction depends on stubbornly material arrangements: seabed routes, landing points, server halls, cooling systems, chip fabrication, code repositories, update chains, trust stores, procurement files, contractor knowledge, and engineers who know where the awkward dependencies are buried. The cloud has an address. Often several.

That materiality changes the argument about national capability. States do not merely need data; they need the means by which data moves, is processed, authenticated, stored, restored, and trusted under stress. Control over those means is rarely total. It is distributed across firms, regulators, infrastructure owners, standards bodies, utilities, and security institutions, often across several jurisdictions at once. A country may therefore sound digitally ambitious while remaining operationally exposed at points so mundane that political leaders barely mention them. A routing choice made years earlier, a procurement shortcut taken under budget pressure, a software component sourced without real scrutiny, a data centre clustered in the wrong place, or an ageing government network left half-integrated can quietly define the limits of state action long before any crisis makes those limits obvious.

This is the central tension: the systems that increase efficiency and scale often concentrate risk and obscure dependence. Centralisation can improve baseline security, reduce duplication, and make services easier to run. It can also create chokepoints that only reveal their political significance when they fail. Distributed systems can reduce single points of failure while producing their own burdens of coordination, interoperability, and uneven protection. Neither posture is inherently sovereign. Neither is inherently reckless. The real issue is whether a state understands its dependencies well enough to govern them, test them, and, when necessary, contest them.

The stakes run deeper than technical resilience. National data infrastructure shapes bargaining power. A government that depends heavily on external network routes, foreign-owned compute, proprietary trust mechanisms, and opaque software supply chains may still function smoothly for long periods. Smooth operation can conceal structural weakness. When disagreement sharpens over sanctions, lawful access, export controls, vendor risk, or crisis response, dependence stops looking like efficiency and starts looking like leverage in someone else's hands. What seemed to be a service relationship may prove to be a political relationship conducted by other means.

This is equally true inside the state. Grand strategies often assume that governments can integrate, share, and secure data once the right policy language is in place. They cannot, unless the underlying estates permit it. Public networks are old in uneven ways. Some are patched and serviceable, others tangled by legacy contracts, fragmented identity systems, weak documentation, and staffing shortages that turn ordinary maintenance into institutional fragility. The bottleneck is often not vision but plumbing. A minister may announce transformation; a civil servant still has to reconcile incompatible systems, recover a neglected interface, or persuade a contractor to explain code nobody in the department now fully understands. Capability is frequently decided in those rooms.

A more realistic way to think about national strength therefore begins below the level of rhetoric. It asks where the physical routes lie, who controls the facilities, how energy and cooling shape compute, which trust anchors allow systems to recognise one another, how public networks actually connect, what legacy burdens prevent migration, and how deeply hardware and software supply chains tie domestic ambition to external production.

The movement that follows runs from the seabed and the exchange point to the server hall and the certificate store, from the government estate to the supplier chain behind it. At each stage, the same question sharpens: where does convenience end and dependency begin?

That question matters because dependency is not automatically failure. Modern states cannot sever themselves from global infrastructure without inflicting damage on their own economies, administrations, and alliances. Interdependence is normal. The strategic challenge is to distinguish tolerable interdependence from brittle reliance, and ordinary outsourcing from the quiet transfer of judgment to suppliers whose incentives only partly align with public need. Trusted supplier debates often miss this point. Trust is not a mood. It has to be built from audit rights, testing, visibility, fallback plans, and the capacity to verify claims rather than merely accept them.

A useful image for the chapter is the cable under the street: out of sight, taken for granted, indispensable until cut. Much of national data infrastructure is governed in exactly that register. The public rarely sees it. Political debate notices it late. Yet whole theories of digital power rise or fall on whether those hidden connections can be relied upon, repaired, substituted, or governed when pressure arrives. The same applies to names in a certificate chain, to electricity feeding a data centre, to a civil service contract nobody intended to become permanent, to a chip supply dependency buried several layers beneath a user interface. Hidden systems make visible politics.

The harder diagnostic, then, is not whether a country calls itself sovereign, connected, open, or secure. It is whether its data infrastructure can survive dispute, shock, and ordinary neglect without turning national power into a story of surprised dependence. Before asking what data can do for a state, it is worth asking what the state is standing on, who else is touching it, and which of those touchpoints could become a choke in the moment that matters most.

Undersea cables, routing, and chokepoints

On 30 January 2008, damage to undersea cables in the eastern Mediterranean disrupted internet and telecommunications connectivity affecting Egypt, India, and parts of the Gulf. The immediate effects were uneven, but the political lesson was sharp. Data that felt placeless suddenly revealed its route. Traffic slowed, services faltered, and governments were reminded that digital dependence runs along physical paths laid across seabeds, funnelled through coastal landing stations, and managed through commercial and regulatory decisions that few citizens ever see. The sea had left a fingerprint.

That moment helps correct a persistent misconception. The internet is often described as if it were naturally decentralised, frictionless, and self-healing in all circumstances. Parts of that description are true in limited technical senses. Yet the global movement of data depends heavily on concentration. Most intercontinental traffic still travels through submarine fibre-optic cables. Those cables land at specific points. They connect to terrestrial backhaul. They pass through exchange facilities and commercial arrangements. They are maintained by ships, licensed by states, financed by consortia, and increasingly shaped by large private firms with global platform interests. What looks virtual from a screen is, at decisive moments, a question of geography and governance.

The strategic importance of undersea cables begins with a simple fact: routes create dependencies. A country connected to the wider network through a small number of cable landings, or through nearby hubs controlled elsewhere, may enjoy rapid access and low latency in ordinary conditions while remaining exposed to concentrated failure. The concept here is not mere fragility, but chokepoint risk. A chokepoint exists when disruption, coercion, or technical failure at a narrow point in the system can produce outsized effects downstream. Undersea cable systems generate such points in several ways - at landing stations, along heavily used maritime corridors, within regional hubs, and inside the commercial arrangements that determine how traffic is handed from one network to another. The implication is blunt. Sovereignty does not end at the shoreline, but it often thins there.

Physical concentration matters because repair is never instantaneous and rerouting is never cost-free. Cable faults occur for mundane reasons as well as strategic ones: fishing activity, anchors, undersea landslides, equipment failure, or accidental damage during maritime works. States do not need to assume sabotage to treat these systems as critical. A country whose public services, financial markets, logistics, cloud access, or diplomatic communications depend on a handful of high-capacity routes faces a resilience problem even in peacetime. The visible signs are practical. Does traffic reroute cleanly when one path fails? Do core services remain usable? Are public authorities able to see where the bottleneck sits, or do they wait for private carriers to explain it after the fact? Risk is rarely abstract here. It appears as delay, congestion, service degradation, and the loss of priority over one's own traffic.

A second named example makes this clearer. In March 2011, the earthquake and tsunami in Japan disrupted a wide range of infrastructure, including communications systems and power networks. The wider lesson for data infrastructure was not that submarine cables alone determine national resilience. It was that network robustness depends on how physical routes, terrestrial facilities, power supply, and restoration capacity interact under stress. A cable may survive while the landing environment, upstream power, or network equipment does not. The strategic concept is layered dependency. Data traffic rests not on one asset but on a chain of assets whose failure modes differ and can compound. The implication is important for national assessment: governments that map only the cable and ignore the landing station, the grid, the exchange point, or the operator relationship are not really mapping the system.

Landing stations deserve more attention than they usually receive in public debate. They are the coastal facilities where undersea cables come ashore and connect to terrestrial networks. Because they sit at the meeting point between international and domestic connectivity, they can become quiet centres of leverage. Their ownership, licensing, physical security, and redundancy shape whether a state can route traffic flexibly, inspect critical infrastructure risks, or recover quickly from disruption. A landing station that appears commercially efficient may still create national exposure if too many routes converge there, if backhaul options are limited, or if governance is opaque. One building can matter. That is the political meaning of infrastructure concentration.

Routing decisions add another layer of vulnerability because data does not necessarily travel by the most geographically direct or politically comfortable path. Packets follow routes shaped by network design, congestion, cost, peering agreements, and commercial preferences. That means data generated inside one country may transit others unexpectedly, pass through foreign exchange points, or depend on carriers subject to external legal and strategic pressures. The concept here is path dependence in motion. Governments often speak about where data is stored, but routing can matter just as much. A service hosted domestically may still rely on international transit for essential components. Sensitive communications may cross jurisdictions that a government would never have chosen if physical path were obvious to the user. The implication is not that every detour is a crisis. It is that visibility into routes is part of sovereignty, and many states possess less of it than they assume.

Peering arrangements help determine those routes. Peering is the set of agreements by which network operators exchange traffic, either directly or through intermediaries. It sounds technical and commercial because it is both. It is also strategic. A network that depends heavily on paid transit from a small number of upstream providers may face higher costs, poorer resilience, and weaker bargaining power than one with diverse peering relationships and healthy exchange infrastructure. A state that permits domestic traffic to hairpin through foreign hubs because local interconnection is thin may be accepting avoidable exposure. The visible behaviour again matters. When users in the same country reach domestic services by way of foreign networks, the issue is no longer merely engineering elegance. It is a question about what national infrastructure has failed to provide.

This is one reason regional hubs acquire geopolitical significance. Singapore, Marseille, London, and other major interconnection points matter not simply because cables land nearby, but because dense commercial ecosystems of carriers, exchanges, cloud providers, and data centres cluster around them. Traffic seeks efficiency. Capital seeks scale. The result is that certain cities become gravitational centres for digital flows well beyond their national boundaries. That concentration can create valuable connectivity and lower costs for surrounding regions. It can also create dependence on infrastructure, firms, and legal environments located elsewhere. States linked through such hubs enjoy access while ceding some control. The trade-off is rarely visible to ordinary users. It becomes visible when disputes over regulation, sanctions, surveillance, or outage response begin to touch the hub itself.

The governance of cable systems complicates matters further. Many cable projects have historically been financed by consortia involving telecom operators from several countries. More recently, large technology companies have played a growing role as investors, capacity buyers, or direct participants in subsea infrastructure. That shift has strategic implications. When platform firms help shape routes, capacity, and interconnection, the boundary between public communications infrastructure and private commercial strategy grows thinner. States then confront not only foreign carriers or foreign governments, but firms whose incentives combine commercial efficiency, service performance, cloud architecture, and geopolitical calculation. A route chosen for business reasons may later carry strategic consequences. Private capital lays public dependency.

This does not mean states are powerless. They regulate landing rights, issue licences, review foreign investment, impose security conditions, shape domestic exchange policy, and in some cases support route diversification or strategic cable projects. They can also require operators to meet resilience obligations, maintain contingency plans, or cooperate with security agencies under defined legal frameworks. Yet formal authority does not guarantee practical command. A ministry may approve a cable landing without possessing the technical depth to assess broader routing exposure. A regulator may oversee market competition while leaving systemic redundancy underexamined. A security service may understand the threat but lack influence over the commercial decisions that actually determine interconnection. Governance fragments easily in this domain, and fragmentation itself becomes a vulnerability.

A credible limitation should be acknowledged. The global internet has repeatedly shown an ability to reroute around faults, and not every cable break produces national crisis. Many countries benefit from substantial redundancy, and network operators routinely manage congestion and restoration in ways invisible to end users. It would be wrong to imagine a world where any single cut plunges a connected society into darkness. The resilience of packet-switched networking is real. But resilience is not evenly distributed. Some states, regions, and sectors enjoy far more alternatives than others. Some services degrade gracefully; others fail sharply. The existence of rerouting does not erase chokepoints. It changes how they bite.

The more serious error lies in assuming that because traffic *can* reroute, questions of power disappear. They do not. Rerouted traffic may become slower, costlier, or more exposed to foreign transit. Emergency capacity may be available for some users and not others. Governments may discover that they have little priority over the networks their essential services depend upon. Commercial operators may restore profit-critical paths before politically sensitive but less lucrative ones. These are governance questions disguised as network questions. They reveal who decides under pressure, whose traffic matters, and what a state can compel when infrastructure it treats as nationally significant is privately owned and commercially optimised.

The older language of sea power offers a useful parallel, though not a perfect one. Control over maritime routes once shaped trade, military reach, and imperial resilience through choke points, ports, shipping lanes, and coaling stations. Undersea cables inherit some of that logic without replicating it exactly. They are easier to ignore until they matter, harder for the public to picture, and more deeply entangled with private ownership and technical standards. But they still organise strategic space. They still create corridors of value and points of pressure. A state that ignores them is not escaping geography. It is merely forgetting where geography now sits.

The quiet motif of the shoreline helps keep the argument honest. The shoreline is where abstraction gives way to infrastructure. Somewhere beyond the screen, the signal comes ashore, enters a station, meets a contract, passes through a router, and becomes subject to institutions. That crossing is where digital dependence becomes visible enough to govern. Or fails to. If a state cannot say with confidence how its most important data enters and leaves, who controls the main exchanges, where domestic traffic unnecessarily departs the country, or how it would cope with a prolonged fault at a major landing point, then its claims about digital sovereignty rest on a surprisingly thin foundation.

The hardest diagnostic is therefore not whether a country possesses internet access, cloud ambition, or a flourishing digital economy. It is whether the country can trace the routes beneath that success and judge which ones are merely efficient and which ones have become politically dangerous. Undersea cables, routing, and peering arrangements do not just carry data. They distribute leverage. The question that follows is simple to ask and difficult to answer: when the next disruption arrives, who decides where the traffic goes, and whose interests are built into that decision before the crisis even begins?

Data centres, energy, and operational resilience

In March 2021, a fire at OVHcloud's facility in Strasbourg, France, destroyed one data centre building and disrupted services tied to others on the same site. Websites vanished. Client systems went dark. Some customers discovered, in the least charitable way possible, that redundancy they had assumed existed either had not been configured properly or had remained too close to the original point of failure. The cloud briefly regained its correct proportions. It looked like a building.

That episode matters because it strips away one of the most persistent illusions in digital politics: the belief that storage and compute float above the material world. They do not. Data lives in places that need land, power, cooling, physical security, maintenance staff, network access, and protection against fire, flood, heat, sabotage, and routine technical failure. A state that depends on digital systems therefore depends on a territorial infrastructure every bit as real as roads, substations, ports, or pipelines. The server hall hums. Politics enters with the electricity.

The strategic value of data centres begins with concentration. Compute and storage gain efficiency when capacity is aggregated, standardised, and operated at scale. That is why large facilities and cloud regions have become so attractive to both firms and governments. They lower certain costs, simplify management, and often deliver stronger baseline security than scattered, poorly maintained server rooms ever could. The concept here is centralisation as capability. A concentrated estate can patch faster, monitor more closely, recover more predictably, and attract more specialised expertise. The implication is real: many states are safer because they moved sensitive workloads out of neglected cupboards and into professionally managed environments.

Yet the same concentration creates a second and harsher concept: systemic dependence. When too much data capability sits in too few places, failures stop being local mishaps and become social events. A cooling failure is no longer only an engineering problem if courts lose access to records, hospitals struggle with systems, or payment services stall. A grid constraint is no longer just an energy issue if it delays new compute capacity for public administration, research, or national industry. Operational resilience turns on whether concentration has been balanced by redundancy, geographic dispersion, fallback plans, and institutional clarity about what must keep running when parts of the estate do not.

Energy sits at the centre of this balance. Data centres consume electricity continuously, and not only for computation itself. Power also supports cooling, network equipment, security systems, and the layers of continuity infrastructure meant to bridge fluctuations and outages. This makes national data capability inseparable from energy policy in ways public debate often understates. A government may speak confidently about digital transformation, artificial intelligence, or sovereign cloud, yet those ambitions must eventually meet the transmission network, the planning regime, the generation mix, and the politics of local consent. A server does not care about a strategy document. It cares about stable current.

The visible decisions that follow are not abstract. Where can a new facility secure reliable grid access? Which users receive priority during stress? How long can backup systems sustain operations before fuel logistics become the real bottleneck? Can critical workloads be shifted if a region faces prolonged disruption? Does the state know which public services depend on which private energy and compute combinations? These questions are strategic because they determine whether data systems remain available under pressure. Availability is often spoken of as a technical property. In practice it is an infrastructural settlement between the digital estate and the energy system beneath it.

The heatwave that affected parts of the United Kingdom in July 2022 offered a useful warning. Google and Oracle both reported service disruption tied to cooling problems in their London-area facilities. The immediate cause lay in environmental stress rather than hostile action, but that distinction is less comforting than it first appears. Extreme weather tests operational resilience by attacking the assumptions built into facility design: expected temperatures, cooling margins, staffing access, equipment tolerances, and recovery procedures. The server hall does not merely hum; it heats. A country that treats data infrastructure as detached from climate, water, and grid realities is not thinking strategically enough.

Cooling deserves attention in its own right because it reveals how thin the line can be between apparent abstraction and material constraint. Compute produces heat. Dense compute produces a great deal of it. To keep systems stable, operators rely on combinations of air handling, chilled water, evaporative techniques, liquid cooling, and careful facility design. Each method links the digital estate to local environmental conditions and physical resources. This has political implications. A data centre may promise jobs, investment, and digital capability while also drawing scrutiny over land use, energy demand, and water consumption. The strategic argument is not that such facilities are undesirable. It is that they belong squarely inside infrastructure governance rather than outside it, as if they were simply neutral warehouses for information.

National capability also depends on the industrial ecosystem around data centres. Building and operating modern facilities requires specialised construction, electrical engineering, cooling expertise, security services, fibre connectivity, backup power systems, monitoring software, and maintenance regimes that can be trusted when things go wrong. This is where industrial capacity quietly enters the story. A state that lacks the skills, suppliers, or regulatory competence to support these environments may still rent world-class compute from abroad, but it will do so on terms shaped elsewhere. Conversely, a country with strong local engineering, dependable utilities, and disciplined planning may secure a more durable data base even without commanding the largest digital firms. Capability is not only what is owned. It is what can be built, repaired, inspected, and expanded without strategic surprise.

A second named example sharpens the point from a different angle. During Hurricane Sandy in October 2012, lower Manhattan suffered major power disruption and flooding that affected numerous data centres and telecommunications facilities in New York. What mattered was not merely that servers were exposed to a storm. The episode showed how urban concentration, power dependency, basement fuel systems, building design, and telecom interconnection could combine into cascading failure. Some facilities remained operational longer than others. Some customers discovered their supposed resilience plans had assumed away the very conditions that now defined the crisis. The lesson was broader than New York. Resilience cannot be purchased as a label. It has to be tested against the full chain of dependency, including the dull parts planners prefer to skip.

This is why governments should treat major data infrastructure as critical infrastructure in more than name. The phrase has been used so loosely that it risks losing force. Used seriously, it means at least three things. It means mapping which public and socially vital functions depend on which facilities, providers, and regions. It means planning for disruption not only at the level of cyber attack, but at the level of fire, flood, heat, fuel shortage, labour shortage, supply delay, and telecom failure. It also means recognising that resilience is a public problem even where infrastructure is privately owned. The facility may belong to a company; the failure will belong to society.

Public authority often stumbles here because procurement encourages abstraction. Agencies buy storage, software, hosting, or cloud services as contractual outputs and lose sight of the physical chains beneath them. They know the service level agreement. They do not always know the substation, the cooling configuration, the regional clustering, or the recovery assumptions built into the provider's design. This becomes dangerous when many agencies converge on similar providers or regions without a whole-of-government view of concentration risk. What appears to each department as a sensible outsourcing decision can aggregate into a national dependence that nobody explicitly chose. The server hall hums behind the contract.

The language of resilience can also mislead when it implies a binary distinction between robust and fragile systems. Real resilience is layered and uneven. A service may survive a power event because backup generation works, then fail later because network congestion, staff access, or downstream software dependencies were not equally protected. A dataset may be safely replicated but still operationally unavailable because identity services or certificate checks sit elsewhere. A cloud region may withstand local failure but create wider vulnerability if too many critical workloads rely on the same provider architecture. The concept that matters is not hardening alone, but dependency mapping. One must know what depends on what, in what order, with what fallback.

A credible limitation belongs here. Centralised professional facilities are often far more resilient than the decentralised estates they replaced. Many public-sector server rooms were insecure, underpowered, poorly documented, and dependent on tiny teams. Hyperscale providers and serious colocation operators have frequently improved discipline, patching, monitoring, and disaster recovery well beyond what small institutions could sustain alone. It would be foolish to romanticise a return to scattered local control as if proximity guaranteed resilience. It does not. Centralisation has real benefits, and many organisations are safer because of it.

But that limitation changes the argument rather than cancelling it. The choice is not between cloud concentration and some fantasy of sovereign self-sufficiency. The real question is whether states can enjoy the security and efficiency gains of concentrated infrastructure without surrendering visibility over clustered risk. Resilience requires more than selecting reputable providers. It requires distribution across sites where appropriate, clear workload prioritisation, tested restoration procedures, contractual access to operational information, and internal public expertise strong enough to interrogate supplier assurances. A backup that has not been tested under realistic conditions is a form of optimism. Optimism does not keep services running.

Operational resilience also depends on the treatment of data centres within wider national emergency planning. If facilities are critical, then transport access for staff matters during disruption. Fuel delivery to generators matters. Priority restoration for power and telecoms matters. Coordination between operators and public authorities matters. So does law enforcement awareness, because physical intrusion or sabotage may target the supposedly dull edges of digital capability rather than the software stack itself. A secure login does not help much if the building cannot stay powered, cooled, connected, and staffed.

The geopolitical dimension follows naturally. States compete not only over who writes software or trains models, but over where compute can be hosted, who can access reliable energy, which jurisdictions attract major facilities, and whose industrial base can support expansion. A nation with constrained grid capacity, uncertain planning, weak supply chains, or brittle political consent may find its digital ambitions throttled by infrastructure long before policy documents acknowledge the problem. Meanwhile, countries that secure favourable energy conditions, strong fibre links, predictable regulation, and credible physical resilience may acquire quiet strategic weight. Data capability is not merely coded. It is sited.

The quiet image of the building should therefore remain in view. The building contains racks, yes, but also power feeds, chillers, generators, access controls, cable trays, fire suppression, loading bays, maintenance routines, and people carrying badges and tools. If political argument forgets the building, it will misunderstand digital power. States do not preserve continuity because they praise innovation or invoke sovereignty. They preserve continuity because the material estate behind their digital systems has been placed, supplied, audited, and rehearsed as though it mattered as much as any other critical infrastructure. It does.

The unsettled question is not whether data centres belong to national strategy. They plainly do. The harder question is what kind of national strategy they demand. Should governments prioritise concentration for efficiency, dispersion for resilience, domestic siting for control, or international integration for scale? Each choice solves one problem by intensifying another. The answer cannot be read from marketing claims or high-level rhetoric. It has to be read in the hum of the server hall, in the grid map behind it, and in the uncomfortable possibility that a state's digital memory is only as durable as the physical systems it has chosen to take for granted.

Domain name systems and trust anchors

In March 2011, browsers began to reject digital certificates issued by DigiNotar after the Dutch certificate authority was compromised. The immediate outcome was technical and abrupt. Users encountered security warnings. Services that depended on those certificates could no longer present themselves as trustworthy. In the Netherlands, the disruption reached government systems as well as ordinary websites, because public services had relied on the same trust relationships that underpinned commercial traffic. A familiar icon vanished. The small padlock that most users never think about became a political fact.

That episode remains useful because it shows how much of digital life depends on agreements about names and trust that feel invisible until they fail. When a person types an address into a browser, sends an email, opens a banking app, or logs into a government portal, several background systems work together to answer questions so basic that they rarely appear as questions at all. What name corresponds to this service? Which machine should receive the request? Is this really the service it claims to be? Can the connection be trusted? These are not ornamental details. They are the conditions under which ordinary digital exchange becomes governable at scale.

The strategic importance of naming begins with the domain name system, the distributed mechanism that translates human-readable names into network addresses. DNS sounds administrative because it is administrative. It is also foundational. Names organise access. They make services discoverable, memorable, routable, and brandable. A government service without a stable name is not merely inconvenient; it becomes harder to find, harder to trust, and harder to distinguish from fraud. A banking site, a customs portal, a tax service, an electoral information page, or an emergency alert platform all depend on a naming architecture that users can rely upon without understanding it in detail. The visible behaviour is simple: people type a familiar address and expect to arrive at the right place. The strategic implication is deeper. Whoever helps govern the naming system helps govern the surface of digital authority itself.

Yet a name alone is never enough. Users also need confidence that the service at the other end of the connection is genuine. That is where certificates and the wider public key infrastructure enter the picture. A certificate binds a domain name to a cryptographic key through an attestation by a certificate authority that the binding is valid. Browsers and operating systems then decide whether to trust that authority based on their internal trust stores, which contain root certificates treated as acceptable sources of validation. The conceptual leap matters. Everyday digital trust rests on chains of delegated confidence. A user does not personally verify the server of a public service, a hospital, or a bank. The device performs a ritual of trust on the user's behalf. The padlock is only the surface.

This arrangement has three strategic features. It is distributed rather than centrally sovereign. It is technical but deeply institutional. And it fails in ways that can become systemic very quickly. Distributed, because no single government fully controls the global set of root authorities, domain registries, software trust stores, and browser policies that shape whether names resolve and certificates validate. Institutional, because trust is not created by mathematics alone. Someone decides which certificate authorities are included, on what terms, after which audits, with what response to incidents. Systemic, because once a root or intermediate authority is distrusted, the consequences can spill across sectors, borders, and public functions. The small warning box on a screen can suddenly expose the hidden map of dependency beneath it.

The DigiNotar incident is instructive precisely because it linked commerce, administration, and security in one failure. Certificate mis-issuance reportedly enabled fraudulent certificates for high-value domains, raising the possibility of interception and impersonation. Once confidence in the authority collapsed, major browser vendors moved to distrust its certificates. That response was rational from the perspective of users' security, but it also revealed a hard truth about national dependence. A state may run its own portals, collect its own taxes, and administer its own services, yet still rely on a trust chain whose decisive judgements sit partly with external software vendors and international technical arrangements. Sovereignty here is conditional. The service belongs to the state; the trust needed to reach it may not.

Naming and certificate validation are often treated as purely technical layers because they function best when they remain unobtrusive. But they also allocate power in highly practical ways. Control over a top-level domain registry can affect who may obtain names, under what conditions, and with what dispute mechanisms. Control over recursive resolvers, enterprise DNS policies, or operating system trust stores can influence which services users reach, which warnings they see, and which certificates are accepted or rejected. Governments may regulate registries, require local presence, impose security obligations, or try to shape browser behaviour through procurement and national standards. Platform firms may do the same through software defaults and device ecosystems. The result is not a neat hierarchy but a layered field of authority in which technical configuration, market share, and legal jurisdiction interact continuously.

This interaction becomes especially important in moments of crisis. When certificate trust fails, the effects are not confined to cyber specialists. Public servants may be unable to reach internal systems. Citizens may hesitate before using online government portals. Payment flows may be interrupted.

Email systems may reject connections. Emergency communication can become less reliable precisely when clarity matters most. Trust, then, should not be spoken of as an abstraction. In this domain it takes visible form. Does the browser warn? Does the app connect? Does the user proceed? Does the administrator rotate certificates and update dependencies fast enough to prevent service disruption? A trust anchor proves its value in behaviour, not rhetoric.

A second named example shows how disputes over trust can disrupt at scale even without a dramatic compromise like DigiNotar. In 2017, Google announced plans to stop trusting certificates issued by Symantec's public certificate infrastructure, citing long-running concerns about mis-issuance and operational practices. The consequences unfolded across a wide range of websites and services that depended on Symantec-issued certificates. Operators had to replace certificates, review inventories, coordinate with vendors, and manage the transition before browser distrust hardened into user-facing failure. What mattered was not merely that one company challenged another. A decision by major browser vendors about certificate trust rippled across the digital estate because browsers mediate so much of everyday access. The visible action was administrative: reissue, replace, audit, test, redeploy. The strategic lesson was plain. Trust stores are governance instruments, even when they appear as product settings.

The politics of naming are no less significant. Domain names signal legitimacy and familiarity. States care about country-code domains because they bundle national presence, regulatory reach, and public expectation into a recognisable naming space. Yet much of daily traffic does not stay neatly inside national namespaces. Governments use global top-level domains. Citizens access public services through app links, search results, bookmarks, and embedded sign-ins rather than by carefully typing official addresses. Private platforms shape visibility through indexing and interface design. Phishing attacks exploit this by mimicking names that appear close enough to fool hurried users. A state's ability to maintain trusted naming conventions, secure domain administration, and clear public communication therefore matters as part of national resilience. Fraud lives in the gap between technical correctness and human habit.

This is also why DNS security cannot be reduced to a question of censorship versus openness, important though that debate is. DNS infrastructures support routing and reachability, but they also provide points of intervention. States can direct blocking, mandate resolver policies, or shape how registries and registrars operate within their jurisdiction. Firms can prioritise security features, choose how strictly to enforce certificate warnings, or determine which roots and algorithms to support. Security agencies may seek faster takedowns of malicious domains. Civil liberties groups may warn about overbroad interference with access and speech. The same infrastructure that helps a person find a tax portal can help a government suppress a dissident site or disrupt a criminal campaign. Naming is mundane until it becomes coercive.

A credible limitation should be acknowledged here. The trust architecture of the modern internet, for all its awkward politics, has enabled a vast amount of secure exchange at global scale. Most certificate issuance works without public drama. Most name resolution succeeds quietly. Most users do not need to understand root stores, chain validation, or DNSSEC for systems to serve them tolerably well. It would be wrong to imply that distributed trust is simply a hidden scandal waiting to happen. The system works often enough to sustain daily life across banking, commerce, messaging, logistics, and public administration. That matters.

But functioning often is not the same as being strategically settled. The same architecture that enables global interoperability also creates dependencies that individual states cannot fully master alone. A government may wish to secure domestic services more tightly, yet still rely on international browser ecosystems, certificate standards, and software update cycles. It may seek more control over its namespace while discovering that users' actual pathways to services run through search engines, mobile operating systems, and app stores it does not govern. It may trust a certificate authority until a compromise, audit failure, or vendor decision changes the calculus overnight. Interoperability gives reach. It also gives others influence over the conditions of trust.

This is why trust anchors deserve to be treated as critical infrastructure in their own right, though of a peculiar kind. They are not warehouses, cables, or substations. They are institutional and technical reference points that permit systems to recognise one another as valid. Their criticality lies in the fact that failure can be disproportionate to visibility. A compromised authority, a revoked certificate, a mistrusted root, or a broken validation chain may not produce dramatic physical scenes. Instead it produces hesitation, blockage, warning messages, workarounds, and the gradual accumulation of doubt. A government service that users approach with uncertainty is already partly weakened, even before any adversary exploits the gap further.

Public-sector dependency on these trust layers is often deeper than officials admit. Agencies inherit certificate management practices from vendors, outsource domain administration, allow legacy systems to accumulate weak cryptographic assumptions, or treat browser trust changes as downstream technical matters rather than strategic dependencies. The result is familiar. Renewals are missed. Inventories are incomplete. Emergency replacements become scrambles. Old internal systems fail when trust policies harden. Procurement documents ask for security in broad terms while neglecting the operational burden of certificate lifecycle management. Capability then narrows not because the state lacks law or ambition, but because the quiet work of trust maintenance was never treated as serious governance.

At the same time, efforts to regain control can drift into illusion. A state can promote national certificate authorities, domestic trust services, or sovereign naming policies, but those moves do not automatically solve the deeper problem. Trust that exists only inside one jurisdiction may reduce external dependency for some uses while increasing incompatibility for others. National control can improve assurance in public administration if executed well. It can also isolate services, burden cross-border commerce, or create new single points of political influence. The choice is rarely between global openness and national control in pure form. It is usually between different configurations of dependency, auditability, and interoperability.

The quiet motif of the padlock is useful because it captures the strange intimacy of this infrastructure. The user sees a tiny icon. Behind it stands a chain of names, keys, roots, audits, vendor decisions, registry practices, browser policies, and administrative routines. That chain reaches from global governance bodies to local system administrators renewing certificates late at night. It is one of the clearest examples of how digital power works through distributed authority rather than simple command. A service can be nationally vital while its recognisability and trustworthiness depend on institutions scattered across sectors and jurisdictions.

The forward test is therefore severe. When a state claims to control its digital future, can it also say who controls the names by which citizens find public services, who decides which certificates devices will trust, how quickly trust can be restored after compromise, and what happens when commercial browser policy collides with national administrative need? These are not peripheral questions. They define whether digital public life rests on a stable grammar of recognition or on a set of dependencies that remain invisible until the next warning window appears.

Public sector networks and legacy systems

In May 2017, hospitals across England felt the effects of the WannaCry ransomware attack with unusual clarity. The National Health Service did not fail because the state lacked policy ambition or because digital transformation had not been praised often enough. It failed in crucial places because older systems remained in service, patching was uneven, networks were difficult to segment cleanly, and local estates carried technical debt accumulated over years of procurement compromise and institutional strain. Screens froze. Ambulances were diverted. Appointments were cancelled. The machine had a history.

That history matters because public debate about state data capability still tends to imagine a government as if it were one organisation with one network, one architecture, and one decision-maker. Real governments do not look like that. They are sprawling estates built by successive administrations, constrained by budget cycles, legal obligations, staffing ceilings, emergency fixes, outsourced functions, incompatible standards, political impatience, and the stubborn fact that public services cannot simply stop while systems are rebuilt. A ministry may speak in the language of integration and interoperability while relying on applications older than some of its staff. A tax authority may run sophisticated analytics beside core databases designed for another era. A police force may digitise frontline reporting while depending on fragmented back-office systems that cannot compare identities consistently across regions. The state is never only modern. It is layered.

The key concept is legacy, though the word is often used too lazily. Legacy does not simply mean old. Some old systems remain dependable, well-understood, and appropriate to their task. Legacy, in the more serious sense, means inherited technical and contractual arrangements that narrow present choices. A system becomes legacy when replacing, connecting, securing, or even properly documenting it demands effort disproportionate to the apparent simplicity of the task. That effort may be technical, but it is also organisational. The application still runs because a few specialists understand it. The interface still exists because it was never budgeted for replacement. The vendor remains because no one wants to risk migration before the next election, audit cycle, or spending review. Legacy is governance sediment.

This is where public sector networks become strategically important. Data capability depends not only on what a government collects, but on whether information can move lawfully and reliably through the estates that hold it. Networks determine which agencies can talk to which, under what permissions, through what identity controls, with what visibility into access, and with what resilience when parts of the estate fail. A fragmented network architecture does more than slow operations. It changes what the state can know in time to act. If a social services team, an immigration authority, a border system, and a fraud unit cannot reconcile identifiers or move relevant records without manual intervention, then the state may possess information in the abstract while lacking it in practice. The visible symptom is mundane: an official retypes data from one screen into another. The strategic consequence is serious: delay, error, duplication, and mistrust become routine features of governance.

Procurement plays a larger role in this than policy language usually admits. Public contracts structure the architecture through which data will later move, sometimes for decades. Systems are purchased for specific programmes, urgent compliance deadlines, or narrow ministerial priorities, then remain in place long after the original rationale has faded. A department seeking speed may accept proprietary formats, limited export rights, weak interoperability, or opaque hosting arrangements because the immediate service need is politically pressing. Later, the same department discovers that these choices have hardened into constraints. Data cannot be shared easily. Integration depends on expensive intermediaries. Audit becomes partial because logs or schema remain controlled by the supplier. Migration is postponed because service continuity cannot be risked. The contract outlasts the strategy.

A named example shows the scale of the problem without reducing it to caricature. The United States federal government has spent years grappling with outdated public systems, a fact repeatedly noted by the Government Accountability Office. One emblematic case has been the Internal Revenue Service's long reliance on ageing core technology, including legacy programming environments that remain critical to tax administration. The point is not that such systems are uniquely incompetent. Quite the opposite. They often continue to function because generations of staff have kept them alive through patching, adaptation, and operational discipline. The deeper problem is that dependence on these systems can make change slow, costly, and politically risky. A state may know that integration, modernisation, or stronger security controls are needed, yet remain trapped between the danger of leaving systems alone and the danger of altering them badly. Stability and stagnation begin to blur.

The same tension appeared in the United Kingdom with the National Health Service National Programme for IT, launched in the early 2000s and eventually dismantled after years of cost, complexity, and governance difficulty. The ambition was sweeping: connect records, standardise infrastructure, and modernise the information base of public healthcare. The practical challenge proved fiercer. Local variation, supplier dependencies, clinical workflows, contract complexity, and changing expectations made central coordination extraordinarily difficult. The lesson is not that integration is impossible or that public systems should remain fragmented. The lesson is that integration work is not a glamour project. It is patient institutional labour. It requires standards that fit real workflows, procurement that preserves flexibility, governance that can arbitrate trade-offs, and staffing stable enough to hold technical memory over time. The database is never the whole story. The interface is where the pain lives.

This is why staffing limitations are so politically consequential. Governments do not merely buy systems. They must understand, operate, challenge, and evolve them. That requires architects, engineers, cyber specialists, procurement lawyers, product managers, service designers, database administrators, and officials capable of translating between policy goals and technical reality. Where those skills are scarce, states become more dependent on vendors not only for delivery, but for judgment. A department may receive a reassuring presentation about migration, resilience, or interoperability and lack the internal depth to interrogate it properly. A contract may specify outcomes while neglecting the practical question of who will own the knowledge required to adapt the system later. The visible behaviour is subtle but decisive: meetings in which only the supplier fully understands the architecture; incidents in which public officials must wait for external interpretation before they can even describe their own problem. Capability drains quietly this way.

Public-sector staffing problems are rarely reducible to salary alone, though pay matters. Career structures often reward generalist movement over technical depth. Procurement cycles discourage long time horizons. Political leadership changes faster than legacy systems do. Crisis work consumes the very teams that should be modernising the estate. Skilled staff burn out maintaining brittle services because downtime is politically intolerable, leaving too little capacity for redesign. Institutional memory then shrinks further. The state becomes dependent not only on suppliers, but on a handful of internal specialists who know which obscure component will break if a configuration changes at the wrong moment. That is not resilience. It is a form of technical patronage produced by neglect.

Fragmented architecture creates a further problem: governments struggle to decide what counts as the same person, event, or case across multiple systems. Identity mismatch is among the least glamorous and most consequential obstacles in public administration. Different departments may use different identifiers, naming conventions, address formats, case structures, or access rules. A benefits agency may classify a household differently from a tax authority. A police record may not reconcile neatly with court data. A health service may guard identifiers for good reason while frustrating cross-agency comparison in situations where comparison would reduce harm. The challenge is not merely to connect everything. It is to connect enough, under lawful and intelligible conditions, without creating a universal identifier culture that overwhelms purpose limitation and public trust. Integration is always political.

Risk accumulates in these seams. A fragmented estate invites manual workarounds, shared passwords, duplicate storage, spreadsheet dependence, and ad hoc exports that keep services moving while weakening security and auditability. Officials do this because they must. A public body cannot stop paying benefits, issuing licenses, or processing cases simply because enterprise architecture is imperfect. Yet each workaround generates its own exposure. Data ends up in places it was never meant to remain. Versions diverge. Permissions blur. A record corrected in one system survives uncorrected in another. These are not dramatic failures. They are the daily texture of institutional fragility. The visible decision - downloading a file, emailing an extract, copying from one register into another - is exactly where risk becomes governance.

A credible limitation should be stated plainly. Not every legacy system is a liability. Some are resilient precisely because they were designed narrowly, changed cautiously, and insulated from the fashion cycles of the software industry. Governments have occasionally harmed themselves by treating replacement as an end in itself, discarding stable systems in pursuit of modern interfaces or procurement prestige. A mature assessment therefore distinguishes between brittle legacy and dependable continuity. Age alone does not condemn a system. The relevant question is whether the system can be secured, understood, integrated where needed, and adapted without disproportionate risk. Sometimes the sensible decision is replacement. Sometimes it is containment. Sometimes it is deliberate coexistence with careful interfaces and clear boundaries.

That limitation, however, does not soften the larger argument. It strengthens it by keeping attention on capability rather than novelty. The real bottleneck is often not the age of a platform, but the absence of disciplined integration work around it. Governments regularly underestimate how much national capability depends on tasks too small to attract speeches: cleaning records, documenting interfaces, rationalising identity stores, retiring duplicated applications, standardising logs, mapping dependencies, rehearsing restoration, writing better contracts, and keeping enough skilled staff inside the public service to know when a supplier is bluffing. These are not decorative improvements. They determine whether data can be used, shared, protected, and challenged with confidence.

The state therefore inhabits a paradox. It seeks to act through data more quickly and more intelligently, yet the machinery through which that data moves is often slow, layered, and patched together by institutional compromise. Political leaders often frame this as a gap between ambition and implementation. That is too flattering. The gap is structural. Public institutions inherit missions broader than private firms, legal duties more complex, tolerance for failure lower in some respects and oddly higher in others, and user populations that cannot be selected for convenience. They must keep old systems running while building new ones, preserve records while reforming services, protect rights while reducing delay, and work through labour markets that do not always reward technical stewardship. A start-up can pivot. A pension system cannot.

The quiet motif of the interface is useful here because it captures where so much of the state's real difficulty sits. The interface may be a technical connector between databases, a procurement boundary between department and vendor, or a human boundary between frontline service and back-office record. It is at the interface that grand policy turns into friction. Does the record move? Does the identifier match? Does the permission hold? Does the audit trail survive? Does the person at the desk trust the answer on the screen enough to act? These are the moments when state capacity becomes visible, and they are rarely solved by slogans about innovation.

A further problem lies in the politics of invisibility. Successful integration work often attracts little credit because it prevents problems rather than announcing new services. No voter notices the database that no longer duplicates identities, the middleware quietly retired, the contract rewritten to preserve audit rights, or the documentation that lets a system survive staff turnover. Politicians therefore gain more from launching platforms than from paying down debt. Budgets follow attention. Attention follows spectacle. The public estate accumulates complexity in part because orderly simplification offers too few rewards until failure forces recognition. By then, options are narrower and tempers shorter.

This is why public sector networks and legacy systems belong in any serious account of national data power. A country may possess strong law, advanced private firms, and impressive rhetoric about digital transformation, yet still find its public capability narrowed by the old and ordinary facts of integration. The limiting factor is often neither AI capacity nor cloud access nor legal authority in the abstract. It is whether government systems can recognise the same case across agencies, move data under proper controls, survive supplier churn, and recover after disruption without descending into improvisation. Much of state strength hides in those dull successes.

The unresolved question is not whether governments should modernise. They have no real alternative. The harder question is how to distinguish renewal that genuinely expands public capacity from renovation that merely adds new layers to an already cluttered estate. Every state wants seamless services, secure data, and interoperable systems. Far fewer are willing to fund the unglamorous, politically thankless work that makes those claims credible. When the next grand strategy promises transformation, the better test may be simpler: who is paying for the interfaces, who is keeping the knowledge, and who will still understand the network when the consultants have gone?

Supply chains for hardware and software

In May 2017, the WannaCry ransomware attack spread rapidly through organisations around the world, disrupting hospitals, firms, ministries, and transport systems. In the United Kingdom, the National Health Service became the most politically visible victim, but the deeper lesson lay elsewhere. The damage did not arise from a single national failure in isolation. It travelled through a supply chain of operating systems, update practices, vendor dependencies, legacy hardware, network configuration, and public-sector purchasing decisions accumulated over years. The breach was not merely an attack on computers. It was an attack on inherited dependency.

That is the right starting point for thinking about hardware and software supply chains. States do not acquire data capability by owning databases alone. They acquire it through stacks of components they did not wholly design, fabricate, write, maintain, or even fully inspect. A government portal may appear sovereign at the surface while depending, several layers down, on chips manufactured abroad, firmware written by contractors, operating systems maintained by foreign firms, open-source libraries assembled by distributed volunteers, cloud orchestration tools updated on external schedules, and security products whose internal workings remain largely opaque to the customer. The screen looks national. The stack is not.

The phrase "trusted supplier" sits at the centre of this politics and often obscures more than it reveals. Trust sounds reassuring. It also sounds static, as though a vendor could simply be sorted into safe and unsafe categories and the matter closed. Real systems are not so neat. Supply-chain trust is never a feeling alone. It is a question of verification, visibility, substitutability, and consequence. Can a state inspect what it buys, test what it deploys, verify what is claimed, constrain what a supplier can do, and recover when a supplier fails or becomes politically contested? If the answer is no, then trust is functioning as a euphemism for dependency.

This matters because digital systems are made of layers, and each layer carries its own politics. At the physical base sit semiconductors, memory, storage devices, network equipment, and specialised processors. Above them sit firmware, hypervisors, operating systems, drivers, middleware, encryption libraries, identity services, and applications. Still higher sit update channels, support contracts, remote management tools, telemetry, and the legal arrangements that define maintenance and liability. A state can be confident at one layer and blind at another. It may trust the visible vendor brand while knowing little about the subcontractors, foundries, package maintainers, or dependency chains beneath. The strategic problem is therefore not simply who sells the final box or licence. It is who shapes the hidden conditions under which the box or licence continues to function.

The semiconductor layer makes the materiality of this dependence unusually clear. Advanced chips emerge from an international production system with deep specialisation across design, fabrication, lithography, packaging, chemicals, and testing. Very few states can reproduce that chain domestically. Fewer still can do so at competitive scale. The implication is not merely economic. Compute capability, cloud expansion, military systems, industrial automation, and increasingly public-sector digital services all depend on a supply structure that remains global and politically exposed. Export controls, sanctions, natural disasters, water stress, energy constraints, or conflict in one part of the chain can reverberate through systems that appear far removed from semiconductor policy. A data strategy that ignores chips is still a slogan.

A named example helps. In 2022 and 2023, the United States expanded export controls intended to restrict China's access to certain advanced semiconductor technologies. The immediate subject was geopolitical competition, especially in advanced computing and artificial intelligence. The broader lesson was simpler and more durable: chip supply is not an inert commercial background. It is a strategic instrument that can be shaped by law, diplomacy, and industrial policy. States had long spoken about digital sovereignty in broad terms. Export controls revealed one of the hard edges of that sovereignty debate. Access to computation depends not only on money or talent, but on where the critical bottlenecks in production and tooling sit, and who can legally intervene.

Hardware dependence, however, is only half the story. Software supply chains shape national data capability just as deeply, and often more opaquely. Modern systems are assembled from reusable components: open-source libraries, package managers, container images, proprietary modules, cryptographic tools, build pipelines, and update services. A single public-sector application may rely on hundreds of dependencies, many of which are maintained outside the contracting state and some of which are only lightly scrutinised by those deploying them. This arrangement produces remarkable efficiency. It also means that vulnerabilities, malicious insertions, abandoned components, or flawed updates can propagate widely across institutions that did not realise they shared the same software ancestry.

The SolarWinds compromise, disclosed in December 2020, remains a defining example. Malicious code was inserted into software updates for Orion, a network management product used by numerous organisations, including United States government agencies. The strategic importance of the incident did not lie only in espionage access, serious though that was. It lay in the method. Compromise travelled through a trusted update channel. Institutions that believed they were maintaining security through routine patching instead received an adversary through the very mechanism of upkeep. This is a different kind of vulnerability from the dramatic breach at the perimeter. It attacks confidence in the supply chain itself. The visible action was ordinary - install update, maintain system, proceed. The strategic implication was corrosive: even disciplined administrators can import risk when verification depends on trust they cannot independently test.

Operating systems create another layer of concentrated dependency. Most public institutions rely on a narrow range of operating systems for desktops, servers, mobile devices, and increasingly cloud environments.

These systems shape security models, update cycles, compatibility, logging, identity integration, and application behaviour. They also create political asymmetry. A government may wish to harden or tailor its estate, but it usually cannot dictate the vendor's release schedule, end-of-support decisions, hardware compatibility rules, or telemetry design. The state can configure, defer, negotiate, or complain. It rarely commands. This is one reason operating systems matter strategically: they define the baseline assumptions of public-sector computing while remaining largely outside public control.

The issue is not only technical dependence but time dependence. Suppliers decide when software reaches end of life, when patches stop, when architectures shift, and when customers must migrate or accept rising risk. Public bodies often struggle to keep pace because procurement cycles, staff shortages, specialised applications, and budget limits make migration slower than vendor roadmaps assume. A system that still works operationally may become insecure or unsupported politically, leaving governments trapped between expensive replacement and rising exposure. The decision to defer upgrade then becomes a security choice produced by institutional constraint, not by ignorance. Supply chains therefore govern the tempo of public administration as much as its tools.

Open-source software complicates the picture in productive ways. It is easy to speak about open source as either salvation or danger. It is neither. It can reduce dependence on single vendors, improve auditability in principle, and permit customisation that proprietary systems often resist. It also relies on maintainers, communities, funding arrangements, and governance processes that vary enormously in quality and resilience. The 2021 Log4Shell vulnerability in the widely used Log4j library exposed how a seemingly modest open-source component could create global risk because it sat quietly inside countless products and services. The lesson was not that open source is inherently unsafe. It was that dependency is often hidden in places procurement documents barely mention. A state may buy from a reputable supplier and still inherit exposure from components several steps removed from the contract.

This is why "trusted supplier" debates are ultimately debates about verification rather than origin myths. Nationality matters sometimes, particularly where legal compulsion, political influence, or strategic conflict is relevant. But nationality alone is a poor risk metric. A domestic vendor can produce insecure software, opaque firmware, or brittle dependency chains. A foreign vendor can submit to strong audits, segmentation, and contract terms that reduce practical exposure. The strategic question is not whether a supplier belongs to a favoured flag. It is whether the buyer can meaningfully inspect, monitor, constrain, and replace what is being supplied. Trust that cannot be tested is branding.

Huawei's role in fifth-generation mobile network controversies illustrated this point with unusual clarity. Debates in the United Kingdom and elsewhere were often framed in terms of national origin and espionage risk, but the more serious issues concerned verification limits, patching dependence, governance of software updates, concentration of vendor presence, and the consequences of political rupture. Some systems can be segmented. Some cannot. Some vendors can be excluded at tolerable cost. Others are already too deeply embedded for clean removal without service disruption. The debate was therefore never only about whether one company could be morally trusted. It was about how to manage a dependency once systems had been built around it, and how much verification was truly possible in a complex software-defined environment.

A credible limitation should be admitted here. Complete autonomy is not a realistic benchmark for most states. Autarky in chips, operating systems, cloud software, cyber tools, and industrial electronics would be punishingly expensive and in many cases technically implausible. Even large powers depend on international supply chains and specialised external production. For smaller and mid-sized states, the fantasy of self-sufficiency can distract from the more practical work of building resilient interdependence. National capability does not require making everything. It requires understanding what cannot be made domestically, what must be diversified, what must be verified, and what cannot be allowed to concentrate without fallback.

That limitation improves the analysis because it shifts attention from purity to management. The most serious states do not ask whether they can eliminate dependence. They ask which dependencies are acceptable, which are monitorable, which can be diversified, which can be segmented, and which would become strategically intolerable under conditions of dispute. These are different questions. A consumer messaging app and a core government identity platform do not carry the same threshold for supplier risk. A laptop procurement can tolerate a different dependency profile from a military communications system or a national tax database. Sector matters. Function matters. Recoverability matters most of all.

Verification is therefore the practical centre of the issue. Can the code be reviewed or at least meaningfully tested? Can updates be staged, signed, and audited? Can firmware integrity be checked? Can telemetry be understood? Can procurement secure access to logs, incident reporting, and exit support? Can a state trace critical components beneath prime contractors to know what is actually deployed? Can teams simulate vendor loss and still maintain essential functions? These are not elegant questions, but they are the only ones that make "trusted supplier" into more than political theatre. Verification does not eliminate risk. It turns vague trust into governed exposure.

Dependency management also requires public-sector competence. Governments routinely sign contracts for software and hardware they do not fully understand, then discover that their leverage ends where the supplier's proprietary knowledge begins. Without internal engineers, architects, procurement specialists, and security teams who can interrogate design claims, review assurance evidence, and maintain continuity plans, the state becomes a passive recipient of vendor narratives. This is one reason staffing and supply chains belong together analytically. A country does not become more sovereign merely by changing suppliers if it still lacks the institutional capacity to verify what any supplier is doing.

The quiet motif of the box is helpful here. A device arrives in a box. So does a software product, in effect, wrapped in contracts, support promises, update channels, and reassuring language about security. The temptation is to treat the box as a stable object. It is not. It is an entry point into a chain of upstream dependencies and downstream obligations. Chips inside came from elsewhere. Code inside calls other code. Updates will alter behaviour later. Support may be withdrawn. Legal conditions may change. A state that buys the box without mapping the chain has purchased uncertainty disguised as convenience.

The strategic challenge, then, is to build enough distance from suppliers to verify them without retreating into fantasies of total independence. That means diversifying where sensible, segmenting critical functions, demanding better software bills of materials and audit rights where possible, investing in open standards that ease substitution, and retaining enough public expertise to know when a dependency is deepening into a chokepoint. It also means accepting that some risks cannot be engineered away and must instead be prioritised politically. Not every vulnerability deserves the same response. Not every foreign component is intolerable. Not every domestic product is safe.

The hardest question comes at the point where procurement, security, and geopolitics finally meet. When a state says a supplier is trusted, what exactly has been trusted: the code, the company, the jurisdiction, the update process, the contractual remedies, the probability of future conflict, or simply the absence of a better option? That question is uncomfortable because it exposes how much modern data capability rests not on clean sovereignty, but on managed uncertainty. The states best prepared for that condition will not be the ones claiming they depend on nobody. They will be the ones that know precisely where the chain bends, where it breaks, and how much of their public life is hanging from each link.

Chapter 4

Cloud Dependence and Sovereignty Debates

What does a state gain when it moves from scattered server rooms and brittle local systems to a handful of professionally managed cloud environments, and what does it quietly surrender in the same move? The question matters because cloud migration is often sold in a language of obvious improvement: stronger security, faster deployment, lower maintenance burdens, cleaner procurement, and more reliable scaling. Much of that sales pitch contains truth. Much of the difficulty begins there.

A ministry that once relied on ageing hardware, uneven patching, and overworked internal teams may genuinely become safer when critical services move into a better-run environment. Baseline security can improve. Backups can become more disciplined. Identity controls can tighten. Recovery can become faster, at least in theory. The practical relief is real. Systems start to behave less like improvised estates and more like managed services. Yet the very concentration that produces those gains also changes the political character of dependence. The state ceases to maintain many weak rooms and begins to rely on a few strong doors.

This is the central tension. Cloud centralisation can reduce ordinary fragility while increasing systemic exposure. It can improve day-to-day security while narrowing the field of suppliers on which essential functions depend. It can shorten procurement and deployment cycles while binding public institutions more tightly to external product roadmaps, contractual terms, audit regimes, and technical architectures they did not design. A government may feel more capable because it can launch faster, store more cleanly, and patch more consistently. It may also discover that it has outsourced part of the terrain on which sovereignty is exercised: visibility, access, prioritisation, and recovery during dispute.

The difficulty is sharpened by the fact that cloud debates are often argued in the wrong register. Too much attention settles on the simple question of location, as though the decisive issue were merely where the data rests. Place matters, but not by itself. Control sits in other places too: in administrative privileges, encryption arrangements, logging rights, incident response procedures, subcontracting chains, software dependencies, support pathways, and the fine print that governs what a customer may inspect, export, or challenge. A database hosted on domestic soil may still be managed through systems shaped elsewhere. A workload hosted abroad may remain better governed than one nominally local but badly overseen. Geography matters. So do the hands on the console.

These distinctions matter because states do not move all workloads into the cloud on equal terms. Some functions are relatively forgiving. Email, document storage, collaboration tools, and routine administrative systems may benefit greatly from scale and standardisation. Other functions carry a different political weight. Identity infrastructure, welfare payments, border control, tax administration, emergency communications, electoral support systems, intelligence workflows, and certain health services sit closer to the constitutional nerve. Their failure is not merely operational. It can produce cascading administrative paralysis, public mistrust, and acute political damage. A system may be technically available and still strategically unsafe if the state cannot guarantee continuity, explain control, or recover on its own timetable.

That is why cloud dependence is not simply a technology choice. It is a question about how a state ranks its own functions and what forms of assurance it considers non-negotiable. Commodity services can tolerate one type of risk. Mission-critical systems require another posture altogether. The temptation, however, is to treat cloud migration as a general modernising logic and only later discover that certain services should never have been folded into the same assumptions as office productivity tools or routine hosting. The cloud promises uniformity. Government does not have that luxury. Its functions differ too sharply in consequence.

The political appeal of "sovereign cloud" emerges from this unease. The phrase sounds decisive, but it often conceals several distinct ambitions: domestic hosting, national legal control, tighter operational oversight, reduced foreign supplier influence, stronger auditability, or symbolic reassurance to anxious publics and legislators. Some of these aims can be compatible. Some pull against one another. A more domestically controlled arrangement may raise costs, narrow access to innovation, or increase concentration inside the national market. A more interoperable arrangement may lower those costs while preserving dependencies that become salient during a crisis. Sovereignty in this domain is less a destination than a series of design choices, each trading one form of comfort for another form of exposure.

The path ahead follows that tension closely. It begins with the operational changes cloud centralisation imposes on security, cost, and concentration, then moves into the harder matter of what control actually means when access, audit, and lawful authority are distributed through contracts and technical roles rather than slogans about place. From there, the question narrows to the workloads that can bear ordinary platform dependence and the ones that cannot, before turning to sovereign cloud proposals as instruments of governance rather than badges of political intent. The issue throughout is not whether states should use cloud services. Most already do, and with good reason. The issue is how to recognise when convenience has become structural dependence.

A useful image for the chapter is the keycard. A keycard grants entry, but only within a building whose rules, logs, locks, and emergency exits someone else may still control. Cloud arrangements often work like that. Governments receive access, dashboards, privileges, and assurances. They do not automatically receive mastery over the whole environment. The distinction is easy to forget when systems function smoothly and procurement language speaks of partnership. It becomes harder to forget during an outage, a dispute over lawful access, a security incident, or a rushed question from a minister who wants to know who can actually do what, and now.

The real test, then, is not whether a cloud contract sounds sovereign, secure, or modern. It is whether the state can explain its control points in concrete terms before stress arrives: who holds the keys, who sees the logs, who can isolate a workload, who can verify a claim, who can restore service first, and who bears responsibility when the answer is politically unbearable. Only then does the argument move beyond branding and into power.

What cloud centralisation changes

On 7 December 2021, an outage in Amazon Web Services' us-east-1 region in Northern Virginia disrupted a striking range of services that many users never realised shared the same infrastructural dependence. Retail systems slowed, logistics tools faltered, media services stumbled, and devices that had been marketed as seamless suddenly looked contingent. The incident did not prove that cloud computing was a mistake. It proved something more important. Systems that feel separate at the screen can fail together underneath. The outage travelled farther still.

That is the right place to begin because cloud centralisation is often described in slogans that flatten a more interesting reality. One slogan presents the cloud as obvious progress: more secure, more efficient, faster to deploy, easier to maintain. Another treats it as a single, looming dependency in which sovereign capacity dissolves into platform power. Both contain part of the truth. Neither is enough. Hyperscale cloud changes the state's digital posture by moving it away from thousands of unevenly managed machines and towards a smaller number of highly standardised, professionally operated environments. That shift can reduce a great deal of ordinary fragility. It can also concentrate failure in ways that are politically and strategically harder to absorb.

The first change is security. Many public institutions ran, and some still run, systems that were never designed for the complexity they now bear. Servers sit unpatched because upgrades threaten service continuity. Access controls drift. Logs are incomplete. Backup routines exist on paper more reliably than in practice. Specialist staff are scarce. In that setting, moving workloads into a well-run cloud environment can improve baseline security quickly and materially. The concept here is pooled discipline. Hyperscale providers standardise hardening, automate patching, centralise monitoring, segment workloads more consistently, and maintain physical security at a level that many agencies would struggle to match alone. The implication is not abstract. Administrators stop nursing failing hardware. Security teams gain better tooling. Recovery becomes something that can be rehearsed rather than merely hoped for.

A named example shows why this mattered to serious institutions early. When the Central Intelligence Agency awarded its Commercial Cloud Services contract to Amazon Web Services in 2013, the significance lay not in fashion but in operational logic. Classified and sensitive workloads required an environment that could scale, standardise controls, and provide technical capabilities that would have been difficult and slow to build repeatedly across separate estates. The move signalled that cloud was no longer just a commercial convenience. It had become a security architecture. What changed was not only where systems sat, but how they were managed: shared tooling, standardised controls, and faster provisioning altered the cadence of institutional work. A server once acquired through prolonged procurement could now be instantiated as needed. That is speed translated into governance.

Speed is the second major change, and it reaches further than deployment alone. In older public estates, obtaining infrastructure often meant buying hardware, waiting for delivery, configuring networks, provisioning storage, securing rack space, and coordinating between multiple internal teams and suppliers before any service could begin. Cloud centralisation turns much of that fixed lead time into a service call. Teams can test sooner, scale more quickly, and retire failed experiments without the same sunk costs. For governments, this matters because policy windows are often short and public demands unforgiving. A department responding to a crisis, launching a benefits portal, or expanding a digital identity function values not merely capacity but tempo. The visible behaviour is straightforward: environments appear in hours rather than months, development teams iterate more freely, and security controls can be applied through shared patterns rather than handcrafted exceptions.

Cost structures change in tandem. Cloud does not simply make computing cheaper. It converts large portions of capital expenditure into operational expenditure and shifts the burden of maintaining core infrastructure from the customer to the provider. That can be beneficial, especially where public bodies have underinvested in their own estates or lack the staffing depth to maintain them properly. Yet the political meaning of this shift is often misunderstood. Costs become easier to start and harder to contain if governance is weak. Consumption-based models reward elasticity, but they also punish inattention. Agencies unused to seeing infrastructure as a continuous meter can discover that convenience encourages sprawl: duplicated workloads, idle resources, poorly governed storage, or services left running because ownership is unclear. The cloud can reduce waste created by obsolete hardware. It can also create waste made of clicks.

This leads directly to the hardest part of the story: concentration risk. Centralisation improves many routine conditions while making correlated failure more plausible. If many institutions rely on the same provider, the same region, the same identity services, the same management plane, or the same update logic, then an error or outage at that level can propagate widely. What had once been many local weaknesses becomes fewer shared dependencies. The strategic concept is not simple brittleness, because hyperscale systems are often highly resilient within their own design. The problem is common-mode risk. Too many important functions can fail in related ways because they are built on the same foundations.

The 2021 outage in Northern Virginia revealed this clearly. The immediate technical cause is less important here than the political lesson. Services that appeared unrelated to users were related where it counted. Shared infrastructure meant that disruption travelled across sectors and organisations that had made separate procurement decisions but inherited common dependency. That is what cloud centralisation changes at national scale. A ministry may believe it has modernised prudently. A bank may believe it has secured commercial advantage. A hospital may believe it has outsourced undifferentiated infrastructure wisely. All three may still discover that their resilience assumptions converge on the same provider architecture.

A second named example sharpens the point from a different angle. In 2019, the Capital One breach exposed the consequences of a cloud misconfiguration involving data stored in Amazon Web Services. The incident did not show that cloud itself was inherently insecure; public estates suffer breaches too. It showed something subtler and more important. Cloud changes the shape of security work. Misplaced credentials, poorly configured permissions, and weak understanding of shared responsibility can turn powerful infrastructure into an efficient amplifier of human error. The organisation had not merely rented servers elsewhere. It had entered a different governance model in which security depended on understanding where provider responsibility ended and customer responsibility began. The implication extends well beyond one breach. Cloud centralisation does not eliminate institutional error. It relocates and redefines it.

That shared-responsibility model is one of cloud centralisation's most consequential but least glamorous features. Providers secure parts of the stack. Customers secure others. The dividing line varies by service model and architecture. This can improve security because responsibilities become clearer than in some fragmented on-premise estates. It can also produce dangerous assumptions. Agencies may assume the provider is handling more than it is. Providers may document their responsibilities in ways that satisfy lawyers more readily than operators under pressure. Auditors may certify controls without capturing how teams actually deploy and configure services. A state that moves to cloud without building internal literacy around these boundaries is not simplifying its security problem. It is changing its vocabulary while hoping the old instincts still suffice.

Operational culture changes too. In cloud environments, infrastructure becomes programmable. That can be a major advantage. Teams can define systems as code, test configurations, replicate environments, and apply policies more consistently across workloads. Done well, this reduces drift and supports recovery. Done badly, it allows misconfigurations to replicate with equal speed. The switch cuts both ways. One flawed template can travel as efficiently as one good control. That is why cloud centralisation rewards disciplined engineering cultures and punishes organisations that treat migration as procurement rather than institutional transformation.

This is especially important for government because public institutions rarely move into cloud as greenfield actors. They bring legacy applications, old identity stores, compliance burdens, procurement habits, and fragmented governance structures with them. Cloud platforms may standardise infrastructure while leaving application portfolios messy, ownership unclear, and interdependencies poorly mapped. The result is a hybrid condition in which old weaknesses meet new complexity. Some workloads benefit immediately. Others become awkwardly suspended between worlds: too important to migrate casually, too outdated to integrate cleanly, too politically sensitive to risk during transition. Centralisation then becomes uneven in practice. The cloud looks coherent in policy papers and layered in the real estate.

A credible limitation should be faced directly. Concentration risk is real, but it can be overstated if analysts treat every use of hyperscale cloud as equivalent. Architecture matters. Workloads can be distributed across regions. Critical services can maintain failover arrangements. Some functions can remain outside the cloud, and some can be designed for portability. Multi-cloud and hybrid approaches sometimes reduce dependence, though they also add complexity and can create fresh governance burdens. More importantly, many public-sector systems were far less resilient before migration than nostalgic critics admit. A brittle local estate is not made strategically superior merely because it is locally owned. Centralisation can be a genuine improvement even when it introduces new forms of dependence.

That limitation strengthens rather than weakens the central argument. The point is not to romanticise old server rooms or to suggest that states should shun hyperscale cloud. The point is to understand that centralisation changes the problem from one of dispersed weakness to one of concentrated reliance. Routine security often improves. Recovery from common local failures often improves. Speed of deployment often improves. But the significance of outage, vendor dispute, control failure, or architectural misunderstanding rises with concentration. The state trades many small rooms for a few strong doors. It must then ask who holds the keys, how many functions sit behind each door, and what happens when one no longer opens.

Cloud centralisation also changes the economics of skill. Some low-level infrastructure burdens fall away, which is one reason migration can be so attractive. But the need for internal expertise does not disappear. It moves upward. Governments require fewer staff replacing disks and more staff who understand identity architecture, permissions models, incident response in cloud environments, vendor negotiation, logging, workload prioritisation, and the security implications of service design. An agency that mistakes cloud adoption for the end of technical dependency rather than its reorganisation will become more reliant on external advice at exactly the moment it most needs internal judgment.

The quiet motif of the switch is useful because cloud centralisation really does feel like a switch being thrown. Systems that once demanded procurement, installation, and local management become configurable services. Capacity appears quickly. Security controls snap into place faster. The attraction is obvious. Yet a switch also changes which circuit you are on. A public body that centralises into a dominant provider does not merely modernise. It joins a larger electrical logic of dependency in which other users, other workloads, and other crises may share the same underlying current.

That is why the question cloud centralisation raises is not whether it is good or bad for state capability. That is too blunt to be useful. The harder question is which kinds of state capacity it strengthens, which kinds of dependence it deepens, and how visible those trade-offs remain after the migration is politically declared a success. If a government becomes faster, safer, and more scalable in routine conditions but also more exposed to common-mode disruption and fewer providers, has it increased sovereignty or merely exchanged one kind of fragility for another? The answer depends less on cloud as a label than on how much concentration a state can afford before efficiency itself becomes a strategic risk.

Jurisdiction, access, and control points

In July 2013, Microsoft challenged a United States warrant seeking customer email content stored on servers in Dublin, Ireland. The case, commonly known as Microsoft Ireland, looked at first like a dispute about where data happened to sit. It became something more revealing. Courts, companies, and governments were forced to confront a harder question: what does control actually mean when a provider can administer a service from one country, store data in another, answer to law in a third, and route support and security operations across several more? The server had an address. Authority did not.

That dispute remains useful because it exposed the limits of a familiar simplification. Public debate often treats data location as if it were the master fact of digital sovereignty. If the data sits domestically, control is presumed stronger; if it sits abroad, control is presumed weaker. Location matters. It affects latency, disaster recovery, regulatory comfort, and the practicalities of certain legal claims. But location does not settle the deeper politics of cloud dependence. Data may rest in one jurisdiction while administrative privileges, logging systems, key management, support channels, and incident response capabilities remain distributed elsewhere. A state can point to a domestic data centre and still struggle to answer the real question: who can do what, from where, under which authority, and with whose knowledge?

This is the practical meaning of control. It is not a slogan, and it is not exhausted by ownership. Control consists of specific rights and capabilities: who can access content, metadata, configurations, and logs; who can create or revoke credentials; who can approve or execute changes; who can isolate a workload during a crisis; who can inspect the infrastructure; who can compel disclosure; who can challenge a request; who can verify whether a supplier's account of an incident is complete; who can restore service first. The list sounds procedural because control in digital systems is procedural. The implication is central to statecraft. A government that cannot answer those questions clearly does not yet know how dependent it is.

Contractual rights are the first place this becomes visible. Governments often speak as though a cloud service were a technical relationship, lightly regulated by procurement language. In practice the contract defines much of the state's real power. It shapes audit access, data export rights, subcontractor disclosure, breach notification, support pathways, retention rules, service credits, termination conditions, and the scope of provider obligations in emergencies. These clauses are not administrative decoration. They determine what the public customer can see, challenge, demand, or recover when conditions worsen. A service may be domestically hosted and still leave the customer unable to inspect critical logs or verify the provider's handling of a security event. The paper trail matters.

This is why jurisdiction must be handled carefully. Jurisdictional claims are often presented in all-or-nothing terms, as though one legal system entirely governs a cloud workload because the servers, customer, or parent company sit within its reach. Real arrangements are less tidy. Providers operate through subsidiaries, support teams, regional infrastructures, and cross-border internal processes. Governments rely on mutual legal assistance, statutory production orders, contractual commitments, and practical cooperation that vary by context and urgency. The relevant issue is not who can make the loudest claim of sovereignty, but which authorities are likely to be asserted, resisted, complied with, or delayed in real cases. What matters is the path from legal demand to operational access.

A named example sharpens the point. The Microsoft Ireland litigation eventually became overtaken by the United States CLOUD Act in 2018, which clarified and adjusted parts of the legal framework for cross-border access to data held by service providers subject to US jurisdiction. The political argument around that legislation was broad, but the practical lesson was narrower and more durable. Cross-border cloud governance turns on a mix of statutory authority, provider structure, comity processes, and the operational reality of who holds access. The data's location did not cease to matter. It simply ceased to be the only meaningful variable. Law followed architecture, and architecture complicated law.

Technical access is the second control point, and often the most misunderstood. A government may contract for storage in a particular region while relying on a provider whose privileged administrators, security tools, or internal support processes retain the capacity to inspect, move, or alter workloads under defined circumstances. Some providers offer customer-managed encryption keys, stronger isolation options, or administrative segmentation designed to reduce this exposure. Those measures can matter a great deal. Yet they do not remove the need for precise questions. Who manages the keys in practice? Who can trigger recovery procedures? Who can access snapshots or backups? Which actions are logged, by whom, and in a format the customer can independently review? Technical control is not one switch. It is a chain of permissions.

Auditing then becomes indispensable. Trust in cloud arrangements depends less on declarations of compliance than on the customer's ability to inspect and challenge what the provider says happened. This is true for security incidents, access requests, service changes, performance failures, and ordinary operational drift. The visible behaviour matters. Can auditors see the relevant logs promptly? Are subcontracting arrangements transparent enough to understand who touched the system? Can a public body distinguish between an incident in its own workload and an incident in the shared service layer beneath it? Can it verify that a provider followed the contractual and legal steps it claimed to follow when handling an access request or service disruption? Oversight lives or dies in these details.

A second named example helps illustrate this from another angle. In 2021, the European Data Protection Supervisor ordered the European Parliament to suspend the use of a Covid testing website after concerns about transfers of personal data via US-based services including content delivery and tracking components. The controversy was not simply about where specific data packets had travelled. It was about whether public institutions understood the full architecture and control surface of the services they were using. Technical convenience had produced a governance problem. The incident showed how easy it is for access pathways and third-party components to outstrip the assumptions of public oversight. The state thought it had procured a service. It had also procured hidden relationships.

Incident response is the fourth major control point, and perhaps the one most likely to expose weak governance under pressure. When a cloud-based public service fails, the crucial questions are not rhetorical. Who is called first? Who can access the diagnostic information? Who decides whether to isolate, restore, or fail over a system? Which party has authority to act immediately, and which must wait for approval? Does the provider's internal severity framework align with the political significance of the public service affected? A commercial outage policy may not fit the needs of a tax filing deadline, a digital identity system, or a health service under strain. The visible decision - restore this workload, defer that one, communicate now or later - becomes a constitutional event when public trust and service continuity are at stake.

This is where "where data sits" becomes most obviously incomplete as a guide. A dataset may be stored domestically, but if incident response depends on teams, tools, or decision rights located elsewhere, then practical control remains distributed. A state may find that the decisive moments in a crisis occur outside its own chain of command. This does not automatically make the arrangement unacceptable. Many public systems rely on distributed expertise, and some providers are better equipped than governments to respond quickly to deep infrastructure failures. But the dependency must be recognised. If political responsibility rests with the state while operational initiative rests elsewhere, then accountability has been split. Split accountability is manageable only when the terms of that split are understood in advance.

A credible limitation should be acknowledged. Jurisdictional alarm can be overstated when it becomes a shorthand for all cloud risk. Not every cross-border support path is dangerous. Not every foreign parent company negates local safeguards. Not every domestic hosting arrangement produces meaningful sovereignty. Some internationally managed services are better documented, more tightly audited, and more securely operated than local alternatives. Strong encryption, clear contracts, segmented administration, and rigorous oversight can reduce real exposure substantially. It would be simplistic to pretend that domestic location alone guarantees safety or that international providers are inherently uncontrollable.

That limitation strengthens the argument because it forces attention onto control points rather than symbols. A national cloud deployment can still leave the state blind if it lacks audit rights, key management clarity, incident visibility, or internal technical literacy. Conversely, a cross-border arrangement may be tolerable for certain workloads if those control points are tightly specified, independently reviewed, and matched to the function's risk. The relevant comparison is not local versus foreign in the abstract. It is governable versus opaque, auditable versus assumed, reversible versus entrapping. Control is measured in actions, not flags.

This is particularly important for lawful access. Public institutions must answer a sequence of hard questions before they can claim that a workload is acceptably governed. Which laws might a provider be compelled to respond to? Under what conditions would the customer be notified? Can the provider challenge or narrow overbroad demands? Are encryption keys structured so that compliance requires customer involvement, or can the provider produce data independently? What logs would be created by such an event, and would the public customer receive them? These are not only legal questions. They are operational ones. A state's comfort with a cloud arrangement should rise or fall with its answers.

The same applies to oversight bodies. Regulators, auditors, courts, and parliamentary committees often examine cloud procurement through a language of value for money, compliance, or abstract cyber risk. Those categories matter but can miss the real substance. Oversight is more effective when it asks concrete control questions. What privileges do provider staff hold? How are those privileges monitored? Which subprocessors can touch the workload? How quickly can evidence be produced after an incident? Can the public body move its data and configurations elsewhere without service collapse? Does the contract permit meaningful forensic review after a serious event, or only a polished summary from the vendor? Oversight fails when it audits paper and ignores access.

The quiet motif of the key helps to hold the matter together. A key does not only open a door. It also tells us who may enter, who may duplicate entry, who records the entry, and who can change the lock. Cloud governance works the same way. A government may possess the service and still not possess the key in the way that matters most. Or it may possess one key but not another: access to content but not to underlying telemetry; the right to request support but not the right to inspect the response; nominal control over a workload but not over the support chain that sustains it. The more serious the public function, the less wise it becomes to speak vaguely about sovereignty and the more necessary it becomes to trace each key.

This also explains why control must be matched to workload sensitivity rather than asserted uniformly. A collaboration tool for internal drafting can tolerate a different mix of jurisdictional uncertainty and provider access than a national identity platform or a system processing intelligence-derived material. The more a function sits near the constitutional core of the state, the more exacting the control questions must become. Can the service fail gracefully? Can it be isolated quickly? Can the state verify access histories independently? Can it continue operations during a dispute with the provider? If not, then the arrangement may still be attractive commercially and still be strategically wrong.

Public agencies often underestimate one further dimension: institutional literacy. Contracts can contain powerful rights that nobody exercises because officials do not know when or how to invoke them. Technical options can exist but remain unused because no one inside the department fully grasps their implications. Providers may offer customer-managed keys, logging integrations, private connectivity, or privileged access controls that sit dormant while procurement teams congratulate themselves on having bought a "sovereign" service. A state without internal competence cannot turn formal rights into real control. The document says access is governed. The console reveals whether that is true.

The resulting test is uncomfortable but necessary. When a minister says a critical public workload is under control, can the responsible institution answer a practical sequence without hesitation: who holds administrative privilege, who sees the logs, who would be notified first of a breach or legal request, who can suspend access, who can export the workload intact, who can challenge a provider's account, and who would still be accountable if none of those steps worked as intended? Those are not side questions. They are the structure of control itself. The next section turns to the workloads for which these questions become most severe, because not every public system can live comfortably with ambiguity about the keys.

Government workloads and strategic prioritisation

On 30 September 2021, Facebook, WhatsApp, and Instagram suffered a major global outage after a network configuration error disrupted their services. For many users, the event was inconvenient. For businesses, it was disruptive. For governments watching closely, it carried a sharper lesson. A platform failure at one company could interrupt communication, customer service, emergency messaging, and daily coordination across multiple societies at once. The systems were private. The dependence was public.

That episode helps frame the real question. Not every digital workload held by the state carries the same strategic weight, and not every dependency on a platform provider poses the same danger. Governments often speak about cloud and platform risk as if it were a single category. It is not. A payroll system, a collaborative document platform, a digital identity service, a customs declaration interface, a police intelligence environment, and a national health record may all run on modern infrastructure, yet the consequences of delay, compromise, or loss differ profoundly. The central task is therefore not to reject platform dependence in the abstract. It is to sort workloads by consequence, recovery tolerance, and the political damage their failure can inflict.

This sorting is more difficult than it sounds because governments have spent years learning to describe digital services in technical terms while under-describing them as instruments of rule. A state function is not sensitive only because it contains classified information or large quantities of personal data. It may also be sensitive because interruption produces cascading social effects, because a false result can trigger legal harm, because the service underpins other services, or because public trust in the state itself passes through that interface. The concept that matters here is strategic centrality. A workload becomes strategically central when its failure disables more than its own immediate purpose.

Digital identity offers the clearest example. A digital identity platform is not merely another service channel. It can serve as the key to tax filing, benefits access, healthcare portals, licensing, education records, company registration, and sometimes private-sector transactions. If such a system goes down, or if its integrity is compromised, the damage radiates quickly. Citizens cannot prove who they are. Frontline services revert to paper or improvised checks. Fraud risks rise. Backlogs spread. Confidence drains. The visible behaviour changes at once: people queue longer, call centres overload, staff start bypassing normal procedures, and officials quietly stop trusting the system they are meant to defend. A digital identity outage is therefore never just an IT incident. It is a test of administrative continuity.

This is why governments need a more disciplined distinction between commodity workloads and mission-critical ones. Commodity services are not trivial, but they are comparatively replaceable, degradable, or delay-tolerant. Email, collaboration suites, basic web hosting, routine file storage, and many internal productivity tools may be important to efficiency without being existential to public authority. If such services fail briefly, institutions can often continue through workarounds, defer tasks, or accept short-term inconvenience while restoration proceeds. Mission-critical workloads are different. They support core state functions that cannot fail gracefully without wider political or social consequence: identity, payments, tax collection, border management, emergency communications, critical health systems, intelligence support, judicial records, and certain forms of benefits administration. These systems do not simply run services. They authenticate the state.

The difficulty is that governments are often tempted to classify workloads by sensitivity of data rather than by consequences of failure. That is too narrow. A dataset may be highly sensitive and still operationally containable if access is tightly limited and continuity demands are modest. Another service may hold relatively ordinary information yet remain strategically indispensable because society has come to depend on constant availability and reliable outputs. A scheduling platform for vaccine appointments, for instance, may become politically explosive during a public emergency even if its underlying data model is comparatively simple. Risk must be measured not only by secrecy but by interruption, manipulation, and dependency.

A named example from Estonia helps show the stakes. Estonia's digital state is often praised, with good reason, for the coherence of its identity architecture and its integration across public services. That success also illustrates why strategic prioritisation matters. Identity and authenticated access sit close to the centre of the Estonian administrative model. If the key system works, many other services flow. If it fails, the interruption affects far more than one website or database. The lesson is not that digital identity is uniquely fragile. It is that some workloads carry constitutional weight because they organise access to many other rights and obligations. Governments that classify such systems as ordinary cloud customers' workloads are misreading their own machinery.

Payment systems present a similar logic. A government payroll system is important; a welfare payment infrastructure may be more strategically delicate if delay quickly becomes hardship and political grievance. Tax systems do not merely collect revenue. They underwrite the fiscal credibility of the state and shape the trust of firms and households in routine administration. Customs platforms do not merely process declarations. They affect trade flows, border security, sanctions enforcement, and supply chain confidence. A mission-critical classification therefore demands more than secure hosting. It demands a clear view of fallback procedures, data recovery, segmentation, incident response authority, dependency mapping, and the legal capacity to direct restoration priorities when commercial and public interests diverge.

Security agencies learned this logic earlier than most civil administrations. Intelligence and defence workloads are generally assessed through doctrines of mission assurance, privilege control, compartmentation, and degraded operations. Civil governments often approach cloud migration more through convenience, cost reduction, and modernisation pressure. The result can be oddly imbalanced. Highly classified systems may receive extreme scrutiny while systems central to daily public authority are treated as if they were only scaled-up versions of commercial workloads. This is a category error. A social security platform can be politically critical without being secret. A licensing system can become nationally salient if failure disrupts transport or commerce. A public health portal can matter more to lived legitimacy than a more sensitive but narrowly used internal database.

A second named example comes from the United Kingdom's experience with NHS digital infrastructure, especially during and after the WannaCry attack in 2017. The incident revealed weaknesses in legacy systems, patching, and operational resilience. It also highlighted something more enduring. Some health workloads are not merely information repositories. They are live dependencies within care delivery. If records cannot be accessed, systems cannot schedule, verify, or communicate safely. The strategic value of such workloads lies in continuity under pressure. Their classification should reflect that. A hospital record system is not "mission-critical" only because it contains sensitive information. It is mission-critical because care and trust both begin to erode when it cannot be relied upon.

This leads to a harder truth about platform dependence. Large commercial providers often offer better baseline security, more disciplined operations, and faster recovery capabilities than the fragmented estates governments previously maintained. For many commodity workloads, moving to a shared platform is not only reasonable but desirable. It can reduce operational chaos and free public teams from maintaining undifferentiated infrastructure badly. The problem begins when those benefits are generalised without enough regard to functional consequence. A ministry may conclude, with some justification, that collaboration tools improved after migration, then assume the same governance model suits identity, payments, or emergency systems. Efficiency in one domain becomes an argument in another where the terms have changed.

Strategic prioritisation therefore requires a more demanding set of questions. What happens if this service fails for an hour, a day, or several days? Who is harmed first, and who can wait? Can the system degrade safely into a manual process, or does the entire workflow depend on digital authentication and machine-readable records? Does the workload serve mainly internal efficiency, or does it mediate rights, payments, legal status, or social protection? Can the state restore it on its own terms, or must it depend entirely on a provider's commercial incident response sequence? These are not only technical questions. They are questions about how a state imagines its obligations to citizens under stress.

A credible limitation should be acknowledged. Not every government should or could build bespoke arrangements for every important function. Excessive insistence on special treatment can create its own fragility by multiplying architectures, complicating oversight, and exhausting scarce technical talent. Some supposedly mission-critical workloads may benefit from standardisation more than from expensive exceptionalism. Commercial platforms can, in certain circumstances, provide stronger assurance than custom-built public systems that never receive proper maintenance. It would be a mistake to romanticise uniqueness as if it guaranteed resilience. Often it guarantees the opposite.

That limitation strengthens the larger point. Strategic prioritisation is not a plea for blanket insourcing or bespoke sovereign systems. It is a plea for matching control and assurance to consequence. Some workloads deserve ordinary commercial treatment with solid governance. Some require enhanced contractual rights, stronger technical isolation, more rigorous audit, and tested fallback plans. A smaller number may require architectures whose recovery, access controls, and governance cannot be left to default market arrangements at all. The state does not need one answer. It needs a ranking discipline.

This is especially important because platform dependence alters failure perception as well as failure risk. When a public service collapses inside a widely used commercial environment, citizens rarely distinguish between provider error, state procurement choices, and underlying architecture. They see the failure as governmental. A customs platform outage becomes a border problem. A digital identity interruption becomes a state credibility problem. A delayed welfare payment becomes a breach of obligation. Strategic prioritisation must therefore include narrative consequence. Which failures remain technical, and which become constitutional in the public mind? That question often matters more than internal severity labels admit.

The quiet motif of the key is useful again here, because some workloads are not simply stored or processed by the state. They unlock it. Identity systems are the obvious case, but they are not alone. Access control layers, citizen account services, payment authorisation mechanisms, and core inter-agency registers often function as keys to broader administrative life. Their compromise or absence changes the meaning of every dependent service. A government can survive the failure of a filing cabinet more easily than the loss of the keys to the building. Digital estates are no different.

Strategic prioritisation also exposes a labour problem. To classify workloads intelligently, governments need officials who understand not only cyber security or procurement, but the operational and constitutional meaning of services. A payment architect, a welfare administrator, a border official, and a security engineer may all see the same platform differently. If those perspectives are not brought together, classification becomes shallow. Commodity systems get overprotected because they are visible to senior officials. Truly critical systems are underprotected because they appear administratively routine. A sophisticated state learns to rank by consequence, not by organisational prestige.

The central test, then, is not whether a workload runs on a cloud platform or inside government walls. It is whether the mode of dependence matches the consequences of failure. For some functions, speed, scale, and standardisation outweigh the costs of shared dependence. For others, continuity, recoverability, auditability, and control over restoration must dominate. The harder cases sit in between, where a service looks ordinary until a crisis reveals that many other functions leaned on it all along.

The question that follows is severe and clarifying. If a provider outage, access dispute, or integrity failure struck tomorrow, which public systems could the state afford to lose briefly, and which would force it to prove what it actually means by continuity of government? That ranking, more than any slogan about modernisation or sovereignty, reveals whether cloud strategy has been shaped by administrative convenience or by a serious understanding of state power.

Sovereign cloud as policy instrument

In May 2021, Google announced a partnership with T-Systems in Germany for what it presented as a sovereign cloud arrangement intended to reassure public and regulated customers about control, compliance, and oversight. The announcement was notable not because it settled the sovereignty question, but because it exposed how unsettled the question had become. A global hyperscaler and a domestic partner were together offering not simply infrastructure, but a political design. The word *sovereign* had moved from constitutional vocabulary into procurement architecture.

That shift matters because sovereign cloud is often discussed as though it were a single thing: a clear answer to foreign dependence, a neat recovery of national control, or a branding exercise masking ordinary outsourcing. It can be any of these, depending on the design. The term does not describe one settled model. It describes a family of arrangements through which states and providers try to rebalance control over data, access, operations, and assurance without giving up the benefits of scale, standardisation, and commercial innovation. The harder task is therefore analytic rather than rhetorical. One must ask what kind of sovereignty is being offered, to whom, against which risks, and at what price.

The first mistake is to treat sovereign cloud as a question of location alone. Data may sit in domestic facilities and still remain entangled with foreign administrative access, foreign software roadmaps, foreign support chains, and foreign legal exposure. Conversely, some risks can be reduced meaningfully through operational and contractual controls even where domestic hosting is not absolute. The concept worth keeping in view is governance design. Sovereign cloud is not best understood as a place. It is better understood as a bundle of decisions about who operates systems, who manages keys, who can access support channels, who audits incidents, which entities hold contracts, and how recovery works when the relationship between customer and provider comes under strain. The label matters less than the control points.

This is why sovereign cloud proposals need to be judged by the specific dependencies they alter. A domestic joint venture may reduce some jurisdictional anxieties while preserving deep dependence on a foreign software stack. A locally controlled operations team may improve auditability while leaving patch cadence, feature availability, and underlying platform architecture in external hands. A national cloud region may improve latency and certain forms of legal comfort while concentrating workloads into a smaller market with fewer alternative suppliers. Risk rarely disappears. It moves. Sometimes that movement is worthwhile. Sometimes it merely replaces one hard question with another politically easier one.

The attraction of sovereign cloud becomes obvious when viewed from the state's perspective. Governments want the security and operational maturity of hyperscale infrastructure without the full strategic discomfort of hyperscale dependence. They want faster deployment, better baseline controls, and access to advanced services, while preserving enough visibility and authority to satisfy courts, regulators, security agencies, and anxious legislatures. They also want to reassure the public that critical digital systems remain meaningfully governable. Sovereign cloud thus emerges as a compromise instrument: not pure independence, not pure market integration, but an attempt to domesticate platform power through architecture, contract, and policy.

A named example helps clarify the appeal and the ambiguity. In 2022, Oracle and Microsoft advanced arrangements for sovereign cloud offerings in Europe, presenting them as ways to combine hyperscale capability with more local control, restricted support access, and stronger assurances for regulated customers. The strategic interest lay not in the marketing language itself, but in the architecture of reassurance. Domestic or regional personnel. Segmented operations. Contractual commitments around support and access. Local data residency. Enhanced audit pathways. Each element addressed a real concern. Yet none of them alone settled the deeper question of dependency. The cloud service still relied on global software development, external product decisions, and complex support ecosystems that no domestic wrapper could fully erase.

This is where cost enters with unusual force. Sovereignty measures are not free, and their price is not limited to money. Domestic control, restricted support models, dedicated staffing, separate operational environments, and specialised compliance arrangements can all raise direct cost. They can also slow access to new services, reduce interoperability with broader cloud ecosystems, and narrow the pool of engineers and suppliers familiar with the resulting environment. A government may gain clearer oversight over one set of risks while losing some of the economic logic that made hyperscale cloud attractive in the first place. The visible signs are practical: slower rollout of features, higher procurement thresholds, more bespoke contract negotiation, more limited portability, and sometimes a smaller market with less competitive pressure.

The innovation trade-off matters because cloud platforms do not merely host workloads. They increasingly provide managed databases, analytics services, identity layers, AI tooling, security services, and development environments. These tools shape what public institutions can build and how quickly they can build it. A sovereign cloud design that isolates customers too completely may reduce external dependence while also depriving them of the wider platform's velocity and tooling depth. This is not a trivial cost. States depend on innovation not for prestige, but because public service expectations rise, threat environments change, and technical debt accumulates quickly in isolated environments. A sovereign arrangement that becomes a museum of frozen capability may satisfy political symbolism while weakening long-term state performance.

Interoperability is therefore central, though it is often treated as secondary. A sovereign cloud design that makes it difficult to move workloads, integrate with suppliers, collaborate across borders, or adopt common standards may create a different form of lock-in under national colours. This is one reason the sovereignty debate must resist nationalism in its laziest form. Domestic control can be valuable. Domestic exclusivity can also become a trap if it narrows exit options and shields weak suppliers from scrutiny. The real question is whether sovereignty measures preserve bargaining power or merely relocate dependence from one dominant provider to one protected local intermediary. A flag on the contract does not guarantee freedom from lock-in.

The French experience around cloud policy makes this plain. France's "cloud de confiance" approach, developed through state doctrine and commercial partnerships, sought to reconcile European control requirements with the technical reality of global cloud dominance. The effort was serious, not theatrical. It recognised that some public and regulated workloads require stronger guarantees around legal exposure, access, and oversight. It also demonstrated how difficult it is to achieve those guarantees without relying, in some form, on the software and operational foundations of large non-European providers. The lesson is not that the effort was futile. It is that sovereign cloud is better judged as a negotiation over dependency than as a declaration of independence.

A second named example lies in the long European debates about GAIA-X, launched in 2019 with strong German and French backing. GAIA-X was often portrayed in public argument as a response to the dominance of American and Chinese platform firms, and as an attempt to create a more European framework for data infrastructure and interoperability. Its significance here is conceptual. GAIA-X revealed that sovereignty can be pursued through standards, governance frameworks, and federation principles as much as through direct state ownership or wholly domestic cloud stacks. At the same time, the project showed how difficult it is to turn sovereignty language into operational coherence when market incentives, technical complexity, and competing national interests pull in different directions. Governance design is demanding work. Slogans travel faster.

A credible limitation should be admitted. Some sovereign cloud criticism assumes that only full domestic ownership and operation count as meaningful control. That standard is too pure to be useful. Most states, even wealthy ones, cannot recreate every layer of the cloud stack domestically without severe cost and technical compromise. Nor should they try. Many public institutions benefit from global scale, mature tooling, and the security investment that large providers can sustain. A hybrid arrangement with local operational controls and external platform foundations may still reduce real risk in important ways. Purity is a poor guide. The task is not to achieve metaphysical sovereignty. It is to govern dependence intelligently.

That limitation, however, does not rescue weak designs. Sovereign cloud deserves sceptical evaluation precisely because it can seduce governments into buying reassurance rather than capability. A public body may be promised local hosting, restricted personnel access, and strong compliance language while remaining unable to audit critical controls, migrate workloads realistically, or preserve continuity during a dispute with the provider. Politicians may claim sovereignty because a local partner sits in the structure, even if the decisive software, patches, tooling, and escalation pathways remain elsewhere. This is the danger of ornamental sovereignty: the appearance of control without the substance required in crisis.

A more serious evaluation therefore asks a disciplined set of questions. Which dependencies are reduced, and which remain? Does the design improve visibility into privileged access, incident response, and subcontracting? Can the customer manage or meaningfully influence encryption keys?

Are audit rights practical or ceremonial? Can workloads be exported and restored elsewhere within a tolerable time? Does the arrangement preserve access to innovation without creating deeper architectural lock-in? Does the domestic partner add genuine operational control or merely political cover? These questions are more revealing than whether the service is marketed with national symbols or hosted in a local region.

The same discipline should apply to cost and market structure. Sovereign cloud can act as industrial policy by nurturing local operators, support teams, compliance expertise, and integration partners. That may be a legitimate public goal. But industrial policy becomes wasteful when protection outruns competence. A domestic provider shielded from competition may become slow, expensive, and technically second-rate while still claiming the mantle of sovereignty. The state's purpose is not to subsidise comforting weakness. It is to ensure that politically important workloads remain governable, auditable, and resilient. Sometimes that will support local industry. Sometimes it will require admitting that no local supplier yet offers what the state needs.

This is why sovereign cloud should be seen as an instrument rather than an identity. Instruments are judged by the tasks they perform. For some workloads, especially in regulated sectors or sensitive public functions, stronger local control over operations, support, and legal exposure may be well worth the cost. For others, ordinary commercial cloud with strong contracts and disciplined architecture may suffice. The mistake lies in treating sovereignty as a universal procurement virtue rather than a targeted response to specific forms of risk. Not every system needs a sovereign wrapper. Not every system should trust one.

The quiet motif of the wrapper is useful here. Sovereign cloud often arrives as a wrapper placed around global infrastructure: a domestic operator, a local legal entity, a segmented support model, a compliance framework, a jurisdictional buffer. Wrappers can protect. They can also conceal what remains unchanged underneath. The question is not whether a wrapper exists, but whether it changes the terms that matter when things go wrong. Does it alter who can access, who can audit, who can restore, who can challenge, who can exit? If not, then the wrapper is political packaging.

States should therefore resist the false choice between naive globalism and defensive autarky. The more interesting space lies in managed interdependence with clear priorities. That means distinguishing workloads that require deeper domestic control from those that do not, preserving interoperability where possible, insisting on verifiable operational safeguards, and treating local capacity not as a romantic end-state but as a practical source of bargaining power. Sovereignty, used wisely, is not the refusal of connection. It is the capacity to remain governable while connected.

The real test comes when a government faces an uncomfortable trade-off and cannot escape into rhetoric. A sovereign cloud proposal may offer stronger domestic control but higher cost, slower feature access, and tighter coupling to a smaller set of approved intermediaries. Another may preserve innovation and scale but leave harder questions about oversight and external dependence. Which risk is actually being reduced, which is merely being relocated, and which political audience is being reassured at the expense of a more honest accounting? Those questions do not disappear once the contract is signed. They only become harder, because by then the wrapper has usually started to look like the system itself.

Chapter 5

Standards and Interoperability Politics

What looks more neutral than a standard? A format, a protocol, an authentication rule, a procurement requirement, an audit control: each arrives in the language of order rather than ideology. Yet standards rarely remain technical housekeeping for long. Once adopted at scale, they decide which systems can speak to one another, which firms can enter a market, which institutions can inspect behaviour, and which forms of state access become routine enough to seem natural. A standard does not merely describe compatibility. It distributes power.

That distribution is easy to miss because standards often work best when they disappear into ordinary use. A login succeeds. A credential travels. A file opens. A payment clears. A public body buys software under a familiar compliance framework and assumes it has acted prudently. The quiet success of these moments hides the harder truth. Technical compatibility is never only about efficiency. It also fixes expectations about identity, trust, auditability, portability, and permissible friction. Once those expectations settle, they become difficult to reverse. The socket in the wall no longer looks political. It still decides what can plug in.

This is the chapter's central tension. Interoperability can reduce dependence, widen competition, and spare institutions the misery of bespoke integration. It can also standardise channels of observation, simplify extraction, and privilege certain architectures over others. A common standard may help citizens move between services more easily while making behavioural tracking more seamless. A compliance rule may improve accountability while quietly favouring vendors already large enough to absorb its costs. A portability mechanism may empower users while strengthening the identity layer through which state and market both learn to know them. Standards make things work together. They also make forms of control travel further.

That is why standards belong inside geopolitics rather than outside it. They shape what kinds of digital order become durable. They influence which states can project regulatory power, which firms can scale internationally, and which public institutions can insist on their own models of identity, security, and oversight. The contest is often conducted in committees, procurement offices, industry groups, and technical forums rather than at summits. It still concerns national power. A country that helps define the default rules of authentication, auditability, portability, or data exchange does more than win prestige. It helps decide which dependencies others inherit.

The stakes are unusually high around identity. Standards for proofing a person, verifying a credential, delegating access, or moving identity claims across institutions do not simply reduce paperwork. They determine who gets included smoothly, who faces repeated friction, who can recover from error, who bears the burden of suspicion, and how far a state can extend its reach through digital systems. Design choices that appear narrow at the moment of adoption can harden into long political commitments. A rule chosen to reduce fraud may later shape welfare access, immigration control, private-sector onboarding, or law-enforcement visibility. A convenience measure can become a governing principle before anyone admits that it has done so.

Procurement and compliance intensify this effect because they turn standards into market facts. Governments rarely choose abstractly between architectures. They choose through bids, accreditation schemes, security baselines, reporting duties, and contractual clauses that reward some forms of technical organisation over others. The resulting market can then look natural, even inevitable, when it is anything but. "Neutral" requirements often reflect the assumptions of incumbent vendors, the habits of large bureaucracies, or the priorities of security agencies whose definitions of auditability and assurance may be sensible in one context and distorting in another. A standard becomes powerful when it stops looking like a choice.

This matters because public institutions often imagine they are buying interoperability when they are actually buying a settlement among rival interests. The settlement may be wise. It may also be captured. A government seeking portability may inadvertently entrench a dominant identity provider. A compliance regime designed to strengthen oversight may favour cloud models that fit existing audit practices while excluding smaller or more innovative entrants. A security standard may reduce some risks while creating systematic blind spots around others simply because it was shaped by the wrong operational history. Standards are not only written. They are lived through procurement and enforced through exclusion.

The path ahead follows that quiet coercion. It begins with the way standards create power by shaping the field of possible action, then moves into the especially charged territory of identity, authentication, and portability, where inclusion, fraud control, market access, and state authority become difficult to separate. From there it reaches procurement and compliance, where ostensibly technical requirements reveal their role in locking in architectures and narrowing competition. The through-line is simple enough to state and difficult to evade: the fight over standards is a fight over the default settings of political and economic life.

A useful image for the chapter is the hinge. A hinge is a small thing. Most people ignore it until a door sticks, swings the wrong way, or proves too heavy to move without force. Standards operate in much the same register. They sit at points of movement between systems, institutions, and users. When the hinge is well chosen, the door opens easily and repeatedly. When it is badly chosen, the whole structure strains around it. More interestingly still, whoever designs the hinge helps decide who may pass, how quickly, and under whose observation.

The harder diagnostic, then, is not whether a standard sounds open, secure, or modern. It is who benefits when that standard becomes ordinary, whose burdens it lowers, whose power it enlarges, and which alternatives become steadily less thinkable once the hinge is fixed in place. That question leads directly to the first problem: how standards acquire power in the first place, and why the most technical decisions so often become the most durable political ones.

Why standards create power

In February 1980, IBM announced the 3270 Information Display System as part of a wider effort to organise how terminals, controllers, and mainframes communicated across large institutions. The immediate result was practical. Offices could connect equipment more predictably, train staff more consistently, and plan procurement around a recognised architecture. The deeper result was political in a quieter sense. Once a standard took hold, it did more than reduce confusion. It shaped which vendors could participate, how organisations built their workflows, and what kinds of information handling became normal. The plug decided more than the machine.

That is the key to standards. They are often presented as technical agreements designed to reduce friction, and often they do exactly that. But friction is never merely an engineering inconvenience. It is also a distribution of power. A standard decides what counts as a valid message, a trusted credential, an acceptable interface, a portable file, a compliant audit log, a recognised identity claim. Once those decisions settle, they shape markets and institutions long after the original debate has been forgotten. People start to treat them as neutral because they become ordinary. Ordinary does not mean apolitical.

The power of standards begins with coordination. Systems built by different organisations, vendors, and governments cannot interoperate reliably unless they share some rules. A payment standard lets banks clear transactions more smoothly. A document format lets agencies exchange files without retyping them. A telecom standard lets networks connect calls across borders. The concept here is compatibility as infrastructure. Compatibility lowers the cost of connection, reduces duplication, and expands the field in which organisations can act. The implication is obvious enough: standards can widen markets and improve public administration. But compatibility also has a hidden side. It fixes the terms on which connection occurs. Whoever helps define those terms helps define the structure of dependence.

This is why standards create lock-in even when they are formally open. Once organisations build systems, train staff, procure tools, and write regulations around a standard, alternatives become more expensive. The lock-in may be technical, because interfaces and data models have hardened. It may be commercial, because dominant vendors have optimised around the standard while smaller rivals struggle to comply. It may be institutional, because regulators and auditors have learned to recognise one pattern of evidence and distrust unfamiliar ones. Lock-in is not always malign. Sometimes it produces stability that users and public bodies genuinely need. But stability has direction. It privileges the actors already aligned with it.

The history of mobile telecommunications makes this unusually clear. The rise of GSM standards in Europe during the late twentieth century did more than enable roaming and equipment compatibility. It helped create a continental market structure, strengthened European industrial coordination, and shaped who could build competitive products. The success of GSM is often told as a story of technical foresight. It was also a story of standard-setting as industrial policy. A common framework let firms and regulators coordinate around scale rather than fragmenting into incompatible national systems. The strategic lesson is larger than mobile telephony. Standards can turn a region's political decision into a market fact, and a market fact into long-term geopolitical weight.

Yet standards do not only widen opportunity. They also define what becomes easy to monitor, extract, and compare. This is the part of the story that optimistic accounts often neglect. Interoperability can reduce dependence by preventing any one vendor or institution from holding data hostage in closed systems. It can also create standard pathways for access that outlast the original justifications for access. A standard data exchange interface built to improve service coordination can become a durable channel for surveillance or automated scrutiny. A standardised logging rule can strengthen auditability while simultaneously making cross-system monitoring more seamless. The same hinge opens both ways.

A named example from telecommunications helps show this darker edge. The lawful interception standards developed through bodies such as the European Telecommunications Standards Institute created common technical frameworks through which authorised access to communications could be implemented by service providers. The rationale was intelligible: governments wanted interception capabilities that could function reliably across changing digital networks. The concept was standardised access. The implication was more complicated. Once access interfaces are standardised, they can lower operational friction not only for legitimate, tightly governed uses, but also for misuse where oversight is weak or compromised. A capability designed for lawful process becomes easier to scale because the standard has already solved part of the technical problem.

This is one reason standards are geopolitical. They do not simply improve efficiency within a settled political order. They help produce that order by deciding what kinds of coordination become normal. A digital identity standard that assumes portable, machine-readable credentials does not merely help users authenticate. It also expands the practical reach of states and firms that can validate, store, and reuse those credentials. A common security logging standard may improve incident response while increasing the ease with which data can be aggregated across public and private systems. A content moderation interface may assist trust and safety operations while also inviting states to demand structured reporting or removal pathways that were once harder to impose. Standards make power travel farther by packaging it into routine procedure.

The geopolitical dimension is easiest to see when states and firms compete to shape standards bodies, procurement frameworks, and regulatory baselines. This competition rarely looks dramatic from the outside. It proceeds through working groups, compliance language, technical committees, reference implementations, and the patient labour of making one architecture appear normal. But the consequences can be profound. If one country's firms dominate a standard, they may gain scale advantages abroad. If one region's regulators embed certain compliance expectations into market access, foreign firms may be forced to adapt globally. If security agencies persuade standards processes to include capabilities they consider necessary, those capabilities may become embedded across networks and products far beyond the original jurisdiction. The room where the standard is written may be smaller than the room where its effects are later felt.

The internet's basic protocols provide a useful counterpoint because they show how standards can diffuse power as well as concentrate it. Open standards for routing, email, and the web helped create an environment in which many actors could interconnect without seeking permission from a single gatekeeper. That openness mattered historically. It lowered barriers to entry, supported innovation, and reduced dependence on closed proprietary systems. A credible limitation therefore belongs here. Not every standard is an instrument of capture. Some genuinely widen choice and protect against domination by any one actor. Open, well-governed interoperability can be a source of pluralism.

But that limitation does not dissolve the argument. Even open standards generate power effects. They privilege those with the capacity to implement them well, influence their evolution, and wrap profitable services around them. They can entrench dominant firms if those firms become the default interpreters of nominally open rules. They can also create new expectations of data portability, identity exchange, or compliance reporting that strengthen institutional control even while reducing vendor lock-in. The crucial question is therefore not whether a standard is open in principle. It is what kinds of order it stabilises in practice.

The politics become especially sharp when standards govern categories that touch identity, authentication, and data exchange. Here a seemingly narrow choice about fields, tokens, schemas, or proofing thresholds can alter who gets included, how easily fraud is detected, how far records travel, and how much discretion frontline officials retain. Once these choices become infrastructural, they are difficult to contest politically because they no longer appear as choices. They appear as the natural way systems work.

This is the quiet triumph of standards power. It shifts debate from "should this be possible?" to "how do we manage what is already built?"

Markets respond accordingly. Vendors design for the standards that customers and regulators reward. Compliance consultancies grow around them. Auditors train against them. Procurement officers learn to ask for them. A standard that began as a coordination device can become a commercial moat. Smaller competitors may struggle not because their products are inferior, but because the cost of proving conformance to the recognised model is too high. Incumbents then defend the standard as neutral good practice, which often contains enough truth to be persuasive. The political challenge lies in seeing how neutrality can be selective. A standard may be sensible and still favour the already powerful.

Procurement is where this often hardens. Public bodies rarely choose among pure technical possibilities. They choose among products and bids framed through compliance requirements, accreditation language, and assurance models. A standard embedded in procurement acquires a force beyond voluntary adoption. It becomes the price of admission. This matters because procurement can freeze a momentary balance of power into long-term dependence. If a government requires a particular audit format, interface model, or credential framework, it may improve oversight and interoperability. It may also lock itself into vendors and architectures that perform well on paperwork while narrowing future options. The decision looks administrative. Its effects are strategic.

A second named example comes from the battle over office document formats in the 2000s, especially the contest between OpenDocument Format and Office Open XML in international standardisation arenas. This was not merely a quarrel among software companies. It was a struggle over public sector dependence, archival durability, procurement freedom, and the future shape of office software markets. File format standards determined whether governments could move between vendors without costly conversion, whether public records remained usable across time, and whose software assumptions would define normal bureaucratic practice. The point is not to reopen that specific dispute. It is to see how a file format became a question of state capacity. A standard for saving documents ended up shaping the politics of administrative autonomy.

Trust should also be placed under pressure here. Standards are often defended as ways to create trust between unfamiliar systems and institutions. That is true. But trust in this context is manufactured through visible mechanisms:

a certificate accepted, a token validated, an audit passed, a message parsed correctly, a log field recognised by a regulator. These visible mechanisms can make large systems work. They can also reduce complex judgments to machine-readable signals that institutions come to rely upon too heavily. A compliant credential may still mask exclusion. A valid log may still conceal meaningful context. A standardised interface may still create a surveillance capability whose political implications were never properly debated. Trust, standardised, is efficient. It is not automatically wise.

A more exacting view therefore asks four questions whenever a standard begins to dominate. What does it make easy? What does it make hard? Who benefits from that distribution? And who gets to revise it later? These questions matter because power often lies less in the initial adoption than in the difficulty of modification. Once standards become embedded in contracts, regulations, and code, change becomes costly. The actors best placed to absorb that cost gain influence over the future direction of the system. Standards create power partly because they create inertia.

The quiet motif of the hinge is useful again. A hinge looks like a small technical object joining two surfaces so that movement becomes smooth. Standards perform exactly that function. They join systems, firms, regulators, and states in ways that make movement possible. But a hinge also determines how far a door opens, which direction it swings, and how much force it can bear. The hinge is not the room, yet it shapes life inside the room. So do standards. They rarely command attention when they work, which is precisely why their political force becomes so durable.

This is why the debate over standards should not be left either to technologists who imagine politics arrives later or to politicians who imagine standards are merely implementation details. The most consequential standards are pre-political only in the way constitutions are pre-political: they structure what later arguments can plausibly achieve. By the time a society realises that an interface normalises extraction, or that a compliance requirement shields incumbents, or that an identity standard has widened the practical reach of surveillance, the standard is often already deep inside the machinery.

The forward test is therefore severe. When a government or regulator supports a standard in the name of interoperability, security, or innovation, can it also say what forms of dependency, visibility, and exclusion that standard will stabilise? Or does the technical language merely postpone a political argument until the architecture has become too ordinary to challenge? The standards that matter most are seldom the ones that announce their power. They are the ones that make a particular arrangement of power feel like common sense.

Identity, authentication, and portability

In September 2018, the Supreme Court of India delivered its judgment on Aadhaar, the vast biometric identity system that had come to sit close to the centre of Indian public administration. The Court upheld the programme in substantial part while placing limits on some uses, especially by private companies. The ruling did not end the argument. It clarified its stakes. Identity infrastructure was no longer merely an administrative convenience or a welfare tool. It had become a constitutional question about who may prove personhood, through what means, for which purposes, and under whose authority. A credential had become a political instrument.

That transformation captures the larger issue. Standards for identity proofing, authentication, and portability do not simply help people log in. They decide what evidence counts as enough to be recognised, how often a person must re-prove who they are, which actors may rely on that proof, and whether a credential granted in one setting can travel into another. The language is technical. The consequences are social, economic, and political. A badly chosen identity standard can exclude the poor, burden migrants, amplify administrative error, or entrench private gatekeepers. A well-chosen one can reduce fraud, widen access, and make the state more legible without making people permanently transparent to it. The key opens more than one door.

Identity proofing is the first decision point, and it is more politically charged than it sounds. Proofing asks what evidence must be presented before a person is accepted into a system as who they claim to be. Passport, utility bill, tax record, mobile number, biometric match, in-person interview, document scan, trusted referee, existing bank account: different systems ask for different combinations. These choices reflect assumptions about fraud, state capacity, and the social distribution of documentation. They also sort populations. A standard built around formal address history will favour the stably housed. A standard built around prior financial records will favour the already banked. A standard built around high-quality biometric capture may work smoothly for some users and fail others because of age, occupation, disability, or local infrastructure. Proofing looks like verification. It often functions as border control inside ordinary administration.

This is why inclusion cannot be treated as an afterthought. Inclusion is visible in behaviour: whether people complete enrolment without multiple failed attempts, whether frontline staff rely on workarounds, whether appeals rise because legitimate users are denied, whether assistance becomes routine rather than exceptional. An identity system that excludes a small but socially vulnerable share of users may still look successful in aggregate while producing sharp local harms. Those harms are not incidental. They feed back into legitimacy, because identity infrastructures are usually attached to services people cannot easily forgo - welfare, healthcare, taxation, licensing, employment checks, migration status, or digital payments. A system that says "prove yourself" more often than a society can realistically comply with becomes a machine for administrative mistrust.

Authentication, the second major layer, is narrower in concept and broader in consequence. Once a person is enrolled, authentication determines how they later prove continuity with that identity. Passwords, one-time codes, cryptographic keys, biometric verification, device-based tokens, smart cards, federated log-ins, risk-based scoring - each method solves some problems and creates others. The strategic point is not merely which method is strongest in a laboratory sense. It is how the method behaves in the real world. Does it fail safely? Can the user recover access after loss, theft, or coercion? Does it require stable connectivity? Can the method be deployed across public services without creating a single point of catastrophic dependence? Does it allow impersonation to be detected and corrected before harm becomes permanent? An authentication standard is not good because it sounds advanced. It is good when it holds under social and institutional stress.

Estonia offers a useful example because it shows how identity standards can become a backbone of public authority rather than a peripheral convenience. Its national digital identity system, supported by strong authentication practices and used across public services, has long been associated with efficient e-government, digital signatures, and relatively seamless administrative interaction. The value lies not only in convenience. It lies in coherence. When public bodies and private actors can rely on the same trusted identity infrastructure, transaction costs fall, services become more portable, and routine dealings with the state change tempo. The visible effects are ordinary and telling: a prescription retrieved, a company registered, a declaration filed, a signature accepted without repeated in-person checks. Standards, in this setting, create a predictable civic rhythm.

Yet the same example shows why identity standards are long-term political commitments rather than neutral technical decisions. Once a digital identity becomes widely used, it attracts more functions. More services rely on it. More private firms seek to integrate with it. More public bodies build assumptions around it. The system then moves from being one service among many to being a gate through which many other rights and obligations pass. This creates strategic value, but also dependency. Outages hurt more. Compromise matters more. Errors travel further. The administrative state becomes more elegant and less forgiving. That is why the design of authentication and recovery pathways matters as much as the existence of the identity itself.

Portability sharpens the stakes further. A portable credential allows proof established in one context to be recognised in another. This is often presented as straightforwardly empowering. Users should not need to prove the same facts repeatedly. Firms should not face endless duplication of compliance checks. Public bodies should avoid wasting effort re-collecting what the state already knows. All true. But portability is not a simple good. It changes the structure of power by deciding who may rely on whose identity decisions, under what conditions, and with what consequences for competition and state reach. A portable identity can reduce friction while expanding the zone within which one successful proof becomes the foundation for many forms of monitoring, transaction, or exclusion.

The European Union's eIDAS framework illustrates this tension. By creating rules for electronic identification and trust services across member states, eIDAS sought to make recognised digital identities and signatures more interoperable across borders. The ambition was practical and important: smoother cross-border transactions, more reliable digital trust, less duplication. The geopolitical significance ran deeper. A framework for portability does not merely help citizens and firms move. It helps create a regional market in which certain credential models, assurance levels, and trust services become more normal than others. Portability becomes a governance tool. The choice to standardise recognition across borders alters competition, administrative expectations, and the possible scope of coordinated public authority.

Fraud sits at the centre of these debates, often as the argument that settles them politically. Governments and firms promise stronger proofing and authentication because fraud is visible, unpopular, and costly in human as well as financial terms. Identity systems that reduce duplicate claims, impersonation, and account takeover can indeed produce real public benefit. But anti-fraud design has a habit of overexpansion. Once a system is built to distinguish genuine from false identities, pressure mounts to use it more widely, to tighten thresholds further, and to pass the burden of doubt onto the user. Fraud prevention then shades into suspicion by design. The question ceases to be "can the state know enough to stop abuse?" and becomes "how much friction can it impose on everyone else in order to do so?" Authentication standards answer that question whether governments admit it or not.

This is also where private-sector competition enters. Identity standards often decide which firms can participate in markets for payments, onboarding, age verification, hiring, digital signatures, or compliance services. If a standard relies heavily on existing banking relationships, banks gain structural advantage. If it depends on mobile network credentials, telecom providers may become indispensable intermediaries. If the state certifies only a narrow set of identity providers, competition may shrink around those already established. Conversely, open and well-governed portability standards can lower barriers to entry by preventing dominant actors from trapping identity inside closed ecosystems. The same standard can either widen or narrow the market depending on how it allocates trust and cost.

A named example from the United Kingdom makes this visible. The Gov.uk Verify programme, launched to create a federated digital identity model for access to government services, was designed partly to avoid a monolithic state-run identity system by relying on certified private providers. The model contained serious thought and genuine principle. It also struggled with adoption, service coverage, and the difficulty of reconciling inclusiveness, usability, and assurance across different departments and populations. The lesson is not that federation was a mistake or that centralisation is automatically better. It is that identity architecture always carries trade-offs. A federated model may diffuse power and support competition while creating inconsistency or access barriers. A more central model may simplify user experience while concentrating failure and state reach. The design commits the polity long before the politics catch up.

A credible limitation should be admitted. Standardisation in identity is not always a route to excessive state reach or private dominance. Fragmented, inconsistent, and weak identity practices can produce harms of their own: fraud that erodes public trust, repeated bureaucratic burdens, exclusion through arbitrariness rather than formal design, and administrative systems that cannot interoperate even where they plainly should. A citizen asked to prove the same facts to multiple public bodies with no reliable reuse of prior verification experiences not liberty but friction. Some degree of standardisation is therefore necessary if digital government is to function at all. The problem is not standardisation as such. It is what kind, for whom, with which escape routes.

That limitation refines the argument rather than weakening it. The true issue is not whether identity should be standardised, but how the standard distributes power between citizen, state, and market. Does it let users recover from loss of access without humiliating burdens? Does it prevent one actor from becoming the unavoidable broker of personhood? Does it allow credentials to move across contexts without allowing every transaction to become linkable by default? Does it permit selective disclosure, or does every proof expose more data than the situation requires? Does it enable competition among service providers without degrading assurance to the point of harm? These are political design questions expressed through technical architecture.

The architecture matters because standards are stubborn once adopted. A proofing threshold chosen to reassure regulators can later exclude people who lack conventional documents. A portability feature introduced to reduce paperwork can later enable broad cross-sector correlation. A biometric authentication method adopted to deter fraud can later produce failure patterns that disproportionately burden manual workers or the elderly. An identity provider market structured around a few large incumbents can become extremely difficult to reopen once all major services depend on their interfaces. What begins as a design preference becomes a path dependence. The key, once cut, fits many more locks than originally intended.

This path dependence is especially significant for the state because identity standards do not merely support administration; they help define the practical boundary of membership and obligation. Who can access benefits, open a business, verify age, prove entitlement, cross a border, register a property interest, or file a tax return may increasingly depend on systems that convert human presence into machine-readable assurance. If those systems are built carelessly, they can turn ordinary public life into repeated contests of recognisability. If they are built wisely, they can reduce fraud and friction together without making the population permanently legible to every actor able to tap the interface. The distinction is hard to sustain. That is precisely why it matters.

The quiet motif of the key remains useful because identity systems are, in effect, key-making institutions. They cut the shapes by which a person opens services, rights, obligations, and markets. A badly cut key sticks, locks out, or opens too much. A well-cut one works smoothly enough that users forget the politics embedded inside it. But the politics stay there. They live in the proofing rules, in the recovery process, in the portability conditions, in the audit logs, in the market structure of credential providers, and in the legal assumptions about what counts as enough evidence to be known.

The harder question, then, is not whether a digital identity standard can be made secure or efficient in isolation. Many can. The sharper question is what kind of social order it invites once it becomes ordinary. Does it build a public infrastructure people can use without fear of routine exclusion or silent overexposure? Does it support competition without letting identity become another rent-bearing bottleneck? Does it strengthen the state's capacity to govern without making every act of recognition a chance for unnecessary extraction? Those questions do not arise after the design is chosen. They are the design.

Procurement, compliance, and institutional capture

In July 2021, the United Kingdom's Competition and Markets Authority cleared Microsoft's acquisition of Nuance, a company whose speech and healthcare tools already sat close to sensitive administrative and clinical workflows. The decision itself belonged to competition law. Its wider significance lay elsewhere. Public institutions do not encounter technology as isolated products. They encounter it through procurement frameworks, compliance requirements, pre-approved suppliers, existing integrations, and the practical comfort of buying from firms already recognised as safe bets. By the time a contract is signed, much of the market has often been sorted already. The tender was the visible moment. The real decision had been maturing for years.

That is the right place to begin because procurement is often misunderstood as an administrative afterlife to strategy, a procedural stage that follows the serious political argument. In practice procurement is where much of the serious political argument is settled. Governments declare ambitions about openness, competition, security, and interoperability. Procurement translates those ambitions into bid criteria, accreditation thresholds, reporting duties, audit requirements, service-level expectations, indemnities, insurance rules, and technical specifications. Those choices do not merely select suppliers. They define what kinds of suppliers can realistically compete and what kinds of architectures will come to dominate public systems. The form writes the market.

Compliance frameworks intensify this effect. A standard or assurance regime may present itself as neutral - a common test of seriousness, a shared language of risk, an efficient means of comparing unlike vendors. Often it does useful work. Without some baseline, public institutions would struggle to distinguish responsible providers from reckless ones. Yet neutrality in compliance is always partial. Someone chooses which controls count, which evidence is acceptable, how often reports must be produced, how audits are structured, what documentation satisfies due diligence, and which operational models fit comfortably inside the framework. These choices can protect the state. They can also privilege the firms already organised to comply.

The concept that matters here is institutional capture, though it rarely arrives as open corruption. More often it appears as the slow alignment of standards, procurement habits, and assurance language with the capabilities of incumbents and the preferences of powerful internal actors, especially security agencies and large administrative buyers. A vendor with mature compliance teams, established legal templates, broad certification portfolios, and armies of consultants can meet complex procurement demands more easily than a smaller rival, even where the smaller rival offers a technically better or more open product. A security body accustomed to certain kinds of logging, segmentation, or access control may press for requirements that make operational sense from its vantage point while narrowing the field of architectures that can qualify. Capture does not always distort rules for private advantage alone. It often distorts them in the name of prudence.

This is one reason public technology markets so often converge on a familiar set of suppliers. The convergence is not simply the result of superior products or lazy officials. It is produced by the interaction of risk aversion and bureaucratic proof. Procurement officers must justify decisions under scrutiny. Auditors want recognised evidence. Legal teams prefer tested contract forms. Ministers want scandal avoided. Civil servants, aware that failure attracts more attention than foregone innovation, choose options that can be defended in conventional language. The visible behaviour is easy to recognise: references to "market-leading" vendors, preference for suppliers already on approved frameworks, repeated reliance on certifications as proxies for deeper understanding, and a quiet reluctance to back solutions that would require the state itself to learn something new. Compliance becomes a shield. It also becomes a filter.

A named example helps show how architecture follows from these filters. The United States Federal Risk and Authorization Management Program, known as FedRAMP, was created to standardise the security assessment and authorisation of cloud services used by federal agencies. It has delivered real benefits by creating a clearer route for cloud adoption in government. It has also demonstrated how compliance design shapes market structure. Achieving and maintaining the necessary authorisation demands documentation, process discipline, staffing, and time that large cloud providers and established contractors are far better placed to sustain than smaller entrants. The framework did not exist to crown incumbents. It existed to manage risk. Yet risk management itself became a market-making force. The state asked for evidence in a particular form, and the firms most able to furnish that form gained advantage.

This does not make the framework misguided. It makes it politically significant. Procurement and compliance never merely observe the market. They organise it. Once a public sector begins to rely on a compliance regime, firms adapt around it. Investors read it. Consultants package services to navigate it. Auditors train against it. Agencies come to treat it as the natural language of seriousness. Over time, the distinction between a secure system and a certifiable system can start to blur. That is where capture becomes subtle. Institutions begin to confuse what is easy to verify with what is strategically best.

Auditability requirements are among the clearest examples of this dynamic. Governments quite reasonably want systems that produce logs, preserve evidence, document access, and support incident investigation. Auditability is not a bureaucratic fetish. It is a condition of accountability. But auditability requirements are not architecture-neutral. Some cloud models, especially those built around highly standardised services and strong centralised logging, satisfy formal audit expectations more comfortably than more distributed or modular designs. A requirement that all relevant events be captured in a particular way, retained under particular conditions, and surfaced through particular tooling may favour hyperscale cloud environments and large managed service providers over smaller firms, open-source assemblies, or federated architectures that do not package evidence so neatly. The consequence is important. A control chosen to strengthen oversight can also narrow architectural diversity.

The same applies in identity and access management. Public buyers often require single sign-on, centralised privilege management, comprehensive event logging, and tightly integrated directory services. These are often sensible goals. They can reduce error, strengthen security, and make audits far more meaningful. They can also tilt markets towards vendors offering broad suites rather than narrower components. A supplier that provides identity, logging, endpoint management, productivity tools, and compliance dashboards in one integrated stack can satisfy procurement language more readily than a set of specialised providers whose products would need to be assembled and governed by the customer. Integration becomes both a benefit and a moat. The state may gain easier administration while deepening dependence on a smaller number of firms.

A second named example lies in the long controversies around electronic health records in the United States, especially the role of certification requirements attached to federal policy under the HITECH era. Certification was meant to encourage interoperability, safety, and modernisation. It succeeded in accelerating adoption. It also helped structure a market in which certain large vendors consolidated formidable positions, partly because they could navigate the certification and procurement environment more effectively than smaller competitors. The lesson is not that certification was a mistake. It is that once compliance becomes the gateway to public money and regulatory legitimacy, certification criteria begin to shape market structure as powerfully as technical merit does.

Security agencies exert a particular influence here because their concerns are institutionally difficult to resist. When they ask for stronger logging, broader retention, better traceability, more granular access controls, or clearer audit trails, they often do so from a real operational need. The problem is not that these demands are cynical. The problem is that they can have second-order effects outside the security frame. A requirement designed to preserve forensic visibility may also encourage architectures that centralise data collection. A demand for lawful access readiness may favour providers able to maintain standardised interfaces to sensitive systems. A preference for uniform telemetry may make public and private systems easier to supervise while also making them easier to monitor across purposes. Security logic can travel far beyond its original domain once embedded in procurement.

This is why institutional capture should not be reduced to vendor lobbying alone, though lobbying matters. Capture also occurs when a state's own strongest bureaucratic actors define neutrality in their own image. A compliance framework may look balanced while carrying the assumptions of intelligence agencies, large ministries, or procurement officials whose experience has been formed by specific kinds of vendors and legacy risks. Those assumptions are often reasonable within their home context. They become more problematic when universalised. What serves a highly classified environment may not suit an innovative civic service platform. What works for a very large department may crush smaller suppliers serving local government. The language of "best practice" often conceals this scaling problem.

A credible limitation should be stated clearly. Formal compliance requirements can also check arbitrary procurement, reduce corruption, and protect public bodies from irresponsible or insecure suppliers. In their absence, governments can drift into opaque contracting, political favouritism, and haphazard technical choices that leave systems more brittle and less accountable. Smaller vendors are not automatically better, nor are open or decentralised architectures automatically safer. Some degree of standardised assurance is indispensable if public institutions are to buy at scale with any coherence. The issue is not whether compliance should exist. It is what kind of compliance produces security without quietly scripting the market around a narrow set of business models.

That limitation sharpens the real question. Good procurement design distinguishes between controls that genuinely protect public interests and controls that mainly reward incumbent capacity to produce paperwork. It asks whether audit requirements can be satisfied in more than one architectural form. It checks whether interoperability obligations reduce lock-in or simply make dominant suites more attractive. It tests whether smaller firms can prove trustworthiness without reproducing the full compliance bureaucracy of a hyperscaler. And it recognises that innovation is often less hindered by technical impossibility than by the cost of entering a public market whose assurance rules have become too heavy for outsiders to bear.

This becomes especially important in cloud markets because compliance and procurement are already closely intertwined with concentration. Public buyers want reliability, incident response maturity, geographic resilience, and detailed audit evidence. The largest cloud providers are unusually well placed to supply all four. That makes their popularity understandable. It also means that every new requirement for detailed logging, sophisticated key management, formal attestations, or rapid evidence production can reinforce the gravitational pull towards those same providers. The process looks rational at every step. The strategic result may still be overconcentration. Procurement officials optimise for defensibility in the individual contract. The state inherits dependence at the system level.

The quiet motif of the form helps keep this argument grounded. A form is meant to record facts neutrally. Yet anyone who has dealt with bureaucracy knows that forms also shape behaviour. They reward certain answers, discourage others, and define what can count as a serious response. Procurement and compliance work the same way. A tender form, a security questionnaire, a certification checklist, an audit template - these do not merely observe the vendor landscape. They teach vendors how to become legible to the state. Over time, firms that learn the form best become the firms the state sees most easily. Visibility becomes advantage.

The more mature response is not to romanticise procurement freedom or to sneer at compliance as a paper exercise. It is to treat both as instruments of market design and state capacity. A public body should ask not only whether a requirement reduces a known risk, but also what market behaviour it is likely to produce. Will it encourage open interfaces or bundled suites? Will it strengthen auditability without standardising unnecessary data extraction? Will it preserve room for smaller trusted suppliers, or quietly eliminate them? Will it align with the operational needs of the actual workload, or has a control designed for one environment been copied into another because nobody wanted the burden of arguing against it? These are governance questions wearing administrative clothes.

Capture, then, should be understood as a pattern rather than a scandal. It appears when institutions repeatedly define neutrality, assurance, and best practice in ways that fit incumbents, reinforce existing bureaucratic habits, and make alternative architectures harder to imagine, let alone buy. It can produce short-term order. It can also hollow out public bargaining power over time. A government surrounded by compliant suppliers may still be strategically weak if those suppliers have become too few, too deeply embedded, and too fluent in the state's own assurance language to be meaningfully challenged.

The harder test is therefore not whether a vendor can pass the form, but whether the form itself has become part of the dependency. If auditability requirements, certification routes, and procurement rules repeatedly favour the same architectures and firms, the state must ask whether it is buying security, buying comfort, or buying a future in which its own standards have quietly narrowed the range of systems it can plausibly govern. That question is less dramatic than a breach or an outage. It may be more consequential, because by the time the answer is obvious, the market has usually already been written.

Chapter 6

Surveillance Capability and Political Legitimacy

What happens when a state becomes technically able to know far more about its population than it can openly justify, lawfully process, or politically survive being seen to know? The question is not rhetorical. It reaches into the ordinary machinery of government: who gets flagged, who gets watched, who gets stopped, who gets audited, who gets profiled, who gets left alone. Surveillance is often discussed as if it were a single dramatic act. More often it accumulates through routine permissions, new interfaces, cheaper storage, better search, more generous data sharing, and the quiet administrative appeal of asking for information that already exists somewhere else. The screen invites one more query.

This is why surveillance capacity rarely expands only through explicit doctrine. Sometimes it does, especially after war, attack, or emergency. Just as often it grows through convenience. A dataset collected for fraud control becomes useful for policing. A commercial feed acquired for marketing turns out to map movement. A platform partnership built for moderation opens a wider reporting channel. A retention rule designed for one purpose lingers long enough to serve another. Technical possibility arrives before political language catches up, and institutions learn to treat the gap as normal. The result is not only more observation. It is a gradual weakening of the old distinction between what a state may do and what it happens to find easy to do.

That drift matters because surveillance sits at the point where state capability and public trust most visibly collide. A government has real obligations to investigate violence, disrupt espionage, prevent fraud, and protect critical systems. Citizens generally understand that some secrecy and some intrusion are necessary for those tasks. Yet the same instruments that strengthen security can also degrade legitimacy when they appear unbounded, weakly supervised, or too closely tied to private data markets. The issue is not simply whether surveillance works. It is whether the public can believe that it works on terms compatible with law, restraint, and error correction. When that belief weakens, capability itself begins to curdle.

The stakes are therefore larger than privacy in the narrow sense. Surveillance affects democratic resilience because people alter behaviour when they suspect that monitoring is broad, opaque, or politically selective. Speech changes. Association changes. Participation changes. Officials become more defensive. Journalists guard sources differently. Citizens grow less willing to trust emergency instructions from institutions they suspect of opportunism. A state may collect more and govern worse. That is the paradox worth keeping in view. Data power that hollows out trust does not merely create a moral problem. It creates a strategic one, because crises require voluntary cooperation that cannot be forced at scale every time it is needed.

This tension is sharpened by the way surveillance now crosses institutional boundaries. Intelligence services share with allies. Police use commercial tools. Regulators encounter data first assembled for advertising. Border systems connect to watchlists built elsewhere. Cloud providers and platforms mediate what public bodies can see and how quickly they can act. Responsibility then becomes oddly diffuse. Who set the terms? Who checked the legal basis? Who audited subsequent use? Who bears the political cost when a capability developed in one domain migrates into another? Shared capability can raise collective security. It can also leave one institution holding the scandal for decisions shaped somewhere else.

The chapter's path follows that widening field. It begins by separating forms of surveillance that are too often blurred together, then moves into the alliances and partnerships through which states borrow tools, data, and analytic reach from one another. From there it enters the murkier territory where commercial brokerage and public power begin to overlap, before turning to the institutional devices that make secrecy bearable or unbearable: warrants, minimisation, auditing, remedies, and the credibility of those who oversee them. The argument then broadens to the social effects of perceived observation and finally to the recurrent cycle in which misuse, breach, and mission creep produce scandal without always producing durable reform.

A useful image for the chapter is the mirror. A state wants a mirror sharp enough to detect threats, trace networks, and verify claims before harm spreads. But a mirror can also unsettle those who live before it, especially when they cannot tell who is watching through the glass, what is being recorded, or how long the image remains. A society that feels perpetually reflected back to authority does not only fear abuse. It often becomes less candid, less trusting, and less resilient. The mirror then starts to distort what it was meant to reveal.

This is why legitimacy must be treated as a component of surveillance capability rather than a check added from the outside. Oversight, minimisation, independent review, disclosure rules, and meaningful remedies do not merely decorate power with ethics. They help determine whether power remains usable without constant backlash. A secret programme can survive if it is tightly governed and credibly bound. A lawful practice can still corrode trust if the public encounters it only through leak, scandal, or bureaucratic evasion. Institutions that rely on surveillance need more than legal authority. They need enough credibility that inevitable mistakes do not turn every revelation into proof of bad faith.

The harder question, then, is not whether states should possess surveillance capabilities. They already do, and many are necessary. The harder question is where capability stops being governed and starts becoming self-justifying - where technical convenience, alliance habit, commercial access, and institutional secrecy combine into a surveillance order too expansive to explain and too normalised to challenge until scandal forces the issue. The first step in answering that question is conceptual discipline: knowing what kind of surveillance is actually being discussed before the mirror starts to look like one thing.

The surveillance spectrum

In June 2013, reporting based on documents disclosed by Edward Snowden revealed details of surveillance programmes operated by the United States National Security Agency, including arrangements for the collection of communications data and the use of broad technical access across global networks. The disclosures did not create the modern surveillance debate, but they changed its grammar. Public argument could no longer proceed as though surveillance meant one thing: a warrant, a wiretap, a suspect, a line listened to in secret. The archive told a different story. Surveillance had become a layered activity ranging from focused investigation to large-scale collection and increasingly to the analysis of patterns no individual had consciously declared.

That mattered because democratic societies often inherit an older moral picture of surveillance that no longer fits the technical landscape. In that older picture, the state wishes to know something about someone specific, seeks authority, acquires the relevant information, and acts. Much surveillance still works that way, and in some circumstances it must. But modern systems do not merely wait for a named suspect. They store first, sort later. They collect because collection is cheap, because retention might prove useful, because technical architecture makes large-scale copying easier than selective filtering, and because analysis now depends heavily on pattern recognition across many records at once. The result is not simply more observation. It is a blurring of categories that were once easier to keep distinct in law and public imagination.

The first task, then, is conceptual discipline. Surveillance is not a single practice but a spectrum, and the distinctions along that spectrum matter politically as much as technically. At one end sits targeted investigation, where an institution focuses on a defined person, account, device, or network on the basis of some prior reason. In the middle sits bulk collection, where data are acquired or retained at scale because future analytic value is presumed, even if only a small fraction will ever be examined closely. Further along sits behavioural inference, where institutions derive conclusions about risk, intent, association, or identity from patterns in data that may themselves appear ordinary or indirect. These modes overlap. They are not interchangeable. Confusing them makes serious oversight almost impossible.

Targeted investigation remains the form most easily defended in liberal legal terms because it matches older doctrines of suspicion and authorisation. A magistrate or judge is presented with grounds. A warrant or order specifies a target or a narrowly bounded set of targets. A surveillance act follows. The visible behaviour is familiar: a named device is monitored, a premises search is conducted, a financial trail is examined, a particular communications account is intercepted. The principle is specificity. The state seeks to know something about this person, this plot, this case. That specificity does not eliminate risk or abuse, but it gives law and oversight a relatively stable object to govern. One can ask who was targeted, on what basis, for how long, under what authorisation, and with what result.

A useful example lies in the conventional use of wiretaps and communications intercepts in organised crime and terrorism investigations. In the United Kingdom and the United States alike, such powers have historically been justified on the basis that covert access can reveal communications that public investigation cannot reach. The concept is focused intrusion. Its implication is operational and legal at once. Focused intrusion can be proportionate because the burden of justification falls before the act rather than after it. Oversight is still imperfect, but the model presumes a chain linking reason, authority, and action. That chain becomes much harder to maintain as surveillance drifts away from named targets and towards environments, populations, or patterns.

Bulk collection changes the logic because the state no longer waits for a fully specified subject before acquiring data. It gathers or compels large volumes of material on the premise that later analysis will identify what matters. The data may include communications metadata, network traffic, travel records, location traces, financial transactions, or other signals whose value emerges mainly when retained at scale and queried retrospectively. The concept here is anticipatory acquisition. Bulk collection treats uncertainty itself as a reason to collect broadly, because not knowing in advance who matters becomes part of the case for storing more. The operational attraction is obvious. After an attack or breach, investigators can look backwards. The political difficulty is just as clear. If broad acquisition precedes particular suspicion, the old grammar of necessity and proportionality comes under strain.

The Snowden disclosures made this visible because they showed how modern intelligence systems had normalised forms of collection that sat uneasily within public expectations shaped by more targeted models. The argument offered by security agencies was not wholly implausible. In a world of transnational networks, ephemeral communications, and fast-moving plots, selective acquisition can miss the relevant trail before anyone knows which trail matters. Yet the move from target to pool changes the legal and moral terrain. The act under scrutiny is no longer only the later search or analytical use. It is also the prior accumulation that made such use possible. Bulk collection creates archives of potential scrutiny. That is a different kind of power.

Behavioural inference takes the logic further. Here the institution may not need direct access to the content of communication, or even to a single obviously sensitive dataset. Instead it compares patterns: repeated movement, contact frequency, device proximity, transaction timing, search behaviour, anomalous travel, common log-in characteristics, social graph overlap, or deviations from normal routine. The result is not always a fact in the classic evidentiary sense. It is often a judgment about likelihood. This person may belong to that network. This device likely belongs to that household. This account behaves like others previously associated with fraud, protest mobilisation, espionage, or radicalisation. The concept is predictive scrutiny. Its implication is particularly significant because it weakens the boundary between data collected for ordinary administration or commerce and data used for security or enforcement.

A second named example helps here. The use of automated number plate recognition, widely deployed in several countries including the United Kingdom, illustrates how behavioural inference can grow from infrastructure originally justified in narrower operational terms. Number plate data can help locate a stolen car or identify a suspect vehicle in a specific inquiry. That is targeted enough in spirit. Yet the same systems also enable pattern analysis across time and place: repeated journeys, common routes, probable associations, unusual deviations, and retrospective reconstruction of movement. The camera records one car. The database makes a behaviour legible. That shift from event detection to pattern inference is the essence of the problem. The same infrastructure supports different surveillance logics depending on how it is queried, retained, and connected.

This is why technical convenience matters so much. Surveillance capability often expands not because a legislature explicitly authorises a new doctrine, but because institutions discover that a system already in place can do more than originally advertised. Storage becomes cheaper. Search becomes faster. Data linkage becomes easier. Commercial platforms create rich behavioural datasets. Machine learning tools lower the cost of classification. Interfaces built for fraud detection can be repurposed for broader monitoring. The institution then experiences a familiar temptation. If the data exists, and the query is possible, why not ask? Convenience becomes the quiet legislator.

That drift is one reason lawful authority must be carefully separated from technical possibility. Technical possibility concerns what a system can do: search all records, correlate many sources, detect anomalies, reconstruct movement, infer networks, rank risk. Lawful authority concerns what an institution may do under defined rules, with defined oversight, for defined purposes. The two are not naturally aligned. A system may technically enable mass retrospective analysis where the legal basis contemplates only narrower use. A commercial dataset may make location tracking easy where public authorities would once have needed stronger formal justification. A social media platform may offer search or reporting tools that encourage state use beyond older investigative boundaries. Serious vocabulary matters here because institutions often describe technical capability as though it were a mere operational option rather than a challenge to legal design.

The practical difference shows up in routine decisions. Does an analyst query a broad database because the tool allows it, or because a warrant and policy authorise it for this case? Does a police unit buy commercially available location data because subpoena is slower, even if the older route carried more oversight? Does an agency retain a dataset longer than necessary because future utility is hard to rule out? These are not theoretical questions. They are the daily points at which surveillance expands. The decisive move is rarely a dramatic declaration. It is the normalisation of asking what the system can do before asking what the institution should do.

A credible limitation should be acknowledged. The spectrum is a tool for analysis, not a perfect map of reality. Some targeted investigations depend on background datasets that were collected broadly. Some bulk systems are subject to stringent filtering and minimisation. Some forms of inference are indispensable to ordinary governance, including fraud detection and cybersecurity, and do not belong automatically in the same moral category as covert political surveillance. It would be unhelpful to flatten every pattern-based analysis into oppression or every large-scale dataset into illegitimacy. Modern institutions often need forms of aggregation and inference to function. The point is not to deny that need. It is to keep categories sharp enough that powers granted for one mode are not silently stretched into another.

That limitation, however, only reinforces the need for clearer language. Without distinctions, political debate swings between panic and denial. Security agencies describe capabilities in the most targeted and necessity-laden terms available, even when those capabilities depend on bulk archives or inferential tools. Critics describe all collection as mass surveillance, even where the operational reality is narrower. Both moves obstruct governance. A state that wants to preserve legitimacy must be able to say, with precision, whether it is authorising targeted access, bulk retention, inferential scoring, or some combination of the three. Only then can oversight, minimisation, and remedy match the real capability rather than a comforting fiction.

The commercial sphere complicates the spectrum further because behavioural inference no longer belongs only to governments. Advertising technology, fraud prevention vendors, social media platforms, and data brokers have spent years building systems that classify users from fragmented traces. States now encounter a world in which inferential machinery already exists and can sometimes be bought, borrowed, or compelled. That changes the political landscape. An institution need not build a mass surveillance stack from scratch if a private intermediary has already assembled relevant profiles, location histories, or behavioural models for other purposes. The state's role shifts from collector to accessor. Yet from the citizen's perspective, the result may look much the same. Observation has been privatised upstream.

This is why the spectrum should also be read as a spectrum of institutional temptation. Targeted investigation tempts institutions to broaden categories of suspicion. Bulk collection tempts them to keep data simply because deletion forecloses future use. Behavioural inference tempts them to treat correlation as enough of a reason to intervene. Each temptation is reinforced by convenience. Each becomes easier to justify internally when the technical system is already in place. Constraints therefore need to be designed around the mode of surveillance, not around a generic claim that "data access" exists. A warrant model that fits targeted investigation may be insufficient for bulk retention. An audit regime designed for bulk access may miss the harms of opaque inferential scoring. Precision in vocabulary is a precondition of precision in law.

The quiet motif of the query helps hold the argument together. A query sounds innocent: a search, a filter, a request for what the database already contains. But every surveillance system ultimately turns on queries. Who may ask them? Against what data? Using which selectors, models, or thresholds? With what record of the asking? The query is where lawful authority meets technical possibility. It is also where institutions most often discover the gap between what they meant to permit and what their systems now make effortless.

The harder question, then, is not whether the state should investigate threats. It must. The harder question is when a capability built for one point on the spectrum starts to slide along it under the pressure of convenience, commercial availability, and analytic ambition. If targeted tools lean on bulk archives, and bulk archives feed behavioural inference, what exactly is being authorised when a government claims it is using surveillance "lawfully" and "only where necessary"? That question cannot be answered by rhetoric alone. It requires naming the mode of surveillance plainly enough that the next boundary can still be seen before it is crossed.

Intelligence sharing and dependency

In 1946, the United States and the United Kingdom concluded what became known as the UKUSA Agreement, laying the foundations for an intelligence-sharing system that later expanded into the alliance commonly called the Five Eyes. The agreement was born in the shadow of war and the onset of a harsher geopolitical order. Its immediate purpose was practical: pool interception, distribute tasks, reduce duplication, and build a shared informational advantage against common adversaries. But the longer lesson lies elsewhere. Intelligence sharing did not merely combine strengths. It also created a structure in which some states would know more, some would rely more, and all would be changed by the terms on which access was granted. The file crossed borders.

That crossing is the starting point for any serious account of intelligence partnerships. States share intelligence because no state, however capable, sees everything alone. Threats move across jurisdictions. Signals travel through foreign infrastructure. Financial flows pass through allied systems. Language expertise, technical access, and analytic tradecraft are unevenly distributed. Cooperation can therefore save lives, prevent attacks, expose hostile networks, and improve strategic warning in ways unilateral collection cannot. The case for sharing is not cosmetic. It is operational. Yet operational value should not obscure the deeper politics. Sharing is never a simple gift. It is a governed exchange shaped by hierarchy, trust, capability, law, and the quiet leverage that comes from being more necessary to a partner than that partner is to you.

This is the core concept: intelligence sharing creates capability and dependence at the same time. A weaker or smaller state may gain access to data, tools, and analytic methods it could not otherwise sustain. A stronger partner may gain geographic reach, local knowledge, legal footholds, or political cover. Both may become safer in immediate terms. But the bargain is rarely symmetrical. One side may define formats, security standards, retention expectations, caveats on dissemination, or the technology through which exchange occurs. One side may audit more than it is audited. One side may decide how much to reveal about source and method, and one side may remain more exposed when misuse becomes public. The alliance raises collective security. It also redistributes control.

The visible signs of this redistribution often appear mundane. A national service adopts a partner's watchlist format. Analysts are trained on a foreign toolset. Shared databases rely on classification practices set elsewhere. Intelligence reports arrive already shaped by another state's analytic priorities and collection biases. A smaller service aligns its legal or technical procedures with the expectations of a more capable ally in order to remain in the exchange. These are not merely bureaucratic details. They are the mechanisms by which dependence becomes normal. Over time, the partnership ceases to be one source among many and becomes part of the operating system of national security itself.

A named example makes the point more concretely. The "Five Eyes" arrangements among the United States, United Kingdom, Canada, Australia, and New Zealand have long been associated with unusually deep forms of intelligence cooperation, particularly in signals intelligence. Public understanding of the full detail remains partial for obvious reasons, but the broad strategic lesson is plain enough. The alliance has allowed participating states to divide collection tasks, pool analytic effort, and gain access to a wider field of information than any one member could easily generate alone. That is real strength. Yet it also means that member states, especially those with smaller domestic capabilities, can become accustomed to strategic vision partly delivered through allied systems. Dependence can feel like partnership when the pipeline works well.

The issue becomes sharper when intelligence sharing extends beyond raw reporting into tools, infrastructure, and analytic capacity. Data exchange is only one layer. States also share software, platforms, training, methodologies, malware analysis, threat signatures, targeting assistance, and technical support for lawful interception or cyber operations. This broadens the meaning of dependency. A government may not simply receive finished intelligence; it may come to rely on another state's ability to process information in the first place. The concept here is embedded assistance. Once a partner's tools and workflows become integral to domestic capability, autonomy narrows even if formal sovereignty remains intact. The state still decides, but it increasingly decides inside someone else's technical frame.

This is not necessarily a flaw. Many states have strong reasons to accept such bargains. Building full-spectrum intelligence capability is expensive, politically difficult, and often unrealistic. A country facing terrorism, hostile espionage, or cyber intrusion may reasonably prefer shared access to strategic blindness. Intelligence partnerships can also improve standards by spreading tradecraft, raising security discipline, and encouraging common procedures for handling sensitive material. A smaller service trained through alliance cooperation may become more professional, not less. The limitation should be stated clearly: dependency is not always a pathology. Sometimes it is a rational response to real threat and finite resources.

But the limitation does not cancel the problem. It clarifies its terms. The real question is not whether states should share intelligence. They always will. The harder question is who sets the terms of sharing and what those terms do over time. Are caveats reciprocal or mostly one-way? Can the receiving state independently evaluate the quality and legality of what it receives, or is trust largely inferred from the relationship itself? Does the partnership improve domestic capacity, or does it slowly substitute for it? Can a state challenge the use conditions attached to shared data without risking wider exclusion? These are constitutional questions conducted through secure channels.

A second named example shows how political cost can become uneven even when intelligence value is shared. In the years following 11 September 2001, intelligence cooperation among the United States and various partners expanded dramatically across counter-terrorism, rendition, interrogation, data sharing, and watchlisting. Some states gained access to operational insights and stronger security relationships. Some also found themselves implicated in controversies over detention, torture, extraordinary rendition, and unlawful transfer. The public record in countries such as the United Kingdom, Canada, and several European states later revealed how alliance logic could blur national responsibility. The operational case for cooperation had been strong. The political and moral aftermath was not evenly distributed. A partner can inherit scandal from a practice it did not fully design but did help sustain.

That example matters because it highlights a frequently neglected point: intelligence sharing can externalise political risk. A state may receive information from an ally while remaining only dimly aware of the exact provenance, legal basis, or coercive practices that produced it. It may choose not to ask too many questions because the intelligence seems urgent or because the alliance relationship is strategically valuable. Later, when courts, inquiries, journalists, or parliamentary committees reconstruct the chain, the receiving state cannot easily claim innocence. The visible action may have been passive - receive, read, act. The political consequence is active complicity. This is one reason oversight in intelligence sharing must reach beyond domestic collection alone. Partnerships generate their own accountability problems.

Data sharing also creates asymmetries in auditability. The state that collects and packages intelligence often knows more about source reliability, collection methods, and analytic uncertainty than the state that receives the product. Caveats can limit onward dissemination, but they can also limit scrutiny. A receiving service may act on a lead without being able to inspect the evidentiary scaffolding beneath it. This can be unavoidable; sources and methods need protection. Yet the democratic difficulty remains. Decisions with legal or coercive effects may depend on information the acting state cannot fully test and the affected person cannot meaningfully challenge. Secrecy here is not only a shield against adversaries. It is also a structural barrier to accountability.

The same issue appears in shared watchlists and no-fly arrangements. Lists can be operationally useful because they allow rapid coordination across borders, transport systems, and policing environments. But a list is also a power-bearing object. It can embed one state's thresholds of suspicion into another state's frontline decisions. A border officer may deny boarding or trigger secondary screening based on a foreign-origin alert that domestic institutions did not create and may not be able to review in full. The concept is imported suspicion. The implication is serious: alliance cooperation can shift practical standards of scrutiny without corresponding public debate or judicial clarity in the receiving state.

Commercial technology compounds these dependencies. Intelligence partnerships increasingly operate through common platforms, cloud services, cyber defence tools, biometrics, and data fusion systems supplied by private firms. Sometimes those firms are local. Often they are not. The alliance then sits atop a shared vendor layer that can standardise exchange and accelerate analysis while also creating a new kind of lock-in. A state may depend not only on a partner government's willingness to share, but on a jointly used proprietary environment for searching, correlating, and storing intelligence. This adds another actor to the chain of control and another location where audit rights, incident response, and legal obligations matter. The alliance becomes partly infrastructural.

A credible counterpoint deserves attention. Intelligence sharing is not always hierarchical in the crude sense of stronger versus weaker. Smaller states sometimes contribute geographic access, language expertise, maritime position, regional contacts, or local legal authorities that larger partners lack. They can extract meaningful concessions, preserve distinct legal traditions, and refuse certain forms of cooperation. Some intelligence communities have also built internal safeguards for received intelligence, including caveat management, minimisation rules, and independent review of foreign-supplied material before it is used domestically. This matters because it prevents the argument from collapsing into fatalism. Dependence is real, but it is negotiated.

Still, negotiation takes place within unequal capability. A country with powerful collection systems, global platforms, advanced analytics, and central alliance roles can usually shape norms more than a country whose value lies in regional access or niche expertise. That shaping function matters because it extends beyond immediate operations into doctrine. Shared definitions of threat, acceptable targeting, suspicious behaviour, data retention, or lawful access can migrate through partnerships and become embedded in domestic practice. This is how intelligence alliances become constitutional by other means. They influence how states see the world, which risks they prioritise, and which intrusions start to feel ordinary. The alliance does not simply provide information. It socialises institutions.

This is why the vocabulary of "sharing" can mislead. Sharing sounds horizontal, reciprocal, almost familial. Sometimes it is. Often it obscures a more complicated political economy of access. Some partners are net providers. Some are net consumers. Some share finished products. Some share raw data. Some dictate technical formats. Some bear the diplomatic or judicial consequences when things go wrong. The real diagnostic is more exacting. Who can withhold? Who can inspect? Who can condition access on policy alignment? Who can terminate a partnership without crippling the other's capability? These questions reveal where dependence sits more clearly than ceremonial language about friendship or common values.

The quiet motif of the bridge helps hold the argument together. Intelligence partnerships are often described as bridges across jurisdictions, bureaucracies, and threat environments. Bridges are valuable. They allow movement that would otherwise be slow or impossible. But bridges also have architects, toll points, maintenance rules, and weight limits. Some parties cross more freely than others. Some control the span. Some can close it. A state that relies heavily on a bridge must know not only where it leads, but who can stop traffic and under what conditions. Otherwise the bridge is not just a route. It is a point of leverage.

The legitimacy question, therefore, does not disappear when sharing improves security. It becomes more demanding. A democratic state must ask whether its oversight institutions can examine the terms on which shared intelligence is used, whether ministers and judges understand the dependencies they are authorising, whether remedies exist when foreign-supplied data cause domestic harm, and whether public trust can survive revelations that national surveillance practices are partly shaped through alliances rather than purely national decisions. Collective security may require secrecy. It does not relieve governments of the duty to know what kinds of dependence they are building in the dark.

The forward test is severe. When a state accepts intelligence, tools, or analytic capacity from a partner, is it merely borrowing strength, or is it also importing priorities, thresholds, and liabilities it cannot fully supervise? The answer cannot be read from the alliance communique. It must be found in the terms of access, the depth of audit, the architecture of the shared systems, and the political courage to ask who would bear the cost if the partnership's hidden bargain were suddenly dragged into public view.

Commercial data brokerage and state access

In January 2022, the United States Federal Trade Commission reached a settlement with Kochava, a data broker accused of selling geolocation data that could be used to trace people to sensitive places, including reproductive health clinics, places of worship, and domestic violence shelters. The case turned on consumer protection law, but its deeper significance lay in a different register. Data collected for advertising had become useful for tracking. A market built to predict consumer behaviour had matured into an infrastructure of quasi-intelligence. The breadcrumb trail had changed owners many times before the public noticed what it could reveal.

That is the correct starting point because the modern surveillance state does not rely only on warrants, subpoenas, and covert collection. It increasingly operates within an information economy where behavioural traces are gathered first for commercial purposes and only later recognised as operationally valuable to public authority. This changes the legal and political texture of state access. The old oversight logic assumed that the state either collected the information itself or compelled it from a defined holder for a defined reason. Brokerage markets unsettle that picture. When location histories, device identifiers, credit attributes, purchase patterns, and social profiles circulate as saleable commodities, the question is no longer simply what the state may seize. It becomes what the state may buy, license, or receive through partnership without triggering the scrutiny that older forms of compelled access were designed to attract.

The concept that matters here is the grey zone. Commercial data brokerage sits between market exchange and public power, between consumer tracking and state intelligence, between formal legal process and practical access. In that zone, datasets assembled through apps, ad networks, loyalty programmes, online forms, software development kits, and countless background interactions can be repackaged into products that appear commercially ordinary yet carry clear surveillance utility. A government need not build a nationwide location tracking system if brokers already sell movement patterns. It need not directly compel a platform to identify social networks if consumer segmentation markets already model affinity, routine, and likely association. The state enters by the side door.

This side door matters because it bypasses some of the political friction that traditionally limited surveillance. A warrant requires a theory of suspicion, a legal basis, and usually some form of judicial or administrative scrutiny. A subpoena, depending on jurisdiction and context, still carries procedural traceability and contestability. A commercial purchase, by contrast, may be processed through procurement channels that frame the transaction as market activity rather than coercive access. Partnership arrangements can blur the matter further by presenting data flows as collaborative, analytical, or service-improving rather than evidentiary. The visible behaviour is often banal: an agency signs a contract, renews a subscription, or acquires access through an intermediary. The strategic implication is severe. Surveillance capability can widen without proportionate public debate because the mechanism of acquisition looks less like force.

Location data is the clearest example because movement is so revealing. A smartphone app may collect GPS coordinates, Wi-Fi signals, Bluetooth information, advertising identifiers, and timestamps to improve advertising performance, refine analytics, or support other business functions. That same data, when aggregated and sold, can reveal repeated overnight stays, workplace routines, visits to clinics, religious practice, political attendance, border crossings, or meetings between devices that appear together over time. The issue is not whether every individual datapoint is perfectly accurate. It is that aggregated traces can support powerful inference even where the raw signal is noisy. A person need not announce who they are or what they believe. The trail often says enough.

A named example sharpens the point. Reporting in 2020 and 2021 described how the United States Department of Homeland Security and related agencies had obtained access to commercially available location data for immigration and border-related purposes. The broader significance was not limited to any one agency or country. It lay in the method. Data originally generated through ordinary consumer applications could become useful for state tracking without the same public confrontation that would have accompanied direct compulsory collection on comparable scale. The breadcrumb trail passed through an advertising market and emerged as an enforcement resource. This is the structural novelty. The surveillance question is displaced upstream into consumer data governance, where many of the decisive choices are made with weaker constitutional drama and much less visible accountability.

Commercial brokerage also complicates the distinction between personal and non-personal data. Industry actors often describe products as aggregated, pseudonymised, or de-identified. Those terms matter legally and technically, but they do not end the matter analytically. A dataset need not include a name to become operationally useful. Repeated location at night can suggest home. Repeated location by day can suggest work. Co-location with another device can suggest association. Visits to clinics, houses of worship, military bases, protest sites, or government offices can suggest circumstance, belief, profession, or vulnerability. De-identification reduces some risks. It does not necessarily remove the capacity to infer. The state may not receive a list of named citizens. It may receive something sufficiently rich to be turned into one.

This is why the phrase *quasi-intelligence* is apt. Commercial datasets are not intelligence in the classic sense of covertly collected state information organised by security institutions. Yet they can function like intelligence once bought, subpoenaed, or partnered into public use. They can identify targets of interest, narrow search spaces, test hypotheses, support profiling, and provide retrospective insight into movement or behaviour. The state does not need the whole dossier to gain advantage. It needs enough fragments, structured well enough, to answer operational questions. Modern brokerage markets specialise in fragments precisely because fragments are saleable, combinable, and reusable.

A second named example lies in the long controversy around Clearview AI, whose facial recognition business drew intense scrutiny after reports in 2020 about its scraping of publicly available images and marketing to law-enforcement agencies. The company did not operate as a traditional data broker in the narrow ad-tech sense, but it embodied the same structural shift. Images harvested for one set of social and commercial purposes were transformed into a searchable identification resource for public power. The operative point was not only the technology of facial recognition. It was the business model of acquisition and repurposing. A firm could assemble a surveillance-relevant database before legislatures, courts, or publics had fully decided whether such a database ought to exist at all. State access then followed entrepreneurial initiative rather than explicit public authorisation.

Purchase is only one route through the grey zone. Subpoena and partnership matter as well, and each has its own politics. A subpoena can compel commercial records from a company that may not think of itself as part of the national-security apparatus at all. A partnership can make access feel voluntary or socially useful. Public health, fraud prevention, safety research, and content moderation all provide legitimate grounds for collaboration between state and platform or broker. The challenge is that the same channels can normalise broader access patterns over time. A company that learns to share data for one urgent purpose may become more institutionally prepared to share for another. The state, having seen what is possible, begins to treat that possibility as part of the ordinary landscape of governance.

Technical convenience drives much of this expansion. Commercial datasets are often already cleaned, indexed, and packaged for query. They may arrive with dashboards, APIs, geofencing tools, link analysis features, or segmentation functions that make them easier to use than older forms of evidence. The traditional burden of state intelligence work - collecting, standardising, and linking messy raw data - has partly been outsourced upstream to markets whose own incentives are advertising, profiling, logistics, fraud scoring, or consumer analytics. Public authority inherits the convenience. The question becomes not whether a particular line of inquiry is possible, but why an agency should refrain when the product already exists and the contract is readily available. Convenience erodes restraint by making action feel administratively normal.

This is one reason oversight regimes struggle. Many surveillance laws and oversight bodies were designed around coercive powers exercised directly by the state. They know how to ask whether a warrant was issued, whether a subpoena was valid, whether minimisation rules were followed, whether interception targets were properly authorised. They are less well adapted to a world in which public bodies can acquire similar practical insight through purchases or voluntary partnerships. The legal categories often lag behind the capability. A dataset may enter through procurement rather than investigation, through a contractor rather than an agency collection programme, through a vendor's analytic output rather than a raw records request. Traditional oversight logics then miss the substance because they are looking for the wrong doorway.

A credible limitation should be stated clearly. Commercial data is not a magic surveillance asset. It can be noisy, biased, incomplete, stale, or misleading. Location traces drift. Device identifiers change. Consumer profiles contain obvious errors. App-based data overrepresent some populations and underrepresent others. Brokers may exaggerate precision or coverage. Some public uses of commercial data are also plainly legitimate, including fraud detection, cybersecurity, certain kinds of public health analysis, and market regulation. It would be simplistic to treat all brokered data as illegitimate and all state use as abuse. The state can learn useful things from markets, just as markets learn useful things from the state.

But the limitation does not relieve the central concern. Precisely because brokered data is imperfect, institutions may be tempted to use it for triage, suspicion, or prioritisation while avoiding the evidentiary burdens that more formal processes would impose. The dataset becomes an initial clue rather than a final proof. That may sound modest. In practice, initial clues shape who gets scrutinised, which leads are pursued, and which populations experience disproportionate official attention. Imperfect commercial data can therefore still produce concrete harms even when it never appears in court. The breadcrumb trail need not be evidentially complete to redirect state attention.

This is also why minimisation and purpose limitation become harder to sustain in the brokerage context. A dataset bought for one mission can often be searched again for another. A subscription product invites repeated use because the marginal cost of one more query is low. A vendor seeking to retain customers will tend to emphasise new use cases rather than narrower boundaries. The architecture of brokerage encourages reuse. That is not a side effect. It is part of the commercial model. Public institutions operating within that model require unusually clear internal rules if they want to resist mission creep, because the market itself pushes towards expansion.

Competition and international politics add further complexity. Brokers often operate across borders, sell to multiple sectors, and draw from supply chains of apps, exchanges, and intermediaries that are difficult even for sophisticated regulators to map. One country's weak consumer data rules can therefore become another country's surveillance loophole. A state may restrict direct government collection while tolerating commercial practices that make equivalent access available for purchase later. Regulatory fragmentation becomes a strategic resource. The law says one thing at the point of state collection and another at the point of commercial circulation. Public authority learns to route around its own earlier constraints.

The quiet motif of the breadcrumb trail helps keep the argument grounded. Breadcrumbs are small. Each seems trivial, easily overlooked. But a long enough trail reveals routine, destination, companionship, and return. Digital advertising and consumer analytics have created breadcrumb trails at industrial scale. The political novelty lies in how readily those trails can migrate from persuasion markets to surveillance uses. A society may think it has accepted personalised advertising, convenience, and app-driven commerce. It may discover later that it has also normalised the upstream production of tracking material useful to the state.

The deeper problem is not only legal but conceptual. Commercial brokerage encourages governments to think of information as available if it is marketable, and therefore as less constitutionally charged than if it had to be compelled. That is a category mistake. A person's movements do not become less revealing because they were first sold to advertisers. A behavioural model does not become less politically significant because a vendor rather than an intelligence service assembled it. The route by which data arrives affects oversight. It does not erase the power of the data once used.

A serious diagnostic must therefore ask the same questions of brokered access that earlier generations asked of direct surveillance powers. What exactly is being obtained? By whom? Under what authority? For which purposes? With what audit trail? Can the subject challenge misuse or error? Does the institution rely on the data merely as a lead, or as a basis for coercive action? Who reviews the transition from commercial signal to official intervention? These questions need not condemn every state use of commercial data. They simply restore political seriousness to a domain that markets have made deceptively ordinary.

The unresolved tension is plain. If governments can buy, license, or partner into forms of insight that once would have required stronger legal process, then what becomes of the old bargain between surveillance power and public oversight? The answer cannot be found only in privacy policies or procurement files. It lies in whether democratic institutions are willing to treat market access to behavioural data as a matter of state power rather than mere commerce, and whether they can still close the side door once the breadcrumb trail has become too operationally useful to ignore.

Oversight, minimisation, and credibility

In December 2019, the Inspector General of the United States Department of Justice released a report on the Federal Bureau of Investigation's applications under the Foreign Intelligence Surveillance Act in the investigation of Carter Page. The subject was politically charged, but the deeper significance lay in something less partisan and more durable. The report did not prove that surveillance oversight was meaningless. It showed that even within a system built around warrants, judicial authorisation, and internal review, errors and omissions could accumulate at the point where secrecy, urgency, and institutional confidence met. The file had been signed. That was not enough.

This is the central problem of surveillance oversight in constitutional states. Public institutions need secrecy to protect sources, methods, investigations, and allied relationships. Without some secrecy, certain threats cannot be tracked at all. Yet secrecy is not self-limiting. It shields necessary operations and, unless disciplined, it also shields error, drift, bureaucratic self-excuse, and the slow expansion of power through routines that outsiders cannot easily see. The challenge is therefore not to choose between secrecy and accountability as though one must destroy the other. It is to build forms of accountability that function under conditions of secrecy, and that remain credible when mistakes inevitably occur.

Credibility matters because surveillance depends on more than legal authority and technical capability. It depends on whether the public, the courts, the legislature, and even frontline officials believe that intrusive powers are being used within intelligible bounds. That belief is not sentimental. It is operational. A security service that loses credibility may still possess broad powers, but its claims are less trusted, its errors cost more politically, and its room to manoeuvre during crises narrows. A state that cannot persuade its own citizens that covert powers are governed will eventually find that every disclosure, however partial or distorted, lands in a climate of presumption against it. Legitimacy is not a moral garnish applied after the hard work of security. It is part of security's working capital.

Warrants are the most visible instrument in this architecture, partly because they fit an older legal imagination of surveillance. A warrant represents specificity. It requires an institution to define what is sought, against whom, on what basis, for what duration, and under what conditions. The visible behaviour matters. Someone signs. Someone records the legal threshold. Someone takes responsibility for asking. This is more than ritual. It slows power just enough to force articulation. A state that must explain itself before intruding is a state forced to distinguish suspicion from curiosity, operational necessity from convenience. The implication is not that warrants solve everything. It is that they preserve a grammar of justification without which covert power easily becomes administratively casual.

Yet warrants only protect legitimacy if the surrounding institutions are capable of making them real. A judge or commissioner must receive enough context to assess necessity and proportionality. The applying agency must present evidence candidly rather than selectively. Internal review must be strong enough to catch sloppiness before it hardens into formal authorisation. Renewal procedures must not become automatic. None of this can be assumed. A warranting system can look stringent from outside while functioning weakly in practice if judges are overloaded, challenge is one-sided, and agencies learn how to package applications in ways that satisfy formal thresholds without exposing their own uncertainty. The signed page matters. So does the culture around it.

Minimisation is the quieter and, in some respects, harder task. It asks what institutions do after collection has been authorised or when incidental collection is unavoidable. Which records are retained? Which are masked, segregated, or deleted? Under what conditions can identifiers be unmasked? Who may search across retained material? When does a dataset acquired for one purpose become off-limits for another? The concept is restraint in use. That restraint is crucial because modern surveillance often produces more information than the initiating rationale strictly requires. Communications with uninvolved people are swept in. Metadata about broad populations accumulate. Commercially obtained datasets contain more than any one inquiry needs. Without minimisation, the logic of "just in case" steadily defeats the logic of "only as necessary".

The intelligence agencies of the United States, the United Kingdom, and other democracies have all developed forms of minimisation, masking, retention schedules, and internal querying rules for precisely this reason. The details vary. The principle does not. Surveillance powers become more politically survivable when institutions can show that collection does not automatically mean unrestricted use. But minimisation only deserves trust if it is visible in conduct. Are analysts trained to treat unnecessary access as a breach rather than a convenience? Are search logs reviewed? Are retention deadlines enforced? Are breaches reported upward rather than buried? Does an oversight body inspect the actual practice rather than the policy manual? A minimisation regime that exists only in legal text is a credibility trap.

Auditing is what turns these ideals into something sturdier than organisational self-description. Audit trails, access logs, compliance reviews, independent inspectors, legislative committees, judicial commissioners, and external watchdogs all serve one basic function: they create records of power's use that can be tested after the fact. In a field where operations often cannot be publicly disclosed in real time, this after-the-fact intelligibility is indispensable. A competent audit system does not guarantee virtue. It makes impunity harder. It also changes behaviour before problems arise, because officials who know their queries, accesses, and decisions may later be examined tend to act differently from those who assume their conduct will remain permanently opaque.

A useful example lies in the post-Snowden reforms and reporting mechanisms introduced in several jurisdictions, including the United States and the United Kingdom. These changes varied in ambition and effect, but the broader lesson was plain. Public reporting about use of powers, inspector general reviews, judicial opinions made public in part, and stronger commissioner roles did not destroy operational capability. They altered the terms on which that capability had to be defended. The point is not that transparency solved the legitimacy problem. It did not. The point is that institutions learned, under pressure, that secrecy without structured visibility was becoming politically unsustainable. Audit, in that setting, was not an obstacle to power. It was part of power's stabilisation.

Remedies matter for the same reason. Oversight without consequence breeds cynicism. If a person is wrongly targeted, unlawfully retained in a database, denied boarding because of a tainted watchlist, or subjected to persistent scrutiny on the basis of bad data, the existence of rules and audit structures means little unless there is some route to correction. Remedies need not always be public or theatrical. Some must remain constrained by secrecy. But institutions that cannot correct their own mistakes in ways that affect outcomes do not merely fail the individuals concerned. They weaken the credibility of the whole surveillance system. A state that can intrude but cannot credibly repair is asking to be distrusted.

This is where secrecy becomes corrosive in a distinctive way. Secrecy is often defended as a shield for legitimate operations, and often rightly so. But when errors occur inside secret systems, the ordinary mechanisms by which institutions reassure the public - open explanation, adversarial challenge, visible correction - are weakened. The agency knows more than the public. The public knows only that mistakes happen somewhere behind a wall. Suspicion then expands to fill the gap. A regime that might have survived individual errors under conditions of ordinary visibility begins to look systematically unaccountable because its corrections, if they occur, remain largely invisible too. Secrecy can therefore convert manageable error into a crisis of belief.

A second named example makes this dynamic clearer. The United Kingdom's Investigatory Powers Tribunal has, on occasion, found intelligence-related conduct unlawful, including in cases touching data retention and sharing practices. These rulings have not destroyed the British intelligence system. They have served a different function. They have shown that secret surveillance powers can still be subjected to legal judgment and that at least some red lines can be enforced retrospectively. The significance lies not in any single decision, but in the existence of a forum where secrecy does not abolish review altogether. A tribunal, commissioner, or inspector general may seem a thin answer to pervasive technical capability. Often it is thinner than we would wish. Yet without such institutions the state's claim to disciplined covert power becomes far less believable.

A credible limitation should be admitted. Oversight is not a mechanical cure. Too much process can become formalism. Excessive reporting can overwhelm rather than clarify. Judicial authorisation can degenerate into routine if applications are rarely contested and judges become overfamiliar with agency logics. Auditing can turn into box-ticking. Remedies can remain too slow or too narrow to matter. Some critics therefore conclude that oversight mainly launders practices the state had already decided to keep. The criticism is not frivolous. Oversight institutions can indeed be co-opted, under-resourced, or deferential.

But that limitation does not rescue the alternative, which is power governed largely by internal assurances. The relevant question is not whether oversight is perfect. It is whether the system contains enough independent friction to make abuse, drift, and concealment materially harder. A weak oversight regime may disappoint. No oversight worth the name is worse. The task, then, is not to romanticise commissioners, courts, or inspectors general. It is to ask what they can actually see, what they can compel, whether they can publish enough to stabilise public confidence, and whether institutions change behaviour after adverse findings. Oversight is not measured by its statutory elegance. It is measured by whether agencies alter conduct when watched.

The most serious systems therefore combine several forms of restraint. Warrants or comparable authorisations slow initial intrusion. Minimisation narrows use after collection. Audit records activity in ways that make later review possible. Independent bodies inspect, question, and sometimes publicly criticise. Remedies create at least the possibility of correction. These elements are not interchangeable. A state strong on authorisation and weak on remedy, or strong on internal compliance and weak on independent review, may still generate political fragility. Legitimacy emerges not from one heroic safeguard but from a pattern of credible constraint.

This has direct strategic consequences. Surveillance institutions operate in environments shaped by leaks, disinformation, political polarisation, and deep public scepticism about concentrated power. In such an environment, credibility is a scarce resource. Agencies with stronger reputations for self-restraint and lawful process are better placed to defend necessary secrecy, obtain renewed authority, and preserve cooperation from firms, courts, allies, and citizens. Agencies that appear dismissive of oversight may gain short-term freedom and lose long-term room for action. The effect is cumulative. A scandal handled well can narrow damage. A scandal met with evasion can poison future operations far beyond the immediate case.

The quiet motif of the file returns here for good reason. Surveillance files are not only repositories of intelligence. They are also records of justification, access, review, retention, and sometimes of institutional failure. A file that can be audited, corrected, and bounded tells one story about the state. A file that cannot be meaningfully challenged tells another. The distinction matters because public trust often rests less on whether citizens believe the state never errs than on whether they believe the state can admit, trace, and repair error without being dragged to that point by catastrophe.

The harder question, then, is not whether legitimacy should constrain surveillance. It already does, whether institutions like it or not. The harder question is whether states are willing to treat legitimacy as a strategic asset substantial enough to justify slower procedures, stronger minimisation, more intrusive audit, and remedies that genuinely bite. Those choices can feel costly in the short term. The alternative is costlier in a different register: a surveillance order that remains technically potent while growing politically unbelievable, until every secret file looks less like protection than proof that the system never learned how to stop itself.

Chilling effects and democratic resilience

In June 2013, after the first disclosures based on documents leaked by Edward Snowden, civil liberties groups, journalists, lawyers, and ordinary users began to describe a change that did not look like a police raid or a courtroom order. It looked quieter than that. People hesitated before searching certain terms, contacting certain sources, or joining certain discussions online. The legal framework had not visibly altered in every case. The architecture of expectation had. A citizen did not need to know precisely what was being monitored to start acting as if the state, or someone close enough to it, might be watching. The pause mattered.

That pause is the political substance of a chilling effect. It is not simply fear, and it is not confined to overt authoritarian settings. A chilling effect occurs when perceived surveillance alters behaviour before any formal sanction is imposed. People self-censor. They avoid meetings, language, associations, donations, or reading habits that feel newly risky under conditions of ambiguous observation. The visible behaviour can be mundane: a source declines a call, a campaign group moves offline, a public servant withholds an internal concern, a young activist attends one fewer meeting, a journalist stores notes differently, a citizen does not search for information about a sensitive issue from their own device. None of these decisions makes headlines. Taken together, they reshape democratic life.

This matters because surveillance debates are too often framed as contests between security and privacy in the abstract. The more serious issue lies elsewhere. Surveillance changes what a population is willing to do voluntarily, and democratic resilience depends heavily on voluntary action. A resilient society is not one in which the state can compel everything. It is one in which people comply with urgent instructions, share truthful information, report wrongdoing, cooperate with institutions during emergencies, and participate in collective life without assuming that every act of visibility may later be turned against them. Chilling effects weaken exactly those habits. They thin the connective tissue that makes democratic states governable under strain.

The mechanism is straightforward. When people believe that data collection is broad, opaque, or weakly bounded, they begin to treat ordinary participation as a form of exposure. The concept here is anticipatory self-restraint. A person no longer asks only whether a given action is lawful or worthwhile. They ask whether it will leave a trace, what that trace might later be made to mean, and whether anyone would help if the meaning were distorted. That final question is crucial. Chilling effects grow fastest where surveillance does not merely exist, but exists in an environment of low remedy and low trust. People tolerate observation more readily when they believe rules are real, mistakes can be corrected, and institutions are not looking for excuses to escalate. When those beliefs weaken, caution spreads.

A named example helps fix the argument in something more concrete. In the aftermath of the Snowden disclosures, researchers and advocacy groups reported evidence of what became widely known as the "Wikipedia effect": readers appeared less likely to visit pages on topics associated with terrorism and national security. The precise measurement and interpretation have been debated, as they should be, but the broader phenomenon fits what many observers already suspected. Public awareness of surveillance capability altered inquiry itself. The visible act was small - choosing not to read. The implication was large. A democracy depends not only on free speech, but on free curiosity. If the act of learning begins to feel like self-registration, the political damage extends well beyond any one programme or law.

This is why chilling effects should be understood as strategic harms rather than only civil-libertarian concerns. A state that wants resilient citizens needs people who will come forward in periods of confusion, contest official decisions when they are wrong, expose corruption, organise lawful dissent, and still cooperate during genuine emergencies. Surveillance that undermines those dispositions can degrade national capacity even when it produces useful intelligence in the short term. The relationship is not sentimental. It is behavioural. A population that distrusts data practices becomes harder to mobilise and harder to reassure. In crisis, delay grows where trust is thin. Compliance becomes grudging or performative. Rumour outruns official instruction.

Public health provides one of the clearest illustrations. During the COVID-19 pandemic, governments asked populations to adopt extraordinary practices quickly: testing, isolation, contact reporting, app use, vaccination appointments, movement changes, and administrative patience under stress. Success depended not only on legal powers, but on whether people believed data given for health purposes would remain within intelligible bounds. In some places, that belief was strong enough to support broad cooperation. In others, suspicion about data sharing, policing, immigration consequences, or long-term retention weakened participation. A contact-tracing system can be technologically elegant and socially brittle at the same time. If citizens suspect that health data, location data, or identity systems will drift into unrelated enforcement uses, they may simply opt out. The immediate consequence is poorer data. The larger one is weakened crisis response.

The same logic applies beyond emergencies. Journalists need sources willing to take risks. Lawyers need clients willing to disclose sensitive facts. Opposition parties need supporters willing to associate publicly. Religious and minority communities need enough assurance to organise without assuming that ordinary practice is being archived for later scrutiny. Democratic resilience lives in these small acts of willingness. A state may never formally ban dissent and still erode it by building a pervasive atmosphere of observed vulnerability. The distinction matters. Repression is not only what the state prohibits. It is also what people quietly stop doing.

Behavioural change under perceived surveillance does not distribute evenly. Those already familiar with state scrutiny - migrants, dissidents, racial or religious minorities, welfare recipients, precarious workers, whistleblowers, and politically marginal groups - often feel the chill earlier and more intensely than well-protected majorities. This creates a dangerous asymmetry. A surveillance system can appear tolerable to those least likely to bear its frictions while progressively narrowing the civic space of those most in need of equal protection. The visible behaviour is often unequal participation: some communities withdraw from formal channels, some avoid reporting harms, some prefer informal networks to public institutions, some stop trusting the state as a neutral guarantor altogether. Resilience then becomes stratified. The state may still claim broad legitimacy while losing it in the places where stress will later concentrate.

A second named example lies in the long controversies around surveillance of Muslim communities in the United States and parts of Europe after 2001. The problem was not only direct investigative scrutiny, though that was real. It was the wider social effect of being treated as a population whose ordinary religious, educational, charitable, and associational life might be read as a field of suspicion. When communities begin to assume that lawful assembly could trigger watchful attention, speech and participation change. The point is not that all counter-terrorism measures were illegitimate. The point is that broad patterns of suspicion can produce durable mistrust even where specific interventions are lawful. A community that regards public authority as a likely misreader of its own ordinary conduct will not easily become an enthusiastic partner in future crises.

A credible limitation should be acknowledged. Chilling effects are difficult to measure with precision. People often change behaviour for several reasons at once, and the line between prudent caution and democratic harm can be blurry. Some forms of surveillance may deter genuinely dangerous conduct without materially burdening wider public life. Some individuals, especially the politically committed, continue to speak and organise despite clear awareness of monitoring. Democracies also ask citizens to tolerate forms of observation that support safety, fraud prevention, and basic administration. It would be simplistic to treat every awareness of surveillance as politically corrosive or every adaptation of behaviour as proof of repression.

But the difficulty of measurement does not make the phenomenon trivial. Many of the most important political goods are hard to quantify cleanly. Trust is one. Institutional credibility is another. A population's willingness to act candidly with the state, or in the presence of the state, is rarely captured by a single metric. It shows itself in patterns of cooperation, complaint, turnout, reporting, compliance, and dissent. When people start telling each other to leave their phones outside, to avoid searchable terms, to use unofficial channels, to decline formal complaint procedures, or not to register for lawful but sensitive activities, democratic resilience is already being taxed. The state may continue to function. It is functioning on thinner social credit.

This is why legitimacy must be placed at the centre of resilience rather than treated as an after-action report. Legitimacy, in this context, means more than legal authorisation. It means that institutions are believed when they say a capability is bounded, when they promise a dataset will not be repurposed, when they explain that oversight is meaningful, and when they claim that mistakes will be corrected rather than hidden. These claims are constantly tested by conduct. If agencies evade scrutiny, if mission creep becomes routine, if commercial data are quietly repurposed, or if scandal reveals that public assurances were artfully incomplete, credibility drains. That loss does not stay inside surveillance policy. It travels outward into every later request for civic trust.

The strategic cost is especially visible during compound crises. A government facing cyber attack, disinformation, public health stress, or civil disorder needs rapid truthful reporting from citizens, firms, and local institutions. It needs people to believe that temporary measures really are temporary. It needs minority communities not to interpret emergency steps as cover for old patterns of discriminatory scrutiny. It needs journalists and watchdogs to remain adversarial without assuming that contact with sources or scrutiny of official narratives will itself trigger disproportionate attention. A state that has normalised expansive, weakly bounded surveillance may find these forms of cooperation harder to secure. People do not suddenly trust in an emergency. They draw on judgments formed beforehand.

This is also why technical arguments about anonymisation, minimisation, or lawful basis, though important, do not settle the political question. Citizens do not experience systems as legal categories. They experience them as repeated interactions with institutions that either merit confidence or do not. A contact-tracing app may be designed with care and still fail politically if introduced by authorities already associated with opacity or mission creep. A lawful protest database may be defended administratively and still deepen fear if people suspect it will later be mined for unrelated purposes. The legal architecture matters. The civic memory around the architecture matters no less. Every past boundary failure lingers inside the next request for trust.

The quiet motif of the pause deserves a return because it captures what is so often missed in formal analysis. A chilling effect is rarely dramatic at first. It is a pause before a search, a hesitation before a meeting, a source who decides against a message, a citizen who does not file a complaint, a volunteer who stays home, a patient who withholds a detail, a community organiser who discourages attendance, a teacher who avoids a topic. No single pause will topple a democracy. A society filled with such pauses becomes measurably less free long before any law announces that freedom has narrowed. Resilience degrades in silence.

States therefore face a hard choice that cannot be evaded with slogans about balance. Surveillance may produce intelligence gains. It may also produce a population more cautious, less candid, and less cooperative than the same state would need in its next emergency. The trade-off is not hypothetical. It is built into the social interpretation of power. A government that extracts too much trust too cheaply through surveillance may later discover that trust is not replenished on command.

The real test comes when public authority asks citizens to do something difficult and urgent without coercion strong enough to make everyone comply. Will people believe the request is bounded by law and directed at a genuine public purpose, or will they hear it through the memory of prior overreach? That question belongs to crisis management, public health, national security, and democratic theory at once. It is also where chilling effects cease to be a secondary concern and become a measure of whether data power has strengthened the state or quietly hollowed out the society on which the state depends.

Boundary failures and scandal cycles

In June 2013, The Guardian began publishing documents disclosed by Edward Snowden in London, exposing a vast architecture of intelligence collection and data sharing that many governments had preferred to describe only in fragments or abstractions. The immediate result was global controversy. Parliamentary hearings followed, lawsuits multiplied, officials defended necessity, and oversight bodies were forced to explain arrangements that had grown in relative darkness. But the most enduring lesson did not concern one leaker or one agency alone. It concerned the pattern by which surveillance systems cross boundaries long before publics are told where those boundaries lie. The line had moved.

That movement is the heart of scandal in surveillance politics. A scandal is not simply the revelation that a state possesses intrusive capabilities. Democratic publics often accept that some covert powers are necessary. A scandal erupts when the revealed use of those powers violates an understood boundary: between security and convenience, between targeted inquiry and broad capture, between lawful authority and technical opportunism, between public purpose and private misuse, between official assurance and the facts that later emerge. Boundary failure is therefore not identical to illegality, though it may include it. It is the moment when an institution's own account of what it is doing no longer matches what its systems, staff, or partners have in fact made possible.

These failures occur in several familiar forms. A breach exposes data gathered for sensitive purposes but protected carelessly. Misuse reveals that personnel accessed, queried, or shared data for reasons detached from public duty. Mission creep shows that a capability built for one function has expanded into adjacent domains without equally visible debate, oversight, or consent. Each form produces a distinct kind of public anger, yet all converge on the same political question: if the institution could not hold its own line in secret, why should anyone trust the next assurance issued in public? The visible behaviour matters. A rogue lookup, an unauthorised disclosure, a silent retention extension, a repurposed dataset, an omitted caveat in an official statement - these are the actual mechanics through which legitimacy drains.

Mission creep deserves special attention because it is so often produced by convenience rather than conspiracy. An agency builds a system to detect fraud and later notices that the same data could help with immigration enforcement. A communications retention rule justified by serious crime quietly becomes useful in lesser cases. A location dataset acquired through commercial means begins to assist routine investigations that once would have required stronger process. A biometric identifier introduced for efficient access to services later becomes attractive for broader policing or profiling. None of these moves requires a dramatic policy declaration. Technical capability and bureaucratic curiosity do much of the work.

The problem is not that institutions set out openly to deceive. It is that systems rewarded expansion while governance remained attached to older, narrower explanations.

A named example makes the pattern concrete. The 2018 Windrush scandal in the United Kingdom was not a classic surveillance scandal in the narrow intelligence sense, yet it remains highly instructive as a case of administrative boundary failure. The Home Office's data-driven immigration enforcement practices, combined with poor records and a hostile compliance culture, subjected lawful long-term residents to wrongful denial of work, housing, healthcare, and security. The scandal did not arise because the state lacked information. It arose because it treated incomplete and ill-fitting information as sufficient basis for coercive action while allowing institutional incentives to favour suspicion over correction. The concept here is administrative overreach through data formalism. The implication is strategic as well as moral. Once publics see that record systems can be used with this degree of rigidity and opacity, trust in adjacent systems weakens too.

The Snowden disclosures offer a second, differently structured example. They did not show only that intelligence agencies possessed powerful collection tools. They revealed a mismatch between public understandings of surveillance and the scale, scope, and indirectness of the actual arrangements in place. Bulk collection, extensive data sharing, and deep platform cooperation had advanced further than many legislators, courts, and citizens grasped. This was boundary failure through accumulated secrecy and analytic expansion. The scandal cycle that followed was equally revealing. There were reviews, reforms, revised authorities, stronger reporting duties, and legal challenges. Some changes were meaningful. Many were partial. The basic capabilities did not disappear. The cycle did what scandal cycles often do: it narrowed the most politically embarrassing edges while leaving much of the deeper architecture intact.

That pattern matters because scandal is rarely a clean moment of reckoning. More often it is a political sequence with a recognisable rhythm. Revelation comes first, usually through leak, litigation, journalism, or catastrophic operational failure. Officials respond by defending necessity, isolating bad actors, and stressing complexity. Investigations follow. Some institutional reforms are announced, often focused on process, reporting, or wording. Public attention then shifts, especially if no fresh outrage immediately renews it. Meanwhile the underlying incentives that produced the failure - incentives to collect more, retain longer, share broadly, classify aggressively, and underinvest in independent review - often remain substantially in place. The result is piecemeal reform: enough change to claim learning, rarely enough to alter the conditions under which the next scandal will grow.

This is not simply because governments are cynical. Scandal management is itself an institutional discipline. Leaders need to restore calm, preserve operational capacity, reassure allies, and protect the morale of agencies that believe - often with some justice - that they are doing difficult work under conditions the public only partly sees. Oversight bodies may be serious and still constrained by secrecy, legal complexity, or resource asymmetry. Legislators may denounce overreach while remaining unwilling to weaken powers they may later want in office. Civil servants may prefer formal compliance adjustments over structural redesign because formal adjustments are legible, defensible, and less disruptive. Scandal cycles therefore persist not only through bad faith but through the deeper alignment of administrative self-protection with political short-termism.

A credible limitation should be admitted. Some scandals do produce important reform. The Church Committee investigations in the United States in the 1970s led to substantial scrutiny of intelligence abuses and contributed to later oversight structures, including the Foreign Intelligence Surveillance Act of 1978. That history matters because it shows that political systems can sometimes translate revelation into more than cosmetic change. Major public inquiries, court rulings, and legislative redesign can alter institutional behaviour when political pressure is sustained, when evidence is clear, and when reform coalitions extend beyond a single moment of outrage. The scandal cycle is not fate.

But the limitation sharpens rather than weakens the central point. Durable reform tends to happen only when incentives change along with procedures. New warrant forms, revised guidance, and public apologies matter less than whether institutions are rewarded differently afterwards. Does a service gain status from restraint as well as reach? Do procurement and design choices privilege minimisation rather than maximal retention? Are audit failures career-limiting rather than reputationally survivable? Do independent reviewers receive timely access to operational detail rather than sanitised summaries? Are legal bases narrow enough to prevent routine repurposing, and are exceptions drafted tightly enough that urgency does not become a permanent solvent of boundaries? Without changes of this kind, scandal produces adaptation, not transformation.

Breaches illustrate the same logic from another angle. When a database is exposed, a partner system compromised, or internal access abused, public focus often lands on the immediate security failure. That focus is justified, but it can be too narrow. A breach is politically explosive not only because secrets escape. It also reveals what was being held, how loosely access had been governed, and whether the institution knew enough about its own systems to explain the damage honestly. A breach can therefore trigger scandal even where the original collection was lawful and publicly defended. The issue becomes not "should the state have had this power?" but "if it was going to exercise this power, how could it have failed so carelessly at the point of stewardship?" Competence and legitimacy fuse here. A state that cannot protect what it collects invites demands that it collect less.

Misuse by insiders is especially corrosive because it punctures the official narrative that only rules and warrants matter. Many systems depend heavily on human discretion: analysts choose queries, police officers run checks, administrators handle accounts, contractors maintain platforms, supervisors decide when an anomaly is serious. When insiders use access for curiosity, harassment, political interest, or personal advantage, the scandal touches something deeper than one individual's misconduct. It suggests that the system's social defences were weak - that logging was not reviewed, culture did not discourage opportunistic access, and leadership had not treated stewardship as part of operational seriousness. The visible acts may be small. Their symbolic effect is enormous. Citizens who hear that an official queried a neighbour, a former partner, a journalist, or a celebrity are invited to imagine what else happens without notice.

This is why public trust is so vulnerable to cumulative scandal. One incident may be survivable if institutions respond candidly, correct harm, and redesign the system in visible ways. Repeated incidents have a different effect. They teach the public to hear official reassurance as pre-scandal language rather than as a credible account. A government then loses one of its most important assets: the ability to stabilise expectations before fear hardens. Once that ability weakens, even well-designed systems may face distrust because they inherit the memory of earlier failures. Boundary failure thus travels across time. The next data initiative arrives already burdened by the last scandal.

The role of secrecy in these cycles is particularly fraught. Some secrecy is necessary to protect current operations and human sources. Yet secrecy also permits institutions to define the pace and shape of revelation, often releasing enough to manage public relations without fully clarifying what happened or why. This produces a familiar asymmetry. The public is asked to trust that mistakes are isolated and reforms meaningful, while lacking the information needed to judge either claim. Oversight bodies may know more, but they are often constrained in what they can say. The result is a credibility gap that scandal can widen dramatically. Each partial disclosure invites suspicion that the undisclosed remainder is worse. Sometimes that suspicion will be unfair. Politically, it is still potent.

The quiet motif of the line is useful here because scandal is nearly always about a line that was thought to exist and was later discovered to be poorly drawn, badly monitored, or already crossed. The line may separate intelligence from policing, advertising from surveillance, security retention from administrative convenience, targeted access from broad pattern analysis, or emergency powers from ordinary governance. Institutions rarely fail because no line existed at all. They fail because they treated the line as self-enforcing. It never is. If organisational incentives favour wider access, more data, and fewer delays, the line will drift unless something pushes back with equal seriousness.

Designing constraints alongside capability therefore becomes a matter of strategy rather than virtue signalling. Constraints are not what come after power. They help determine what kind of power survives public scrutiny without needing constant emergency repair. A system built with clear purpose limitations, narrow access rules, robust logging, workable remedies, independent review, and deletion defaults is not merely more ethical. It is more resilient politically. When the inevitable error or misuse occurs, such a system gives institutions better tools to explain, contain, and correct. The scandal may still be painful. It is less likely to become existential.

That is the deeper reason piecemeal reform so often disappoints. It fixes what was most visibly embarrassing rather than what was structurally generative. One access pathway is tightened while the incentives for broad retention remain. One programme is renamed while adjacent datasets remain linkable. One internal approval step is added while independent audit remains underpowered. One contractor is dismissed while the architecture that enabled excessive sharing is left intact. The public sees motion. The system experiences continuity. Trust recovers only partially, then degrades again when the next boundary failure reveals how little changed beneath the surface.

The hard question is therefore not whether scandals are useful. They often are, because without revelation many boundary failures would remain politically invisible. The harder question is what a political system learns from them. Does it respond by narrowing the most indefensible practices while leaving the expansionary logic untouched? Or does it redesign incentives so that the next official considering one more retention rule, one more data-sharing agreement, one more commercial feed, one more quiet repurposing must confront friction equal to the convenience of saying yes? The answer will determine whether scandal remains a periodic embarrassment or becomes the only real oversight architecture the system still has.

Chapter 7

Cyber Operations and Data Integrity

What harms a state more: the theft of its data, the temporary loss of a service, or a silent alteration that leaves the service running while decisions built on it turn false? The question unsettles because popular discussion still treats cyber conflict mainly as a drama of breach and outage. Stolen files feel tangible. Dead screens feel dramatic. Manipulated data often feels abstract until the wrong train is routed, the wrong shipment is cleared, the wrong patient record is trusted, or the wrong official assessment hardens into policy. The system still answers. That is the danger.

This is why cyber operations cannot be understood only through the language of confidentiality. Theft matters. Service denial matters. But integrity may matter more, because integrity sits closest to judgment. A government can survive the loss of secrecy more readily than the corruption of the information on which it must act. If decision-makers no longer know whether telemetry is genuine, whether logs were altered, whether a database entry is authentic, or whether a warning reflects reality rather than manipulation, the state loses something deeper than information. It loses confidence in its own instruments. The screen no longer clarifies. It begins to deceive.

That tension gives the chapter its centre. Cyber operations are often discussed as technical contests over access, intrusion, and recovery. They are also contests over credibility. A confidentiality breach can embarrass, expose, and coerce. A denial-of-service attack can interrupt and intimidate. An integrity attack strikes at the state's ability to distinguish signal from fabrication while preserving enough normal appearance to delay recognition. The more digital systems are woven into transport, energy, health, payments, logistics, and administration, the more this distinction matters. A state may continue functioning visibly while the quality of its own decisions has already begun to erode.

The stakes reach well beyond specialist agencies. Critical infrastructure now depends on streams of data that operators trust because they must. Sensors, control systems, dashboards, alerts, scheduling platforms, dispatch tools, and operational records all compress reality into machine-readable form. This compression is indispensable. It is also a strategic vulnerability. A false reading can be safer for an attacker than a broken machine, because it invites the target to make the mistake itself. A service interruption announces hostility immediately. A manipulated data stream can travel further before anyone agrees that an attack has occurred. The distinction between accident, malfunction, and adversarial action then becomes politically consequential.

This is why incident response belongs at the heart of state capacity rather than at its edge. The question is not only whether a state can prevent every intrusion. It cannot. The harder test is whether it can detect compromise, establish facts, coordinate institutions, communicate honestly, preserve evidence, restore service, and reassure the public without compounding the damage through confusion or denial. States often discover that fragmented authority is as dangerous as the initial technical event. Agencies dispute competence. Firms delay disclosure. Operators protect reputation. Ministers demand certainty too early. The result is slower recovery and deeper mistrust. A cyber incident is never only a technical episode. It is also a test of administrative coherence.

Attribution sharpens these difficulties because it forces governments to act in public under conditions of incomplete visibility. To attribute is not merely to identify a likely culprit. It is to decide when evidence is good enough for accusation, retaliation, sanction, warning, or restraint. That decision has strategic costs either way. Speak too quickly and a state risks error or exposure of sensitive methods. Wait too long and it appears hesitant, divided, or unable to protect what matters. Attribution therefore sits between intelligence and politics. It is judged not only by what happened, but by how a government explains what it believes happened and what it intends to do about it.

The path ahead follows that chain of difficulty. It begins by separating theft, disruption, and manipulation so that cyber harm can be seen in terms more precise than spectacle, then moves into the infrastructures where data and physical consequence meet most dangerously. From there it turns to response itself, where coordination, forensics, reporting, and public communication become part of deterrence rather than a postscript to it, before arriving at attribution and signalling, where states must make strategic meaning out of evidence they can never fully disclose. The through-line is simple enough to state and hard enough to practice: a digital state depends not only on keeping systems running, but on knowing whether the information inside them can still be believed.

A useful image for the chapter is the gauge. A gauge looks like a small, obedient thing. Operators glance at it and act. Citizens never see it, but their safety may depend on it. If the gauge breaks, the fault is visible. If the gauge lies, the whole system becomes harder to govern because action continues under false assurance. Cyber operations increasingly target states in that second register. They do not only knock doors down. They alter the dials and let institutions walk themselves into error. The real damage begins when trust in the gauge has not yet collapsed but no longer deserves to hold.

That is why integrity should be treated as a national security concern in its own right, not as a technical subset of cybersecurity jargon. A state that cannot trust its records, telemetry, controls, and communications cannot govern confidently even if its networks remain online. The harder question, then, is not simply how to prevent breaches, but how to recognise when a system is still available, still responsive, and already dangerous. Once that question is taken seriously, the familiar categories of cyber debate begin to look thinner than they first appeared.

Data theft, manipulation, and disruption

On 27 June 2017, screens across ministries, banks, logistics firms, and infrastructure operators began to fail as NotPetya spread outward from Ukraine. In Kyiv, government agencies and companies confronted locked machines, paralysed networks, and corrupted systems that did not yield to ordinary recovery. The incident was first described in much public commentary as ransomware, because ransom notes appeared and disruption was immediate. That description captured the surface and missed the deeper point. The damage did not lie chiefly in secrecy lost or even in temporary downtime. It lay in destroyed records, crippled operations, and the collapse of confidence in what systems could still be trusted to say. The screen was still there.

That is the right place to begin because cyber conflict is too often narrated through the simplest and most dramatic image: the stolen file. Theft is tangible. It produces a visible victim and a recognisable harm. Confidential information leaves the building, and the injured institution can point to what was taken. Yet states, firms, and critical services can sometimes absorb theft better than they can absorb corruption. A stolen archive may expose secrets, embarrass leaders, compromise sources, or enable blackmail. A manipulated dataset can do something more insidious. It can cause decision-makers to act on false premises while still believing the system before them remains serviceable. The gauge has not gone dark. It has started to lie.

This distinction matters because cyber harm takes at least three analytically different forms. The first is confidentiality breach: data are accessed, copied, or exfiltrated without authorisation. The second is disruption or denial: services become unavailable, degraded, or unusable. The third is integrity attack: data, logs, telemetry, or operational settings are altered so that records and system outputs no longer correspond reliably to reality. These forms can overlap, and often do. A campaign may steal first, corrupt later, and deny service at the end. But they are not interchangeable. Each strikes a different element of state capacity. Theft targets secrecy. Disruption targets availability. Manipulation targets judgment itself.

Confidentiality breaches are the most familiar because their consequences have long been understood in intelligence, defence, and corporate governance. The 2015 breach of the United States Office of Personnel Management made this painfully clear. Sensitive background investigation files, fingerprints, and personal histories linked to federal employees and contractors were compromised in Washington. The strategic damage did not consist only in embarrassment or administrative expense. The stolen files could be mined for patterns of vulnerability, relationships, and access. The concept is exposure. Confidentiality loss enlarges an adversary's field of knowledge. It helps them identify targets, pressure points, and future opportunities. The implication is serious and durable. A state that cannot protect sensitive repositories gives an adversary a quieter route to long-term advantage.

And yet confidentiality, for all its importance, does not always produce immediate breakdown. A government can continue operating after secrets are stolen, often for some time, if it can rotate credentials, protect affected personnel, alter procedures, and contain downstream effects. The damage is real, but it is often strategically mediated. Disruption is different. Denial-of-service attacks, ransomware, destructive malware, and network outages can stop action at once. Ports cannot clear shipments. Hospitals postpone procedures. Courts lose access to records. Transport networks fall back to manual operation or stall altogether. The harm is visible because the service fails publicly. That visibility can itself be a weapon. A disrupted state looks weak, and weakness seen by citizens, markets, and rivals carries political force beyond the immediate technical incident.

The 2017 WannaCry attack illustrated this logic in the United Kingdom's National Health Service. Hospitals and clinics faced cancelled appointments, disrupted systems, and hurried workarounds. The issue was not only the temporary inaccessibility of data. It was the interruption of care and the public recognition that a health system had become dependent on digital infrastructures it could not always defend or restore quickly. The concept here is operational stoppage. Disruption damages by preventing institutions from doing what they are expected to do in public view. It can therefore erode trust swiftly, especially when the state appears unprepared or unclear about what failed.

Manipulation, however, reaches deeper still because it strikes at the relation between information and action. An integrity attack does not need to make a system unavailable. It can leave dashboards active, records accessible, and workflows seemingly normal while changing the content on which people rely. Telemetry may be falsified. Logs may be altered to conceal unauthorised actions. A sanctions list may be modified. A patient record may be changed. A maintenance report may be edited. A payment instruction may be rerouted. A procurement database may be quietly polluted. The concept is corrupted reliance. Institutions continue to act, but the informational ground beneath their action has shifted without their knowledge.

This is why integrity deserves to be treated as a national security concern rather than merely as a technical property of good data hygiene. States govern through records. They move troops, funds, patients, cargo, electricity, welfare payments, and legal judgments through systems whose outputs are taken as reliable enough to support action. If those outputs are manipulated, the state may become an instrument of its own compromise. Theft gives the adversary a copy. Disruption forces the state to stop. Manipulation invites the state to proceed, wrongly, by its own hand. Strategically, that can be more damaging because it attacks confidence and interpretation together. Once institutions begin to doubt whether their systems tell the truth, recovery becomes not simply a matter of restarting services, but of reconstructing reality.

The practical difference shows up in decision tempo. After a theft, an institution may ask what was taken and who must be protected. After a disruption, it asks what can be restored and how quickly. After a manipulation, it must ask whether any current output can be trusted at all. That question is paralysing because it extends beyond the originally affected system. If logs may have been altered, can investigators trust their timeline? If telemetry may be false, can operators trust alarms, gauges, and readings? If a database entry may have been changed, can downstream systems using that data still operate safely? Integrity attacks force institutions into an epistemic crisis. They do not merely damage assets. They damage assurance.

A second named example makes the point through industrial control rather than administrative databases. The Stuxnet operation, publicly analysed after 2010 in relation to Iranian nuclear facilities at Natanz, demonstrated how cyber effects could combine manipulation and physical consequence. The episode is often remembered for its sophistication, but its lasting significance lies in the logic of deception. Systems were not simply shut down in obvious fashion. Normality was partly simulated while sabotage unfolded. This is not a model to be copied, and its specifics remain a matter of continuing study, but its strategic meaning is clear enough. Integrity attacks can be powerful because they make operators misread their own environment. The visible system and the actual system diverge.

Critical infrastructure makes this especially dangerous. Power grids, transport systems, water networks, hospitals, and industrial sites rely on streams of data that operators must read quickly. False telemetry can mislead maintenance decisions. Altered sensor data can conceal overheating, pressure changes, contamination, or abnormal network states. Manipulated scheduling data can misroute goods or staff. Corrupted records in health systems can affect treatment choices. In such environments, availability is not the only issue. A system that goes offline may at least announce its own failure. A system that remains online while telling operational lies can stretch damage across time before detection. The strategic advantage belongs to the attacker who turns the target's own trust into a vulnerability.

This does not mean that disruption is somehow secondary. Sometimes denial is exactly the point. Ransomware, destructive wipers, and service outages can impose immediate economic costs, degrade morale, and send a clear signal of reach. They also shape political narratives. A stolen intelligence file may trouble specialists. A nationally visible service outage becomes an event ordinary citizens feel directly. That public salience matters. States often fear disruption more because disruption is legible. It produces images, queues, delays, missed care, halted travel, frustrated users, and ministerial embarrassment. These are real strategic effects. But legibility should not blind analysts to the possibility that the less visible integrity attack may be the more profound one.

A credible limitation should be admitted. In practice, the boundaries between theft, disruption, and manipulation are not clean. Exfiltration tools can also modify systems. Ransomware may destroy logs, reducing both availability and integrity. Defensive recovery after a disruptive event often depends on preserving trustworthy backups, making integrity central even where denial was the first symptom. Some institutions may also rationally prioritise confidentiality because exposure of sources, military plans, or diplomatic secrets could have catastrophic consequences even without further interference. The point is not to construct a rigid hierarchy of harms applicable in every case. It is to keep analytical categories clear enough that strategic priorities are not dictated only by what is most visible.

That limitation strengthens the argument because it shifts attention from spectacle to function. A state should ask not merely whether a cyber incident stole, stopped, or touched data, but what element of governance it impaired. Did it widen an adversary's knowledge? Did it interrupt essential services? Did it cause the state to misperceive and misjudge? Different answers imply different national-security implications. Too much public and even official language still collapses cyber harm into breach or outage, as if the decisive question were whether systems were entered or halted. The more demanding question is whether the incident damaged the state's capacity to know what was true and to act accordingly.

This is also why integrity must be built into resilience planning rather than treated as a specialist concern for database administrators and forensic teams. Backup strategies matter, but so do provenance, logging, change control, segregation of duties, validation routines, and tested methods for distinguishing trusted from untrusted states after an incident. An institution that can restore services but cannot verify what has been restored may regain speed without regaining safety. The issue is not only technical correctness. It is organisational confidence. Frontline staff, ministers, regulators, and citizens need to know when the state believes its own data again, and why.

The quiet motif of the gauge helps keep the distinction in view. A stolen manual is serious. A smashed gauge is obvious. A gauge that continues to function while reporting false readings is something else. It recruits the operator into the failure. Cyber operations increasingly aim at precisely that effect because modern states depend so heavily on mediated representations of reality. Dashboards, alerts, databases, and control systems are trusted not because officials are naive, but because action at scale demands trust in instruments. National security in such a setting depends as much on the integrity of those instruments as on the secrecy of the information they contain.

The political implications follow directly. A state that cannot protect confidentiality may suffer exposure. A state that cannot preserve availability may suffer interruption. A state that cannot defend integrity may suffer strategic self-deception. Of the three, the last is often hardest to explain to the public and hardest to recover from institutionally, because the damage lies partly in confidence itself. How does a government persuade citizens, markets, and allies that a compromised system is trustworthy again? How does it reassure operators that the readings now reflect reality rather than residue of an attack? How does it make decisions under uncertainty about whether the very records guiding response have been altered? These are not just technical recovery questions. They are questions about state credibility.

That is why integrity cannot remain the neglected term in cyber debate. The hardest incidents are not always the loudest. They may be the ones that leave the service standing while confidence in its outputs quietly collapses. Once that possibility is taken seriously, the standard map of cyber harm begins to look incomplete. The next question is not only which systems might be breached or stopped, but which systems a state cannot afford to mistrust for even a short period without beginning to govern against its own interests.

Critical infrastructure data and operational technology

In December 2015, parts of Ukraine's power grid were disrupted in an incident that quickly became a reference point for discussions of cyber operations against critical infrastructure. The event was not important only because the electricity supply was interrupted. It mattered because it showed that digital compromise could travel through the operational layers of a public utility into the routines by which humans monitor, trust, and act. Operators do not govern a grid by touching every wire. They govern through screens, signals, alarms, and commands. The reading mattered.

That is the essential fact about critical infrastructure in the digital state. Energy systems, transport networks, hospitals, water utilities, ports, and industrial facilities increasingly depend on data streams that compress physical reality into forms operators can manage. Sensors report pressure, temperature, voltage, speed, occupancy, dosage, route status, and device health. Control systems translate that information into dashboards, alerts, and decisions. This makes modern infrastructure more responsive, scalable, and efficient. It also makes it vulnerable in a distinctive way. Attack the machinery and the damage may be visible. Attack the data by which the machinery is interpreted, and the damage may begin before anyone agrees on what is happening.

The term operational technology is often used to distinguish the systems that monitor and control physical processes from the more familiar world of information technology. The distinction is useful if handled carefully. It reminds us that a hospital infusion pump, a railway signalling system, a pipeline control environment, and a power distribution network are not simply office networks with higher stakes. They are socio-technical systems in which digital data and physical consequence meet directly. But the distinction can also mislead if it suggests that operational technology is somehow separate from ordinary data politics. It is not. Operational systems rely on naming, identity, logging, remote access, updates, vendors, cloud services, and supply chains just as administrative systems do. The difference lies in what follows from error. In operational environments, a corrupted record is not merely an archival problem. It may become a safety problem.

Energy systems make this vividly clear. A modern grid is not governed by instinct or line-of-sight. Operators depend on telemetry from substations, switches, generators, and network nodes to judge load, stability, and fault conditions. That telemetry supports routines that are meant to keep electricity flowing and equipment within safe limits. The concept that matters is mediated control. Operators act through representations. The implication is severe. If the representations are false, delayed, incomplete, or selectively altered, the operator may make a harmful decision while believing it to be corrective. In such a setting, cyber risk is not only about whether systems go dark. It is about whether the state's understanding of physical reality remains trustworthy enough to support action.

False telemetry is the clearest illustration. A gauge that fails visibly tells an operator something useful: do not trust this reading. A gauge that continues to display plausible but incorrect information is far more dangerous. In power systems, transport control, and industrial processes alike, plausible falsehood can produce delay, misallocation, or unsafe action. This is why integrity matters so much. Not every critical infrastructure incident involves dramatic sabotage or shutdown. Some of the most consequential risks arise when systems remain online, alarms remain silent, and decision-makers continue to act through data that no longer corresponds to the physical environment. The screen still glows. That is the problem.

Transport systems exhibit the same structure in a different register. Railways, ports, airports, road networks, and logistics hubs all rely on continuous data about position, timing, capacity, maintenance status, and access control. These systems have always involved information, but digitisation has increased speed and interdependence. A port operator now depends on linked schedules, customs records, cargo manifests, and yard management data. A rail network depends on signalling data, scheduling systems, and increasingly automated support for routing and maintenance. A civil aviation environment depends on flight planning systems, navigation data, communication networks, and intricate layers of operational record. The strategic issue is continuity under trust. When data streams are reliable, the network works faster and more efficiently. When they are compromised, the same dependency creates a multiplier for disruption.

The 2017 NotPetya incident demonstrated this multiplier particularly clearly through shipping and logistics. Maersk, among others, faced severe disruption to business systems and operational processes after the malware spread. The strategic lesson was broader than one company. Ports and shipping are not only commercial services; they are arteries of national supply, trade, and sometimes crisis response. The systems affected were not simply bookkeeping tools detached from movement. They were part of the informational infrastructure through which movement was coordinated. This is the concept of logistical dependence. A cargo network can be physically intact and still fail to function at speed if the data environment that orders it has been corrupted or disabled.

Health systems offer perhaps the most politically sensitive version of this problem because the link between data integrity and human consequence is so immediate. Hospitals depend on electronic records, lab systems, imaging archives, scheduling platforms, prescribing databases, and device telemetry. These systems help clinicians act under time pressure. Their value lies partly in speed and partly in trust. A patient record does not need to be spectacularly wrong to be dangerous. A corrupted allergy field, a delayed lab result, an altered medication list, or a misleading device reading can change clinical judgment in ways that are hard to detect in the moment. The point is not to induce melodrama. It is to recognise that in digitally mediated care, informational integrity is inseparable from patient safety.

The WannaCry attack on the National Health Service in 2017 remains instructive for this reason. Public discussion often focused on cancelled appointments, locked systems, and general disruption, all of which were serious. The deeper lesson lay in the way digital fragility translated into operational strain across a health system whose public legitimacy depends on continuity and safety. Hospitals could improvise with paper in some contexts. They could not easily improvise trust in records, scheduling, or communication once the informational environment became unstable. This is why cyber incidents in health systems are politically potent. They expose the state not merely as a data custodian or purchaser of technology, but as guarantor of care under pressure.

Critical infrastructure risk also resists the comforting assumption that operational technology is mostly isolated or static. Many such systems were indeed designed with assumptions of separation, longevity, and specialised access. Over time, however, remote management, vendor support, cloud-connected analytics, enterprise integration, and cost pressures have eroded simple boundaries. Operational environments are linked to corporate networks, external contractors, update services, monitoring tools, and shared administrative platforms more often than public imagination suggests. The line between the plant floor and the office network has thinned. This does not mean every system is recklessly exposed. It means the governance question has become more complex than old images of isolated control rooms allow.

A credible limitation should be acknowledged. Not every critical infrastructure system is equally digitised, equally exposed, or equally dependent on continuous networked data. Many operators maintain manual fallback procedures, segmented environments, and hard-won operational discipline. In some sectors, conservative engineering and layered safety mechanisms still provide significant protection against catastrophic failure. Public discussion can lapse into melodramatic assumptions that every compromise will produce immediate physical disaster. That is not accurate, and it can obscure the actual variation across sectors and systems. Some infrastructures are more resilient than the cyber commentary surrounding them implies.

But the limitation does not alter the core argument. Even where direct catastrophic physical consequences remain unlikely, disruption to data and operational technology can still produce serious harm through degraded continuity, slower decision-making, delayed services, misallocation of resources, and declining public confidence. A railway need not crash for a nation to feel the effects of compromised signalling or scheduling. A hospital need not lose life in visible numbers for trust in digital care systems to weaken. A power grid need not collapse nationally for local outages and operator uncertainty to produce strategic concern. Risk in these domains is cumulative and systemic as often as it is apocalyptic.

This is why cyber resilience in critical infrastructure cannot be reduced to perimeter defence or procurement of security products. The harder task lies in governance of data dependence. Which signals are most safety-critical? Which systems must continue under degraded conditions? Which records can be independently validated if digital integrity is in doubt? Which operators know how to recognise the difference between technical malfunction and adversarial manipulation? Which public authorities can coordinate across private operators, sector regulators, emergency services, and political leadership when the event begins as ambiguous noise? These questions matter because infrastructure crises often start with uncertainty, not certainty. A state that waits for perfect clarity may already be late.

Public communication is part of this resilience, though it is often treated as secondary. When critical infrastructure incidents occur, citizens and markets do not only watch whether systems recover. They watch whether institutions seem to understand what failed, what remains trustworthy, and what they are asking others to do in response. Fragmented, contradictory, or prematurely confident communication deepens mistrust. So does visible reluctance to admit that the state does not yet know whether data can be relied upon. Infrastructural credibility therefore depends partly on epistemic honesty. The public can tolerate uncertainty better than it can tolerate confident error followed by reluctant correction.

The private sector's role complicates all this because much critical infrastructure is privately owned, contracted out, or technologically dependent on vendors whose incentives do not perfectly match public expectations. Operators may hesitate to report incidents quickly for reputational reasons. Vendors may control diagnostic tools or update channels. Cloud and software providers may hold crucial logs. Sector regulators may have incomplete visibility into the actual dependencies linking operational technology to enterprise systems and external services. The result is that state capacity in a crisis often depends on relationships, reporting regimes, and legal authorities shaped long before the incident begins. A government that does not understand those relationships may find that it can demand accountability after the fact more easily than it can secure coordination in the moment.

The quiet motif of the gauge remains useful because operational technology is, in the end, a system of gauges and commands mediating the physical world. The gauge can show pressure, load, movement, dosage, occupancy, route status, or device health. It condenses complexity so that people can act. A state whose infrastructure depends on such gauges is strong only so long as the gauges remain trustworthy enough to support judgment. The danger is not merely that they can break. It is that they can continue to function as interfaces while failing as representations. Once that gap opens, the operator's confidence becomes a target in its own right.

This leads to a more serious understanding of cyber risk in critical infrastructure. The issue is not simply that digital systems might be attacked. It is that the data stream has become part of the infrastructure itself. In energy, transport, and health alike, the record and the machine increasingly govern together. A false record can create a true consequence. A corrupted signal can produce a real stoppage. A misleading reading can generate a harmful human choice. That is why integrity belongs beside availability and confidentiality as a strategic concern. The state cannot treat infrastructure data as mere administrative support once physical continuity and public safety depend on it so directly.

The unresolved question, then, is not whether critical infrastructure should digitise. Much of it already has, and for good reasons. The harder question is how a state decides which data streams must be treated as safety-critical and which institutional arrangements are strong enough to preserve trust in those streams when systems are under pressure. Until that question is answered with more seriousness than slogans about innovation or resilience usually permit, the next incident will not only test machines. It will test whether the state knows which readings it can still believe.

Incident response as state capacity

On 8 July 2022, Rogers Communications suffered a major outage across Canada that disrupted mobile service, internet access, payment systems, emergency calling, and ordinary business activity. The event was not a conventional cyber attack, yet it exposed something cyber strategy often prefers to treat as an afterthought. A society can be brought into visible disorder not only by intrusion, but by the failure of institutions to restore, explain, and coordinate under pressure. The breakdown was technical. The lesson was governmental. A network failed; the state was tested.

That test matters because public discussion still treats cyber power too narrowly. Prevention, patching, deterrence, and threat intelligence dominate the conversation. They matter. But no state can prevent every failure, whether caused by attack, software flaw, operator error, supply-chain weakness, or some mixture of all four. The harder question is what happens after the first alert, the first call, the first contradictory signal, the first public rumour. At that point, cyber security stops being a specialist matter and becomes a problem of state capacity: who coordinates, who reports, who investigates, who communicates, who decides what remains trustworthy, and who can restore service without creating new confusion. The clock starts immediately.

This is why incident response deserves to be treated as part of national capability rather than as the dreary aftermath of someone else's failure. A successful response limits damage, preserves evidence, restores continuity, and protects public confidence. A weak response lengthens disruption, multiplies error, and tells adversaries something useful about the target's governing competence. The concept here is response as power. States deter not only by threatening punishment or building thicker defences, but by demonstrating that attacks and failures will not produce the social and political effects an adversary hoped to create. Recovery speed, institutional clarity, and credible communication all shape that calculation.

Coordination sits at the centre of this problem because cyber incidents rarely respect administrative boundaries. A ministry may own the legal authority, a regulator may hold sector knowledge, a private operator may control the affected system, an intelligence service may have contextual insight, police may handle criminal investigation, and a national computer emergency team may provide technical support. Each actor sees only part of the event at first. The visible danger is fragmentation. One body waits for confirmation. Another waits for permission. A company delays disclosure while lawyers assess exposure. Ministers demand certainty before technical teams can honestly provide it. By the time the picture sharpens, recovery has already been slowed by institutional hesitation.

A named example makes this vivid. During the WannaCry attack in May 2017, the United Kingdom's National Health Service experienced serious disruption across hospitals and services. The technical causes involved unpatched systems and exposed weaknesses. The governance lesson lay in how difficult coordinated response can become inside a sprawling public service with local variation, uneven digital maturity, and multiple lines of operational authority. Hospitals improvised. Central institutions intervened. Public communication struggled to keep pace with what was happening on the ground. The incident showed that response capacity is not just the possession of skilled analysts or national plans. It is the ability to make many institutions act coherently under ambiguity.

Reporting is where coherence often first falters. Organisations hit by cyber incidents frequently face conflicting incentives. They may want help, but also fear reputational damage, regulatory scrutiny, legal liability, customer loss, or political blame. Public bodies are no exception. A department may delay internal escalation because it hopes the problem is local and manageable. A private infrastructure operator may understate severity while checking facts. A regulator may receive incomplete information and therefore hesitate to trigger broader coordination. The result is a familiar pathology: everyone reports too late for the collective system to function well. The concept is delayed legibility. A state cannot coordinate what it cannot see, and it often cannot see because the institutions nearest the problem have reasons to keep the picture partial.

Mandatory reporting rules are often offered as the cure. They help. They also reveal a deeper truth. Reporting obligations matter less as abstract duties than as social signals about what the state values. If the system punishes early disclosure more than silence, institutions learn the wrong lesson. If reporting brings practical technical assistance, legal clarity, and a credible public process, disclosure becomes more likely. The visible behaviour tells the story. Do operators call early, share logs, and preserve evidence? Or do they wait until public failure forces admission? Response capacity depends on shaping those choices before the crisis, not merely condemning them afterwards.

Forensics then becomes the bridge between response and knowledge. A state cannot decide how to restore, whom to notify, or whether to attribute unless someone can reconstruct what happened with reasonable confidence. That work is painstaking. Logs may be incomplete. Systems may already be altered by emergency actions. Vendors may hold critical telemetry. Cloud environments may distribute evidence across several providers. In critical infrastructure, the additional burden is acute: investigators must preserve enough of the record to understand the incident without freezing the very systems people rely upon for safety and continuity. The strategic point is not only technical. Forensics determines whether the state can move from anxiety to explanation without bluffing.

This is one reason fragmented authority deepens mistrust. When different institutions control different pieces of the evidentiary puzzle, the public encounters confusion rather than competence. One agency says there is no indication of compromise. Another speaks of suspicious activity. A minister frames the event as contained. An operator quietly expands the scope of affected services. Each statement may be defensible at the moment it is made. Collectively they create a picture of uncertainty managed through overconfidence. Publics can tolerate uncertainty more easily than they can tolerate being managed by institutions that sound certain before they have earned it. Credibility is built not by pretending to know quickly, but by showing how knowledge is being assembled.

A second named example helps here. The Colonial Pipeline ransomware incident in the United States in May 2021 revealed how cyber events in privately operated infrastructure can become national governance problems with remarkable speed. Fuel supply disruptions, public anxiety, political pressure, and questions about federal and corporate response all converged quickly. The episode was not only about ransomware. It was about whether reporting channels, inter-agency coordination, public messaging, and recovery decisions were strong enough to manage cascading effects beyond the compromised network itself. The incident forced visible choices about when to disclose, how to characterise the threat, and what kind of federal role was appropriate in a private sector crisis with national implications. That is what response as state capacity looks like in practice.

Public communication is often treated as the soft edge of incident response. It is nothing of the sort. Communication determines whether citizens know which services remain safe to use, whether firms understand reporting expectations, whether markets perceive control or drift, and whether adversaries see confusion as part of the damage already achieved. The visible behaviour matters immediately. Does the state give practical guidance without pretending to know more than it does? Does it distinguish clearly between confirmed facts, working hypotheses, and speculation? Does it avoid the opposite errors of false reassurance and theatrical alarm? Poor communication can turn a containable technical incident into a broader crisis of trust. Good communication can narrow panic even while systems remain under repair.

This is where legitimacy and deterrence meet. An adversary contemplating disruption does not ask only whether the target can prevent access. It also asks how much social disorder, political embarrassment, and loss of trust the incident might create. A state known for coherent response, credible communication, and fast restoration offers a less attractive target than one known for bureaucratic confusion and reputational evasiveness. Deterrence is therefore not only about offensive retaliation or denial through hardening. It is also about reputational resilience. If a state can convince rivals that incidents will produce limited strategic return, it has strengthened deterrence by reducing the expected payoff of attack.

A credible limitation should be admitted. Strong incident response cannot neutralise every harm. Some adversaries seek costs that will be felt regardless of competent management. Some technical events unfold too quickly or opaquely for institutions to build certainty before political pressure mounts. In decentralised democracies, fragmented authority is not always a design flaw; it can reflect legitimate constraints, sectoral expertise, and the refusal to centralise power too heavily. A state with many relevant actors may still be healthier than one with a single commanding centre that suppresses bad news. Centralisation alone is not competence.

That limitation sharpens the real argument. The issue is not whether one office should command everything. It is whether a state has built enough prearranged clarity that plural institutions can act together when ambiguity is high. Who leads technical triage? Who owns sector liaison? Who can compel timely disclosure? Who coordinates forensics with law enforcement? Who decides what can be said publicly, and on what evidentiary basis? Which body speaks when the operator is private but the consequences are public? These questions should be answered before the incident, not improvised during it. Where they are left vague, fragmentation becomes a force multiplier for damage.

Institutional memory matters here more than glossy strategy documents. States often learn the wrong lessons from cyber incidents because political attention rewards visible procurements and legal reforms more than the patient work of rehearsals, cross-sector relationships, joint playbooks, trusted reporting channels, and retention of experienced responders. Response quality depends on people who know whom to call, which logs matter, which ministerial anxieties will distort judgment, which suppliers hold decisive knowledge, and which public phrases calm rather than inflame. Lose that memory through turnover, outsourcing, or bureaucratic churn, and incident response becomes slower even if the formal structures remain intact.

The same is true of relationships with private operators. Much critical infrastructure is owned, run, or maintained outside the state. No doctrine can wish that away. The real question is whether those relationships are governed closely enough that cooperation remains possible when incentives diverge. Companies may want to minimise reputational harm.

Governments may want faster disclosure. Regulators may seek evidence. Security services may want silence around sensitive context. Response fails when these interests collide without any pre-existing means of reconciliation. It succeeds more often when the state's authority, the operator's obligations, and the practical channels for joint action have already been tested in less dramatic times.

The quiet motif of the clock helps keep the whole issue grounded. Incident response is a race against three losses at once: loss of service, loss of evidence, and loss of trust. Restore too slowly and the disruption spreads. Investigate too clumsily and the record is spoiled. Speak too badly and the public concludes that authority itself has become unreliable. The clock begins before the first press conference and keeps running after the last server is restarted. That is why response is not a coda to cyber strategy. It is the moment strategy becomes visible.

The hardest question is therefore not whether a state can write an incident response plan. Most can. It is whether the plan corresponds to the actual distribution of authority, expertise, incentives, and fear that will shape behaviour when a real crisis arrives. Can the state make fragmented institutions act as if they belong to one response without pretending that uncertainty has vanished? Can it tell the truth quickly enough to deserve belief later? And can it recover in a way that teaches adversaries a lesson about futility rather than teaching citizens a lesson about drift? Those answers determine whether incident response remains a technical chore or becomes what it truly is: a measure of how governable the state remains under pressure.

Attribution, signalling, and escalation control

On 15 February 2018, the governments of the United Kingdom and the United States publicly attributed the NotPetya attack to the Russian military. The statements arrived months after the malware had spread from Ukraine into firms, ministries, logistics systems, and public services far beyond the original point of compromise. By then, the technical damage was well known. What remained politically unsettled was the question of authorship and meaning. Public attribution did not repair corrupted systems or restore lost data. It did something else. It assigned responsibility in a domain where responsibility is often contested, delayed, and strategically rationed. The name mattered.

That moment helps explain why attribution in cyber conflict is never merely a forensic exercise. It is a political act built on technical evidence, intelligence judgment, diplomatic timing, and calculations about what should be revealed, withheld, or made deliberately ambiguous. The common complaint that cyber attribution is impossible is too crude to be useful. States often possess enough information to reach highly confident internal judgments about likely perpetrators. The harder problem is whether they can turn those judgments into public claims without exposing sources and methods, compromising allied access, overstating certainty, or triggering a response cycle they do not fully control. Attribution, then, is not simply about finding out who did it. It is about deciding what to say, when to say it, and what strategic burden the statement is meant to carry.

This makes attribution unusually contested. Technical investigators may examine malware families, infrastructure reuse, coding patterns, operational timing, victim selection, and overlaps with known campaigns. Intelligence agencies may add human sources, intercepted communications, partner reporting, and classified context. Diplomats and political leaders then confront a different question: what level of confidence is sufficient for public accusation, sanctions, expulsion, criminal indictment, covert response, or studied silence? The concept here is layered certainty. Different institutions hold different types of evidence, and they are rarely equally shareable. The implication is important. Public statements about cyber attribution are not simple mirrors of technical truth. They are negotiated products of evidentiary asymmetry and strategic purpose.

This is one reason cyber incidents invite scepticism without justifying cynicism. The public often encounters attribution through short official statements that present confidence without disclosing the chain of reasoning that produced it. That can sound unsatisfying, even manipulative. Sometimes it is. But the state may also be protecting access that would be strategically foolish to reveal in detail. A government may know because it can see operational traffic, because a partner shared sensitive reporting, because a human source had access to planning, or because it can correlate technical behaviour with other clandestine indicators unavailable for public use. The visible behaviour is therefore often elliptical: "we assess", "we are confident", "based on all-source intelligence". Such phrasing is not neutral. It signals that the public is being asked to accept a claim without seeing most of the evidence. Democratic trust then depends on the prior credibility of the institution making the claim.

A named example helps clarify how attribution and signalling interlock. In October 2018, the Netherlands publicly described its disruption of a Russian military intelligence operation targeting the Organisation for the

Prohibition of Chemical Weapons in The Hague. The Dutch government paired the account with physical details about the operatives' equipment, travel, and proximity to the target. This was more than a law-enforcement disclosure. It was a signal. By releasing unusually concrete material, the Dutch authorities increased the credibility of attribution while warning that hostile activity had been observed closely enough to expose methods and presence. The concept is demonstrative attribution. The implication reaches beyond one case. States sometimes reveal more than usual not simply to persuade the public, but to shape an adversary's expectations about detection, exposure, and future operational cost.

Signalling, in this sense, is the language through which attribution becomes strategy. A state may attribute privately to an adversary and remain silent publicly. It may attribute publicly but respond modestly. It may coordinate statements with allies to show collective judgment rather than unilateral accusation. It may file indictments against individuals, expel diplomats, impose sanctions, harden defences, conduct counter-operations, or merely warn that malicious activity has been observed and monitored. Each move says something different about confidence, resolve, and appetite for escalation. The visible act matters less than the pattern. A sanction without public detail may signal caution. A joint attribution with several governments may signal coalition strength. A criminal indictment of named officers may signal persistence and record-building rather than immediate punishment.

This is why cyber attribution should not be read only through the question of proof. It also belongs to deterrence and escalation control. States need ways to impose costs, communicate boundaries, and avoid accidental spirals. Public attribution can support deterrence by eroding an adversary's plausible deniability and attaching reputational or economic costs to particular forms of activity. But it can also sharpen confrontation by forcing the accused state to respond, deny, counteraccuse, or retaliate elsewhere. The concept here is calibrated exposure. A government tries to reveal enough to support its strategic purpose without revealing so much that it degrades intelligence access or narrows its own future options. That calibration is difficult, and many public misreadings of cyber politics arise from not seeing how much is being balanced inside a short official statement.

A second named example comes from the public attribution of the 2017 "WannaCry" attack to North Korea by the United States, the United Kingdom, and others. The incident had already caused severe disruption before those statements were made. Public attribution did not reverse the damage. It helped assign meaning to it. It located the event within a broader pattern of hostile state activity and justified subsequent political and diplomatic actions. Yet the case also illustrates the limits of attribution as remedy. A state can publicly name an attacker and still struggle to produce immediate consequences proportionate to the harm. This is one reason some observers dismiss attribution as theatre. The dismissal goes too far. Attribution may not stop a campaign already completed, but it still shapes norms, sanctions, alliance coordination, and the strategic vocabulary available for the next incident.

Still, scepticism is warranted. Attribution statements can serve domestic political needs as well as genuine security ones. Governments may speak with more confidence in public than the evidence fully merits, especially when pressure mounts to appear decisive. They may also choose timing that aligns with diplomatic convenience rather than technical clarity. Some incidents are politically useful as examples of foreign hostility. Others are quietly downplayed because they cut across sensitive negotiations or expose domestic vulnerability. The reader should therefore resist two temptations at once: uncritical faith and reflexive dismissal. A serious interpretation asks what evidence is likely being held back, what policy objective the attribution supports, which allies are joining the claim, what forms of response accompany it, and what the government seems unwilling to say.

This is also why attribution is difficult to separate from alliance politics. Joint statements are often stronger than unilateral ones because they suggest convergence across independent intelligence systems. They can also reflect alliance discipline rather than fully equal evidentiary confidence. A smaller ally may join a statement partly out of trust in a partner's classified assessment, partly out of strategic solidarity, and partly because it wishes to reinforce broader geopolitical alignments. This does not make the attribution false. It does mean the politics of coalition must be read alongside the language of evidence. Public consensus among allies may signify shared proof, shared interests, or both.

Attribution becomes harder still when incidents involve proxies, criminal groups, semi-autonomous contractors, or state tolerance rather than direct command. Cyber operations thrive in this space because responsibility can be distributed across infrastructure providers, front companies, criminal marketplaces, patriotic hackers, and intelligence services whose relationships are deliberately blurred. A government may know that a campaign served another state's interests and benefited from that state's permissive environment without being able to prove direct tasking to public satisfaction. The concept is graduated responsibility. Strategic response then depends not on impossible certainty about every link in the chain, but on judgments about sponsorship, shelter, tolerance, or control sufficient to justify action. This is politically uncomfortable because public discourse often demands a cleaner answer than the intelligence picture can honestly provide.

A credible limitation belongs here. Sometimes states genuinely do not know enough to attribute publicly with confidence, or they know but choose not to speak because intelligence access is more valuable than public accusation. Silence is not always weakness. It may reflect prudence, covert response, or the wish to avoid escalating an incident whose effects can still be managed quietly. Likewise, an absence of dramatic retaliation after public attribution does not necessarily mean the claim was hollow. Costs can be imposed through sanctions, private warnings, cyber countermeasures, intelligence adjustments, and alliance coordination that remain partly or wholly out of sight. Public observers often overvalue visible drama because it is visible.

That limitation, however, does not remove the need for better public literacy about cyber signalling. Official language deserves close reading. Terms like "likely", "highly likely", "confident", and "we assess" are not filler. They are calibrated markers of how much certainty a government is willing to perform publicly. Joint attributions matter differently from solo ones. The gap between technical detail and policy response matters too. A highly detailed attribution followed by minimal response may signal limited escalation appetite. A sparse attribution paired with sanctions or expulsions may indicate stronger political resolve than the underlying public evidence suggests. The reader should also notice whether governments frame incidents as criminal acts, hostile state behaviour, reckless conduct, or violations of international norms. Those categories are part of the signal.

Escalation control is where all this becomes most delicate. States want to show they are not passive victims, but they also want to avoid locking themselves into response ladders that could spill into broader confrontation. Cyber incidents are especially awkward because their effects range from espionage, which states routinely practise against one another, to disruptive or destructive operations that look more like overt coercion. Public attribution helps governments sort incidents into categories legible enough for domestic and international audiences. Yet the act of sorting can itself escalate. Label an incident too weakly and deterrence suffers. Label it too strongly and the state may create expectations for retaliation it cannot or should not meet. The art lies in preserving room to manoeuvre after the statement has been made.

This is why some governments increasingly combine attribution with what might be called bounded disclosure. They release enough technical indicators, contextual evidence, or law-enforcement detail to support credibility while withholding the most sensitive intelligence. They coordinate with allies to widen the base of trust. They choose sanctions, indictments, public advisories, or expulsions in combinations that signal seriousness without forcing immediate kinetic analogy. None of this eliminates ambiguity. It manages it. The point of escalation control is not to make ambiguity vanish. It is to keep ambiguity from being exploited equally by the adversary and by domestic critics who read every incomplete statement as proof of incompetence or deceit.

The quiet motif of the fingerprint helps unify the problem. A cyber operation leaves traces, but traces are not self-interpreting. A fingerprint at a scene may suggest presence, but not alone motive, chain of command, or strategic meaning. Digital fingerprints are more ambiguous still, because they can be copied, routed through intermediaries, or mixed with deliberate deception. States therefore do not attribute from one print. They attribute from patterns, context, intelligence, and judgment. Publics, lacking most of that material, see only the gloved hand of official assertion. Trust becomes the missing variable. That is why credibility built elsewhere - through honest communication, careful wording, and a reputation for restraint - matters so much here.

The strategic reader should therefore approach cyber attribution statements with structured doubt rather than suspicion for its own sake. Ask what the state appears to want the statement to accomplish. Ask why it is speaking now. Ask which allies are aligned, what responses accompany the accusation, and which sensitive details remain absent. Ask whether the incident is being treated as espionage, coercion, or something in between. Ask whether the public evidence is thin because the case is weak or because the stronger evidence cannot be exposed without cost. These questions do not solve the attribution puzzle. They prevent the common mistake of treating public statements as either transparent truth or empty propaganda.

The unresolved tension remains. A state must often show enough confidence to deter, reassure, and justify response while withholding enough detail to preserve future access and keep escalation under control. That makes public attribution permanently vulnerable to contestation. The harder question is whether democratic states can sustain enough credibility that such contestation does not automatically collapse into disbelief, while still preserving the secrecy on which sound attribution often depends. That tension will not disappear. It is one of the prices of trying to govern cyber conflict without either surrendering to opacity or pretending that every fingerprint can safely be laid on the table.

Chapter 8

Data Localisation and Cross-border Flows

What does a state actually gain when it insists that data stay within its borders, and what does it merely gain the appearance of controlling? The question has grown harder because localisation is rarely presented as one thing. It can be argued as a law-enforcement necessity, an industrial policy, a resilience measure, a privacy safeguard, or a declaration of sovereign seriousness. Sometimes it is all of these at once. That is exactly why it needs disentangling.

The appeal is easy to grasp. A government faced with foreign platforms, external cloud providers, opaque jurisdictional claims, and politically embarrassing dependence may look at data localisation and see a line it can still draw. Keep the data here. Keep the servers here. Keep the firms answerable here. The promise is clarity: a territory, a regulator, a warrant, a rule. Yet digital systems do not become governable merely because they are pinned to a map. Data may be stored locally while support, software control, encryption keys, analytics, and legal pressure remain distributed elsewhere. The border on paper can feel firmer than the system beneath it.

This is the chapter's central tension. Localisation can mitigate real risks, but it can also become a performance of control that confuses geography with authority. Some forms of localisation do improve response speed, narrow jurisdictional ambiguity, and reduce certain dependencies. Others mainly fragment architecture, raise costs, limit innovation, and create domestic chokepoints while leaving deeper power relations substantially unchanged. A state may reduce one exposure and intensify another. The policy question is therefore not whether localisation is good or bad in the abstract. It is what kind of problem it is actually solving, for whom, and at what price.

That price is often misunderstood because the benefits of cross-border flows are easy to treat as mere convenience. They are more than that. International data movement supports trade, cloud efficiency, security operations, research collaboration, payments, logistics, and the ordinary functioning of firms that serve several markets at once. Restricting those flows can create friction that is economically real and politically strategic. Compliance costs rise. Architectures fragment. Smaller firms struggle more than dominant ones. Services become harder to scale across jurisdictions. At the same time, governments may still discover that "local" systems depend on foreign software, foreign suppliers, foreign capital, or foreign legal entities in ways that no simple localisation rule can dissolve. The server may sit here. The leverage may not.

The stakes grow sharper when states press conflicting demands on the same firms. A company operating across several jurisdictions may be told by one government to retain more data, by another to delete it sooner, by one to disclose on request, by another to resist foreign disclosure, by one to localise sensitive categories, and by another to preserve integrated global operations for security or compliance reasons. The conflict is not merely legal. It is architectural. Firms then have to decide whether to split products, duplicate infrastructure, redesign data paths, narrow services, or absorb the contradiction and wait for the next conflict. What looks like regulatory nuance from the outside becomes a structural burden inside the system.

This is where regional blocs acquire unusual importance. They can stabilise expectations by making rules predictable across a larger market, yet they can also create new borders within the digital economy. A regional regime may reduce internal friction while increasing external incompatibility. Compliance then becomes not only a legal duty but a competitive fact. Firms capable of redesigning systems around one bloc's standards gain an advantage. States inside the bloc gain normative reach. States outside it may find their firms adapting to foreign expectations simply to remain commercially viable. Localisation, in that setting, is no longer a narrow domestic measure. It becomes part of a wider contest over standards, market access, and the political geography of data flows.

The path ahead follows that layered conflict. It begins with the motives that drive localisation demands and the need to distinguish serious risk reduction from symbolic closure. It then moves into the corporate dilemma created by extraterritorial pressure, where compliance, user trust, and operational coherence rarely align neatly. From there it broadens into the role of regional regimes in creating both order and fracture, connecting the politics of data flows to the larger questions already raised about cloud dependence, standards, and legitimacy. The through-line is simple enough to state and difficult to honour: borders still matter, but they do not govern digital systems in the straightforward way many politicians would prefer.

A useful image for the chapter is the fence. A fence can protect, signal ownership, and slow intrusion. It can also reassure the owner while leaving the deeper vulnerability elsewhere - in the gate, the key, the utility line, the contractor, the path around the side. Data localisation often works in a similar register. It may create real protection. It may also create a visible perimeter around a system whose decisive dependencies remain external. The policy challenge is to tell the difference before the fence becomes a substitute for diagnosis.

The harder diagnostic, then, is not whether a government can say that data are stored domestically. It is whether domestic storage changes the real balance of access, auditability, continuity, and bargaining power enough to justify the costs and the fragmentation it imposes. Until that question is asked with more precision, localisation will remain attractive partly because it looks like action even when it is only rearrangement. The next step is to examine why states reach for it so readily, and why some of the reasons are more serious than others.

The logic of localisation

In July 2015, Russia's data localisation law came into force, requiring certain personal data about Russian citizens to be stored on servers located in Russia. The legal change looked, at one level, straightforward: keep the data here. Yet the measure quickly revealed the wider politics of localisation. It was argued in terms of sovereignty, jurisdiction, public order, and national interest. It also imposed architectural choices on firms whose services had previously treated borders as secondary to scale and efficiency. The server acquired a passport.

That image matters because localisation is rarely only about storage. A government does not usually reach for localisation because it has suddenly developed a sentimental attachment to national server racks. It does so because data crossing borders raises old state anxieties in newly technical form. Who can compel access? Who can resist lawful process? Who can disrupt service in a crisis? Who benefits economically from data-intensive sectors? Who gets to say that a system is under national control? Localisation speaks to all of these questions at once, which is why it attracts such varied coalitions: police and intelligence agencies, industrial policy advocates, privacy campaigners, national security officials, domestic technology firms, and politicians eager to demonstrate firmness in public. The fence promises many things.

The first motivation is law-enforcement access, and it is perhaps the most intuitively persuasive. States have long insisted that evidence relevant to crime and security should be reachable within lawful process. Cross-border data storage complicates that expectation. It may require slower mutual legal assistance procedures, engagement with foreign courts, negotiation with global firms, or confrontation with legal frameworks not designed around domestic urgency. Localisation appears to simplify the problem. If the relevant records sit domestically, authorities imagine that warrants will bite faster, evidence will be easier to preserve, and institutional control will rest closer to home. The concept is jurisdictional compression: bring the data within the state's practical and legal reach. The implication is real, but not absolute. Domestic storage can reduce some forms of delay while leaving other control points - support access, encryption management, platform administration, software updates - substantially external.

This is why localisation often overpromises to law enforcement. The visible demand is for data "to be here". The harder question is which part of the data environment actually matters for access. A dataset may be stored in-country while replicated, indexed, or administered through systems subject to external influence. A local subsidiary may operate under a foreign parent's legal and technical constraints. A warrant may secure faster service of process while not resolving whether the provider can meaningfully comply without cross-border engineering or policy decisions. Localisation can help. It is not a magic solvent of jurisdictional complexity. States that present it as such risk confusing proximity with power.

The second motivation is industrial policy. Data localisation can be framed as an economic development tool: a way to attract investment in domestic data centres, cloud services, telecom infrastructure, and associated technical skills. Governments sometimes see a chance to keep more of the value created by digital activity within the national economy rather than letting it flow outward through global platforms and hyperscale providers. The concept here is territorial capture of digital rents. If firms must store and process data locally, domestic infrastructure providers, contractors, lawyers, auditors, and engineers may gain work and influence. The political appeal is obvious. Localisation begins to look like a jobs policy wrapped in sovereignty language.

And yet industrial policy through localisation has its own contradictions. A domestic market may indeed benefit from new server capacity, compliance services, and regulatory leverage. It may also become more concentrated, more expensive, and less innovative if the protected environment narrows competition or traps customers inside weaker local alternatives. A firm forced to duplicate systems for one jurisdiction spends resources on compliance architecture rather than product development. Smaller firms may struggle most because they cannot absorb the cost of local build-out as easily as global incumbents. What appears nationalist and anti-platform can therefore end by entrenching the largest firms, which alone can afford architectural fragmentation. The local cloud grows. So does the moat.

Resilience forms the third and often most serious rationale. States do not localise only because they want easier access or domestic profits. They also worry about continuity. If essential public or economic functions depend on foreign infrastructure, foreign legal disputes, foreign sanctions, or remote technical operations, then a crisis can quickly become a problem of external dependency. Localisation promises a degree of operational shelter. Local hosting may reduce latency, support faster incident handling, and place critical workloads nearer to national emergency planning. In some sectors, especially where continuity under stress matters more than marginal cost, that can be a rational choice. The key question is whether localisation genuinely reduces fragility or merely moves it.

This distinction becomes especially important in critical public functions. A state may plausibly conclude that certain identity, health, tax, or emergency systems should not depend heavily on cross-border data flows or distant support chains. That is not merely symbolism. It may be prudent design. But prudence is specific. It requires identifying which functions need geographic and administrative proximity, what kind of failover is required, and which external dependencies remain even after localisation. A domestically hosted identity service still relying on foreign cloud software, foreign identity standards, or foreign hardware supply chains is not non-dependent. It is differently dependent. Genuine resilience starts with dependency mapping, not with patriotic confidence in rack location.

The fourth motivation is political symbolism, and it should not be dismissed simply because it is symbolic. States often use localisation to demonstrate seriousness to domestic audiences unsettled by foreign platform power, intelligence disclosures, or the sense that governments have lost command over information flows. A localisation law can therefore serve as a visible line: we have acted, we have fenced the field, we have made data stay.

Symbolic measures can have political value, especially when publics demand reassurance. The difficulty begins when symbolism displaces diagnosis. A state may gain applause for building a visible perimeter while leaving less visible vulnerabilities - vendor lock-in, privileged remote access, software dependence, weak auditing, inadequate incident response - largely untouched. The fence stands. The gate remains open.

A named example from India shows the political complexity of this logic. Debates around data localisation intensified in the late 2010s as questions of privacy, law-enforcement access, domestic digital industry, and strategic autonomy converged. Localisation was argued not only as a privacy measure, but as a tool of state capacity and economic development. The attraction was understandable. India possessed scale, a growing digital public infrastructure, and strong reasons to worry about foreign platform dominance. Yet the debate also revealed the multiplicity of aims bundled into localisation: user protection, easier access for authorities, domestic cloud growth, and the politics of digital sovereignty. One policy instrument was being asked to solve several different problems at once. That is often the first sign that a localisation measure may do some of them only partially.

The costs, meanwhile, are often underestimated precisely because they are dispersed. Efficiency suffers when firms must duplicate storage, engineering, legal review, and operational workflows across jurisdictions. Innovation can slow because product teams must design around divergent regulatory boundaries rather than common architectures. International trade is affected because cross-border services, compliance support, payments, advertising, analytics, fraud detection, and logistics all rely on data moving where the service design expects it to move. Localisation can therefore function like a non-tariff barrier, even when framed in the language of security or rights. Domestic users may see a familiar service. Behind the interface, the system has become more fragmented, costlier to maintain, and sometimes poorer in function.

These costs are not distributed evenly. Large multinational firms often cope better than small entrants, which means localisation can reinforce incumbency while being sold as a challenge to external dominance. Domestic start-ups trying to scale internationally may also suffer if they must maintain fragmented data architectures early in their growth. Universities, researchers, and public-interest organisations may confront more friction in cross-border collaboration. Consumers may not see the missing service, the delayed feature, or the absent competitor that never entered the market. They will still feel the longer-term effect if digital markets become less open, more expensive, and more concentrated around those best able to navigate regulatory fragmentation.

A credible limitation should be admitted. Not every criticism of localisation is neutral economic wisdom. Some industry opposition is self-interested, and some cross-border flow advocacy treats global efficiency as an unquestioned good when it may rest on weak accountability and asymmetric power. States do face real problems of foreign legal exposure, slow access, brittle dependence, and underdeveloped domestic infrastructure. It would be complacent to treat localisation as inherently backward or protectionist. In some contexts, especially for highly sensitive data and critical public systems, more territorial control may be justified and strategically prudent. The issue is not whether localisation ever makes sense. It plainly can.

That limitation sharpens the real test. A serious localisation measure should be judged by whether it addresses a specific, demonstrable dependency or legal problem and whether the chosen remedy matches the problem's structure. Does it improve lawful access in a way that survives technical scrutiny? Does it materially strengthen continuity for a critical function? Does it build domestic capacity without simply sheltering weak providers? Does it preserve enough interoperability that security, commerce, and innovation do not pay an excessive price? Or does it mainly create the performance of sovereignty by fixing one visible variable - where the data rests - while leaving the decisive relations of control substantially unchanged? Those are not ideological questions. They are design questions.

The same policy can therefore be either prudent or performative depending on context. Localising certain public records tied to national identity or electoral administration may be a proportionate response to a real strategic concern. Requiring broad categories of ordinary commercial data to remain in-country, without clarity about the actual problem being solved, may produce more theatre than security. The temptation for governments is to blur these cases because broad rules are simpler to announce than narrow ones. The temptation for critics is to attack them all as digital mercantilism. Both habits are analytically lazy. The harder work lies in classifying the function, the threat, the remaining dependencies, and the likely cost of fragmentation.

The quiet motif of the fence helps keep that classification in view. A fence can protect livestock, define property, reassure anxious neighbours, or signal political intent. It can also mislead the owner into neglecting the weak point that matters more: the gate, the road, the supplier, the water source, the guard. Data localisation works much the same way. It can be a sensible perimeter control. It can also become a substitute for the deeper work of governing access, auditability, continuity, and supply chains. The state that confuses the fence with the whole security architecture will eventually discover that the symbolic comfort was real and the strategic protection incomplete.

The question that follows is therefore harder than the slogan suggests. When a government says it wants data to stay at home, is it trying to solve a concrete problem of access, resilience, or industrial weakness, or is it trying to convert territorial instinct into digital policy whether or not the system actually behaves territorially? The answer matters because the costs of getting it wrong are not merely economic. A state that mistakes performative control for real mitigation may end up more fragmented, less innovative, and no more sovereign where it counts. The next step is to see how these pressures look from the other side of the relationship, where firms are asked to comply with several states at once and discover that no architecture can fully satisfy all of them.

Extraterritorial pressure and corporate dilemma

In August 2020, Apple removed popular applications from its China App Store, including services used for encrypted messaging and information access, after changes in local legal and regulatory pressure made continued availability increasingly difficult to sustain. The immediate event looked like a familiar story of corporate compliance in a major market. The deeper significance lay elsewhere. A global platform had once again been forced to decide which mattered more in practice: one architecture for all users, public claims about privacy and rights, or continued access to a state large enough to shape the terms of the global digital economy. The code met the border.

That meeting is now one of the defining pressures on large technology firms. Global platforms, cloud providers, telecom companies, payment networks, and software services are no longer merely commercial actors moving through a stable legal environment. They operate inside overlapping claims of jurisdiction, access, and political authority that increasingly collide. One state demands retention. Another demands deletion. One requires disclosure on request. Another restricts transfer. One insists on local hosting. Another penalises fragmentation or insists on common global controls for safety or compliance. A company trying to maintain one coherent service across these demands discovers that legal conflict quickly becomes architectural conflict. Law writes itself into the system.

This is the central corporate dilemma. Firms are asked to remain compliant, preserve user trust, and maintain operational coherence at the same time, even when the three goals no longer fit together. Compliance means obeying the laws or commands of the jurisdictions in which they operate. User trust means persuading people that their data will not be used, exposed, or repurposed in ways they find intolerable. Operational coherence means keeping products and infrastructure sufficiently unified that they remain efficient, secure, maintainable, and intelligible. These aims can coexist under settled legal conditions. Under extraterritorial pressure, they begin to pull against one another. The result is not a single dramatic clash, but an accumulation of compromises that slowly fragments the global digital stack.

Extraterritorial pressure takes several forms. A state may assert authority over data held by a company because the company is headquartered, listed, staffed, or incorporated within its jurisdiction. It may demand disclosure from a local subsidiary even where the relevant records are stored elsewhere. It may threaten fines, market exclusion, criminal liability, or licensing consequences if the company fails to comply. It may require local presence, local staff, local key management, or local content moderation capacity. The company then faces a problem deeper than mere legal disagreement. It must decide whether to adapt its architecture to the jurisdiction's demand, withdraw from the market, or try to hold a middle ground that satisfies no one for long. The cloud is told to choose a side.

The Microsoft Ireland litigation, which unfolded between 2013 and 2018, remains a valuable marker of this tension. The United States government sought access to emails stored in Dublin by Microsoft, arguing that the company, as a US-based provider, could be compelled to produce them. Microsoft resisted, framing the case as a clash of sovereignty and process. The legal details shifted over time, especially after the United States enacted the CLOUD Act in 2018. What matters here is the structural lesson. The question was not simply where the emails were located. It was whether a global firm's legal obligations to one state could reach into data arrangements that another state or region might regard as its own regulatory concern. The server sat in Ireland. The pressure travelled from Washington. The company stood in the middle.

This middle position is not merely uncomfortable. It is constitutive of how modern digital firms operate. A company offering email, cloud hosting, social media, ride-hailing, payments, or app distribution across many markets necessarily builds services that move data, support, and software across borders more fluidly than most legal systems were designed to contemplate. Engineers optimise for scale, latency, resilience, and common code bases. Lawyers then discover that the very integration that makes the product work smoothly also makes compliance harder when states want different things from the same information. A shared user database may improve security and fraud detection globally while creating impossible disclosure conflicts. A single retention policy may simplify governance while violating one jurisdiction's deletion rules and another's preservation demands. The architecture itself becomes a legal battlefield.

This is why divergent retention and disclosure requirements are so consequential. Retention rules determine what exists to be sought, sold, or stolen. Disclosure rules determine when the company must hand it over and to whom. When states differ sharply on these matters, firms face a three-sided pressure. Retain more and the company may satisfy one government's demands while increasing exposure under another's privacy regime and under its own trust commitments to users. Retain less and it may reduce risk and align with minimisation principles while angering law-enforcement agencies or breaching sectoral obligations elsewhere. Hold different data for different markets and it may satisfy immediate legal conflict while turning a previously integrated service into a patchwork of local rules, higher cost, and uneven functionality. Fragmentation is not an accident here. It is a compliance outcome.

A named example from messaging and social media makes this concrete. Meta, like other large firms, has repeatedly faced conflicting demands across jurisdictions over encrypted services, user data, and content moderation. European privacy obligations, United States law-enforcement interests, and legal requirements in countries with much lower tolerance for user secrecy or dissent have not formed one coherent expectation. A company that presents itself as globally connected and privacy-aware must therefore decide, jurisdiction by jurisdiction, whether to store, separate, disclose, resist, or redesign. The public often sees only the outward policy statement. Beneath it sits a more consequential series of questions: where are the logs kept, how are keys handled, what metadata remain available, which teams can access them, and which local laws are now shaping what the product can promise at all.

This is where user trust becomes difficult to sustain. Trust sounds like a matter of public relations until one asks what visible behaviour users are actually expected to rely on. Can the firm tell them honestly who may obtain their data? Can it explain whether that answer varies by country? Can it resist overbroad requests without losing market access? Can it keep one set of privacy commitments across all jurisdictions, or must it quietly degrade protections for users in more coercive environments? A company may publish transparency reports, legal process guidelines, and broad statements of principle. Those help. They do not erase the fact that trust is being strained by a world in which a platform's relationship with one state may alter what every user elsewhere can reasonably expect.

Operational coherence, meanwhile, is more fragile than many outsiders assume. Large-scale digital services gain security and efficiency partly because they avoid needless fragmentation. Shared infrastructure allows common patching, consistent identity systems, unified detection of abuse, and standardised incident response. Once governments push firms towards local hosting, local moderation, local staff restrictions, local retention schedules, and jurisdiction-specific product versions, coherence begins to erode. This can reduce some forms of dependence on foreign systems, but it can also make platforms harder to secure and govern well. A service with one strong architecture may become several weaker ones stitched together by legal necessity. The company obeys. The system becomes less elegant and sometimes less safe.

A second named example lies in TikTok's efforts to reassure governments in Europe and North America about data access, local storage, and governance, especially as scrutiny intensified after 2020. The company's various regional data and trust arrangements were not merely technical upgrades or public relations gestures. They were attempts to manage competing political demands: reassure host governments that local data would be insulated from foreign state access, reassure users that their information was not being casually exposed, and preserve enough of the platform's global operational logic to keep the service viable. Whether one judges those efforts convincing is less important here than recognising their structure. The company was trying to answer several states at once by redesigning architecture around suspicion.

A credible limitation belongs here. Large firms are not helpless victims of sovereign conflict. They often cultivate ambiguity where it suits them, overstate the impossibility of compliance when pushing back against regulation, and use privacy language strategically while pursuing business models built on extensive data collection. Some corporate pleas for coherence are really pleas to avoid constraints that would reduce profit or expose governance weaknesses. It would be naive to frame the company simply as the innocent object of competing state demands. Firms help create the transnational architectures that later complicate public authority.

But that limitation sharpens the core argument rather than weakening it. Even self-interested firms still confront genuine structural conflict when states make mutually incompatible claims. A platform can neither fully localise and remain globally integrated, nor fully integrate and remain responsive to every local sovereignty demand. Something has to give. Sometimes the sacrifice is user trust. Sometimes it is market access. Sometimes it is operational simplicity. Often it is all three in varying degrees across different jurisdictions. The modern corporation becomes, in effect, a site where incompatible theories of digital order are translated into product decisions.

This is why extraterritorial pressure matters geopolitically rather than merely legally. A state able to force architectural change in global platforms exercises power well beyond its borders. It does not need to control the firm outright. It only needs enough market size, legal leverage, or political will to make non-compliance too costly. The company's engineers and lawyers then do the work of translating that state pressure into global product realities. Data pathways shift. Moderation policies change. Storage arrangements multiply. Support teams are restructured. What appears as a local legal demand can therefore become a worldwide design fact. Extraterritoriality enters the product through compliance engineering.

The private firm's dilemma is thus also a public dilemma. Citizens, regulators, and policymakers need to understand that "global service" and "national control" no longer coexist easily. Every demand for local obedience risks fragmenting the service. Every defence of global coherence risks sounding like evasion of democratic accountability. Every promise to users risks being qualified by a jurisdiction they may never see. The ordinary consumer experiences a single interface. Behind it stands a layered map of state pressure, market calculation, and engineering compromise that no terms-of-service summary can really disclose.

The quiet motif of the seam helps hold the matter together. A seam joins pieces into one garment. It also marks where different materials meet and where strain will show first. Global digital firms are now full of seams: between jurisdictions, between retention rules, between disclosure obligations, between trust claims and access realities, between one code base and many regulatory orders. When the garment stretches, the seam tells the truth about its construction. So do these conflicts. They reveal that the supposedly borderless internet was always stitched together through political bargains that are now fraying.

The harder question, then, is not whether global firms should obey the laws of the states in which they operate. Of course they must, within the bounds of law and conscience. The harder question is what happens when obedience to one state deforms the service for users elsewhere, when trust can no longer be promised in universal terms, and when architectural fragmentation becomes the price of staying in the market. That is the pressure point at which corporate governance, state sovereignty, and user rights stop looking like separate debates and start appearing as one conflict conducted through the design of systems. The next step is to see how entire regions try to stabilise that conflict by building legal blocs of their own - and how those blocs, in turn, create new borders in the digital economy.

Regional regimes and interoperability breaks

On 16 July 2020, the Court of Justice of the European Union struck down the EU-US Privacy Shield in the Schrems II judgment. The legal result was immediate enough: a major mechanism for transatlantic personal data transfers could no longer serve as a secure bridge in the way many firms had hoped. The political result was larger. A regional legal order had asserted that cross-border data flows could not be treated as routine commercial plumbing when the surrounding surveillance and redress arrangements failed to meet its standards. The bridge had not collapsed for technical reasons. It had failed a constitutional test.

That moment captures the double character of regional data regimes. They stabilise expectations within a bloc by clarifying what counts as acceptable processing, transfer, access, and remedy. They also create new borders in the digital economy by forcing firms, states, and institutions outside the bloc to adapt or accept friction. The logic is neither trivial nor parochial. A regional regime says, in effect, that interoperability is not merely a technical property. It is a legal and political achievement conditioned by trust, accountability, and shared standards. Data may move only if the surrounding order is judged sufficiently legible and disciplined. The passport is no longer enough. The legal habitat matters.

This is why regional regimes should be understood as instruments of ordering power. They reduce uncertainty for actors inside the regime by setting common rules, common supervisory expectations, and common vocabulary for compliance. A hospital system, cloud provider, bank, or public authority operating across a regional bloc can design around one broad set of assumptions rather than several unrelated national ones. The concept here is internal stabilisation. Stability has obvious value. It lowers legal ambiguity, makes procurement more predictable, and allows regulators and firms to speak a shared language about transfers, security, minimisation, and redress. The implication is significant. A regional bloc can function as a market-maker not only through scale, but through the credibility of its rule set.

But that same rule set can generate interoperability breaks at the boundary. A company moving data between jurisdictions must now ask whether legal protections, oversight structures, transfer mechanisms, and state access rules outside the bloc satisfy internal standards. If the answer is unclear or negative, the flow becomes contested even when the technology works perfectly well. This is where the phrase interoperability break becomes useful. The systems can still connect physically. The legal and political order says they do not connect cleanly enough to be trusted. A regional regime therefore creates borders that are not visible in cables or packets but in adequacy decisions, contractual clauses, audit requirements, and the threat of enforcement. The interface still exists. Its legitimacy is fractured.

The European Union provides the clearest example because it has turned data protection and digital governance into a form of external influence as well as internal order. The General Data Protection Regulation, in force from 2018, did not merely harmonise expectations within the Union. It forced firms around the world to account for European standards if they wished to serve European users or process European data at scale. This was not only a privacy event. It was a geopolitical one. Compliance became a condition of market access. Regional law acquired extraterritorial effect through ordinary business necessity. The strategic lesson extends well beyond Europe. A bloc with enough market weight and regulatory confidence can write rules that others obey without formal jurisdiction over them.

That obedience, however, comes at a cost that falls unevenly. Large firms often absorb regional compliance demands more easily than smaller ones because they can hire counsel, redesign workflows, segment infrastructure, build internal transfer mechanisms, and maintain documentation at a level smaller rivals cannot. Compliance thus becomes a competitive factor in a very practical sense. It does not only weed out reckless actors. It can also strengthen incumbents whose scale allows them to turn regulatory burden into an entry barrier. The visible behaviour is familiar: large providers advertise regional compliance packages, local hosting options, dedicated controls, and legal assurances, while smaller firms retreat from certain markets, narrow their offerings, or accept subordinate roles as suppliers to better-resourced platforms. Regulation shapes competition even when competition is not its explicit target.

This is why regional regimes are also diplomatic instruments. Adequacy decisions, transfer agreements, sector-specific understandings, and regulatory dialogues become tools through which blocs recognise, pressure, or refuse one another. The legal vocabulary can sound dry, but the political meaning is sharp. To declare another jurisdiction adequate is to acknowledge that its legal order provides sufficiently trustworthy protection for data moving under the bloc's rules. To withhold adequacy is to signal that legal uncertainty, state access, weak remedies, or broader governance concerns remain unacceptable. Diplomacy thus becomes infrastructural. Recognition determines whether flows remain smooth, expensive, provisional, or politically fraught.

A named example beyond Europe clarifies that this is not a single-region phenomenon. The African Union Convention on Cyber Security and Personal Data Protection, adopted in 2014, and subsequent national and regional developments across Africa have reflected a growing effort to build common expectations around digital governance, even if implementation has remained uneven. The significance lies not in claiming that one cohesive African data regime already exists at the same density as the European model. It lies in recognising the strategic aspiration: regions increasingly understand that digital fragmentation can be reduced internally through shared norms, even as those norms create new questions about external interoperability. Regionalism in digital governance is no longer an eccentric legal project. It is part of how states try to avoid being merely rule-takers in a system designed elsewhere.

Interoperability breaks also reveal how closely localisation, cloud dependence, and standards politics now intertwine. A regional bloc may not demand strict localisation in every case, yet its transfer conditions can still encourage local processing, regional cloud offerings, and compliance architectures tailored to internal law. Cloud providers respond by building "regional" or "sovereign" variants, promising restricted support access, local controls, and more auditable arrangements. Standards bodies and procurement officers then translate those expectations into technical and contractual requirements. The result is a layered regionalisation of digital infrastructure. Data flows continue, but under thicker legal wrapping and more segmented operational design. The border becomes a pattern of systems engineering.

This can improve governance. It can also produce new fractures. A firm serving several regional blocs may end up maintaining several versions of what was once a more unified system: separate retention schedules, separate hosting patterns, separate legal review channels, separate user flows, separate audit structures, perhaps even separate product features. That fragmentation is often defended as necessary respect for legal diversity, and sometimes it is. It can also reduce security coherence, slow innovation, and make cross-border services more brittle. One system becomes several cousins rather than one platform. The challenge is not that regional law creates borders. It is that every border introduced into the system has technical, economic, and political afterlives that are easy to underestimate at the moment of drafting.

A credible limitation should be admitted. Not every interoperability break is a sign of dysfunction or protectionism. Sometimes a break reflects a serious and justified refusal to treat incompatible legal orders as if they were interchangeable. A regional regime that insists on stronger redress, tighter limits on state access, or more disciplined transfer mechanisms may be doing exactly what a constitutional order ought to do. Smooth flow is not the only value at stake. Friction can be principled. A world in which data moved effortlessly between any systems willing to process it would not necessarily be freer, fairer, or safer. Some breaks deserve to exist.

But that limitation sharpens the real problem. Once several regional regimes begin to insist on their own principled conditions, the cumulative result may be a digital economy divided not only by infrastructure and market power, but by partially incompatible theories of lawful data order. Firms then become the engineers of diplomatic tension. They must build workarounds, seek adequacy, negotiate transfer tools, redesign products, and reassure users whose data now travel through increasingly political pathways. The state, meanwhile, discovers that regional law can amplify sovereignty and constrain it at once. A bloc gains normative power internally and externally. Individual member states may lose some unilateral flexibility in return for a stronger collective position. Regionalism strengthens one layer of authority by disciplining another.

This is why compliance becomes more than a legal burden. It becomes a diplomatic language. A firm that can say it meets the standards of a powerful regional bloc is not merely claiming procedural tidiness. It is claiming admissibility into a political order. A state seeking recognition or adequacy is not merely negotiating a trade convenience. It is bargaining over the legitimacy of its institutions, the constraints on its intelligence services, and the credibility of its remedies. Compliance documents, audit reports, supervisory decisions, and transfer instruments all become fragments of geopolitical argument. The border is administered by lawyers, regulators, cloud architects, and standards professionals as much as by customs officers.

A second named example helps illuminate the diplomatic dimension. The negotiations and repeated instability around EU-US data transfer arrangements, from Safe Harbor to Privacy Shield and then beyond Schrems II, show how regional regimes can turn ongoing allied relations into recurring disputes over legal trust. The United States and the European Union are close partners across defence, trade, and diplomacy. Yet cross-border data flows between them have repeatedly become contested because the surrounding legal orders, especially on surveillance and redress, do not align cleanly enough. The lesson is not that alliance dissolves regulatory difference. It is that even close allies can generate interoperability breaks when legitimacy standards diverge. Digital cooperation requires more than friendly rhetoric.

This connects directly to the book's broader concern with legitimacy. Regional regimes do not only regulate firms. They embody claims about what kind of authority deserves to handle data across borders. A bloc that insists on stronger rights, more independent supervision, or tighter transfer conditions is making an argument about the relation between data power and lawful order. That argument may be defensible, performative, selective, or all three at once. But it is never merely technical. When the break occurs - when a transfer tool fails, when adequacy is denied, when a regional cloud becomes necessary - the underlying issue is not really whether packets can travel. It is whether institutions on the other side of the border are believed to behave in ways compatible with the regime's own understanding of trust.

The quiet motif of the bridge deserves a return here. Regional regimes build bridges internally: shared rules, common expectations, routine transfers, repeatable compliance. At the same time, they decide which external bridges may remain open, which need reinforcement, and which no longer deserve traffic at all. A bridge is useful precisely because it joins places that remain distinct. But the stronger the bridge inside the region, the more exacting the question becomes at the boundary: who is allowed to cross, under what conditions, and with what assurance that the legal ground on the other side will still hold? Interoperability is not just connection. It is trusted passage.

The harder question, then, is not whether regional regimes will continue to proliferate. They almost certainly will, because they offer states a way to regain leverage in a system otherwise dominated by global platforms and cross-border infrastructures. The harder question is what kind of digital world those regimes will produce together. Will they stabilise lawful pluralism while preserving enough interoperability for trade, research, security, and civic exchange? Or will they harden into rival legal blocs whose standards are strong internally and only awkwardly translatable across borders? That question will not be settled by technology alone. It will be settled in the uneasy space where compliance becomes diplomacy and the bridge becomes an argument about whose order is trusted enough to carry the weight.

Chapter 9

Privacy Regulation as Statecraft

What does a state really do when it writes a privacy law: protect dignity, restrain firms, discipline itself, or redraw the market in its own image? The honest answer is usually all four. Privacy is often presented in public argument as a moral claim about the individual standing against intrusion. That claim matters. It is not the whole story. Once translated into rules about consent, retention, minimisation, access, correction, and transfer, privacy becomes an instrument for organising power. It tells institutions what they may know, how long they may know it, what they must explain, and what kinds of business models or administrative habits will remain viable under law. The notice on the screen is only the surface.

This makes privacy law unusually easy to misunderstand. Critics sometimes treat it as symbolic reassurance for anxious citizens, a layer of forms and banners that leaves the deeper data economy intact. Admirers sometimes treat it as a principled shield whose value is self-evident once enacted. Both views miss the harder point. Privacy regulation is a governing technology. It changes incentives, administrative burdens, contractual defaults, technical design choices, and the distribution of bargaining power between state, firms, and individuals. A deletion right can alter storage architecture. A purpose-limitation rule can narrow the ease with which data slide from welfare administration into policing or from customer service into behavioural profiling. A consent standard can shift liability, but it can also legitimise extraction if written carelessly. The rulebook becomes a map of permissible ambition.

That dual character creates the chapter's central tension. Privacy law is strongest when it shapes conduct before harm occurs, yet it only remains credible when it can be enforced after harm occurs. A state may draft elegant rights and precise duties, but if regulators cannot investigate, compel, interpret, and punish with consistency, the law does more than disappoint. It creates false reassurance. Citizens are told they are protected;

firms learn that delay and contestation are often enough; public bodies begin to cite legal compliance as evidence of trustworthiness even where practice remains opportunistic. A weak privacy regime does not merely fail to constrain power. It launders it through official language.

This matters because privacy is one of the few domains where legitimacy, market design, and state capacity converge so directly. A serious privacy framework can rebalance power by forcing both government agencies and private firms to justify collection, narrow reuse, maintain records, respond to challenges, and build systems that are more intelligible to those affected by them. A weak one can harden the opposite lesson: rights are decorative, complexity defeats ordinary people, and large institutions will continue to know more than they can be made to explain. The difference is not only legal. It is civic. Citizens learn from how rights operate. If rights are cumbersome, obscure, and rarely effective, public trust does not grow merely because the statute book has become more ornate.

The stakes are sharpened by national security. Every privacy regime must answer the same uncomfortable question: what happens when the state claims that ordinary limits cannot fully apply because intelligence, counter-terrorism, cyber defence, or serious crime require broader access? Exemptions are unavoidable. The issue is their design. Write them too loosely and they become corridors for mission creep, swallowing the restraint the law was meant to impose. Write them too rigidly and the state may impair legitimate investigations or create incentives for informal workarounds. Boundary setting here is not a technical afterthought. It is one of the places where a society declares what kind of emergency language it is willing to live with in normal time.

The same is true of data rights and remedies. Rights that cannot be used are politically revealing. A right of access that produces incomprehensible disclosures, a correction right that vanishes into a customer-service maze, a deletion right defeated by hidden retention chains, a complaint route that takes years to resolve - none of these is neutral failure. Each teaches the public that the legal order recognises the injury without seriously intending to rebalance the relationship. A usable remedy does something more demanding. It makes the institution answer in a form the ordinary subject can understand and act upon. That answer, repeated often enough, becomes part of how trust is built or squandered.

Privacy law also travels. Once a jurisdiction builds a regime that is large enough, coherent enough, and credibly enforced enough, others must position themselves in relation to it. Some copy it. Some adapt it. Some resist it while still redesigning products to preserve market access. Cross-border data flows, adequacy judgments, contractual transfer tools, and mutual recognition arrangements then become instruments of diplomacy as much as commerce. A privacy regime stops being a domestic settlement and becomes a way of projecting standards outward. The law begins to govern beyond its territory not only through formal reach, but through the practical need of firms and states to remain interoperable with the order it has created.

The path ahead follows that broader understanding. It begins by treating privacy not as a noble sentiment attached to data policy, but as a way of governing markets and institutions through design choices that shape who may know what and for what purpose. It then turns to the harder matter of enforcement, where expertise, resources, and independence determine whether law is felt as pressure or merely read as promise. From there it moves into the architecture of exemptions, the operability of rights, and the diplomatic life of privacy rules once they begin to structure market access and regulatory recognition across borders. The through-line is simple enough to state and difficult enough to sustain: privacy becomes statecraft when it stops being only a declaration of values and starts allocating power in durable, inspectable ways.

A useful image for the chapter is the valve. A valve does not abolish flow. It regulates pressure, direction, and release. Privacy rules operate in much the same manner. They do not end data collection, nor should they if governments and economies are to function. They decide where data may move freely, where it must slow, where it must be justified, where it must stop, and who has the authority to open or close the channel. A valve badly designed may reassure the eye while failing under pressure. A good one becomes part of the system's reliability precisely because it constrains excess before the pipe bursts.

The harder question, then, is not whether a privacy regime sounds principled. Many do. It is whether the regime can force both public and private power to act as though the principles actually cost something. Can it make rights usable, exemptions narrow, enforcement credible, and cross-border recognition conditional on more than diplomatic convenience? Or does it mainly produce a more sophisticated language in which the same old asymmetries are defended with better paperwork? That question leads directly to the first issue: how privacy rules function not only as restraints, but as technologies of governance in their own right.

Privacy as a governance technology

In May 2018, as the General Data Protection Regulation came into force across the European Union, users around the world were confronted by a sudden flood of consent notices, updated privacy policies, and redesigned settings pages. For many, the moment felt faintly absurd. The internet seemed to have responded to a major legal change by producing more banners and more clicks. Yet the real significance lay beneath that surface clutter. A regional legal regime had just altered the terms on which firms could collect, combine, justify, and retain data, and in doing so it had changed not only what companies said to users, but what engineers built, what lawyers feared, what regulators could demand, and what kinds of market practice now required a more careful public defence. The pop-up was trivial. The redesign was not.

That moment helps correct a persistent misunderstanding. Privacy is often treated as if it were mainly a moral vocabulary for objecting to intrusion - important, worthy, but secondary to the real business of administration, commerce, and security. In practice, privacy rules do something more exacting. They organise the movement of information through institutions. They decide when data may be collected, on what grounds, for which purposes, under what conditions of reuse, with which obligations of deletion, correction, explanation, and challenge. They do not merely protect a sphere of personal dignity from external interference. They structure the incentives of states and firms alike. Privacy law, used seriously, is a technology of governance.

This becomes clear the moment one asks what any privacy regime actually changes. It changes product design. It changes internal documentation. It changes procurement. It changes the ease with which one database can be linked to another, one service purpose can drift into another, one customer relationship can become a source of behavioural profiling, one welfare record can become law-enforcement intelligence, one platform feature can become an extraction channel. The concept here is regulated informational discipline. The law does not eliminate power. It forces power to travel through narrower gates. The implication is political rather than decorative. A society that regulates data flows intelligently redistributes practical advantage among state, firm, and individual before any court case begins.

Consent is the most publicly visible of these instruments, and also the most misunderstood. Consent sounds straightforward: people should agree before their data are used. In practice, consent rules govern how institutions package choice, how much burden falls on the user, and which activities require justification beyond "the user clicked yes". The visible behaviour is familiar: a service asks permission, presents defaults, offers toggles, links to a policy, and records an answer. This can be empowering. It can also be a ritual of exhaustion. If consent is demanded too often, framed opaquely, bundled across unrelated purposes, or attached to services people cannot realistically avoid, it functions less as a transfer of control than as a legal performance through which extraction is laundered into apparent choice. A privacy regime that relies on consent too heavily may therefore entrench the asymmetry it claims to soften.

That does not make consent worthless. It makes its design decisive. A carefully framed consent rule can force firms to separate functions they would rather bundle, reduce the ease of background tracking, and make controversial uses of data visible enough to become contestable. A carelessly framed one can train users to click through coercive architecture and teach firms that fatigue is an acceptable substitute for legitimacy. This is why privacy as governance technology requires more than good motives. It requires a realistic understanding of institutional behaviour. Firms optimise around legal thresholds. States do too. The question is not whether consent exists. It is what forms of conduct the consent rule actually rewards.

Purpose limitation often does more serious work because it aims at one of the central pathologies of data power: function creep. Data collected for one reason have a habit of becoming tempting for another. A hospital record can look useful for policing. A tax register can look useful for social sorting. A customer account can look useful for targeted advertising, then for credit scoring, then for fraud analytics, then for political influence. Purpose limitation resists this slide by insisting that data collected under one justification do not automatically become available for adjacent uses merely because the institution now finds those uses convenient. The concept is boundary preservation. Its implication is profound. A state or firm forced to justify secondary use must expose ambitions it would otherwise have smuggled through routine.

A named example helps here. The controversy surrounding the care.data programme in England in 2014 illustrated what happens when purpose is insufficiently understood and insufficiently trusted. The scheme aimed to expand the use of NHS patient data for planning and research, goals that can be defensible and socially valuable. The backlash came not from hostility to public benefit in the abstract, but from uncertainty about access, reuse, safeguards, and whether data given in one intimate context might travel further than patients had reasonably understood. The visible behaviour was public refusal and political withdrawal. The lesson was not that health data should never be shared. It was that purpose limitation is not a technical obstacle to efficiency. It is part of the social contract that determines whether efficiency remains governable.

Data minimisation is the third pillar, and perhaps the most strategically important because it asks a question institutions rarely ask themselves voluntarily: what can be left uncollected? The logic of both bureaucracy and commerce tends towards accumulation. More data might be useful later. Storage is cheap. Analytical tools improve. New uses emerge. Minimisation pushes in the opposite direction. It treats absence as a form of protection. Data not collected, or not retained beyond genuine need, cannot be misused, breached, repurposed, or compelled in the same way. This is governance through restraint. The visible decision may be modest - dropping a field from a form, reducing retention, separating identifiers, declining to log by default - but the strategic effect can be considerable. It narrows the future bargaining power of the institution holding the system.

Minimisation also redistributes risk. Large firms and large states often benefit from accumulation because they possess the infrastructure and legal support to extract value from broad archives. Individuals bear much of the downside when those archives are breached, correlated, sold, or used in ways they cannot foresee. By forcing institutions to justify each category of collection and each period of retention, minimisation shifts some of the burden back onto the collector. The collector must now defend the future value of the record against the present cost of holding it. That is not anti-innovation. It is a demand that innovation stop treating the public as a free reservoir of optional knowledge.

A second named example shows how these ideas can travel beyond Europe. Brazil's Lei Geral de Protecao de Dados, which took effect in 2020, drew on international privacy principles while adapting them to a distinct institutional and political context. Its significance lies not only in the rights it created, but in the way it signalled that privacy regulation could be used to reorder digital markets and public authority in an emerging major economy rather than being dismissed as a niche European preoccupation. The law's long-term impact depends on enforcement and institutional capacity, but the design ambition itself matters. Privacy regulation was being used as a tool of statecraft: part market governance, part civic reassurance, part diplomatic positioning.

This is why privacy rules should be evaluated less by their rhetoric than by their effect on institutional incentives. A good regulatory design does not merely announce that individuals deserve respect. It changes what firms build and what agencies find easy. Does the rule make broad secondary use harder than narrow, declared use? Does it reward deletion rather than indefinite hoarding? Does it force clearer separation between public functions that would otherwise drift into one another? Does it give the individual a real point of leverage, or only a point of notice? These are governance questions, not only rights questions. They ask whether the law changes behaviour upstream, where power usually takes shape before the affected person even knows there is a problem.

There is, however, a credible limitation that any serious account must acknowledge. Privacy regulation can generate bureaucracy without generating restraint. A regime heavy on consent notices and internal paperwork may create the appearance of discipline while leaving the dominant business model and the dominant administrative instinct substantially intact. Firms can become highly skilled at formal compliance while continuing to profile aggressively inside the permitted space. Public bodies can cite lawful basis and public interest while steadily widening the practical reach of data sharing. In such cases privacy becomes administrative theatre, and theatre can be politically useful to the very institutions it was meant to discipline.

That limitation does not weaken the broader argument. It sharpens it by forcing attention onto design quality rather than symbolic ambition. The point is not that privacy law always rebalances power. It is that it can, if drafted and enforced in ways that alter the default behaviour of institutions rather than merely surrounding them with documentation. Consent must be specific enough to matter. Purpose limitation must be operational rather than aspirational. Minimisation must reach architecture and retention, not remain a slogan in policy text. Otherwise the law teaches the wrong lesson: that regulation is something clever institutions route around while keeping their legitimacy gains.

This is also why privacy governance cannot be cleanly separated from market structure. Large firms often cope with privacy obligations more easily than smaller competitors because they can redesign systems, hire compliance teams, and spread legal cost across wider revenues. That can make privacy law pro-competitive in one respect, by restricting data extraction and reducing arbitrary dominance, while anti-competitive in another, by raising the threshold for market entry. The same is true for the state. A disciplined privacy framework can restrain administrative overreach while also increasing the leverage of regulators and data protection authorities. Power does not disappear. It is rechannelled. The real question is whether the new channels are more visible, reviewable, and contestable than the old ones.

The quiet motif of the valve is useful here. A valve does not abolish flow. It governs pressure, direction, and release. Privacy rules work best when they function in precisely that way. Consent regulates the opening. Purpose limitation directs the route. Minimisation narrows the volume. None of these mechanisms guarantees justice by itself. Together, they can prevent systems from treating unlimited collection and unrestricted reuse as the natural baseline of digital life. They make institutions justify the flow rather than simply enjoying it.

That is why privacy should be read as a practical language of constitutional design in the information age. It decides whether data collection begins from presumption of institutional entitlement or from presumption of bounded purpose. It decides whether users encounter genuine leverage or merely ritual acknowledgement. It decides whether the future belongs to archives whose uses multiply faster than oversight, or to systems built with enough restraint that later temptation meets friction instead of automatic access. The law becomes a device for teaching institutions what they may not easily become.

The harder question, then, is not whether privacy matters. The harder question is what kind of privacy rule actually governs, rather than merely decorates, the systems it addresses. A consent banner may satisfy a formal requirement and change almost nothing. A carefully enforced purpose rule may quietly reshape an entire business model. A minimisation obligation may look modest and still prevent a later scandal that would otherwise have been treated as inevitable. The reader should therefore ask of every privacy regime: where does it place the valve, who controls it, and what forms of power does it leave flowing as though no governance choice had ever been made?

Enforcement capacity and institutional credibility

In July 2021, Luxembourg's data protection authority issued a major privacy fine against Amazon under the European Union's General Data Protection

Regulation. The headline travelled quickly because large fines always do. Yet the more consequential question was not the number attached to the decision. It was whether the case reflected an isolated spectacle or part of a wider pattern of regulatory pressure capable of changing how large firms built systems, documented purposes, handled consent, and responded to supervisory scrutiny. Punishment can attract attention. Credibility requires repetition.

That distinction goes to the heart of privacy enforcement. A law on the books can reassure citizens, guide procurement, and shape political rhetoric even before it is tested. But a law without credible enforcement can become worse than legal absence, because it teaches the public to mistake vocabulary for protection. People are told they have rights, that firms face duties, that the state has drawn lines around acceptable conduct. If those lines are rarely inspected, weakly defended, or selectively ignored when powerful actors are involved, the law becomes a device for false reassurance. Institutions continue to collect, combine, and repurpose data, while those affected are invited to believe that the problem has already been solved in statute. A promise has been printed. Nothing else follows.

This is why enforcement capacity belongs at the centre of privacy regulation rather than at its administrative edge. Privacy law is often discussed as a matter of principle, drafting, or jurisprudence. Those matter. But the lived force of a privacy regime depends heavily on whether some institution can investigate meaningfully, compel evidence, interpret complex systems, resist political pressure, and insist on remedies that alter conduct rather than merely narrate disapproval. The concept here is regulatory force. Without it, even elegant rights and carefully worded obligations remain fragile aspirations. With it, ordinary bureaucratic and commercial habits begin to change because the cost of ignoring the law becomes harder to discount.

Resources are the first and most obvious determinant of that force. Data protection authorities, sectoral regulators, courts, and inspectors cannot supervise complex digital systems by moral seriousness alone. They need staff who can read contracts, inspect code-related documentation, understand cloud architectures, question data flows, evaluate retention claims, and distinguish symbolic compliance from operational reality. A regulator asked to oversee multinational platforms, advertising technologies, public-sector databases, biometric systems, data brokers, and cross-border transfers without enough technically literate staff will quickly become dependent on what the regulated entities choose to disclose. The visible symptom is delay. The deeper problem is asymmetry. The institution charged with restraint knows less, later, and under tighter constraint than the institutions it is meant to discipline.

Expertise matters as much as headcount because privacy enforcement now sits at the intersection of law, engineering, business process, procurement, security, and administrative design. A regulator that understands only legal form may be impressed by policies, notices, and contracts while missing the architecture that keeps extraction or repurposing alive beneath them. A regulator that understands only technical design may miss the strategic importance of interpretation, remedy, and institutional precedent. Serious enforcement therefore depends on mixed competence: investigators who can map a data flow, lawyers who can turn that map into a robust theory of violation, and leadership able to decide whether to pursue a precedent-setting case, a negotiated correction, or a broader supervisory campaign. Enforcement quality lies in that combination, not in righteous language.

Independence is the second determinant, and it is harder to secure than most statutes admit. A privacy regulator that is formally independent but practically reliant on ministries for budget, appointments, or political cover may hesitate when the target is a major state programme, a national champion, or a strategically sensitive foreign investor. A regulator that fears being portrayed as anti-innovation, anti-security, or hostile to domestic industry may prefer guidance and persuasion long after stronger intervention is warranted. The same applies inside government. Officials responsible for reviewing public-sector data practices often sit close enough to executive power that institutional loyalty blunts scrutiny. Independence, then, is not only legal separation. It is the practical ability to inconvenience important actors without risking institutional retaliation.

This is where symbolic fines and sustained supervisory pressure begin to diverge. A symbolic fine can matter. It may generate publicity, sharpen internal boardroom attention, and signal that a regulator has awakened. But a one-off penalty, however large, does not necessarily change business models or administrative routines. Large firms may treat it as litigation risk or a cost of operating at scale. Public bodies may absorb it into reputational management. Sustained supervisory pressure works differently. It combines repeated scrutiny, iterative findings, orders to change process, close review of remediation, and the willingness to return if the institution adjusts the wording rather than the conduct. The visible behaviour is not the press release. It is the redesign of dashboards, the narrowing of retention, the abandonment of dubious lawful bases, the restructuring of internal approvals, the changed tone in product meetings when privacy officers are no longer decorative. That is what credibility looks like in practice.

A named example helps sharpen the contrast. The Irish Data Protection Commission has played an outsized role in enforcing the GDPR against major technology firms because many of them have their European headquarters in Ireland. This has made it a focal point for both praise and criticism. The relevant lesson is not to turn one authority into hero or villain. It is to notice the enforcement dilemma built into concentration. When a small number of regulators carry responsibility for supervising some of the world's most powerful data-intensive firms, delay and pressure acquire systemic significance. If the regulator acts slowly, the whole regime looks hesitant. If it acts aggressively, diplomatic, commercial, and domestic political pressures intensify. The case reveals that enforcement capacity is not only about law. It is about whether institutional design matches the scale of the actors being regulated.

The same principle appears outside Europe. The United States Federal Trade Commission has, over time, used consumer protection authority to challenge privacy and data security practices in ways that do not depend on a single omnibus federal privacy statute. This has sometimes allowed it to intervene where deception, unfairness, or inadequate security were visible. It has also exposed the limits of enforcement without a more coherent underlying statutory framework. The lesson is subtle. A powerful regulator can do meaningful work even with imperfect tools. But where the legal basis is fragmented, enforcement often becomes reactive, negotiated, and case-specific in ways that make long-term discipline harder to sustain. Credibility requires not only institutional will, but a rulebook clear enough to turn precedent into routine expectation.

This is why laws without enforcement can become actively corrosive. They encourage three false beliefs at once. Citizens believe they are protected because rights exist on paper. Firms believe they can postpone hard changes because supervision is likely to be slow or selective. Governments believe they can present themselves as rights-respecting while continuing to build expansive data systems under the cover of formal legality. These beliefs can coexist for years. The public sees privacy notices, regulators publish guidance, ministries invoke safeguards, and companies assemble compliance teams. Then a scandal, breach, or investigative report reveals that the operational practices changed far less than the legal language suggested. Trust does not merely decline. It curdles, because the public has learned that legal performance may be part of the problem.

A credible limitation should be acknowledged. Enforcement through fines alone is not always the most effective route, and regulators who focus only on punishment can distort their own priorities. Some sectors require guidance, phased adjustment, or standard-setting more than dramatic sanctions. Smaller firms may need clarity more than fear. Public agencies may need redesign support as much as blame. It would be a mistake to imagine that good enforcement always looks punitive or adversarial. In some cases, the most valuable regulatory work happens through audits, consultations, corrective orders, and supervisory dialogue that never produce a headline. Quiet correction can be real correction.

But that limitation reinforces the larger argument. The issue is not whether every violation should end in a fine. It is whether regulated actors believe that non-compliance, evasion, or strategic ambiguity will meet sustained and competent scrutiny. A credible regulator may use guidance first and sanctions later. It may reserve large penalties for recalcitrant or especially harmful conduct. It may push sectors through repeated thematic reviews rather than isolated showpiece cases. The common element is seriousness. Institutions must come to believe that privacy obligations are not optional interpretive gloss but operating constraints that someone with knowledge and authority will revisit until conduct changes.

Public-sector credibility is especially delicate here because the state is regulator and regulated at once. A government that imposes duties on firms while underfunding oversight of its own agencies or drafting expansive exemptions for its own purposes teaches a dangerous lesson. It suggests that privacy law is a tool for disciplining others while preserving executive convenience. This does not only undermine legitimacy. It weakens enforcement culture more broadly. Officials inside regulators absorb the message. Firms do too. If the state exempts itself easily, why should anyone believe that the next privacy rule reflects constitutional principle rather than bargaining power?

Cross-border enforcement adds another layer. Privacy regulation now often functions through cooperation among data protection authorities, adequacy decisions, mutual assistance, and shared standards. This can strengthen the regime by widening oversight and reducing forum shopping. It can also expose inequalities in institutional capacity. A state with a prestigious privacy law but weak supervisory institutions may benefit diplomatically from the law's symbolism while contributing little to collective enforcement. Another with stronger institutions may end up carrying disproportionate practical burdens. Here again, credibility depends not on the elegance of the statute but on the boring question of whether somebody answers the phone, investigates the complaint, and follows the data trail far enough to matter.

The quiet motif of the valve from the previous section is useful again. A privacy rule may define where the valve sits and who nominally controls it. Enforcement determines whether the valve actually closes under pressure. A stuck valve is worse than no valve if everyone believes the system is protected when it is not. Institutions continue to increase pressure on the pipe while the public assumes that law has already contained it. By the time a breach, scandal, or misuse reveals the failure, the very presence of the formal safeguard deepens the sense of betrayal. The mechanism existed. It did not work.

This is why credibility must be understood as cumulative and behavioural. It is built when regulators choose cases wisely, explain decisions clearly, inspect actual practice, impose remedies that can be observed in institutional redesign, and return often enough that targets know the first investigation was not the last time anyone would look. It is weakened when fines are announced without follow-through, when major complaints disappear into procedural fog, when politically sensitive actors are handled with conspicuous caution, or when technical complexity becomes a standing excuse for inaction. The public may not track every enforcement file. It notices the pattern.

The strategic implication is broader than privacy alone. A state that cannot enforce its own data rules convincingly forfeits part of its claim to govern the information economy rather than merely comment on it. Market actors adapt to credible enforcement much more readily than to rhetoric. Foreign governments assess seriousness partly through supervisory practice. Citizens decide whether rights are real not by reading the law but by watching what happens when powerful institutions overstep. Regulatory authority therefore contributes to national power in a quiet but meaningful way. It signals whether the state can turn normative ambition into lived institutional discipline.

The harder question, then, is not whether a privacy regime contains impressive rights or sanctions. Many do. The harder question is whether the institutions behind the regime possess enough resources, expertise, and independence to make those provisions bite repeatedly and fairly, including against actors whose size, political importance, or technical opacity would make a weaker authority retreat. Without that capacity, privacy law becomes a public comfort and a private loophole at once. With it, the law begins to act less like an announcement and more like a governing force. That distinction will determine whether the next claims about rights and protections are heard as assurance or as another carefully drafted delay.

National security exemptions and boundary setting

On 16 July 2020, the Court of Justice of the European Union delivered its judgment in Schrems II and struck down the EU-US Privacy Shield. Much of the public attention focused on transatlantic data transfers. The deeper constitutional issue was plainer and harder: how far could national security claims reach before they consumed the privacy protections that made those transfers lawful in the first place? The case did not assert that states could do without intelligence or lawful access. It forced a sharper question. When a legal order says privacy matters, what exactly remains outside that promise, and who decides how wide the outside should become?

That question sits at the centre of every serious privacy regime. No state writes data protection law on the assumption that intelligence agencies, police, border services, and security institutions can function under the same rules as ordinary commercial actors in every circumstance. Exceptions are inevitable. A government must investigate threats, disrupt espionage, detect plots, and protect critical systems. The trouble begins when inevitability becomes elasticity. National security exemptions are often drafted as necessary escape valves. They can easily become unmarked corridors through which the most ambitious forms of data access travel with the least friction. The label says emergency. The practice becomes routine.

This is why boundary setting matters more than rhetorical commitment. The real political work of privacy law lies not only in the rights it grants or the duties it imposes, but in the shape of the exemptions that qualify them. A narrow exemption may preserve investigative capability without hollowing out the rule. A vague one may allow almost any institutional appetite to describe itself as security-related and thereby evade meaningful scrutiny. The concept here is perimeter design. An exemption is not an accidental hole in an otherwise complete wall. It is part of the structure. The implication is fundamental. A privacy regime is only as credible as the boundaries it draws around its own exceptions.

The first danger is vagueness. Terms such as national security, public safety, public order, serious crime, essential interests, or state security can each be defensible in context. They become dangerous when left undefined enough to absorb ever wider categories of activity. Vagueness gives administrators room to argue that adjacent aims belong inside the exemption because they support the broader security mission. The visible progression is familiar: data access justified for counter-terrorism later assists immigration control, sanctions screening, fraud detection, disorder monitoring, critical infrastructure protection, or political risk analysis. Some of these uses may be legitimate. The problem is that a vague exemption does not force institutions to explain the transition with enough precision for courts, regulators, or the public to judge whether a genuine boundary remains.

This is how mission creep usually enters. It seldom begins with open repudiation of privacy principles. It begins when a dataset, system, or legal authority built for one high-salience purpose proves technically useful in another and the exemption language is loose enough to accommodate the shift. A communications retention rule created in the name of grave threat is soon said to be useful in more ordinary investigations. A border screening dataset begins to support welfare compliance or policing tasks. A cyber defence exception widens into broad visibility over network activity that many unrelated agencies then wish to query. The move can be explained each time as modest, sensible, and temporary. The cumulative result is different. The exception becomes a parallel legal order.

A named example helps fix the point. The history of the United Kingdom's Investigatory Powers framework, especially the long controversies over bulk powers, data retention, and the scope of access available to public authorities, shows how difficult it is to contain expansive security and investigatory claims once technical capability and statutory language begin reinforcing one another. The legal architecture includes warrants, oversight, and review mechanisms, but the public debate has repeatedly returned to the same underlying anxiety: whether powers justified by extreme scenarios gradually become normal tools of administration and investigation. The significance lies not in claiming that all such powers are illegitimate. It lies in observing how much trust depends on whether exemptions appear tightly linked to stated purposes rather than endlessly adaptable.

The second danger lies at the opposite extreme. An exemption drafted too rigidly can obstruct legitimate investigation or intelligence work in ways that are not merely inconvenient, but strategically harmful. Security services do not operate in cleanly bounded worlds where every threat announces itself under the right legal heading. Investigators often need to move quickly across uncertain facts, changing networks, and incomplete evidence. A privacy regime that denies any practical route for exceptional access may force institutions into delay, legal improvisation, or informal workaround. The consequence is not only weaker security. It can also be worse governance, because agencies under operational pressure may begin to treat privacy law as unrealistic and therefore something to be circumvented rather than internalised.

This limitation must be taken seriously if the argument for strong boundaries is to remain credible. A privacy rule that treats every access question as if it were a routine consumer matter will fail to command respect inside security institutions and may not deserve to. The state does possess obligations that justify secrecy, urgency, and, in some contexts, forms of collection and analysis unavailable to ordinary actors. The issue is not whether exemptions should exist. It is whether the law forces those exemptions to remain exceptional in practice by tying them to clear thresholds, competent authorisation, defined use conditions, and meaningful review. Good boundary design is not absolutist. It is discriminating.

The United States offers a useful example of how difficult this discrimination can be. The long controversies around Section 702 of the Foreign Intelligence Surveillance Act illustrate the problem with unusual clarity. Supporters view the authority as an important intelligence tool for collecting foreign intelligence information in a digital environment where communications routes and identities are not neatly territorial. Critics point to incidental collection, querying practices, and the danger that foreign intelligence authorities may become a route to information about citizens and residents that would otherwise face stricter constraints. The dispute is not merely ideological. It is about boundary mechanics: targeting rules, query rules, minimisation, oversight, and the degree to which an authority designed for one class of activity can drift into another through institutional convenience.

This is where interpretation becomes as important as drafting. Legislatures may write exemptions with apparent care, only to discover that agencies, courts, regulators, or ministers interpret key terms in ways that widen or narrow them substantially over time. "Necessary" can become "useful". "Serious threat" can become "material relevance". "National security" can be read narrowly around espionage and terrorism or broadly enough to cover economic resilience, public disorder, foreign influence, critical supply chains, and strategic technology policy. Some expansion may reflect real changes in threat environment. Some reflects institutional incentives. Interpretation is therefore part of boundary design, not an afterthought to it. A narrow statute can still yield a broad exemption culture if the interpreters are deferential and the oversight weak.

The practical question is always the same: who has to explain what, to whom, before the exemption can be used? A meaningful boundary requires more than a legislative phrase. It requires a chain of justification. Which official authorises access? What threshold must be met? Which datasets or systems may be touched? For how long? Under what retention and dissemination rules? Can the rationale later be audited? Are downstream uses restricted to the original purpose, or does the exemption silently legitimise wider reuse? Does a court, commissioner, inspector general, or regulator see enough to test whether the security label was apt? These are not procedural niceties. They are the architecture through which legitimacy survives necessary secrecy.

Oversight bodies matter especially because national security exemptions tend to operate in environments where public transparency is necessarily partial. The public will rarely see the full case for why a power was used. That makes intermediating institutions indispensable. If judges, commissioners, parliamentary committees, or independent inspectors lack technical knowledge, timely access, or political independence, the exemption becomes difficult to contest in practice. The government then ends up asking for trust on the basis of self-description alone. In the short term, that may suffice. In the long term, it produces fragility, because every future disclosure or scandal invites the public to assume that the invisible space behind the exemption has expanded further than officially admitted.

A credible counterpoint deserves attention. Some democratic systems have, at times, managed to write and supervise security exemptions with more discipline than critics assume. Targeted warrant systems, independent commissioners, sunset clauses, ex post review, and minimisation requirements can genuinely narrow the risk of drift. National security and privacy are not always engaged in a zero-sum struggle. In some cases, clear exemptions make privacy law more durable precisely because security institutions know where exceptional access is allowed and do not need to fight every privacy rule as if it threatened their mission. That is an important insight. The point is not to create permanent war between privacy and security. It is to create terms under which both can remain governable.

That said, terms degrade under pressure unless they are regularly renewed. Emergencies, technological shifts, public fear, and geopolitical rivalry all create incentives to widen what counts as security-relevant. The expansion may be defended sincerely. Officials may genuinely believe that old distinctions no longer fit new threats. Sometimes they are right. But institutions also learn from convenience. A power once obtained is rarely abandoned voluntarily if it continues to yield intelligence, investigative speed, or administrative advantage. This is why sunset clauses, periodic review, and public reporting in aggregate matter. They force the state to restate and defend boundaries rather than treating them as settled once written.

The diplomatic dimension should not be overlooked. National security exemptions do not only shape domestic legitimacy. They influence cross-border trust. Data transfer arrangements, adequacy decisions, and mutual recognition frameworks often turn on whether one jurisdiction regards another's security exemptions as too broad, too secretive, or too weakly supervised. The Schrems II judgment made exactly this point in an especially visible way. A state may view its own exemptions as necessary. Others may view the same design as incompatible with meaningful rights. Boundary design therefore becomes a matter of external credibility as well as internal constitutional order. The exemption speaks beyond the state that writes it.

The quiet motif of the line is useful here. Privacy law draws lines around ordinary collection, ordinary processing, ordinary reuse. National security exemptions redraw those lines under pressure. The question is not whether the line moves. It must. The question is whether the line still exists as something institutions can see, justify, and be held to after it moves. A line that no one can describe except by invoking general danger is not much of a line. It is a claim of discretion.

This is why legitimacy depends less on the abstract existence of exemptions than on whether the public can believe that the exemption remains narrower than the rule. That belief is shaped by visible behaviour: how often exemptions are invoked, how candidly their logic is explained in public terms, whether oversight bodies ever say no, whether misuse leads to consequence, and whether powers recede when the justifying emergency does. Citizens do not need full operational detail to judge whether a system appears bounded. They need enough evidence that the state regards the boundary as real rather than as a drafting inconvenience.

The hardest question, then, is not whether national security should override privacy in some cases. It plainly must. The harder question is how a legal order signals that override without teaching every ambitious institution to speak in the language of security whenever ordinary limits become inconvenient. That is a problem of design, interpretation, and institutional character at once. If the exemption becomes the place where pressure always wins, privacy law will survive mainly as rhetoric. If the exemption is drawn too rigidly to accommodate real threat, privacy law may provoke the very evasions that later discredit it. Boundary setting is therefore not a compromise tucked inside the regime. It is one of the main places where the regime proves what kind of state it is trying to build.

Data rights, remedies, and public understanding

In May 2014, the Court of Justice of the European Union ruled in Google Spain that individuals could, in certain circumstances, ask search engines to remove links from name-based search results when those links were inadequate, irrelevant, or no longer relevant. The judgment was quickly reduced in public debate to a catchy phrase - "the right to be forgotten" - but its deeper significance lay elsewhere. A court had not merely declared a value. It had forced the question of what it means for a person to act upon a data-related right in the face of a powerful intermediary whose systems had become part of ordinary memory. The form had to work.

That is the starting point for any serious discussion of data rights. Rights to access, correct, delete, object, or seek redress are often described as protections for the individual against large institutions. They are that. But they are also something more practical and politically revealing: tests of whether a legal order can convert abstract promises into usable leverage. A declared right does little by itself. It becomes real only when an ordinary person can identify the relevant institution, understand what the right means in context, trigger it without specialist help, receive a response that is intelligible, and obtain correction or remedy within a timescale that still matters. Rights that fail this test do not merely disappoint. They teach the public what the law is really for.

This is why operability matters more than rhetorical generosity. A privacy regime may list many rights and still leave individuals functionally powerless if exercising them requires excessive persistence, literacy, technical understanding, or tolerance for bureaucratic delay. The concept here is rights as working tools. A tool that cannot be grasped, or that breaks under ordinary use, does not become noble because it is engraved with good intentions. The same is true of data rights. Their public value lies not mainly in their aspirational language, but in whether they alter institutional behaviour by making challenge possible. A right that can be exercised by only the most informed, confident, and well-resourced subjects will tend to reproduce the inequalities it claims to address.

Access rights are the clearest example because they sit at the threshold of all the others. One cannot correct or delete what one cannot see. One cannot contest a profile, a category, a score, or a decision pathway without some knowledge of what data exist and how they are being used. The visible behaviour matters. A person submits a request and receives something back: a structured file, an unreadable data dump, a legalistic letter, a refusal, or silence. That response teaches an immediate lesson about power. A meaningful access right reveals enough for a person to orient themselves inside the system. A hollow one overwhelms them with raw fields, hides key inferences behind commercial secrecy, or answers in language no ordinary user could turn into action. Transparency that paralyses is a form of refusal.

This is one reason public understanding cannot be treated as an optional civic garnish. Institutions often assume that because a right exists in law, its exercise is merely a matter of individual initiative. That assumption is false. Data systems are complex, terms are specialised, and the social meaning of records is often obscure even to the people affected by them. Many individuals do not know which organisation holds what, which right applies to which context, or whether a troubling outcome arose from error, lawful discretion, automated scoring, stale records, or unlawful processing. A right without public intelligibility therefore remains formally present and socially absent. The institution can continue speaking the language of accountability while the individual struggles even to frame the question.

A named example shows how access rights can nonetheless matter when made usable. The GDPR's data portability and access provisions prompted many firms to build request interfaces that ordinary users could find and activate without litigation. The quality of those interfaces has varied sharply, but the shift itself was revealing. Once law required access in a more systematic way, firms had to organise internal systems around the possibility of being asked. That altered design incentives. It forced data mapping, retention awareness, and, in some cases, more disciplined thinking about why particular categories were being held. The right's value therefore extended beyond the user who clicked "download my data". It worked as a governance device because the firm had to prepare for the click.

Correction rights appear narrower but can be even more significant where records shape opportunity or sanction. A misspelt name is one thing. A wrong address, false debt marker, outdated risk flag, inaccurate immigration note, mistaken watchlist entry, or erroneous welfare record is quite another. Correction matters because data systems often acquire authority precisely by appearing mechanical. A flawed human judgment can sometimes be argued with directly. A flawed database entry tends to travel further and be believed more readily. The concept here is administrative sediment: once an error hardens into a system, it becomes harder to dislodge because other systems begin to rely on it. A correction right is therefore not simply about factual tidiness. It is a means of interrupting the spread of institutional error.

This is especially clear in the public sector. If a benefits record, tax file, immigration register, or criminal justice database contains an error, the effects may cascade across agencies that trust the original source more than the person contesting it. The visible consequence can be denial of service, delay, suspicion, or forced administrative labour by the affected individual. A correction process that is slow, fragmented, or incomprehensible pushes the burden of system repair onto the person least equipped to carry it. A serious correction right, by contrast, obliges the institution to treat the claimant not as an inconvenience to data hygiene but as someone with standing to challenge the state's own memory.

Deletion rights are more politically charged because they confront one of the central instincts of the digital age: keep everything. Institutions retain records because future utility is hard to rule out, storage is cheap, analytics improve, and deletion feels like forfeiture. A deletion right cuts against that instinct by forcing institutions to justify continued retention rather than assuming it. It matters most not where deletion is absolute - it often cannot be, given legal obligations, public records duties, and security needs - but where it changes the default from indefinite accumulation to bounded purpose. The right says, in effect: if you wish to keep this, explain why. That is not anti-memory. It is anti-inertia.

The Google Spain case remains useful here because it showed that deletion-like rights need not always erase underlying records in order to alter power relations meaningfully. Delisting from search results did not rewrite history or destroy newspaper archives. It changed accessibility under a specific mode of search. That distinction is easy to caricature and difficult to govern well, but it reveals something important. Data rights often work by reshaping visibility rather than by abolishing existence. In an information environment where discoverability confers power, modifying how data are surfaced can be as consequential as removing them outright. The law, in that sense, governs attention as much as storage.

A second named example helps expose the difficulty from another angle. The Dutch childcare benefits scandal, which unfolded publicly in the late 2010s and early 2020s, involved tax authorities using risk-based and discriminatory logic in ways that wrongly harmed thousands of families. The scandal was not only about a bad algorithm or a bad rule. It was about the inability of affected people to understand, challenge, and correct the data-driven administrative judgments being made about them before devastating consequences had already followed. The right to redress mattered less in the abstract than the fact that it arrived too late and through a system that had made itself difficult to question. This is why remedies belong inside the architecture of trust rather than after it.

Redress is the point where a right demonstrates whether it can force institutional consequence. An access request may produce information. A correction request may amend a record. A deletion request may narrow future exposure. None of these is sufficient if the individual has already suffered harm and the institution faces no meaningful obligation to explain, apologise, compensate, redesign, or alter downstream consequences. The concept is remedial credibility. A regime without usable redress invites the public to learn that rights exist mainly for the well-informed and the unharmed. By the time the ordinary person reaches the point of formal remedy, the opportunity, service, reputation, or administrative standing at issue may already be gone.

This is why public literacy and remedy are linked. A system can proclaim rights and still deter their use if complaint routes are obscure, time limits are unclear, forms are intimidating, legal language is dense, and outcomes are delayed beyond usefulness. Literacy here does not mean asking every citizen to become a privacy lawyer. It means designing rights around realistic user capacities. Is the route visible? Is the explanation plain? Is the institution obliged to answer in terms a non-specialist can understand? Are support organisations, ombuds offices, or regulators accessible enough to bridge the gap when the first-line controller refuses? Operability lives in these design choices.

A credible limitation must be acknowledged. Not every data right can be absolute or universally simple. Public records obligations, free expression, scientific research, fraud prevention, and national security all create contexts in which access, correction, deletion, or disclosure must be qualified. Some systems are genuinely complex, and some rights claims conflict with other legitimate interests. It would be unserious to imagine a world in which every record can be deleted on request or every algorithm fully opened without trade-offs. Rights design must therefore discriminate among contexts rather than pretending that one clean answer can govern them all.

But that limitation does not rescue regimes in which rights are mostly decorative. The serious question is whether qualifications are narrow, intelligible, and reviewable, or whether they function as a standing excuse for institutional opacity. A person can accept that some data cannot be erased if the institution can explain why, show what remains possible instead, and offer a route to review. People tolerate limits better than indifference. The corrosive case is not the qualified right. It is the right that collapses into procedural fog whenever it threatens to inconvenience power.

This becomes especially important as data rights increasingly mediate the legitimacy of both public and private institutions. A platform that responds clearly to access and deletion requests may build more trust than one that offers grand language and baffling workflows. A welfare agency that corrects records promptly and explains decisions plainly may preserve legitimacy even under difficult conditions. A tax authority, hospital, or university that forces individuals into endless loops of referral and silence teaches a different lesson: that the institution's data are more important than the person's standing before them. Rights are where legitimacy becomes tactile.

The same is true internationally. Privacy regimes are now judged not only by the existence of rights, but by whether those rights are usable enough to support cross-border trust. Adequacy decisions, transfer mechanisms, and diplomatic claims about data protection all depend partly on whether individuals have meaningful routes to challenge misuse and obtain remedy. A jurisdiction can publish impressive statutes and still look untrustworthy if practical redress is too remote, too expensive, too technical, or too deferential to the institutions being challenged. Operable rights therefore contribute to national power in a quiet but real sense. They help make a legal order legible and acceptable to others.

The quiet motif of the form is useful here. A form can be a gateway or a maze. It can invite a person into a process that genuinely responds, or it can be a ritual by which institutions exhaust claimants while preserving the appearance of openness. Data rights live or die in forms, interfaces, help pages, response letters, and complaint routes. The law may reside in statutes and judgments, but the citizen encounters it in menus, deadlines, and explanatory text. That mundane encounter is where trust is made or lost.

The harder question, then, is not whether a privacy regime recognises rights. Many now do. The harder question is whether those rights can be exercised by ordinary people before harm becomes irreversible, and whether their exercise changes institutional conduct rather than merely generating paperwork. A state or firm that wants trust cannot rely on declarations alone. It must show that when a person asks to see, fix, remove, or challenge what has been done with their data, the answer comes back in a form that redistributes power rather than explaining why power must remain where it already sits. That is the threshold at which rights stop being moral ornaments and become part of governance.

Regulatory competition and diplomatic spillovers

On 25 May 2018, the European Union's General Data Protection Regulation came into force across the bloc. The immediate consequences were familiar enough: privacy notices multiplied, compliance teams expanded, contracts were rewritten, and firms serving European users recalculated what data they could justify collecting and moving. The larger consequence was geopolitical. A regional privacy regime had become a global reference point. States outside the Union did not need to copy it word for word to feel its presence. They only needed firms within their borders to want access to European markets, or policymakers to decide that the language of rights, adequacy, and accountability now offered a useful vocabulary for their own political aims. The rule crossed the border before the data did.

That is the core of regulatory competition in privacy. States do not only compete over tax, labour, investment, and industrial policy. They also compete over the legal design of information order. A privacy regime can become a model, a warning, a bargaining chip, or a diplomatic instrument depending on how credible it is, how large the market behind it may be, and how far firms must adapt to remain inside it. The competition is not merely ideological. It is institutional and commercial. A law that changes how firms store records, design interfaces, write contracts, and justify transfers is already shaping market structure. Once other governments notice that effect, privacy regulation stops looking like a domestic moral settlement and starts to look like statecraft.

This is why privacy regimes travel in different ways. Some are adopted because local reformers admire their rights language or institutional logic. Some are adapted selectively, taking the parts that strengthen domestic control while leaving aside the parts that empower individuals too much for local political taste. Some are resisted explicitly, not because they are irrelevant, but because they threaten existing models of state access, platform governance, or economic advantage. The concept here is normative circulation. A privacy law may begin as one jurisdiction's attempt to govern its own information economy and then become a template that others copy, trim, harden, or reject in ways that reveal their own priorities. What travels is not just a statute. It is a theory of who should hold power over data, under what conditions, and with what forms of public accountability.

A named example makes this visible. Brazil's Lei Geral de Protecao de Dados, which took effect in 2020, was shaped in part by international privacy debates and by the perceived need to provide a coherent framework that would support both domestic governance and international trust. The result was not a simple export of European law into Latin America. It was a process of adaptation through local institutions, political pressures, and economic calculation. That distinction matters. Regulatory influence rarely works through mechanical replication. It works through selective borrowing. A state takes what fits its administrative ambitions, its constitutional language, its diplomatic needs, and its market strategy. The law arrives wearing local clothes.

This is where adequacy decisions become especially significant. An adequacy decision says, in effect, that another jurisdiction's privacy protections are trustworthy enough for personal data to move there without extraordinary friction under the originating regime's rules. That sounds technical. It is deeply political. To grant adequacy is to recognise not merely a set of legal clauses, but a broader institutional order: supervisory authorities, remedies, limits on state access, enforcement practices, and the practical seriousness of rights. The visible result is smoother data transfer. The strategic implication is diplomatic recognition through regulatory means. A jurisdiction judged adequate gains easier access to a market and a measure of legal legitimacy in the eyes of the granting bloc. A jurisdiction denied adequacy receives the opposite message, however politely phrased.

This transforms privacy into a lever of market access. Firms prefer legal certainty. Governments know this. If access to a major market depends on the adequacy or comparability of a jurisdiction's privacy regime, then that regime becomes part of economic strategy rather than a separate rights conversation. A government seeking investment, cloud partnerships, research collaboration, financial services integration, or platform presence has reason to ask whether its privacy law helps or hinders recognition abroad. The law's audience is no longer only domestic courts and citizens. It includes foreign regulators, multinational compliance teams, and trading partners evaluating whether shared data flows will be politically and legally stable. Privacy becomes part of export infrastructure.

The European Union has made this especially plain, not because it is uniquely virtuous, but because its combination of market size and regulatory density gives its privacy judgments unusual force. When Brussels treats adequacy as conditional on meaningful limits to surveillance, independent supervisory institutions, and usable remedies, those standards radiate outward. Governments beyond Europe may resent the posture, adapt to it, or both. The important point is that privacy law is now one of the ways a regional bloc projects normative influence without deploying military force or traditional trade sanctions. The passport is regulatory. The border is legal confidence.

Yet regulatory competition is not a one-directional story of European diffusion. Other states and regions have begun to develop their own privacy frameworks not only in imitation but in strategic distinction. Some want regimes compatible enough with powerful blocs to preserve transfer pathways while retaining more state flexibility over security exemptions or domestic industrial policy. Others want to demonstrate sovereignty by resisting imported rights language and advancing different balances between user protection, platform control, and national authority. The competition is therefore not between privacy and no privacy. It is among different privacy settlements, each embedding a different understanding of permissible collection, enforcement seriousness, exemption breadth, and the political role of the regulator. The field is crowded now.

This is why mutual recognition arrangements matter as much as formal adequacy decisions. States and blocs often seek ways to reduce friction without fully harmonising their laws. They negotiate sectoral agreements, standard contractual mechanisms, interoperability frameworks, and supervisory cooperation that allow transfers or cross-border operations under managed conditions. These instruments can be useful and often necessary. They are also diplomatic tools. They allow governments to signal trust incrementally, preserve commercial exchange, and avoid the binary symbolism of full recognition or total refusal. But they can also conceal unresolved differences. A mutual recognition mechanism may smooth immediate tensions while leaving deeper conflicts over surveillance, redress, and enforcement to resurface later. The bridge holds. The foundations still differ.

A second named example lies in the repeated instability of transatlantic transfer arrangements between the European Union and the United States, from Safe Harbor to Privacy Shield and beyond. The legal forms changed, and the diplomatic language changed with them. The underlying issue kept returning: whether US surveillance law and available remedies were compatible enough with European rights standards to justify stable data movement. The importance of these disputes was never only commercial, though commerce felt the strain. They showed that privacy regimes can become recurring diplomatic questions even among close allies. Shared strategic interests do not automatically produce shared thresholds of legal trust. Privacy law, in that sense, acts as a persistent test of how far alliance can smooth constitutional divergence.

A credible limitation should be acknowledged. Not every state adopts or adapts privacy regulation because it has been normatively persuaded by another jurisdiction's rights discourse. Some do so for instrumental reasons: to attract investment, to satisfy trading partners, to modernise administrative practice, or to gain leverage against foreign platforms. A law may resemble a respected model externally while functioning quite differently in enforcement, exemptions, or user remedy. Regulatory competition can therefore reward mimicry as well as substance. A state can speak the language of rights without building the institutions that make rights real. Privacy diplomacy is vulnerable to surface convergence.

But that limitation does not weaken the larger argument. It clarifies the terrain on which real influence operates. A regime becomes powerful not merely when others copy its text, but when they feel compelled to justify deviations from its assumptions, negotiate with its institutions, or reshape domestic practice to preserve access to markets governed by it. That is the deeper meaning of normative influence. A standard matters when others must position themselves relative to it, even if they do so through adaptation or resistance rather than imitation. Privacy regulation now does this. It structures the menu of respectable digital governance.

This has competitive implications inside markets as well. Firms able to comply with high-standard privacy regimes can use that capacity as a commercial asset. They advertise trustworthy processing, local compliance options, audited controls, and transfer-ready structures. Smaller firms may struggle to match that signalling even where their actual data practices are less extractive. Compliance thus becomes both a burden and a moat. Regulatory competition among states spills into competition among firms, and the border between the two can become thin. A government that exports a privacy model may indirectly strengthen the global position of firms already adapted to that model. Regulation is never only rights architecture. It is also industrial terrain.

The same applies to cloud, standards, and procurement, which is why privacy diplomacy cannot be separated from the rest of the book's argument. A privacy regime influences which cloud arrangements appear trustworthy, which technical standards are treated as acceptable, which audit models gain favour, and which procurement clauses become ordinary in both public and private contracts. Adequacy and recognition are therefore not free-floating legal concepts. They rest on views about encryption, access logging, oversight, vendor risk, and lawful process. The diplomatic spillover of privacy law reaches into system design. It shapes what kinds of infrastructure and organisational practice are regarded as politically admissible across borders.

Public legitimacy also travels through these regimes. When a state seeks adequacy or mutual recognition, it is not only asking that its firms be allowed to move data more easily. It is asking other jurisdictions to trust something about its domestic legal order. Does it constrain state access credibly? Does it offer independent supervision? Can individuals complain and receive remedy? Are exemptions narrow enough to preserve the meaning of the rule? These are not technical checkboxes. They are judgements about institutional character. Privacy diplomacy therefore forces states to confront what their laws say about themselves as well as what they demand of others.

The quiet motif of the passport is useful here. A passport does not erase borders. It tells other authorities something about the order that issued it and asks them to treat its bearer accordingly. Privacy regimes increasingly work in much the same way. They grant data, firms, and institutions a kind of regulatory passport - but only if the issuing state's legal order is trusted enough by others. Some passports move easily. Some are scrutinised. Some are refused. The value of the passport depends not only on the document, but on the reputation of the issuing authority.

That is why regulatory competition in privacy has become a form of national power. A state or bloc that can set terms others must consider gains more than legal prestige. It gains leverage over market access, influence over institutional design abroad, and a voice in defining what counts as legitimate digital governance. This is not absolute power, and it is not always benign. It can become paternalistic, self-serving, or unevenly enforced. But it is power all the same, exercised through rules that decide who may move data across borders with confidence and who must live under permanent qualification.

The harder question, then, is not whether privacy regimes influence one another. They plainly do. The harder question is what kind of international order this competition is building. Will it produce a more plural but still interoperable world in which jurisdictions can differ without breaking every bridge? Or will privacy become another front in a wider fragmentation of the digital economy, where recognition is scarce, transfers are precarious, and every major market seeks to make others adapt to its preferred balance of rights, state access, and institutional trust? That question matters because once privacy becomes statecraft, every regulatory choice speaks in two directions at once: inward to the citizen, and outward to the world.

Chapter 10

Markets, Competition, and Data Control

What kind of market is being governed when the most important asset is not only price, product, or scale, but the ability to learn faster than rivals from the behaviour of millions of people? Traditional competition policy was built for industries where dominance could be seen in factories, pipelines, rail lines, shop shelves, or merger balance sheets. Data-driven markets do not erase those older structures, but they add a new one: control over the feedback loops through which firms observe, predict, and refine conduct. The result is a form of power that often looks convenient to users long before it looks dangerous to regulators.

That is why concentration in digital markets rarely arrives as a simple story of one firm charging too much for one service. It arrives as a system of reinforcement. A platform attracts users because many others are already there. It improves because those users generate more behavioural traces. It expands into adjacent services because the resulting data make prediction, targeting, recommendation, and risk management cheaper and more effective there too. What begins as success in one line of business starts to reshape several others. The market no longer turns only on who produces best. It turns on who can see most, infer most, and keep that advantage compounding.

This creates the chapter's central tension. States want markets that remain competitive, innovative, and open enough to support domestic capability. They also want secure infrastructures, trusted services, and institutions capable of governing concentrated digital power without accidentally deepening dependence on the very firms they seek to discipline. Breaking concentration may increase rivalry and choice. It may also complicate security, interoperability, and administrative coherence if done crudely. Supporting domestic firms may strengthen resilience or simply create protected weakness. The issue is not whether markets should be left alone or directed from above. It is how to organise competition when data control itself has become a strategic resource.

The stakes reach well beyond consumer welfare. Behavioural data now influence credit, logistics, labour management, cloud architecture, health technology, advertising, retail, transport, and public administration. A firm that commands a large behavioural reservoir does not merely understand its own customers better. It can shape standards, procurement expectations, research priorities, and the practical terms on which other firms enter the market. It may also become indispensable to the state as supplier, contractor, or technical partner. Market concentration, then, does not remain confined to economics. It spills into sovereignty. A government that relies on a handful of data-rich firms for cloud, analytics, identity, or secure communications is governing through a market structure it may no longer meaningfully direct.

This is why industrial policy returns in altered form. The question is no longer simply whether a state should back "national champions" in the old style. That language is too blunt for data-intensive sectors where success depends on research depth, procurement design, cloud access, skilled labour, standards participation, and the mundane reliability of public institutions. A state may spend lavishly and still fail if it cannot act as a serious customer, regulator, and coordinator. It may refuse industrial policy rhetorically while practising it anyway through public contracts, technical standards, university funding, and mission-oriented demand. The more useful distinction is not between free market and state intervention. It is between institutional design that cultivates durable capability and political theatre that mistakes branding for strategy.

Competition tools therefore look different here too. Portability and interoperability mandates can widen choice, lower switching costs, and prevent dominant firms from treating user relationships as private property. They can also create fresh security and privacy risks if the interfaces are poorly specified, the incentives misaligned, or the compliance burden structured in ways only the largest firms can absorb. A market made more contestable on paper may become more fragile in practice if the mechanisms of opening it expose users, weaken accountability, or entrench new intermediaries. Competition and security are often treated as rival values in digital policy. More often they are engineering problems that must be solved together or they will fail together.

None of this works without people. Engineers, statisticians, auditors, procurement specialists, investigators, product managers, and policy staff determine whether laws become architecture or remain aspiration. Public institutions often speak grandly about digital capacity while treating talent as an afterthought: underpaid, outsourced, rotated too quickly, or trapped in career structures that do not reward technical depth. Private firms know better. They compete for scarce expertise because they understand that institutional memory and operational competence are forms of capital. States that neglect this lesson end up buying what they cannot build, regulating what they cannot fully inspect, and announcing strategies that no one inside the machinery can actually deliver.

The path ahead follows that chain of dependence. It begins with the economic logic through which data concentration produces platform advantage and then moves into the harder question of how states try to cultivate domestic capability without falling into slogans about prestige or protection. From there it turns to the legal and technical tools used to open markets back up, asking how rivalry can be encouraged without degrading privacy, security, or public trust, before arriving at the human foundations of all of it: the skills, careers, and institutional memory that determine whether market governance exists anywhere beyond speeches and white papers.

A useful image for the chapter is the flywheel. Once it turns, each rotation makes the next easier: more users, more data, better prediction, more adjacent expansion, stronger bargaining power, deeper lock-in. States often confront data markets only after the flywheel is already spinning fast enough to look like nature rather than policy. They are then tempted either to smash it dramatically or to shelter a domestic version of it and hope that national ownership will make concentration less politically troubling. Neither instinct is reliable. The real task is to understand who built the flywheel, who can slow it, who benefits from its speed, and which public institutions are strong enough to govern its momentum without pretending that momentum itself is a strategy.

The harder question, then, is not whether data markets should be more competitive or more secure. They must be both, and the price of treating those goals separately is usually failure in both domains. The harder question is what kind of state can keep behavioural power from hardening into permanent market rule while still building the domestic capacity needed to avoid dependence on foreign incumbents. That question leads directly to the first issue: how data concentration becomes platform advantage, and why the competitive consequences extend far beyond the firms that first appear to hold the data.

Data concentration and platform advantage

In August 2012, Facebook acquired Instagram, a company then still small enough in public imagination to look like an app rather than a strategic position. The transaction was discussed at the time in terms familiar to technology reporting: growth, mobile photographs, youthful users, social media rivalry. Its longer significance was economic. A firm that already possessed extraordinary reach into social behaviour was buying not only a product, but another stream of human attention, another flow of behavioural signals, another place where future habits could be observed before rivals could build around them. The deal was about more than photographs. It was about seeing more of life in one corporate field of vision.

That is the correct place to begin because data concentration does not usually announce itself as monopoly in the old industrial style. It rarely arrives with a single dominant factory, rail network, or oilfield. It grows through behaviour. A platform attracts users because others are already there. Those users generate data as they search, click, pause, share, buy, move, watch, rate, and compare. The platform then uses those signals to improve recommendation, targeting, ranking, fraud detection, pricing, logistics, moderation, and product design. The service becomes more useful or more addictive, often both. More users arrive. More data accumulate. The flywheel turns again.

This is the first mechanism: network effects. A network effect exists when a service becomes more valuable as more people use it. In a messaging service, the logic is obvious: one joins because friends, colleagues, and family are already present. In a marketplace, more buyers attract more sellers, and more sellers attract more buyers. In a search engine, more queries and more clicks generate better signals about relevance. The concept itself is not new. What matters in data-intensive markets is that network effects and data effects increasingly reinforce one another. The larger platform is not only socially more useful. It is also informationally more capable. Each additional user improves not just the network's scale, but the platform's understanding of how the network behaves.

The visible consequence is a market that becomes harder to contest even when consumers pay no explicit price. A new entrant may build a technically elegant service and still struggle because it lacks the behavioural reservoir that allows the incumbent to rank, predict, personalise, and optimise with far greater confidence. The incumbent appears more convenient because it has already watched more people make more choices across more contexts. This is why data concentration cannot be reduced to raw volume alone. What matters is repeated, structured, context-rich observation linked to the ability to turn signals into operational advantage. A platform that sees what users do across search, maps, payments, email, browsing, devices, and cloud services does not merely possess "more data". It possesses a more complete behavioural picture.

Switching costs deepen the problem. These costs are not confined to money. They include time, habit, social loss, compatibility trouble, credential migration, retraining, loss of history, and fear that a new service will not work as smoothly. A person may dislike a dominant platform and still remain because all their contacts are there, because their files are stored in proprietary formats, because their business depends on visibility inside that ecosystem, or because leaving would mean rebuilding years of routine. Firms face the same trap. A retailer relying on one marketplace's analytics, fulfilment tools, and advertising systems does not switch lightly. A public agency running on one cloud stack, one identity layer, and one analytics environment discovers that exit is not a button. It is a programme of institutional disruption.

This is the second mechanism of concentration. Once behaviour, social connection, and workflow are deeply embedded, the incumbent's advantage becomes self-reinforcing even if its service quality deteriorates or its prices rise indirectly through advertising dependence, worse terms for business users, or tighter control over adjacent markets. The user sees one interface. Underneath sits a thicket of dependencies. The service has become not only popular but infrastructural. That matters because competition policy built for simpler switching assumptions can miss the depth of entrapment in data-intensive markets. People do not only use the platform. They build life and work inside it.

Vertical integration adds a third layer. A dominant firm that controls several stages of the same digital chain can collect behavioural signals at each stage and use them to strengthen the whole. A company may operate the operating system, the app store, the payment rail, the advertising network, the cloud environment, the recommendation engine, and the hardware itself. Each layer generates its own data. Combined, those layers produce something more valuable than their sum: a map of habits across contexts. The firm can observe not only what a user buys, but where they discovered it, how long they considered it, what device they used, what payment method they preferred, and what other behaviours correlated with the final decision. This is not merely efficiency. It is informational enclosure.

A named example helps clarify the scale of this shift. Amazon's growth beyond online retail into logistics, cloud computing, marketplace infrastructure, advertising, and smart devices made it something more than a shop. It became an observing system distributed across commerce and infrastructure. A merchant selling through Amazon does not simply gain access to customers. The platform also gains insight into demand patterns, pricing behaviour, fulfilment performance, inventory movement, and product response across categories. When a firm sits at once as marketplace host, cloud provider, advertising intermediary, logistics coordinator, and consumer-facing brand, it occupies a strategic vantage point few rivals can match. The advantage is not any single line of business. It is the ability to learn across them.

This is why access to behavioural data shapes sectors far beyond advertising. Advertising remains the most discussed case because it made the early economics of tracking visible. Yet the same observational advantage now affects finance, healthcare technology, retail, transport, labour management, insurance, cybersecurity, and public administration. Behavioural data help firms predict churn, detect anomalies, rank job applicants, target loans, optimise delivery routes, score fraud, anticipate maintenance, personalise prices, and design interfaces that guide user conduct. A platform that has learned how people behave in one domain can often transfer that knowledge, or at least the technical systems built from it, into another. The data do not always travel directly. The advantage does.

This is where the phrase "data monopoly" becomes tempting and also slightly misleading. It is useful because it captures the fact that some firms acquire privileged control over the behavioural raw material from which market power can be extended. It is misleading if it suggests that monopoly means one company literally owns all relevant data in a sector. In practice, concentration works through asymmetry rather than total possession. One firm need not know everything. It only needs to know enough more than rivals, and to know it in more reusable forms, for the competitive gap to widen over time. The relevant economic lens is not absolute exclusivity. It is compounding informational advantage.

The attraction of this lens is that it explains why price alone often fails as a diagnostic. A service may appear free or cheap to users while still consolidating extraordinary power. Search, navigation, messaging, social networking, or productivity tools may not charge consumers directly, yet they can still create concentrated markets because users pay with dependency, exposure, behavioural trace, and reduced exit options. Meanwhile business users may face rising costs through advertising auctions, platform fees, ranking dependence, or demands to buy ancillary services to remain visible. A consumer-focused competition test that asks only whether prices have risen may therefore miss the more important question: who controls the behavioural infrastructure through which other firms must now reach customers?

A credible limitation should be stated plainly. Data concentration does not always produce unassailable dominance. Some data are perishable, context-specific, or easily replicated. In certain markets, innovation, regulation, consumer shifts, or technological change can erode incumbent advantage more quickly than pessimists assume. Large firms can also become clumsy, bureaucratic, and overextended. More data are not automatically better if they are noisy, poorly governed, or disconnected from a useful business model. A small specialist firm with sharper focus may outperform a giant in specific tasks despite the giant's broader reservoirs of information. It would be simplistic to claim that any platform with a great deal of data must inevitably dominate forever.

But that limitation does not weaken the structural argument. It refines it. The real issue is not whether data alone guarantee monopoly. They do not. The issue is whether network effects, switching costs, and vertical integration allow certain firms to turn behavioural observation into durable strategic advantage across multiple markets. When they do, competition becomes harder not because rivals cannot code a service, but because they cannot reproduce the social graph, the recommendation history, the logistics data, the trust signals, the identity layer, or the organisational knowledge extracted from years of repeated interaction. The incumbent's advantage sits partly in its servers and partly in the habits it has trained users and business customers to treat as normal.

This also explains why data concentration has political as well as economic consequences. A firm that mediates attention, commerce, cloud storage, identity, or mobility at large scale becomes difficult for the state to ignore and difficult to discipline. Regulators rely on its disclosures. Public agencies procure from it. Political actors campaign through its interfaces.

Researchers depend on its access terms. Media outlets adjust to its ranking logic. The market leader becomes part of the environment in which policy itself is made. That is why "platform advantage" is a more revealing phrase than "market share" in many digital sectors. The platform shapes the terms under which everyone else acts.

The labour dimension matters too, though it is often missed in discussions of concentration. Data-rich firms do not only accumulate behavioural insight. They attract engineers, researchers, product managers, economists, security specialists, and legal teams who know how to convert that insight into durable systems. Talent follows data because data-rich environments offer more learning, more experimentation, and often more money. The result is a second-order concentration: the skills needed to challenge dominant platforms cluster inside them. Rivals, regulators, and public institutions then struggle not only against the incumbent's dataset, but against its accumulated human understanding of how to use that dataset well.

The quiet motif of the flywheel is useful because it captures both the power and the danger of these markets. A flywheel stores momentum. Once it turns fast enough, it seems to sustain itself. Data-rich platforms operate the same way. More users generate more data; more data improve the service; a better service attracts more users and business partners; greater scale attracts more talent and capital; stronger integration raises switching costs; higher switching costs stabilise the flow of data. None of this requires conspiracy. It is the ordinary logic of accumulation in a market where behavioural visibility has become a productive asset.

That logic does not mean that every large platform should automatically be broken up or every integrated service treated as suspect. Some integration creates genuine user benefit, stronger security, and lower transaction costs. Some data use supports fraud prevention, accessibility, and better service quality. The problem begins when these real benefits are used to obscure the degree to which concentration has altered the competitive baseline. A market may still look dynamic from the outside - new apps appear, investments continue, acquisitions multiply - while the underlying terms of success have narrowed around firms already controlling the richest behavioural loops.

The harder question, then, is not whether data are valuable. That is obvious. It is how to judge when behavioural data have ceased to be one input among many and have become a barrier so central that competition, innovation, and even state autonomy begin to bend around the firms that hold them. Once that threshold is crossed, the issue is no longer merely whether one platform is too large. It is whether an entire market structure has been built on observational privilege that others cannot realistically match without the intervention of law, policy, or institutional redesign. That is where the economic analysis must lead before any serious political choice can begin.

Industrial policy for data ecosystems

In 2013, when the Central Intelligence Agency awarded a landmark cloud contract to Amazon Web Services in the United States, the immediate story was about procurement and classified computing. The deeper story was about industrial policy by other means. A public institution with unusual demands and unusual purchasing power did not simply buy a service. It helped validate an architecture, strengthen a supplier, shape a market, and signal that certain technical capabilities now counted as strategically serious. The tender did not wave a flag. It still built a sector.

That is the right place to begin because industrial policy in data-intensive markets is too often discussed in slogans about sovereignty, innovation, or national champions. Those slogans conceal more than they reveal. Data ecosystems do not become nationally capable because a minister declares them important or because a government anoints a favoured firm. They become capable when a state learns how to align research, procurement, standards, finance, and institutional demand in ways that reward competence rather than rhetoric. The crucial question is not whether the state intervenes. It always does, whether openly or through quieter mechanisms. The real question is how it intervenes, on whose behalf, and with what kind of discipline.

This matters because data ecosystems differ from older industrial sectors in a politically important way. Their success depends not only on factories, patents, or export markets, but on infrastructures of trust, reuse, and organisational learning. A capable data ecosystem needs research institutions that generate methods and talent, public and private buyers willing to adopt emerging services, standards that make integration possible, regulators that are predictable enough to support investment, and public agencies competent enough to act as demanding customers rather than confused supplicants. The concept here is coordinated demand. The state does not merely subsidise supply. It helps make a market in which useful capability can mature.

Research funding is often the most visible lever because it is easiest to announce. Governments fund laboratories, university centres, fellowships, testbeds, innovation missions, and strategic research programmes in areas such as cybersecurity, data science, privacy engineering, digital identity, and trusted cloud services. This matters. A country that neglects the upstream generation of methods and skilled people will struggle later to govern or supply advanced digital systems. But research funding alone rarely produces durable ecosystem strength. The path from laboratory to operational deployment is full of institutional gaps. Promising tools fail to travel because procurement is rigid, agencies cannot specify what they need, or promising firms die in the valley between prototype and public contract. Money enters. Capability leaks out.

This is why procurement is so often the decisive lever. Procurement can look dull compared with venture capital, flagship research programmes, or speeches about technological leadership. It is often more important. When the state acts as a serious anchor customer, it gives emerging firms revenue, reference cases, operational feedback, and the confidence that a domestic market exists for products meeting real public needs. The phrase *anchor customer* is not a metaphor of prestige. It describes a concrete function. A government that buys secure digital services intelligently can help a firm survive long enough to improve, hire, and compete more widely. A government that buys badly can trap the same firm in endless pilots, impossible tender requirements, or politically driven contracts that teach the wrong lessons.

The difference between those paths lies in institutional design. A state that wants domestic capability must know what it is buying, why it is buying it, and how to write requirements that reward substance. That sounds obvious. It is rare. Public procurement often favours incumbents because incumbents know how to answer compliance questionnaires, absorb liability demands, and navigate lengthy bid processes. Smaller or newer firms may have technically better products and still fail because the state writes tenders as if it were purchasing mature office furniture rather than emerging strategic capability. The visible behaviour is familiar: bids ask for years of prior public-sector experience, large insurance cover, exhaustive certifications, and integration with legacy systems no outsider could understand without prior incumbency. Procurement says it wants innovation. The paperwork says otherwise.

A named example from Estonia helps show another path. Estonia's digital governance model did not emerge from one heroic national champion. It emerged from sustained state-building around identity, interoperability, public service digitisation, and a relatively coherent institutional willingness to use public demand to shape the market for secure digital services. The lesson is not that Estonia offers a universally exportable template. It does not. The lesson is that state capability matters more than nationalist branding. Governments cultivate ecosystems successfully when they define demanding but usable standards, purchase strategically, build internal technical competence, and allow firms to grow through solving real public problems rather than through political favour alone.

Standards are the quieter infrastructure of this process. They decide whether services can connect, whether credentials are portable, whether data can move safely, whether compliance is legible, and whether smaller firms can plug into a wider architecture without bespoke integration for every contract. Industrial policy for data ecosystems therefore works partly through standard-setting. A state that shapes trusted standards around identity, security logging, interoperability, privacy-preserving data use, or procurement evidence is shaping the field in which firms compete. The concept is market choreography. Standards do not choose the winner directly. They decide what kinds of capabilities are legible and valuable enough to win. That is why standards policy and industrial policy are often the same conversation wearing different clothes.

This also explains why slogans about national champions are so unreliable. They are attractive because they compress a complex problem into a single image: find or build a powerful domestic firm, support it aggressively, and let it stand for national capability. That strategy may work occasionally in sectors with high fixed capital and clear export structures. In data ecosystems, it often creates distortion. One firm becomes politically favoured, procurement narrows around it, criticism is softened in the name of sovereignty, and the domestic market grows less contestable. The protected firm then learns to perform strategic importance rather than to earn it. A weak state often mistakes this for success because the company is large, visible, and national. The deeper ecosystem remains thin.

A credible limitation should be acknowledged. Large firms are not always signs of policy failure. In some data-intensive sectors, scale really does matter. Cloud services, semiconductors, telecommunications equipment, cybersecurity tooling, and advanced analytics often require deep capital, long time horizons, and operational breadth that smaller players cannot always sustain. A state may need some large domestic firms or at least some large trusted suppliers to avoid total dependence on foreign incumbents.

It would be childish to pretend that every concentrated outcome is a pathology or that every policy should privilege fragmentation for its own sake.

But that limitation strengthens the main argument rather than weakening it. The issue is not whether scale matters. It is whether scale emerges inside a disciplined ecosystem or inside a politically sheltered one. A disciplined ecosystem still permits scrutiny, competition at the margins, open standards where possible, and procurement rules that do not assume the national champion should win by default. A sheltered ecosystem substitutes patriotic vocabulary for institutional seriousness. It confuses ownership with capability and visibility with resilience. When stress arrives, the difference becomes clear. One system has several firms, skills pipelines, and public institutions capable of acting intelligently. The other has a logo.

The public sector's own digital competence is therefore part of industrial policy whether governments admit it or not. A ministry that cannot write a good technical specification, evaluate a security claim, manage a pilot, or retain skilled staff is incapable of cultivating a healthy ecosystem because it cannot distinguish real capability from sophisticated salesmanship. The result is familiar. The state outsources judgment as well as delivery, relies heavily on large consultancies or dominant vendors, and loses the ability to act as an intelligent buyer. This is not neutral. It shapes the domestic market by rewarding those best able to manage bureaucratic weakness. Industrial policy fails not only when it backs the wrong firms, but when the state is too institutionally thin to know what a good firm looks like.

A second named example lies in the long role of the United States federal government as a customer for advanced computing, networking, and security-related services. The state did not always proceed coherently, and much of its contracting has reinforced concentration as well as innovation. Still, the broader historical pattern is instructive. Defence, intelligence, civilian research agencies, and procurement bodies have repeatedly helped create or stabilise markets by buying demanding technologies early, funding research linked to real operational needs, and normalising standards that later travelled into commercial life. The point is not to romanticise that record. It is to recognise that data ecosystems do not spring from entrepreneurial talent alone. They are often cultivated by public demand that is technically serious enough to matter.

This is where secure digital services offer a particularly useful case. Many governments now want trusted cloud, identity, cybersecurity, data-sharing, and privacy-enhancing services without depending entirely on a handful of foreign hyperscalers or dominant platforms. The temptation is to declare a sovereign alternative and hope that naming the ambition helps build the market. The harder but more promising route is to become a disciplined buyer. Government can specify security, auditability, portability, privacy safeguards, and continuity needs in ways that allow capable firms to compete while also creating a domestic reference market. This works best when tenders are staged sensibly, interoperability is required, lock-in is constrained, and technical teams inside government are empowered enough to learn from procurement rather than merely administer it.

Labour, again, sits underneath everything. A data ecosystem is not a pile of start-ups plus a ministerial strategy. It is a social structure of engineers, statisticians, auditors, product managers, cyber specialists, procurement officials, standards experts, and public-interest technologists who circulate through institutions and accumulate operational memory. Research funding without career pathways pushes talent abroad or into a few dominant firms. Procurement without internal expertise rewards superficial compliance. Standards without capable participation become imported rules. Industrial policy is therefore also a policy about where technically literate people can build long careers without having to choose between political frustration and private monopoly.

The quiet motif of the anchor helps hold the argument together. An anchor does not drive the ship forward by itself. It provides stability, reference, and holding power in uncertain water. The state can play that role in a data ecosystem. By funding demanding research, buying wisely, setting usable standards, and retaining institutional competence, it gives firms and public institutions something to build around. But an anchor can also drag if placed badly. A government that buys from favoured suppliers regardless of performance, writes tenders that exclude emerging capability, or mistakes political loyalty for strategic value will stabilise the wrong things. It will still be shaping the market. It will be shaping it badly.

This is why industrial policy for data ecosystems should be judged less by how loudly it speaks of sovereignty and more by the quality of the institutions through which it acts. Does research funding connect to operational demand without collapsing into political patronage? Does procurement create a route from prototype to trusted public service? Do standards widen participation or quietly entrench incumbents? Can the public sector retain enough expertise to evaluate claims independently? Does the ecosystem produce several forms of competence, or just one protected supplier with good access to ministers? These questions are more revealing than speeches about leadership.

The harder question, then, is not whether the state should try to build domestic data capability. It already does, even when pretending not to. The harder question is whether it can do so without turning industrial policy into a story about trophies rather than systems. A government can fund research, award contracts, and praise innovation while still deepening dependence if the underlying institutional design is weak. The real test is whether public action leaves behind a broader field of capable firms, skilled people, trusted standards, and intelligent public demand - or merely a handful of politically useful winners. That is the line between ecosystem building and strategic theatre.

Competition tools and interoperability mandates

In March 2004, the European Commission found that Microsoft had abused a dominant position and required, among other remedies, the disclosure of interoperability information so that rival work group server products could communicate more effectively with Windows-based personal computers and servers. The case belonged to an earlier phase of digital competition policy, yet it remains instructive because it showed a truth that has only grown sharper since: market power in information industries often rests not only on what a firm sells, but on who can connect to its systems, on what terms, and with how much friction. A product may look closed because it is popular. Often it stays popular because closure has been built into the conditions of switching away.

That is the starting point for portability and interoperability mandates. They are not decorative additions to competition law. They are attempts to change the technical and organisational terms on which rivalry becomes possible. Portability aims to let users take data, contacts, histories, or settings from one service to another without prohibitive loss. Interoperability aims to let different systems work together so that entry into a market does not always require building a complete substitute for the incumbent's entire environment. Both tools respond to the same problem: digital dominance frequently persists because users are locked into systems whose value depends on accumulated relationships, learned habits, and data-rich feedback loops that do not travel easily. The door stays shut because the room is connected to everything else.

This makes portability and interoperability especially attractive to policymakers frustrated by the limits of traditional antitrust remedies. Breaking up a firm is difficult, often slow, and not always well matched to the actual mechanism of power. Preventing a merger may matter greatly, but it does not necessarily loosen entrenched dependence once a platform already controls the relevant interface. By contrast, a well-designed portability or interoperability rule can alter competitive dynamics without pretending that scale alone is the problem. The concept here is contestability by design. The law does not merely punish dominance after the fact. It changes the market architecture so that rivals can enter and users can leave with less penalty. The implication is practical. Competition stops being a theoretical possibility and becomes a technical option.

Portability is the more familiar of the two because it appeals to a basic intuition of fairness. If a person has built a social graph, music library, transaction history, health record, or creative archive inside one service, they should not have to abandon it all to try another. A portability right therefore aims to reduce switching costs by making movement less destructive. The visible behaviour is easy to picture: export the file, move the playlist, transfer the contacts, carry the archive. This can genuinely increase user choice. It can also change firms' incentives long before users move at scale, because the incumbent knows that the cost of exit is no longer entirely within its control.

Yet portability is often weaker in practice than in policy imagination. The reason is simple. Data do not speak for themselves. A raw export may be technically complete and functionally useless if it arrives in obscure formats, without meaningful metadata, or stripped of the context needed for another service to make it legible. A social media export may preserve posts but not the surrounding interaction that made the posts meaningful. A financial export may move transactions without the classification and verification layers that another service needs to provide equivalent utility. A health data export may be legally portable yet clinically awkward if formats do not align with actual care workflows. The concept is formal portability without practical portability. The user has moved the box and lost the key.

A named example helps clarify the tension. The European Union's data portability right under the GDPR was widely praised for expanding user control, and rightly so. It obliged firms to think harder about exportability and, in some cases, to build tools that users could actually find and use. But experience also revealed the limitations of treating portability as a simple matter of downloading one's data. Much of what gives a platform value lies not only in individual records, but in network position, rankings, feedback signals, and the surrounding social or technical environment. A person may take their data and still be unable to take the relationships or the algorithmic advantages that made the service useful. Portability changes the market. It does not automatically equalise it.

Interoperability addresses that harder problem by reducing the need to leave entirely before competition can begin. If a new messaging service can connect to an established one, a new social tool can communicate across networks, or a new cloud service can integrate more easily with a dominant environment, users and firms do not always have to choose between total dependence and total exit. Interoperability can therefore be more powerful than portability where network effects are strong. The concept is connection without submission. A rival need not reproduce the entire incumbent ecosystem from scratch if it can communicate with it on fair and secure terms. The political attraction is obvious. Competition can grow at the edges of dominance rather than waiting for users to make implausibly clean breaks.

But interoperability creates its own risks, and these risks are often minimised by those who speak about openness as if it were always benign. Every interoperable interface is also an access point. A system designed to let competitors connect may expose personal data, security processes, or content moderation pathways to actors whose incentives and standards differ from those of the original provider. A platform required to open messaging interfaces to rivals may improve user choice while making abuse handling, encryption guarantees, and fraud controls harder to maintain if the rule is drafted crudely. A cloud interoperability mandate may reduce lock-in while creating new attack surfaces and ambiguity about responsibility when something goes wrong. Competition gains can be real. So can privacy and security losses.

This is why competition and security must be co-designed rather than traded rhetorically. The issue is not whether openness is good and security is inconvenient, nor whether security justifies permanent closure. The issue is what kind of technical and institutional design can widen market access without producing irresponsible exposure. This requires more than legal ambition. It requires standards for authentication, liability allocation, auditing, abuse response, and data minimisation that are specific enough to govern actual interconnection. Poorly specified interoperability rules can hand dominant firms a new line of defence - they can claim, often plausibly, that opening the system would endanger users. Poorly governed opening can prove them right.

The Digital Markets Act in the European Union has brought this challenge into particularly sharp focus, especially around interoperability obligations for certain core platform services. The significance of these provisions lies not in any final judgment about their success, which remains a matter of implementation and contestation, but in the seriousness of the problem they are trying to solve. Policymakers recognised that some platforms had become so central that ordinary competition law and ordinary consumer switching could no longer provide enough discipline. The proposed answer was not simply punishment. It was redesign of the market interface. Yet that redesign immediately raised harder questions. How should end-to-end encrypted services interoperate without lowering security? How should smaller entrants access necessary functionality without over-collecting metadata? How should regulators verify compliance in systems too complex for superficial inspection?

A second named example comes from the history of open banking, especially in the United Kingdom and the European Union. Here interoperability and portability have been used to encourage competition in financial services by requiring banks to provide secure, standardised access to customer-authorised data through regulated interfaces. The ambition was substantial: make it easier for new entrants to offer account information services, payment initiation, and tools that could challenge incumbents without forcing consumers to abandon existing banks. The case is important because it shows both promise and difficulty. With strong authentication rules, accreditation, standard setting, and supervisory oversight, interoperability can widen competition in a sector where trust and security matter intensely. It also shows that such success depends on thick governance. Open banking did not work because lawmakers simply declared data should move. It worked, where it did, because the interfaces, permissions, and liabilities were specified with considerable care.

This brings out a central truth. Portability and interoperability are not "light-touch" remedies, even when framed as market-opening tools. They are governance-heavy. Someone must decide what travels, in what format, with what timing, under what user control, through which authentication steps, with what redress when misuse occurs, and with what restrictions on onward use. These decisions shape the actual balance between competition and protection. A shallow mandate can produce checkbox compliance and high-risk connection. A serious one demands regulatory capacity, technical expertise, and continuous revision as firms adapt and adversaries probe the new seams. The state must know enough about systems to open them without breaking them.

A credible limitation should be acknowledged. Not every concentrated market requires interoperability, and not every portability right meaningfully improves competition. In some cases, users benefit more from simpler remedies such as merger control, data access limits for dominant firms, procurement reform, or targeted structural separation. Interoperability can impose heavy engineering and compliance costs on smaller entrants as well as on incumbents. It can also entrench the dominant standard if the terms of connection are shaped around the incumbent's architecture. A rival allowed to connect may still end up living inside the dominant firm's grammar. Openness, in other words, does not guarantee pluralism.

But that limitation refines the argument rather than weakening it. The key question is not whether portability and interoperability are universally desirable. It is whether they can be specified in ways that reduce dependence without merely relocating it. A well-designed portability regime should help users move meaningful aspects of their digital life rather than generating useless archives. A well-designed interoperability regime should widen participation without forcing everyone into insecure, overbroad, or incumbent-biased interfaces. The regulator must ask what kind of rivalry is actually being created. Is the new entrant able to develop distinct services and governance choices, or only to plug into the incumbent's system at the cost of accepting its technical assumptions and risks?

The labour and institutional implications matter here too. Competition agencies, digital regulators, standards bodies, and sectoral supervisors need people who understand protocol design, encryption, authentication, security testing, abuse patterns, and product architecture, not only market definition and legal doctrine. Without that competence, interoperability rules will either be timid or naive. Incumbents will be able to invoke security against every opening, or, worse, regulators will impose access regimes whose weaknesses become visible only after users suffer the consequences. A mandate to open systems is therefore also a mandate to build public expertise. Markets do not become fairer simply because lawmakers choose a technically ambitious remedy. Someone must know how the hinges work.

The quiet motif of the door is useful here. Portability helps people carry their belongings out of a house they wish to leave. Interoperability asks whether the doors between houses can be opened without letting in every threat from the street. A society concerned only with competition may throw the doors wide and regret the result. A society concerned only with safety may bolt them permanently and call captivity security. The harder work lies in designing locks, keys, and thresholds that allow movement and connection without surrendering stewardship. That is what co-design means in practice.

This is also why these tools matter for national power as well as market fairness. A state dependent on a handful of dominant platforms may find its public agencies, firms, and citizens locked into architectures shaped elsewhere. Portability and interoperability can reduce that dependence if they genuinely broaden the field of possible suppliers and services. But if they are mis-specified, they may deepen vulnerability by scattering sensitive functions across weakly governed connections or by making domestic markets more contestable only to foreign incumbents already best positioned to comply. The question is not simply whether markets open. It is who opens them, on what terms, and to whose advantage.

The harder question, then, is whether policymakers are willing to treat competition remedies in digital markets as questions of institutional engineering rather than slogans of liberation. Portability and interoperability can widen choice. They can also expose users, entrench incumbents in new ways, and weaken accountability if drafted by people who understand competition but not systems, or systems but not power. The task is not to choose competition over security or security over competition. It is to design interfaces through which both can survive. That is a more demanding project than either side of the debate often admits, which is precisely why it has become unavoidable.

Labour, skills, and institutional memory

In March 2011, the United Kingdom created the Government Digital Service in London with a brief that sounded administrative and turned out to be strategic. The task was not to invent a new theory of the state. It was to improve how government used digital systems, procured technology, designed services, and worked with data. Yet the longer significance of that moment lies in a harder lesson. Digital capability did not turn on software alone. It turned on whether government could gather, retain, and empower people who knew how systems actually worked. The code was not enough.

That is the proper starting point for any serious discussion of data power. States often speak as though capability lies in infrastructure, law, or procurement strategy, and of course it does. But none of these operates without people who can specify a system, inspect a contract, question a model, read an audit trail, challenge a vendor, interpret a dashboard, explain a risk to ministers, or redesign a workflow that no longer matches public need. Engineers, statisticians, designers, auditors, security specialists, procurement officers, product managers, and policy staff are not support characters in the story of digital government. They are the operating condition. Institutions remember through them.

This is why labour and skills should be treated as a strategic problem rather than a human-resources footnote. A state may pass ambitious laws, fund cloud migration, announce AI strategies, and sign large technology contracts while remaining surprisingly weak if it cannot recruit and keep enough technically literate people to translate policy into systems. The concept here is applied capacity. Capacity does not mean a generic headcount. It means the practical ability to make a public institution understand what it owns, what it is buying, what its systems are doing, and what its legal promises actually require in code and process. Without that ability, the state becomes dependent even when it is spending heavily.

The visible signs of this weakness are often mundane. A ministry cannot explain how a dataset moves between contractors. A regulator struggles to inspect a complex advertising or cloud architecture because too few staff understand the technical stack. A procurement team writes a tender so broad and risk-averse that only the largest incumbent can bid. A department launches a new service but cannot maintain it once the consultancy contract ends. An agency receives an audit, agrees to recommendations, and still cannot implement them because no one inside the institution can sequence the operational change. None of these failures sounds grand. Together, they define whether public power is real or rented.

Retention is therefore not just a staffing concern. It is a constitutional concern. A public institution that constantly loses experienced technical staff loses more than productivity. It loses memory: why a database was structured in a certain way, which vendor promise turned out to be misleading, where the security exception in the workflow really sits, which legacy system cannot be touched without breaking a downstream service, which ministerial instruction created a hidden dependency, which past reform failed because the frontline process was never redesigned. These things are rarely captured fully in documents. They live in the judgments of people who have seen the system behave under pressure. When they leave, the institution becomes easier to impress and easier to manipulate.

A named example from the United States makes the point clearly. The launch of Healthcare.gov in October 2013 exposed severe weaknesses in federal digital delivery, including fragmented contracting, inadequate coordination, and the absence of enough empowered in-house technical leadership to challenge assumptions before failure became public. The later recovery effort is often told as a story of emergency expertise and managerial resolve. It is also a story about institutional learning. The state improved not only because it spent money or hired contractors, but because it brought in people capable of reading the system as a living whole rather than as a chain of procurement milestones. The lesson is not that crises are useful. It is that technical judgement inside government is most visible when its absence becomes impossible to hide.

This is one reason career pathways matter so much. Public institutions often recruit a few talented specialists for short tours, fellowships, or crisis-response roles and then act surprised when capability fades once the tour ends. That model can help seed change. It cannot substitute for a profession. A state needs durable roles in which technically skilled people can enter, advance, specialise, move between functions, and remain influential without having to abandon technical work for pure management or policy theatre. Otherwise the public sector becomes structurally junior: good at importing insight, bad at compounding it. Every new ministerial ambition then begins by rediscovering the same organisational weaknesses.

The problem is sharpened by pay, status, and culture, but it is not reducible to them. Private firms often outpay governments for engineers, security specialists, and product managers. That matters. It does not settle the matter. Many technically skilled people will accept lower pay for public purpose, mission depth, or unusual responsibility if the institution is serious enough to use their skills well. Too often it is not. Technical staff are hired into bureaucracies that distrust unfamiliar expertise, isolate them from decision-making, or treat them as implementers of decisions already made elsewhere. The result is predictable. The public sector does not merely lose talent to higher salaries. It loses talent to environments where talent can act.

This has direct consequences for data governance. A privacy law requiring data minimisation, access rights, and auditability will remain half-real if departments cannot redesign forms, retention policies, and back-end systems accordingly. A competition remedy requiring interoperability will fail if regulators cannot evaluate security claims made by dominant firms. A cyber incident response plan will remain theatrical if agencies lack forensic staff, product owners, and communications leads who understand the underlying systems. A procurement strategy for sovereign or trusted cloud will drift into vendor marketing if nobody inside the state can distinguish contractual reassurance from genuine control. Human capacity is what converts legal ambition into operational truth.

Statistics and analysis deserve special emphasis because data capability is often imagined too narrowly as software engineering. States also require people who can clean and compare records, detect anomalies, assess model quality, understand administrative bias, communicate uncertainty, and resist the institutional temptation to treat dashboards as neutral mirrors of reality. A public agency rich in data and poor in statistical judgement is not strong. It is vulnerable to self-deception. The same applies to auditors and inspectors. Without people who can interrogate data flows, logging practices, access controls, and model governance, oversight institutions risk becoming ceremonial, dependent on the explanations of those they are meant to supervise.

This is where institutional memory becomes a strategic asset in the strongest sense. A seasoned public-sector engineer may know why one form of portability is more dangerous than it looks. A long-serving procurement official may recognise the vendor language that signals hidden lock-in. A regulator who has watched the same platform adapt across several enforcement cycles will be harder to distract with cosmetic changes. A policy official who has seen a data-sharing scandal unfold will write narrower exemptions next time. Memory disciplines optimism. It also disciplines fear. Institutions with memory can distinguish genuinely new problems from old problems dressed in new technical language. They waste less time being impressed.

A second named example lies in Estonia's long development of digital public infrastructure. The country's success is often discussed through systems, not staffing, as though interoperable registries and digital identity arose mainly from clever architecture. They did not. They were built and sustained through a state that managed, over time, to align technical competence, administrative continuity, and political seriousness well enough that institutional knowledge could accumulate rather than constantly disperse. Estonia is not a universally transferable model; it is smaller, more coherent, and differently situated than many countries. But it still demonstrates the broader point. Public-sector digital capacity is not a one-off project. It is a long institutional apprenticeship.

A credible limitation should be admitted. Not every state needs a huge internal engineering corps, and not every capability should be built in-house. Contractors, consultancies, vendors, universities, and temporary fellows can all add real value. Specialist knowledge is unevenly distributed, and some services are reasonably bought rather than built. The point is not bureaucratic self-sufficiency. It is strategic intelligibility. A government can outsource some delivery and still remain capable if it retains enough internal expertise to specify what it needs, judge what it is getting, supervise change, and recover when relationships fail. Total in-house control is unnecessary. Total dependence is dangerous.

That limitation clarifies the real diagnostic. The question is not "build or buy?" in the abstract. It is "what must the state know for itself in order to govern what it buys?" If the answer is "very little", public power is already thinning out. A department that cannot independently test a security claim, understand a data schema, or evaluate whether a service-level promise is operationally meaningful is not using the market from a position of strength. It is relying on the market to explain reality back to it. That may look efficient in calm periods. It becomes expensive in crisis, scandal, procurement failure, or regulatory confrontation.

Labour structure also shapes national capability indirectly through prestige and imitation. If the most ambitious technical graduates and mid-career specialists learn that public service means slow advancement, weak influence, and endless administrative friction, the state loses more than applicants. It loses a social signal. Technical prestige consolidates elsewhere, often in dominant firms whose interests the state later struggles to govern. If, by contrast, the public sector can offer demanding roles, visible responsibility, and real institutional respect for technical judgement, it alters the labour market around digital power. It creates a path by which expertise can circulate between state, academia, civil society, and industry without being captured entirely by the most data-rich firms.

The consequences for democratic legitimacy are not abstract. Citizens experience public-sector technical weakness through broken services, inscrutable decisions, poor correction processes, recurring breaches, badly explained incidents, and grand digital reforms that somehow leave frontline life more confusing than before. Each failure has an institutional backstory, and very often that backstory includes missing skills, high turnover, or a lack of people empowered to raise uncomfortable truths early enough. Conversely, when digital services work well, when agencies explain systems honestly, when regulators challenge firms effectively, and when reforms survive changes of minister or scandal, citizens are often seeing the outward sign of something less visible: enough institutional memory to keep relearning from zero.

The quiet motif of the hand is useful here. Systems do not govern themselves. Someone builds the model, reviews the exception, writes the contract clause, approves the retention rule, interprets the audit, patches the service, challenges the ministerial assumption, and explains the dashboard's limits. The public often sees the interface and forgets the hand. States sometimes do the same. But the hand matters because law, infrastructure, and procurement all depend on it. When the hand is absent, overruled, undertrained, or constantly replaced, the system becomes brittle no matter how modern it appears.

This is why labour policy is inseparable from market policy and statecraft. A country that wants competitive digital markets, trusted public services, enforceable privacy rules, resilient infrastructure, and credible procurement cannot treat engineers and auditors as interchangeable functionaries. It must create institutions in which technical and analytical work can become a durable public vocation rather than a temporary detour before the real career begins elsewhere. That does not require romanticising the state. It requires admitting that public institutions need specialised competence badly enough to design around its absence is no longer a serious option.

The harder question, then, is not whether people matter. Everyone now says they do. The harder question is whether governments are willing to organise careers, authority, pay, procurement, and prestige as though they believe it. A state can publish digital strategies indefinitely while losing the people required to make those strategies real. It can buy advanced systems and still remain operationally naive. It can pass laws and remain unable to inspect how they are implemented. At that point, capacity has not merely weakened. It has become performative. The real test is whether institutional memory is being built faster than it is leaking away, because that is what determines whether the next law, platform reform, cloud contract, or crisis response will be an act of governance or another exercise in forgetting.

Chapter 11

Public Services and National Identity Systems

A woman stands at a public counter with the right name, the right need, and the wrong record. The clerk's screen says one thing. Her papers suggest another. Somewhere inside government, another agency may already hold the missing fact, the corrected address, the earlier verification, the proof that would settle the matter in minutes. But the systems do not speak, the official cannot see, and the citizen is left to carry the burden of stitching the state together by hand. The queue moves. Trust drains.

That scene is mundane enough to be mistaken for administrative bad luck. It is not. It reveals something structural about modern governance. States do not govern only through laws, budgets, or speeches. They govern through the practical ability to know who a person is for public purposes, what prior decisions have already been made about them, which agency can rely on which records, and how quickly those records can be checked, corrected, and acted upon. Identity and data sharing are therefore not technical add-ons to public service. They are the hidden spine of public authority. When the spine is weak, every promise made by the front end of government starts to wobble.

This is why identity systems sit so close to the centre of political legitimacy. A digital identity is not merely a convenience for signing in. It is a decision about how the state recognises persons, allocates entitlements, deters fraud, enables access, and defines the conditions under which public and private institutions may trust one another's claims. Some systems centralise heavily. Some federate. Some rely on smart credentials, some on registers, some on layered combinations of both. None of these choices is neutral. Each settles a different bargain between efficiency, inclusion, resilience, and control. When identity fails, the damage is unusually visible because it does not stay in one programme. It cascades across the services that rely on it.

The tension at the heart of this chapter is simple to state and difficult to resolve. Governments want to share data across agencies because fragmented information produces waste, wrongful denial, duplicated checks, and missed fraud. The same governments fear sharing because past misuse, breaches, and scandals have taught them that pooled visibility can also become pooled vulnerability. Politicians demand seamless services and airtight safeguards at once. Administrators inherit legal ambiguity, ageing systems, outsourced infrastructure, and unequal technical capacity. Citizens are told that government should know enough to act intelligently, but not so much, or in so many ways, that they begin to feel legible beyond necessity. Public service now lives inside that contradiction.

The stakes are high because identity and internal data sharing determine whether the state appears coherent or arbitrary. A tax authority that cannot reliably recognise the same person as a welfare agency will make both fraud control and fairness harder than they need to be. A health system that cannot link records safely may expose patients to error or delay. A benefits system that links records badly may pay the wrong person, deny the right one, or do both in different cases. These are not merely service design defects. They shape whether citizens experience the state as competent, trustworthy, and corrigible. The public rarely sees the architecture. It sees the consequences with painful clarity.

This is also where market structure enters the story with unusual force. Identity systems and data-sharing arrangements are increasingly built, hosted, integrated, and maintained through layers of vendors, consultancies, cloud contracts, middleware, and standards bodies. Governments do not simply choose a policy model and then implement it in a vacuum. They procure architectures that privilege some kinds of control, some forms of auditability, and some dependencies over others. Accountability can blur quickly once one supplier manages authentication, another hosts the data, a third provides analytics, and a fourth maintains interfaces that few civil servants fully understand. The citizen encounters a single state. The state itself may be operating through a chain of commercial abstractions.

That is why the chapter moves as it does. It begins with identity not as a narrow technical credential, but as a governance backbone through which service delivery, fraud control, and inclusion are organised. It then turns to the stubborn difficulty of sharing data inside government, where legal caution, incompatible systems, and institutional memory of scandal often pull against obvious administrative gain. From there it follows the market trail, asking what happens when the capacity to recognise, verify, and coordinate public action depends on contracts and vendors whose incentives do not perfectly align with public accountability. The through-line is constant: public capability cannot be separated from the systems and suppliers through which it is built.

A useful image for this chapter is the keyring. Every modern state carries many keys: identity credentials, agency databases, entitlement records, authentication tools, and the formal permissions that let one office rely on another's information. The promise of good government is that the right key should open the right door without forcing the citizen to stand outside proving themselves again and again. The danger is equally plain. Put too many keys on one ring, or hand the ring to too many people, and convenience becomes exposure. Lose track of who cut the keys, who holds duplicates, and who can change the locks, and the state may discover that its own authority has become harder to audit than the lives it seeks to organise.

The harder question, then, is not whether digital identity and data sharing are necessary. They already are. The harder question is what kind of political order they produce once they become ordinary: one in which recognition is reliable, correction is possible, and accountability survives technical complexity, or one in which the state knows unevenly, acts through brittle linkages, and blames the citizen when its own systems fail to meet. That question begins with identity, because the first test of any data-driven state is how it decides who counts as the person standing at the counter.

Digital identity as a governance backbone

In September 2018, the Supreme Court of India upheld the Aadhaar programme in substantial part while placing limits on some of its uses by private actors. The case was argued in legal language about privacy, proportionality, and constitutional order. Its real force was more concrete than that. A state identity system had become central enough to welfare delivery, financial access, verification, and administrative coordination that the Court was being asked not merely to judge a database, but to judge a theory of governance. The card, the number, the biometric match - each had become a political instrument.

That is the right point of departure because digital identity is often misunderstood as a convenience layer: a quicker login, a cleaner form, a modern substitute for paper credentials. In reality, identity systems sit much closer to the core of public power. They determine how the state recognises persons, how agencies trust one another's decisions, how fraud is deterred, how benefits are delivered, how records are linked, and how inclusion is performed or denied in everyday administrative life. A digital identity system is not merely a tool for proving who someone is. It is a machine for deciding which forms of proof count, who may issue them, who may rely on them, and what happens when they fail. The key opens many doors.

This is why identity functions as a governance backbone rather than an isolated service. Once a state begins to rely on digital identity across tax, welfare, health, licensing, voting registration, migration control, or digital signatures, the identity layer becomes the quiet point of coordination beneath many other systems. It enables speed. It can reduce duplication. It helps agencies rely on each other's checks rather than endlessly re-verifying the same facts. The concept here is administrative legibility with operational consequences. When identity works well, public services feel more coherent because recognition is stable enough to travel. When it fails, the damage spreads quickly because the same recognition error is repeated by every service built atop it.

This helps explain why identity failures produce outsized political damage. A late payment, a broken website, or a minor clerical error may anger users without discrediting the whole model of governance. Identity failure is different. If the wrong person gains access, the right person is locked out, a biometric match fails repeatedly, a credential cannot be recovered, or the underlying register contains an error that cascades across services, the citizen experiences the state not as slow or underfunded but as fundamentally unable to know them correctly. That kind of failure feels existential because identity systems are supposed to settle the most basic administrative question: is this person who the system says they are, and is the system prepared to act on that answer consistently? When the answer turns unstable, trust falters quickly.

Design choices therefore matter enormously, and they matter politically as much as technically. Centralised identity systems gather core functions - enrolment, verification, credential issuance, and often authentication - inside a strong common framework. This can make services more coherent and lower transaction costs for both state and citizen. It can also concentrate risk. A central register or common authentication layer may become a single point of failure, a tempting target, or a politically charged symbol of state overreach. Federation offers a different settlement. Different institutions verify or authenticate identity under common rules, allowing the state to rely on several trusted issuers rather than one commanding centre. Federation can diffuse power and improve resilience. It can also create inconsistency, uneven assurance, and disputes over who is responsible when identities do not travel cleanly across systems.

Credential type adds another layer to the choice. A state may rely on smart cards, mobile credentials, passwords, cryptographic keys, biometrics, paper-to-digital hybrids, or combinations of these. Each carries a different political bargain. Biometrics may reduce certain forms of impersonation while introducing failure modes linked to ageing, labour, disability, or device quality. Mobile-based systems may widen access for some populations while excluding those without stable connectivity or trusted devices. Smart cards may support secure offline verification yet impose renewal burdens and distribution costs. The wrong mistake in this domain is to imagine that credential type is merely a technical preference. It is better understood as a choice about who will find the system natural, who will need workarounds, and where the burden of proving identity will fall when routine assumptions break down.

A named example from Estonia remains instructive because it shows what happens when identity is treated not as a narrow programme but as a durable public infrastructure. Estonia's digital identity system has long supported access to public services, digital signatures, and broad administrative coordination. Its significance lies not only in convenience, though convenience matters. It lies in coherence. When a state can establish a trusted identity layer and align institutions around it, many other services begin to function with less friction and less duplication. The visible effects are ordinary and telling: filing documents, signing contracts, retrieving records, proving status, authorising transactions. Identity, in such a setting, becomes the backbone because it allows the rest of the administrative body to move more smoothly.

And yet the Estonian case also reveals the fragility hidden inside apparent success. A sophisticated identity system still depends on cryptographic trust, secure issuance, reliable recovery procedures, public confidence, and institutional ability to respond when vulnerabilities are found. In 2017, when a security flaw in widely used chips affected Estonian identity cards, the episode did not discredit the system wholesale, but it did demonstrate a crucial truth: identity infrastructures are trusted until they are suddenly tested at scale. The state needed not only technical remedies but also enough credibility to explain, update, and preserve confidence under pressure. Identity systems do not fail solely at the point of design. They fail when recovery, communication, and institutional honesty prove weaker than the architecture assumed.

Inclusion is the other side of this same story. Digital identity is often defended in terms of efficiency, fraud control, and seamless service delivery. Those are real goals. But a governance backbone that excludes certain populations, even intermittently, can produce harms far greater than a slower but more forgiving paper regime. The visible behaviour is simple: a person cannot authenticate, cannot enrol, cannot update a detail, cannot recover access, cannot make one agency accept what another has already verified. The strategic implication is larger. Exclusion is not a side effect that can be tolerated indefinitely in the name of modernisation. It shapes whether the public experiences digital government as an expansion of citizenship or as an administrative sorting machine that rewards the already legible.

This is one reason Aadhaar generated such intense controversy in India. Its defenders pointed to scale, speed, and the benefits of cleaner authentication in welfare and other services. Critics pointed to exclusion risks, privacy concerns, function creep, and the way identity infrastructures can become hard to refuse once they are tied to daily necessity. Both sides were responding to the same reality: once digital identity becomes a backbone, it stops being optional in any meaningful sense. It structures access to the state and often to markets closely tied to the state. That is precisely why the design of enrolment, verification, recovery, and limitation matters so much. A backbone cannot be judged only by how many services rest on it. It must also be judged by what happens to people whose fit with the system is poor.

Security and inclusion are therefore not opposites to be balanced by vague political instinct. They are co-dependent design requirements. A system that is highly secure in the abstract but impossible for many users to navigate will generate workarounds, appeals, local discretion, and informal exceptions that weaken both trust and security. A system that is radically permissive may widen access while creating fraud patterns that undermine legitimacy and provoke political backlash. The real task is to specify enough assurance for the relevant transaction while preserving recovery routes, fallback options, and clear methods of contesting error. Identity must be strong enough to be trusted and flexible enough to be corrected. That sounds modest. It is institutionally demanding.

A credible limitation should be stated clearly. No identity system, digital or otherwise, can eliminate fraud, error, or exclusion entirely. Paper credentials can be forged, local officials can discriminate, and fragmented systems can be both abusive and inefficient. It would be naive to compare real digital systems only against an imaginary analogue world in which discretion is wise, records are accurate, and people are always known properly by face and file. Many digital identity systems do improve service delivery, reduce some forms of fraud, and make public administration less arbitrary than the alternatives they replace. The problem is not digitisation as such. It is whether digitisation hardens error and dependence faster than it improves recognition and redress.

That limitation sharpens the argument rather than softening it. The important question is not whether a digital identity system is perfect. It is whether the state has designed one whose failure modes are politically survivable and administratively corrigible. Can a citizen recover access without humiliation or endless delay? Can an erroneous record be corrected and propagated across dependent systems? Can agencies rely on the credential without treating it as infallible? Can security vulnerabilities be addressed without freezing whole sectors of public life? Can the state explain the system's limits honestly enough that trust survives the first major breakdown? These are governance questions expressed through authentication, enrolment, and credential architecture.

They are also market questions. Identity systems rarely exist outside vendor chains, standards bodies, hardware suppliers, cloud providers, integration contractors, and software intermediaries. A state may proclaim sovereign control over identity while depending on chips, cryptographic modules, mobile platforms, outsourced issuance, or cloud support it does not fully govern. This does not make digital identity impossible. It does mean the backbone is partly built from market relationships that can blur accountability. When the citizen is denied access, the political blame returns to the state regardless of whether the immediate fault lay in procurement, integration, contractor failure, or standards mismatch. That is one reason identity failures are so damaging. They reveal how much public authority now depends on systems the public cannot see and the state may not fully master.

The quiet motif of the key remains useful because identity systems really are key-making institutions. They cut the shape through which a person opens services, rights, records, and transactions. A badly cut key jams, excludes, or opens too much. A carefully cut one disappears into ordinary use, which is often the highest compliment public infrastructure can receive. But even the best key depends on the lock, the hand that turns it, the record of who issued it, and the process for replacing it when it is lost or broken. That is why digital identity must be judged not as a piece of software or a database, but as a full chain of governance stretching from enrolment and proof to authentication, recovery, audit, and remedy.

The harder question, then, is not whether identity should become digital. In many places it already has, formally or by accumulation. The harder question is what kind of state a digital identity backbone quietly creates: one capable of recognising persons consistently without making them permanently transparent, one capable of sharing trust across agencies without turning every administrative act into a demand for deeper exposure, one capable of correcting itself before error becomes exclusion. That question cannot be answered by ideology alone. It must be answered in the design of the key, and in the institutional honesty with which the state admits what the key can and cannot safely open.

Data sharing inside government

In July 2013, the United Kingdom's care.data programme was announced as a way to make better use of health information for planning and research across the National Health Service. The administrative logic sounded persuasive. Why should one part of the state remain blind to data that another part already holds, especially when better linkage might improve care, reduce waste, and inform public policy? Yet the programme quickly ran into public resistance and was ultimately abandoned. The failure was not caused by an excess of technical possibility. It arose because the state had not persuaded the public that it knew where the lines were, who would cross them, and why the crossing could be trusted. The file could move. The justification did not.

That episode captures the paradox at the heart of internal government data sharing. On paper, the case for sharing often looks overwhelming. Agencies duplicate checks, citizens resubmit the same information, fraud patterns go undetected, services fail to recognise changed circumstances, and decisions are made with partial records even though some other part of government may already know what is missing. The costs are visible in delay, waste, and injustice. And yet governments routinely struggle to share data well, even where the practical benefits appear obvious. This is not simply because civil servants are timid or systems are old. It is because data sharing inside government is one of the places where efficiency, legality, architecture, and legitimacy collide most sharply.

The first misconception to discard is that government data sharing fails mainly because officials do not appreciate the value of joined-up information. They usually do. A benefits administrator can see the administrative logic of checking employment records, tax data, housing status, and identity information more coherently. A public health authority can see the value of linking records across service boundaries. A tax authority can see why agencies working from disconnected identifiers create both error and opportunity for abuse. The real problem lies elsewhere. The state does not share data inside a single mind. It shares across institutions with different legal mandates, risk cultures, technical systems, and political memories. The concept that matters is fragmented sovereignty within government itself. Each agency holds a piece of public power and often guards it accordingly.

Legal barriers are the most obvious part of this fragmentation, though they are often overstated and misunderstood at the same time. Some laws genuinely restrict sharing for good reason. Purpose limitation, confidentiality duties, sector-specific secrecy rules, and constitutional protections exist because unrestricted internal circulation of personal data is not neutral simply because the recipient is another branch of the same state. A tax office is not entitled to become a general intelligence service for all of government. A health record is not automatically a policing resource. The law is supposed to slow the assumption that public ownership of data by one institution confers public availability to all others. That slowing function is often justified. The difficulty is that legal ambiguity can be almost as paralysing as legal prohibition. Agencies frequently do not know whether sharing is forbidden, permitted, or permitted only under conditions they cannot easily satisfy.

This uncertainty breeds caution, and caution becomes organisational habit. Officials who have lived through breaches, press scandals, tribunal findings, or political blame learn that unauthorised sharing is punished more visibly than failure to share. The visible risk sits in disclosure. The invisible risk sits in non-use. A department may therefore refuse or delay data sharing even where the legal case for it is perfectly arguable, because no individual official wants to become the person who authorised the transfer later described as overreach. The concept here is asymmetrical accountability. The implication is crucial. Governments often under-share not because privacy law is absolute, but because institutional incentives reward the avoidance of visible scandal more than the reduction of administrative harm.

Past scandals intensify this asymmetry. Once a public controversy teaches agencies that data linkage can trigger accusations of surveillance, overreach, or mission creep, even defensible projects are treated with a kind of anticipatory fear. The memory of care.data in the United Kingdom has had exactly this effect in parts of the public sector. The lesson drawn inside institutions is not always "build stronger trust and clearer governance next time". Often it is "avoid becoming the next example". That defensive reaction is understandable. It is also costly. A state traumatised by one badly explained sharing initiative may become more reluctant to pursue better-designed ones, even where the social benefits are real and the safeguards stronger. Political memory then becomes a technical constraint.

Incompatible systems create a second barrier, and this one is more stubborn than legal reformers sometimes admit. Government does not usually fail to share because data exist in one clean national register waiting to be joined. It fails because identifiers differ, fields are inconsistent, records are incomplete, timestamps do not align, procurement decisions were made in isolation, legacy systems encode categories that no longer match current policy, and the people who built or maintained the older links have moved on. The visible symptom is often mundane: one agency records household composition differently from another, one system uses a legacy identifier while another uses a newer one, one database treats address change as a historical event while another overwrites the old record. These are not small inconveniences. They are the practical grammar of whether the state can recognise the same person, claim, or event across institutional boundaries.

This is why data sharing is inseparable from data quality. A government that shares poor records more aggressively does not necessarily become smarter. It may become more confidently wrong. In benefits administration, this matters acutely. Poor linkage can drive both fraud and wrongful denial because the absence of a reliable cross-agency picture harms the state in two directions at once. A claimant whose circumstances have changed may continue receiving an entitlement that should have stopped because one system does not see what another knows. Another claimant may be wrongly flagged, delayed, or denied because records have been matched too crudely or not updated consistently. The familiar political habit is to discuss these failures as opposites: fraud on one side, unfair denial on the other. In practice, both often arise from the same underlying weakness -

a state that neither sees clearly enough nor doubts its own partial sight sufficiently.

A named example from the Netherlands brings this into focus. The childcare benefits scandal, which became widely public in the late 2010s and early 2020s, showed how data-driven administrative systems can produce devastating injustice when records, risk classifications, and institutional assumptions combine without adequate correction or humane review. The issue was not a simple failure to share data. It was a failure to govern shared and linked data with enough care, context, and correctability. Yet the broader lesson still holds. Governments need data to coordinate entitlements and detect abuse. They also need legal and institutional disciplines strong enough to prevent linkage from becoming overconfident punishment. Sharing more is not the answer by itself. Sharing governably is.

A second named example shows the other side of the problem. Estonia's public sector has often been cited for the way it enables agencies to exchange information while maintaining strong logging and governance structures around who accessed what and why. The important lesson is not that Estonia has solved the problem in universally transferable form. It has not. The lesson is that successful data sharing inside government depends on more than the decision to connect systems. It requires a political settlement about identifiers, access rules, auditability, technical standards, and public expectations. The state must decide not only how agencies may rely on one another's data, but how that reliance will be made reviewable enough to preserve legitimacy.

That legitimacy question is never optional. Internal data sharing sounds administrative until citizens experience it as unexplained circulation of intimate facts through agencies they did not know were connected. The state may regard the transfer as efficient. The person affected may experience it as exposure. This gap in perception matters because data sharing inside government often happens far from the public eye. If a state cannot explain why one agency needs another's records, what safeguards apply, how mistakes are corrected, and what access is logged, the efficiency case will not carry political weight for long. Citizens rarely object to sharing in the abstract. They object when they suspect that the state is using the language of service improvement to normalise a much wider field of administrative visibility.

A credible limitation should be acknowledged. Some governments really do invoke privacy or legal caution as excuses for deeper organisational failings. An agency may claim it cannot share because the law forbids it when the real problem is that its systems are too old, its identifiers too messy, its procurement too fragmented, or its leadership unwilling to prioritise integration. Privacy language can become a bureaucratic shield behind which institutions avoid difficult modernisation work. It would be naive to romanticise every refusal to share as a principled stand against overreach. Sometimes it is inertia dressed as constitutional scruple.

But that limitation strengthens rather than weakens the central argument. The task is not to choose between privacy and sharing as though one must simply defeat the other. The task is to build arrangements in which sharing is specific enough to be useful and bounded enough to be legitimate. That requires several disciplines at once. Legal gateways must be clear enough that officials know when sharing is allowed and for what purpose. Technical systems must use identifiers and standards stable enough to support accurate matching. Access must be logged and reviewable. Frontline staff must be able to correct errors rather than treating cross-agency data as infallible. Citizens must have some practical understanding of what data move where, and some route to challenge the consequences when the movement produces harm.

This is where internal government data sharing becomes a test of state maturity. A weak state either under-shares and blunders through fragmentation, or over-shares and discovers too late that it has damaged public trust. A mature one can draw narrower, better-justified pathways: enough to reduce duplication, catch some abuse, and improve service decisions, but not so broad that every administrative function becomes a pretext for total visibility. Such maturity is difficult because it depends on institutional memory, technical competence, and political restraint all at once. It also depends on ministers accepting that not every potentially useful data flow should be made available merely because it is now technically possible.

The market dimension should not be ignored either. Internal government data sharing increasingly depends on middleware, cloud services, analytics vendors, integrators, and identity platforms supplied by private firms. This complicates accountability. When data move badly, who is responsible - the department that authorised the transfer, the contractor that built the interface, the cloud provider that hosts the environment, the legacy vendor whose schema shaped the mismatch, or the minister who demanded rapid integration without governance work? The citizen will blame the state, and rightly so. But the state may struggle to locate responsibility inside its own contracted architecture. That is one reason data sharing is never only a legal or technical issue. It is also a procurement issue, a labour issue, and a question about how much institutional understanding the state has retained rather than outsourced.

The quiet motif of the bridge helps hold the problem together. A bridge between agencies can reduce distance, duplication, and delay. It can also carry traffic too quickly if no one has agreed what should cross, under what conditions, and with what inspection at the toll. Governments often speak as though the mere existence of unconnected systems were proof of failure. Sometimes it is. Sometimes the failure lies in building bridges without traffic rules, without maintenance, and without public explanation of why the route exists at all. Internal data sharing becomes legitimate not when everything connects, but when the bridge is narrow enough, strong enough, and governed enough that the crossing does not feel like quiet annexation of one part of life by another.

The harder question, then, is not whether government should share more data internally. In many domains it probably should. The harder question is what kind of state such sharing produces once it becomes ordinary. Does it produce a state that sees citizens more clearly without forcing them to become couriers between agencies, or a state that accumulates visibility faster than it accumulates judgment? Does it reduce both fraud and wrongful denial, or merely automate both more confidently? And can it explain its own bridges well enough that administrative coherence feels like service rather than like a system whose appetite for connection no one inside government is still fully able to limit?

Procurement, vendors, and accountability

In August 2020, the United Kingdom abandoned the centralised contact-tracing app it had been developing through NHSX and turned instead to a model based on the Apple-Google exposure notification framework. The decision was explained in technical and practical terms: performance problems, device limitations, the need to deliver something workable under pressure. Yet the episode revealed a deeper truth about public digital systems. Governments do not simply choose policy goals and then translate them into code under their own command. They govern through procurement choices that bind them to platforms, standards, vendors, and technical constraints shaped elsewhere. The contract had already narrowed the state.

That narrowing is often misunderstood because procurement sounds like administration rather than strategy. It evokes tender documents, evaluation scores, legal clauses, and budget lines. In reality, procurement is one of the places where governance is most concretely decided. A public authority that buys an identity system, a cloud environment, a case-management platform, a fraud analytics tool, or a data-sharing interface is not merely acquiring a service. It is choosing an architecture, a dependency profile, a future audit problem, and a distribution of knowledge between itself and the firms on which it will rely. The public may never see the contract. It will live with its consequences for years.

This is why procurement must be treated as a constitutive act of state capacity. Design decisions are often made through market instruments rather than direct public engineering. An agency may contract for enrolment services, credential issuance, cloud hosting, authentication, analytics, call-centre support, and systems integration through several layers of suppliers. Each layer may look reasonable on its own. Together they create a chain of operational dependence in which no single actor fully governs the system and no single contract captures the whole public risk. The concept here is outsourced architecture. The state still owns the political responsibility, but parts of the system's technical reality now sit inside commercial relationships whose incentives do not perfectly match public accountability.

The first effect of this arrangement is architectural. Contracting shapes what kinds of systems are built because firms bid against specified requirements, and those requirements privilege some models over others. A tender that prizes rapid deployment and low upfront cost may encourage heavy reuse of proprietary components and cloud services that later prove hard to exit. A tender that prizes formal compliance over operational intelligibility may reward vendors skilled at documentation while disadvantaging smaller firms with technically stronger but less bureaucratically polished offerings. A tender written by officials who do not fully understand the long-term implications of identity linkage, access logging, or data portability may lock a public service into a structure whose weaknesses only become obvious after citizens are already inside it. Procurement is not downstream of design. It is design in legal clothing.

This is one reason outsourcing often blurs accountability. When a service fails, citizens and ministers naturally ask who is responsible. But digital public services rarely fail in ways that map cleanly onto one organisational box. The problem may sit partly in the procuring department's specification, partly in the prime contractor's implementation, partly in a cloud provider's operational model, partly in an inherited middleware product, and partly in an integration decision made years earlier under another contract. The visible institution remains the state. The explanatory trail leads through several corporate layers, each able to say that it met its contractual terms or relied on another supplier's interface. The result is a familiar pattern: responsibility is public, causation is distributed, and correction becomes harder because the entity answerable to citizens does not fully command the entities that know the system best.

A named example from the Netherlands is instructive here. The SyRI system, used to combine data from multiple public sources for fraud and risk detection, was eventually struck down by a Dutch court in 2020. Public debate often focused on opacity, proportionality, and the rights implications of predictive state systems. Just as important was the institutional setting in which those systems take shape. Risk scoring tools and data-linkage infrastructures do not emerge from policy intention alone. They are procured, configured, maintained, and often partly understood through external expertise. That matters because opacity is not only the result of secretive political intent. It can also arise from layered technical procurement in which the state loses the ability to explain how its own system reaches or operationalises a result. A government that cannot fully narrate its own machinery cannot govern it with confidence.

Long-term dependence is the second major effect, and it is frequently underestimated at the point of purchase. Public agencies often believe they are buying a service. In practice, they are entering a relationship. That relationship may include proprietary data models, custom integrations, vendor-managed security processes, platform-specific tooling, and support arrangements that become progressively harder to replace. The supplier learns the state. The state, unless it has retained unusual internal capability, does not learn the supplier's system to the same depth. Each renewal then becomes less a fresh competition than a negotiation under asymmetrical familiarity. The incumbent vendor can point to switching risk, continuity concerns, retraining costs, and compliance burdens, all of them often real. Lock-in is rarely a trapdoor. It is a sedimentary process.

This is especially consequential in identity systems and public services because these are not peripheral tools. Once an identity provider, benefits platform, or records system becomes embedded in daily administrative action, change becomes politically risky. A failed migration can deny entitlements, disrupt authentication, confuse frontline staff, or trigger public scandal. Governments know this. Vendors know it too. The state therefore negotiates future changes from inside the fear of breaking essential services. That fear can be strategically exploited even without malice. The incumbent need only understand that the public authority's appetite for disruption is lower than its own appetite for preserving market position. Procurement choices made in one cycle begin to govern what can be plausibly chosen in the next.

A second named example lies in the long history of large public-sector IT outsourcing in the United Kingdom, where major service contracts have often concentrated around a relatively small number of large integrators and technology suppliers. The specific systems vary, as do their success and failure. The broader lesson is persistent. Governments outsource partly because they lack time, specialist staff, or delivery confidence. Yet repeated outsourcing can deepen those very weaknesses if internal teams stop learning how systems are assembled, audited, and changed. The state buys capacity and quietly sells understanding. Over time, this makes future procurement less intelligent, because the institution specifying the contract no longer possesses enough technical judgment to recognise what a good contract would need to preserve.

This is not an argument against vendors as such. A credible limitation should be stated plainly. Public institutions cannot and should not build every component themselves. Specialist suppliers provide real expertise, scale, security operations, hardware, software maintenance, and engineering capacity that many states would struggle to match internally. Some services are appropriately bought rather than built. A romantic faith in total in-house sovereignty can produce brittle systems, under-resourced teams, and unrealistic expectations. The issue is not whether governments should use markets. They must. The issue is whether they can govern through markets without allowing market structure to hollow out public judgment.

That limitation clarifies the real diagnostic. A state remains capable when it can specify requirements wisely, evaluate bids with technical seriousness, preserve rights to audit and portability, retain enough internal knowledge to challenge vendor claims, and avoid contracting patterns that turn every future reform into a hostage negotiation with incumbents. It becomes weak when procurement substitutes for understanding. The weak state believes it has solved complexity by buying it. The capable state knows that buying complexity increases the need for internal competence, because someone must still decide what the public interest requires when the vendor's commercial logic diverges from it.

Oversight is where this divergence becomes most visible. Regulators, auditors, parliamentary committees, ombuds institutions, and courts increasingly confront systems built through multiple supplier layers. A right of access, a correction request, an inquiry into bias, a data breach investigation, or a procurement review may all run into the same problem: the public body is answerable, but the operational detail sits in vendor logs, subcontractor processes, third-party tools, or proprietary models. The concept here is procedural distance. Every additional layer between the citizen and the actual operation of the system makes accountability slower, murkier, and more dependent on what the contracted chain is willing or able to reveal. Transparency clauses help. They do not eliminate the problem if the state lacks people who can interpret what they receive.

This is why procurement and labour policy are inseparable. A department with strong internal engineers, product owners, auditors, and technically literate lawyers can contract externally while still preserving public control over key decisions. A department without such staff will often rely on vendors not only for delivery but for diagnosis, roadmap design, and even interpretation of public obligations. The vendor becomes builder, guide, and witness in the same case. That is a precarious arrangement in any sensitive public service and especially in identity systems, where access, exclusion, and redress depend on the details of how systems authenticate, log, recover, and share data. Market dependence becomes constitutional dependence by quieter means.

Procurement also shapes competition beyond the immediate contract. Public purchasing can either widen the field of capable suppliers or entrench a small oligopoly of firms best able to absorb compliance burden, bid preparation, liability clauses, and long sales cycles. A tender written around incumbent assumptions may speak the language of openness while structurally excluding challengers. Requirements for prior public-sector experience, bespoke certifications, high insurance thresholds, and legacy integrations often reward those who already dominate public contracts. The state then reproduces the market concentration it later complains about. Public money becomes a mechanism for narrowing the supplier base under the banner of risk management.

The political temptation is to respond to this with patriotic procurement: favour domestic firms, invoke sovereignty, and hope the problem resolves into national loyalty. Sometimes domestic capability deserves support, and not all foreign dependence is wise. But procurement that mistakes nationality for accountability solves little. A domestic vendor can produce opacity, lock-in, and weak auditability just as readily as a foreign one. The more serious question is whether contracting structures preserve contestability, transparency, and exit options while meeting real public needs. Sovereignty in procurement is not a flag on the supplier's headquarters. It is the state's continuing ability to understand, challenge, and change the system it has bought.

The quiet motif of the chain is useful here. Outsourced public services are often chains of contracts, interfaces, dependencies, and support obligations. A chain can be strong. It can also conceal the point at which strain will snap. Citizens do not experience the chain. They experience the service. When the service fails, the chain suddenly becomes visible as a sequence of excuses: one supplier blames integration, another blames legacy data, another cites contract scope, the department invokes vendor assurances, and the public is left with the unmistakable impression that everyone can explain the failure and no one can own it. That is the accountability cost of poorly governed outsourcing.

The deeper issue is therefore not whether states should contract with private firms. That is inevitable. It is whether the procurement system is designed to preserve public agency rather than to displace it. A government that knows what it is buying, why it needs certain audit rights, how to avoid unnecessary lock-in, when to separate layers of dependency, and how to retain enough in-house skill to supervise the result is still governing through markets. A government that signs broad contracts because it lacks the internal strength to do otherwise is being governed by them in return. The distinction is subtle at the point of purchase and enormous over time.

This is why procurement, vendors, and accountability belong at the centre of any serious account of public services and identity systems. Architecture is contracted. Oversight is conditioned by supplier relations. Long-term dependence is often written in clauses that seem, at the moment, like harmless risk allocation. The state does not lose capacity in one dramatic surrender. It loses it across renewals, integrations, urgent fixes, and small decisions to trust external expertise a little more because internal expertise is thin. By the time the political consequences become visible, the market structure is already embedded in the service logic.

The harder question, then, is not who signed the last contract. It is what kind of public authority emerges after years of building essential systems through layered procurement. Does the state remain able to explain and alter its own machinery, or has it become the nominal face of systems whose real operational knowledge sits elsewhere? That question cannot be answered by procurement law alone, nor by anti-outsourcing sentiment. It must be answered in the design of contracts, the retention of public expertise, and the discipline to recognise that governance capacity is never separate from the market structures through which governance now moves.

Chapter 12

Trust, Consent, and Democratic Legitimacy

A government launches a new data initiative with lawful authority, technical confidence, and a careful case for public benefit. The safeguards are documented. The lawyers are satisfied. The ministers speak of efficiency, fraud reduction, and modern service delivery. And still the public turns against it. Not because every claim is false, nor because every fear is rational, but because legality has not answered the deeper question of whether people believe the state deserves this additional sight into their lives. The notice has been given. Permission has not.

That gap matters because democratic governance does not rest on coercion or compliance alone. It rests on a reservoir of willingness: willingness to provide information, accept inconvenience, trust official assurances, and believe that exceptional powers will not quietly become ordinary habits. This willingness is often described as trust, but the more exact term is social licence. Social licence is not a legal instrument and not a moral mood. It is the practical tolerance citizens extend to institutions when they judge that collection is proportionate, benefits are real, safeguards are credible, and correction remains possible if something goes wrong. It is granted unevenly, withdrawn quickly, and rebuilt slowly.

This creates the chapter's central tension. States increasingly need data to govern well, especially where public services, fraud control, public health, security, and crisis response depend on timely coordination. Yet the very systems built to make the state more capable can weaken its legitimacy if they feel extractive, discriminatory, or impossible to contest. A programme may be lawful and still politically unsustainable. A transparency measure may reassure one audience while alarming another. A data-sharing initiative may look efficient from the centre and invasive from the citizen's side of the screen. The problem is not simply whether the state can justify what it collects. It is whether the public continues to accept the terms on which that justification is made.

That acceptance is fragile because trust is distributed unequally. Those who have historically been misclassified, over-policed, poorly served, or administratively ignored often encounter state data systems not as neutral instruments but as mechanisms through which old inequalities are reproduced in new forms. Profiling, proxies, feedback loops, and uneven access to correction can turn technical systems into engines of administrative harm. The state then discovers that a governance failure is not only a matter of ethics or service quality. It becomes a strategic liability. Communities that feel watched, misread, or routinely disadvantaged become harder to persuade, harder to mobilise in emergencies, and less likely to believe that future assurances are offered in good faith.

This is why transparency cannot be treated as a simple cure. Governments often promise to be more open about data practices, and sometimes they should. But transparency that is improvised under scandal, framed defensively, or detached from intelligible explanation rarely restores much. It can even deepen suspicion by confirming that officials speak clearly only when forced. More useful transparency is structured: regular reporting, stable categories, plain description of powers and safeguards, and institutions willing to explain not only success but limitation. The point is not total exposure. It is predictable visibility strong enough to stabilise expectations before a leak, breach, or controversy does the explaining on the state's behalf.

The difficulty is intensified by the media environment in which these questions now unfold. Leaks, partisan amplification, selective disclosure, disinformation, and ambient distrust all shape how data governance is perceived. A technically well-designed system can fail politically if public narratives harden against it before institutions have earned credibility. A flawed system can survive longer than it should if criticism is dismissed as panic or conspiracy. This means political risk and technical risk do not always travel together. The state may fix the architecture and still lose the story. Or it may tell a reassuring story while the architecture remains brittle beneath it. Democratic legitimacy depends on recognising the difference and governing both.

The path ahead follows that uneasy terrain. It begins with the idea of social licence and the limits of extraction, then moves into the hard problem of how states speak about secrecy without allowing secrecy to become the whole answer. From there it turns to the way inequality and profiling corrode legitimacy from below, to the media dynamics that magnify or distort those injuries, and finally to the question of repair: what institutions must do after breach, scandal, or failure if they want trust to become more than a press strategy. The through-line is straightforward and severe. Trust is not what remains once systems are built. It is one of the conditions under which they can endure.

A useful image for the chapter is the receipt. Citizens hand over data every day, sometimes knowingly, sometimes because there is no meaningful alternative. What they receive in return is not always obvious. Sometimes it is a service, a payment, an entitlement, a warning, a diagnosis, a smoother transaction. Sometimes it is only the state's assurance that the collection was necessary. A receipt becomes politically meaningful when people can compare what was taken with what was returned, and when they can challenge the terms of the exchange if the bargain turns sour. Without that possibility, consent starts to look less like agreement and more like administrative inevitability.

The harder question, then, is not whether democratic states need data. They do. The harder question is what kind of relationship with the public those needs are creating over time. Does each new system deepen a sense that collection is bounded, explainable, and corrigible, or does it teach citizens that lawfulness and legitimacy have drifted apart? That question cannot be answered by compliance alone. It has to be answered in the lived politics of trust, where one badly handled scandal can outweigh a decade of quiet competence and where the state's most sophisticated systems may still fail if too many people no longer believe the receipt is honest.

Social licence and the limits of extraction

In February 2014, England's care.data programme was paused after rising public concern over how National Health Service patient information might be shared and used. The stated aims had sounded administratively reasonable: improve planning, support research, make better use of records the state already held. Yet the programme met a reaction far stronger than ministers appeared to expect. What failed was not only communication, though communication failed badly. What failed was a deeper political bargain. The state believed it had legal authority and practical justification. Much of the public concluded that legality had outrun legitimacy. The file was available. Permission was not.

That episode is one of the clearest modern illustrations of social licence in data governance. Social licence is not a statute, not a formal consent screen, and not a vague synonym for popularity. It is the public's practical willingness to tolerate data collection, linkage, and use because the purpose appears intelligible, the benefits appear real, and the safeguards appear credible enough to deserve provisional trust. It is a political condition rather than a legal entitlement. A state may possess the law and still lack the licence. That is why data extraction can be lawful yet unsustainable.

The concept matters because modern states increasingly depend on information flows that cannot be secured by compulsion alone. Citizens supply data to tax authorities, health systems, schools, border agencies, welfare offices, licensing bodies, and digital identity platforms. They also tolerate passive forms of collection embedded in infrastructure, security systems, and public-private administrative processes. Much of this collection is necessary. The harder question is what turns necessity into toleration. The answer is never simply "the law permits it". People do not experience legality as an abstract constitutional fact. They experience it through whether the request seems bounded, whether the explanation rings true, whether the institution has behaved well before, and whether correction remains possible when something goes wrong. Trust is cumulative. So is distrust.

This is why social licence should be understood as a form of political capital. A government with strong social licence can ask for more information, impose more administrative coordination, and introduce more ambitious digital services without immediately provoking defensive backlash. That does not mean the public becomes passive or gullible. It means the institution has earned enough credit that citizens give it the benefit of the doubt while they assess the next request. The visible behaviour may look modest: fewer refusals, more willingness to adopt a new service, less immediate suspicion when records are linked for a stated public purpose. The implication is larger. A state with social licence governs more easily because it spends less time fighting the presumption that every new data initiative conceals a different and darker purpose.

The reverse is equally important. Social licence is easier to lose than to regain because data governance operates through memory. Citizens remember scandals, leaks, mission creep, and official evasions long after ministers have moved on. Once people conclude that an institution uses "public benefit" language to normalise expanding access, or that promised safeguards are thin, each future initiative inherits the mistrust created by the last one. This is not irrational. It is a practical reading of institutional character. A state that has previously blurred boundaries cannot expect the public to treat the next boundary as secure merely because a different spokesperson now offers reassurance. Legitimacy degrades by association.

A named example beyond care.data makes the point from another angle. During the COVID-19 pandemic, digital contact tracing and exposure-notification systems produced strikingly different public reactions across countries. The technical architecture mattered. So did the epidemiological case. But another factor mattered just as much: whether citizens believed the institutions behind the system would keep health data within the purposes announced. In some places, the public accepted extraordinary collection because the state was seen as competent, bounded, and genuinely focused on public health. In others, suspicion about onward use, policing, immigration consequences, or state opportunism weakened adoption and cooperation. The issue was not whether the law could authorise the system. The issue was whether the state had enough social licence to make the authorisation politically and behaviourally effective.

That reveals something essential about extraction. States extract many things from society: taxes, compliance, time, documentation, testimony, deference at borders, and, increasingly, data. Extraction becomes politically durable only when those subjected to it judge the bargain tolerable. This does not require enthusiasm. It requires a workable sense that what is being taken is proportionate to what is being returned. The returned good may be security, speed, entitlements, public health, fraud control, or administrative coherence. If that exchange begins to feel one-sided, social licence weakens. The request may still be obeyed. It is obeyed more reluctantly, more conditionally, and with more readiness to revolt when the next scandal arrives.

This is why social licence is not the same as consent, though the two are often confused. Consent is usually transactional and formalised. A person ticks a box, accepts terms, or continues using a service under conditions presented to them. Social licence is broader and more ambient. It reflects the public mood around an institution's right to ask in the first place. A person may formally consent because the service is unavoidable, because the form is opaque, or because the administrative cost of refusal is too high. That says very little about whether the surrounding system enjoys real legitimacy. Consent can be coerced by structure. Social licence cannot be manufactured so easily. It depends on the institution's accumulated reputation for boundedness and fair dealing.

This distinction helps explain why legality can become politically unsustainable. A government may point, correctly, to statutory authority, regulatory approval, judicial review, or administrative necessity. Yet legality answers only part of the public question. Citizens also ask, often implicitly:

why this much information, why now, why by these means, why under these institutions, and why should anyone believe the use will remain within the announced purpose? Those are not anti-legal questions. They are the conditions under which law acquires social durability. A state that responds to them only with "it is lawful" is usually revealing that it has mistaken legal clearance for political settlement.

The pressure becomes sharper where the benefits of extraction are distributed unevenly or remain invisible. It is easier for people to tolerate broad collection when the public return is tangible and widely shared: a reliable health service, smoother benefit delivery, fewer duplicate forms, faster emergency response. It is harder when the gains seem abstract, deferred, or concentrated in institutional convenience. "Better analytics" and "improved planning" may be true. They rarely move public judgment on their own. Social licence grows when benefits are legible in ordinary life, not merely legible in policy briefings. A citizen who sees no improvement but hears that more sharing or retention is required for long-term efficiency is being asked to trust in a bargain the state has not yet made visible.

The issue becomes still more difficult where burdens fall unevenly. Data extraction often affects different populations in different ways. A middle-class citizen with stable housing, easy access to documents, and confidence in dealing with institutions may experience a new data-sharing regime as a mild administrative improvement. A migrant, welfare claimant, religious minority, or heavily policed community may experience the same regime as intensified exposure. Social licence is therefore not uniform across society, and governments that measure it only through broad general sentiment can miss the places where distrust is already hardening. This matters strategically. It is often precisely those communities under greater administrative scrutiny whose cooperation becomes most important in crisis or in the detection of policy failure.

A credible limitation should be acknowledged. Social licence is not a veto and cannot be treated as one. Some necessary state actions will be unpopular, contested, or poorly understood in the short term. Governments cannot govern only where public comfort is already secure. Nor can they abandon legitimate security, public health, or anti-fraud measures simply because they are politically difficult. Social licence should not become a euphemism for timidity or a licence for disinformation campaigns to block every significant reform. The public can misjudge. Narratives can harden unfairly. Some beneficial systems will be resisted before they are understood.

But that limitation does not weaken the argument for taking social licence seriously. It clarifies the difference between temporary contestation and durable unsustainability. A state may need to act amid doubt. It cannot flourish indefinitely by burning through trust faster than it replenishes it. A government that repeatedly imposes lawful but socially brittle extraction may discover that each subsequent initiative encounters greater suspicion, lower adoption, more litigation, harsher media framing, and less voluntary cooperation. The result is a state that remains formally empowered but increasingly unable to mobilise compliance without rising coercive and political cost. That is a strategic weakness, not merely a communications problem.

This is one reason social licence should be treated as an institutional achievement rather than a public-relations task. It is built through boundary discipline, usable remedies, clear purpose statements, visible benefits, honest communication, and credible restraint after earlier controversies. Citizens do not infer social licence from slogans. They infer it from whether the state behaves as though limits are real even when more access would be technically possible or administratively convenient. A government that declines to repurpose data casually, that explains what it will not do as well as what it will do, and that corrects harms visibly when they occur builds a sturdier basis for future extraction than one that treats every available dataset as a temptation to which policy must eventually yield.

The quiet motif of the receipt is useful here. Every act of data collection is a kind of exchange, whether or not it is framed that way. The citizen hands something over: a record, a biometric, a location trace, a pattern of behaviour, a link between one file and another. In return, the state offers some mixture of service, order, security, or convenience. Social licence depends on whether the public believes that receipt is honest. Not perfect. Honest. Does the state take only what the transaction plausibly requires? Does it keep its side of the bargain? Does it honour the limits printed on the political receipt, or quietly alter the terms once the data are safely in hand? The answer to those questions shapes whether future requests are met with patience or hostility.

This also explains why repair is so difficult after a breach of trust. A single scandal rarely destroys legitimacy in isolation. What it destroys is the presumption that future promises can be accepted without proof. From that point onward, every new initiative must overcome not only its own complexity but the residue of what came before. Governments often underestimate this. They imagine that if they tighten language, appoint a review, or replace a programme name, the social licence account has been replenished. It has not. Repair requires investigation, remedy, redesign, and, above all, time in which the institution behaves differently enough for the public to notice. Trust is not restored by assertion. It is restored by altered conduct repeated long enough to become credible.

That is why "legal" can still be politically unsustainable. Legality is a floor, not a guarantee. It tells us something important about authority, procedure, and formal permission. It does not tell us whether the governed continue to regard that authority as bounded, intelligible, and worth cooperating with. A state that forgets this may win the immediate legal argument and lose the longer political one. It may collect more data and command less trust. It may strengthen its administrative sight while weakening the willingness of citizens to stand still for the camera.

The harder question, then, is not whether governments need social licence before they can govern with data. They always do, whether they acknowledge it or not. The harder question is how much extraction a democratic state can normalise before the public begins to revise its understanding of what the state is for. Once that revision starts, the next lawful initiative may encounter not debate but accumulated refusal. At that point the problem is no longer simply how to justify a particular system. It is whether the state still knows how to ask for information without making the request itself feel like a warning.

Transparency, secrecy, and selective disclosure

In June 2013, after Edward Snowden's disclosures began to appear in *The Guardian* in London, governments across the United States, the United Kingdom, and allied states were forced into a familiar but unusually public dilemma. Intelligence and security officials argued that secrecy was indispensable to protecting capabilities, sources, and lawful operations. Critics argued that the public had been denied a meaningful account of what was being done in its name and with its data. Both claims contained truth. The real failure lay elsewhere. Transparency had not been built as a stable practice before the crisis arrived, so disclosure became reactive, adversarial, and politically corrosive. The file opened too late.

That episode remains instructive because it shows why transparency in data governance cannot be treated as a simple moral preference for openness. States do need secrecy. Intelligence methods, ongoing investigations, cyber operations, and some forms of technical assurance cannot be fully exposed without degrading the very public goods they are meant to protect. Yet secrecy becomes politically dangerous when it expands into a habit of under-explanation. Citizens do not need to know every operational detail. They do need a durable account of powers, safeguards, review structures, and limits robust enough to prevent every future revelation from feeling like a first glimpse into a hidden constitutional order. The point is not to abolish secrecy. It is to govern it.

This is why transparency must be understood as structured disclosure rather than improvised confession. Improvised disclosure usually comes in one of two forms, both weak. The first is forced release under scandal, leak, litigation, or parliamentary pressure. The second is emergency reassurance after the public has already concluded that an institution spoke too little for too long. Neither form builds trust well because both are shaped by defensive incentives. Officials reveal what they must, conceal what they still can, and frame the narrative around damage control. The concept here is reactive openness. It may produce facts. It rarely produces legitimacy, because the public can see that the institution is speaking only under duress.

Structured transparency works differently. It establishes in advance what kinds of information will be disclosed routinely, in what categories, on what timetable, and through which institutions. It is not total openness. It is repeatable visibility. A government might publish aggregate reporting on data requests, categories of legal authority used, approval pathways, audit findings, error rates in particular administrative systems, or summaries of how safeguards operate in practice. A regulator might publish thematic findings rather than raw operational detail. An oversight body might release declassified annual assessments of compliance problems, boundary disputes, or remedial steps. These forms of disclosure do not satisfy every critic. They do something more important. They stabilise expectations before a crisis forces the state to speak from panic.

Aggregate reporting is especially valuable because it gives the public a way to understand scale and structure without exposing individual cases or operational methods. A transparency report that states how many requests were made under different authorities, how many were rejected or modified, what internal approvals were required, and what categories of data were involved can help citizens and journalists judge whether official powers appear bounded and reviewable. The visible behaviour matters. Instead of simply asserting that safeguards exist, the institution shows that requests move through a system with recognisable friction. The implication is political. A public that sees a stable pattern of explanation is less likely to assume that every unseen act hides unlimited practice.

A named example from the United Kingdom is useful here. The Investigatory Powers Commissioner's Office has published annual reports that describe, in aggregate form, how investigatory powers are used, where compliance problems have arisen, what error categories have appeared, and how oversight has responded. These reports do not disclose the full operational world behind intelligence and law-enforcement activity, nor could they. Their value lies elsewhere. They provide a standing mechanism through which the public can see that powers are not governed only by ministerial assertion. Oversight becomes visible as a routine practice rather than as a story told only after scandal. That does not eliminate controversy. It reduces the epistemic vacuum in which distrust grows fastest.

The same logic appears on the private side of public power. Major technology firms now publish transparency reports about government data requests, content restrictions, and legal process demands. These reports are incomplete, strategically framed, and sometimes shaped by reporting constraints imposed by governments themselves. Even so, they have altered expectations. Once aggregate reporting becomes routine, the public begins to expect that state access and platform response should be counted, categorised, and periodically explained. This matters because public understanding of state data practices now often depends on a hybrid informational environment: part official disclosure, part court record, part journalistic investigation, part corporate reporting. Structured transparency helps prevent this mixed ecosystem from becoming entirely crisis-driven.

Still, transparency has limits, and serious analysis must acknowledge them. A government cannot publish detailed operational techniques without inviting evasion. It cannot always release granular information about intelligence partnerships, vulnerable systems, or live counter-terrorism investigations. Nor can every public system disclose all internal thresholds, model parameters, or detection criteria without compromising safety, fairness, or anti-fraud effectiveness. Transparency advocates sometimes understate this, while state institutions often overstate it. The harder task is to identify what can be disclosed safely enough to support legitimacy without rendering the system strategically naive. This is not a problem that disappears. It must be managed.

That management depends on distinguishing between secrecy about methods and secrecy about norms. Methods may need concealment. Norms generally do not. A government may have good reason to withhold the technical details of how a cyber defence system flags anomalies or how a lawful interception capability is operationalised. It has far weaker reason to withhold the categories of authority under which such systems operate, the approval path required, the oversight body responsible, the existence of redress, or the broad kinds of data involved. When states conflate these two forms of secrecy, they often end up defending unnecessary opacity by sheltering it beneath genuinely necessary confidentiality. That is one of the main ways political trust is squandered.

Selective disclosure becomes dangerous at precisely this point. All disclosure is selective in the simple sense that no institution can reveal everything. The question is whether selection is principled, stable, and intelligible, or opportunistic and politically tailored. Opportunistic selection occurs when governments release reassuring fragments while omitting the categories of information most necessary for judging the real balance of power. It also occurs when they publish in forms designed to minimise scrutiny: over-aggregation, shifting categories, irregular timing, or reports so technical that only specialists can interpret them. The visible product may still be called transparency. In practice it functions as narrative management.

This is why the design of reporting categories matters more than many public debates admit. If requests are grouped too broadly, the public cannot distinguish exceptional powers from routine ones. If error reporting is vague, recurring failure patterns disappear into generic reassurance. If oversight findings are published only as celebratory summaries, the state teaches citizens that transparency means ceremonial confidence rather than disciplined candour. A good disclosure regime therefore requires classification choices that remain stable enough over time to permit meaningful comparison. Structured transparency is not just about saying more. It is about saying comparable things repeatedly enough that patterns become visible.

A second named example comes from the repeated publication of surveillance and access reports by institutions in democratic states after the Snowden era. One of the lessons of that period was that once publics discover a large gap between what they assumed and what was happening, every subsequent official statement is heard against the possibility of further undisclosed scope. Governments responded in part by making some reporting more regular. The exact quality of those efforts has varied.

Their deeper significance lies in the acknowledgement that public trust cannot rely forever on the formula "trust us, but we cannot tell you". Even where secrecy remains necessary, the authority to invoke secrecy must be surrounded by visible practices of counting, review, and explanation.

A credible limitation should be stated plainly. Transparency alone does not guarantee trust. Institutions can publish volumes of material and remain untrusted if the public already believes the disclosures are selective, delayed, or fundamentally cosmetic. Reports can become rituals. Dashboards can create false precision. Aggregate numbers can reassure while masking harms concentrated in specific communities or systems. Transparency without remedy, oversight without consequence, and disclosure without comprehensibility may even deepen cynicism by confirming that institutions know how to appear accountable without altering much beneath the surface. Openness is not a substitute for restraint.

But that limitation strengthens the central argument rather than weakening it. Precisely because transparency is not enough, it must be designed as part of a larger legitimacy architecture. It works best when joined to independent oversight, usable rights, visible correction, and a willingness to disclose not only success but failure. A report that acknowledges compliance problems, explains what changed in response, and returns the following year with enough continuity to show whether the promises were kept does more for legitimacy than a polished statement of principles delivered in the middle of scandal. The public does not require perfection. It requires evidence that institutions can see their own defects clearly enough to govern them.

Media dynamics make this particularly urgent. In a polarised environment, leaks, partial disclosures, and hostile narratives will shape public understanding whether institutions prepare for them or not. States that rely on silence until crisis effectively allow the first coherent story to be written by whoever reveals the problem. Sometimes that will be journalists performing a democratic service. Sometimes it will be political opportunists or foreign actors exploiting ambiguity for their own ends. Structured transparency does not immunise institutions from hostile framing. It gives them a more credible baseline from which to respond. A public already familiar with the broad architecture of powers and safeguards is harder to shock into absolute distrust than one encountering everything under crisis conditions.

The quiet motif of the file is useful here. A file can be locked for good reasons. It can also remain closed because opening it would reveal embarrassment, drift, or ungoverned expansion. The public rarely sees the file itself. What it sees are the rules about who may open it, what is said about its existence, and whether institutions acknowledge the difference between what must stay closed and what should never have been hidden. Transparency is not the abolition of the locked file. It is the discipline of telling the public enough about the filing system that the locked drawer does not become a metaphor for arbitrary power.

This is why transparency should be treated as infrastructure rather than sentiment. It needs categories, schedules, institutions, and habits. It needs officials who understand that aggregate reporting is not a concession to critics but part of the state's own long-term capacity to govern with public trust. It needs legislatures and oversight bodies willing to demand stable disclosure rather than theatrical bursts of openness when headlines require it. It also needs restraint in what is promised. Institutions that claim radical openness and then retreat into vague secrecy at the first operational difficulty teach the public the wrong lesson twice.

The harder question, then, is not whether democratic states can be fully transparent about data practices. They cannot, and should not pretend otherwise. The harder question is whether they can build disclosure regimes strong enough that secrecy remains exceptional in political effect as well as operational necessity. When a crisis comes - and one always does - will the public be hearing from an institution that has spoken consistently enough to deserve provisional belief, or from one that has left a silence so large that every revelation now sounds like proof of deception? That question determines whether transparency functions as a stabilising practice or arrives, too late, as another file opened under force.

Inequality, profiling, and administrative harm

In February 2020, a Dutch court struck down the SyRI system, a government risk-scoring tool designed to identify potential welfare and benefits fraud in the Netherlands. The court's reasoning turned on proportionality, privacy, and the opacity of a system that assembled data from multiple public sources in order to classify risk. But the deeper significance of the case lay in something harsher and more ordinary. A state had built a method for seeing some citizens more intensely than others, while offering too little explanation about how suspicion was produced or how error could be corrected. The signal travelled in one direction.

That is the central problem of inequality in data governance. Data systems do not simply reflect society from a neutral height. They sort, rank, flag, match, score, and route people through institutions built on prior histories of unequal contact. A government database may look impersonal. The choices embedded in it are not. Which variables are collected, which proxies stand in for risk, which records are linked, where human review enters, who gets audited, and who can correct an error quickly enough to matter - all of these decisions distribute burden unevenly. The result is that a state can become more administratively intelligent on paper while becoming more discriminatory in practice. The file grows cleaner. The citizen's experience grows rougher.

This is why inequality in data systems must be analysed not only as a moral problem but as a governance problem. The concept at issue is administrative harm: injury produced not through dramatic repression, but through repeated encounters with systems that misclassify, over-scrutinise, delay, deny, or expose some groups more than others. Administrative harm is easy to underestimate because it often arrives in small units. A benefits claim is flagged for extra review. A housing application is slowed. A border crossing triggers repeated secondary checks. A fraud score prompts a more intrusive questionnaire. A police patrol route is drawn around yesterday's data and therefore tomorrow's suspicion. None of these incidents alone may look historic. Together they teach a population what kind of state it lives under.

Profiling is one of the main mechanisms through which this harm is produced. A profile is not simply a description. It is an operational judgment about what someone is likely to do, need, owe, conceal, or risk. In commercial life, profiling may shape advertising or credit offers. In public administration, it can shape investigations, entitlements, inspections, and the intensity of oversight. The visible act may be small - a score, a flag, a category, a queue position. The implication can be decisive. A person is no longer treated only according to what they have done or formally declared. They are treated partly according to what a system infers from their resemblance to others. That resemblance is often built from proxies rather than direct evidence.

Proxies matter because many discriminatory systems do not mention race, poverty, disability, migration status, or religion explicitly. They use correlates. Postcode stands in for neighbourhood and class. School type stands in for family resources. Language preference stands in for migrant status. Gaps in employment history stand in for instability. Prior contact with welfare or policing stands in for future suspicion. The concept here is indirect sorting. Proxies give institutions a way to deny intentional bias while preserving stratified outcomes. A system can claim not to see protected categories and still reproduce them with grim efficiency because the social world has already encoded inequality into the variables the system does recognise.

This is where feedback loops enter. A feedback loop occurs when past patterns of intervention generate the data that justify future intervention. Police are sent more often to certain neighbourhoods; more recorded incidents then appear in those neighbourhoods; the data support sending more police there again. Welfare fraud teams scrutinise certain claimant profiles more intensely; more anomalies are found there because scrutiny is heavier; the findings justify further scrutiny of the same groups. Child protection systems focus on families already entangled with social services; more records accumulate around those families; the record itself becomes evidence of future concern. The system looks empirical. It is partly self-confirming. The state mistakes the trail of its own attention for the map of objective risk.

A named example from the United States makes this clear. Predictive policing systems that emerged in several jurisdictions over the past decade were often defended as neutral tools that analysed crime data to allocate patrol resources more efficiently. Critics argued, persuasively, that historical crime data reflected prior policing choices as much as underlying harm. If some communities had long been more heavily policed, their recorded offences and police contacts would be denser, and systems trained on those records would send attention back to the same places. The visible output was a map or patrol suggestion. The deeper mechanism was a recursive politics of suspicion. The technology did not invent inequality. It hardened and operationalised it.

Administrative harm becomes especially corrosive when error correction is uneven. A middle-class citizen with a lawyer, stable internet access, administrative confidence, and time to complain may eventually fix a mistaken tax record, challenge a false fraud alert, or navigate a complex appeal. A precarious worker, recent migrant, disabled claimant, or person with limited literacy may not. This difference is not incidental. It is part of the system's distributive logic. Rights and remedies exist formally for everyone. Their effective use depends on resources distributed very unevenly across society. A state that prides itself on due process while allowing correction to depend heavily on personal stamina and social capital is not neutral. It is externalising the cost of its own uncertainty onto those least equipped to absorb it.

This is one reason inequality and profiling cannot be reduced to bias in the narrow algorithmic sense. Public debate often asks whether a model is biased as though the answer lay entirely in the mathematics. Sometimes it does. More often the problem is institutional. Which cases are sent to the model? Which harms count? Which outputs are reviewed? Which agencies can query the result? Which burdens fall on the individual when the system is wrong? A perfectly calibrated model operating inside a lopsided administrative process can still produce unfair and politically toxic outcomes. The machine may be statistically careful. The state around it may not be.

A second named example brings the point back to welfare administration. The Dutch childcare benefits scandal, which unfolded publicly between the late 2010s and early 2020s, demonstrated how data-rich systems can devastate families when suspicion, automated logic, and harsh institutional cultures converge. Parents were wrongly accused, pushed into debt, and treated as suspect in ways that reflected not only bad individual decisions but a system structurally disposed towards overconfidence and weak correction. The scandal is often discussed in terms of algorithmic injustice, and rightly so. It should also be read as a lesson about administrative harm. Once a state uses data systems to intensify scrutiny without proportionate pathways for contestation and repair, governance itself becomes a source of injury.

This matters for democratic legitimacy because harmed groups do not experience these systems as abstract policy tools. They experience them as repeated lessons in who the state expects to be honest, orderly, and intelligible, and who it expects to explain themselves again. A citizen wrongly flagged once may remain irritated. A community repeatedly profiled, delayed, and doubted begins to revise its relationship to authority. Cooperation falls. Fear of engagement rises. People avoid services to which they are entitled because scrutiny feels more dangerous than deprivation. Administrative harm thus spills outward. It reduces service uptake, weakens civic trust, distorts public-health outreach, complicates policing by consent, and turns routine governance into a generator of political resentment.

The phrase strategic liability is not rhetorical overstatement here. A state that governs unevenly through data systems undermines its own resilience. During crises, it may need rapid compliance, accurate information, and cooperation from precisely those populations whose trust it has been quietly eroding. In ordinary periods, it may need people to disclose vulnerabilities, claim entitlements, report harms, or accept official guidance. If the state's data systems have taught those populations that visibility invites suspicion, the state's effective reach contracts even as its technical reach expands. That is a self-inflicted weakness. It is easier to build a profiling system than to rebuild a public's willingness to be seen by it.

A credible limitation should be acknowledged. Not every use of profiling or classification inside government is illegitimate. States do need to prioritise inspections, detect fraud, allocate scarce attention, identify children at risk, and anticipate service needs. A government that refused all forms of categorisation would not become fairer; it would become blinder, more arbitrary, and often more dependent on informal discretion. Nor is every unequal outcome proof of prejudice. Some communities do face distinct burdens, and administrations need ways to respond to real variation in risk and need. It would be childish to replace serious analysis with the slogan that all data-driven differentiation is discriminatory by definition.

But that limitation makes the central test more demanding, not less. The question is not whether the state classifies. It always does. The question is how it classifies, what evidence it relies on, whether proxies are doing the work of forbidden categories, whether past intervention is being mistaken for future truth, whether affected people can understand and challenge the classification, and whether error costs fall disproportionately on those already least able to bear them. If the system cannot answer these questions clearly, its practical intelligence is not much of a defence. It may simply be automating old inequalities with newer confidence.

This is why governance failures become strategic liabilities even when they begin as technical or administrative questions. A badly designed model, an overbroad fraud programme, an unreviewable score, or a biased dataset does not stay in its administrative lane. It becomes part of the state's political character. Citizens infer from it how the state sees them. Courts infer from it whether official claims about proportionality deserve belief. Journalists infer from it whether secrecy and complexity are being used to shield injustice. Civil servants infer from it what kinds of risk the institution really cares about. Each inference shapes future cooperation. The system is not only processing records. It is teaching a lesson about power.

The quiet motif of the queue is useful here. Data systems often promise to shorten queues, sort cases faster, and direct attention more efficiently. They do. They also decide who is quietly moved into the slower line, the suspicious line, the line requiring extra proof, the line from which it is hardest to step out once entered. A fair state cannot abolish queues. It can decide whether the queue is intelligible, contestable, and bounded by rules that do not quietly turn social hierarchy into administrative destiny. When the same people keep finding themselves in the slow line and no one can explain why in terms they can meaningfully challenge, legitimacy has already begun to drain away.

This is why public institutions need more than technical fairness tests or occasional bias audits. They need a political understanding of what profiling does inside unequal societies. That means examining data provenance, proxy variables, feedback effects, remedy pathways, and frontline discretion together rather than pretending that the model can be judged in isolation. It also means asking a question bureaucracies often dislike: whose confidence is the system built to protect? If the answer is mainly the confidence of the institution - its need to appear vigilant, efficient, and data-driven - then the burden of doubt is likely being shifted downwards onto citizens who will have to prove themselves repeatedly against the state's own uncertain inferences.

The harder question, then, is not whether data systems can be made more accurate. Many can. The harder question is whether they can be made more just without changing the organisational incentives that reward over-classification, weak correction, and politically invisible harm. If those incentives remain, the next profiling tool may be cleaner in design and still reproduce the same pattern of unequal burden. A democratic state that ignores this will continue to mistake governance convenience for public legitimacy. The costs will not remain confined to the wrongly flagged individual. They will accumulate in the wider civic fabric until a system built to improve administration becomes one more reason people no longer believe the administration is on their side.

Media ecosystems and distrust dynamics

In June 2013, *The Guardian* began publishing Edward Snowden's disclosures in London, and the politics of data governance changed almost overnight. Programmes that had previously existed in the technical and legal language of intelligence oversight were suddenly reframed through headlines, leaks, televised argument, and social media interpretation. The underlying facts mattered enormously. So did the medium through which they became public. A surveillance capability can be lawful, secret, and politically tolerated right up until the moment a leak transforms it into a narrative of betrayal. The file is one thing. The story about the file is another.

That distinction is at the centre of modern data politics. States often evaluate data systems in technical, legal, and operational terms: does the system work, is the authority clear, are the safeguards adequate, are the risks manageable? Citizens rarely encounter systems at that level of abstraction. They encounter fragments - a newspaper report, a whistleblower revelation, a ministerial interview, a rumour online, a corporate transparency report, a viral anecdote about wrongful targeting or hidden access. Media ecosystems do not merely report on data governance. They shape what data governance means in public life. A well-designed system can fail politically if the dominant narrative around it hardens into one of secrecy, abuse, or manipulation. A flawed system can survive longer than it should if the story told about it neutralises or confuses the harm.

This is why technical risk and political risk must be distinguished without being separated. Technical risk concerns what a system can actually do or fail to do: whether records are secure, whether access controls are weak, whether profiling is inaccurate, whether logs are sufficient, whether safeguards are real. Political risk concerns how the system will be perceived, contested, narrated, and mobilised in public discourse. The two overlap, but not neatly. A system with relatively modest technical risk may still become politically explosive if it touches deep anxieties about state overreach or private manipulation. Another with serious technical vulnerabilities may attract little public concern if it remains obscure, boring, or wrapped in a reassuring public script. A government that sees only one of these dimensions is not seeing the whole problem.

Leaks are one of the most potent mechanisms through which this gap becomes visible. A leak does more than reveal information. It rearranges authority over timing, framing, and trust. The state loses the ability to decide when a system will become legible and under what interpretive conditions. Instead of gradual explanation through official channels, the public often encounters the system as revelation, often accompanied by the implication that ordinary oversight failed, concealment was deliberate, and a larger undisclosed architecture may still exist beyond what has been revealed. Even if the leaked material is partial or technically complex, its political meaning can be immediate. It tells citizens that what mattered was not judged safe to disclose voluntarily. That alone can damage legitimacy.

This is one reason why leaks should not be analysed only as breaches of secrecy. They are also symptoms of communicative failure. When the public lacks a stable, structured understanding of how a system works, what authorities govern it, and what oversight exists, any leak is likely to be interpreted against a vacuum of prior trust. The revelation then fills the entire frame. Snowden's disclosures were especially consequential because they did not merely expose particular programmes. They suggested to many citizens that the state's operative map of surveillance had been much broader than the public map. That gap between operative and public understanding became the political fact, whatever one thought of the specific capabilities.

Disinformation complicates matters further because it exploits precisely that gap between complexity and trust. Data governance is technically dense, legally qualified, and often partly secret. Those conditions create fertile ground for distorted narratives. A real breach can be exaggerated into total omniscience. A lawful but controversial system can be recast as an instrument of dictatorship. A routine data-sharing arrangement can be framed as proof that all public services are covert surveillance networks. False claims spread easily when the official explanation is delayed, jargon-heavy, or historically unreliable. Disinformation does not need to invent public suspicion from nothing. It usually feeds on real ambiguity, real secrecy, or real past misconduct.

A named example from the COVID-19 period is revealing. During debates over digital contact tracing and exposure-notification systems in 2020, several democracies discovered that technical design choices which looked prudent to public health officials could still become politically toxic once interpreted through polarised media environments. In some countries, decentralised systems using privacy-preserving approaches still attracted suspicion that they were hidden instruments of location tracking or long-term surveillance. In others, centralised architectures became lightning rods not only for legitimate privacy critique but for broader anti-state narratives that exceeded the systems' actual design. The issue was not that all fears were irrational. It was that political meaning quickly outran technical description. Once narratives hardened, careful architectural distinctions became harder to communicate.

Polarisation intensifies this tendency by making data governance a proxy battlefield for wider struggles over legitimacy, expertise, and authority. In a low-trust environment, people do not assess a new identity system, fraud tool, or data-sharing arrangement only on its own terms. They assess it through their prior beliefs about the government proposing it, the media ecosystem describing it, and the social groups expected to bear its burdens. The visible behaviour is familiar. One side hears "better administration" and imagines creeping control. Another hears "privacy concern" and imagines obstruction or bad faith. A debate that might once have turned on system design, scope, and safeguards now becomes a conflict over who gets to define reality. The system's actual properties matter, but they are filtered through factional trust before they reach public judgment.

This makes distrust dynamic rather than static. Distrust is not merely the absence of confidence. It is often a self-reinforcing interpretive style. Once citizens begin to assume that official explanations are strategic half-truths, each new clarification can be read as evidence of a larger concealment. Each correction becomes suspicious. Each technical nuance sounds like evasion. This dynamic is especially dangerous in data governance because many systems genuinely do require qualification. They rely on thresholds, exceptions, layered access, and context-dependent safeguards. A state that needs complexity to describe its own rules can sound deceptive even when speaking accurately. That is a structural disadvantage in a media environment that rewards clarity, outrage, and moral simplification.

A second named example lies in the long afterlife of the Cambridge Analytica scandal, which became public in 2018. The episode concerned corporate data harvesting and political campaigning rather than state administration in the narrow sense. Its relevance here is profound. It taught millions of people to see data systems through a lens of hidden influence, behavioural manipulation, and unseen extraction. After such moments, subsequent state or public-private data initiatives do not arrive on a blank slate. They arrive in a political culture already primed to suspect that collection exceeds stated purpose and that institutional actors know more about them than they admit. One scandal in one domain alters trust conditions in another. That is how media ecosystems create spillover.

This spillover is why even well-designed systems can fail politically. A government may build a service with strong minimisation, decentralised storage, independent oversight, and limited retention. It may still fail if its public story is weak, if its institutional reputation is poor, or if prior scandals have made any new request for data sound like strategic encroachment. Technical virtue does not interpret itself. It has to travel through media systems populated by journalists, partisans, experts, activists, influencers, and ordinary citizens with differing incentives and differing reasons for trust. A state that treats communication as a decorative afterthought will often discover that its strongest safeguards arrived too late to shape the first durable narrative.

A credible limitation should be admitted. Media-driven distrust is not always irrational, manipulated, or politically immature. Some scepticism is earned. Leaks sometimes reveal genuine overreach. Investigative journalism performs an indispensable democratic function. Whistleblowing can expose precisely the kinds of secrecy that structured transparency was supposed to prevent. It would be a mistake to speak as though the problem were merely one of public misunderstanding. Sometimes the narrative hardens because the institution deserved it. A government that has misled before cannot blame the media for making its next reassurance harder to believe.

But that limitation reinforces the central argument rather than softening it. The point is not that governments need better messaging to overcome public irrationality. It is that democratic legitimacy now depends partly on understanding how technical systems are narratively received and contested. Public trust cannot be sustained by engineering alone, nor by legal authority alone. It requires institutions to communicate in ways that are anticipatory rather than reactive, plain enough to survive distortion, and humble enough to admit what a system cannot safely do. If a data practice would look indefensible once briefly and vividly described to a suspicious public, that is not only a communications problem. It is often a design warning.

This is where the distinction between technical and political risk becomes practically useful. Technical risk asks whether a system might leak data, misclassify citizens, enable abuse, or suffer unauthorised access. Political risk asks how the system will behave once inserted into a polarised narrative field. Which past scandals will it evoke? Which communities will see themselves as the likely targets? Which features will be impossible to explain quickly? Which forms of secrecy will be read as normal and which as sinister? Which actors, domestic or foreign, have incentives to turn the system into a symbol of broader institutional decay? These are not cynical questions. They are now basic elements of responsible governance.

The quiet motif of the echo is useful here. Information about data systems rarely reaches the public once. It echoes. A parliamentary statement becomes a headline, then a clipped video, then a partisan post, then a rebuttal thread, then a rumour, then a meme, then an official correction, then a second-order argument about why the correction appeared at all. By the time a careful technical explanation enters the stream, the echo may already be louder than the original signal. That is why one cannot judge the public meaning of a system by official description alone. The description is only the first sound.

This has important implications for repair after scandal too. A state that thinks the problem ends once factual corrections are issued has misunderstood the nature of distrust dynamics. Once a narrative has crystallised around hidden access, profiling, or extraction, repair requires more than saying the system was limited, lawful, or misunderstood. It requires visible institutional changes that alter the next cycle of interpretation: new reporting practices, narrower powers, independent review, user-facing remedies, or clearer boundaries that can be publicly described without immediately collapsing into abstraction. The media environment rewards visible acts more than quietly improved internal process. Governments may dislike this. They still have to govern within it.

The larger strategic point is that media ecosystems are now part of data infrastructure in the broadest sense. They do not store or process the underlying records, but they determine whether the public will tolerate the systems that do. A state that ignores this may find itself technically sophisticated and politically brittle. It may invest in secure architectures, oversight mechanisms, and careful legal design, only to discover that these assets carry little public force once trust has already migrated elsewhere. The informational environment in which citizens encounter a system is not external to governance. It is one of the conditions under which governance succeeds or fails.

The harder question, then, is not whether governments can control the story. They cannot, and should not aim to. The harder question is whether they can build systems and disclosure practices strong enough that the first credible public account is not always a leak, a partisan simplification, or a hostile interpretation of silence. If they cannot, then even good systems will remain politically fragile, while bad systems may continue to stumble forward until the next disclosure turns weakness into crisis. That is the point at which technical risk becomes political risk in full: not when a system breaks, but when too many people no longer know why they should believe the people explaining how it works.

Repair after breach or scandal

In October 2021, Facebook, now Meta, announced that internal documents released by the former employee Frances Haugen had shown the company knew far more about some of its harms than it had publicly admitted. The disclosures did not create all the underlying problems. They changed the political conditions under which those problems could be denied, deferred, or cosmetically managed. The scandal was not simply that a platform had failed. It was that outsiders now had reason to believe the institution had understood the failure and allowed the incentives producing it to remain largely intact. The archive became evidence of character.

That is why repair after breach or scandal is so much harder than public institutions and powerful firms often imagine. A breach can be patched. A board can be reshuffled. A minister can apologise. A review can be commissioned. None of these actions is meaningless. None of them, by itself, repairs trust. Repair is not the act of saying that a lesson has been learned. It is the slower and more costly act of proving that the conditions making the failure likely have been altered in ways that outsiders can see, test, and rely upon. The central issue is not message but structure. A scandal becomes politically enduring when the public concludes that the institution's deeper incentives remain untouched.

This is why credible repair usually begins with investigation, but cannot end there. Investigation matters because without a serious account of what happened, who knew, what decisions were made, what warnings were ignored, and what systems or cultures allowed the problem to persist, all later reform is guesswork or theatre. The concept here is institutional diagnosis. A weak diagnosis narrows the scandal to the most convenient cause - a coding error, a rogue employee, an isolated misunderstanding, a bad communications decision. A strong diagnosis traces the chain further. It asks whether procurement pressures, performance metrics, legal loopholes, staffing gaps, commercial incentives, ministerial demands, or oversight failures made the breach or abuse more probable than leaders had publicly admitted. The implication is severe. If the institution investigates only the event and not the ecosystem that made the event legible, it has not begun to repair itself.

The visible signs of weak investigation are familiar. Terms of reference are narrow. External reviewers lack access to the systems that matter most. Reports emphasise procedural lessons while leaving incentive structures intact. Timelines are vague where accountability would become awkward. Recommendations are written in language broad enough to promise change and soft enough to avoid conflict with existing power. This is not merely frustrating. It is informative. It tells the public that the institution is treating scandal as a reputational interruption rather than as evidence of a governing failure. The investigation then becomes part of the damage.

A named example from the United Kingdom makes this plain. The care.data controversy did not end because better leaflets might have reassured the public. It ended because the programme's underlying political settlement had failed. The state had not persuaded the public that secondary use of health data, however potentially beneficial, was governed by limits and institutions strong enough to deserve confidence. Attempts at repair that focus only on communication after such a breakdown mistake the depth of the injury. The public is not asking only what happened. It is asking whether the state still recognises why the earlier account of necessity and safety no longer carries weight. Repair must therefore begin with an inquiry broad enough to address not just the broken programme, but the broken bargain.

Remedy is the second element, and it is often the most neglected because it requires institutions to acknowledge that scandal does not only damage abstract trust. It harms people. Data are misused, denied, exposed, or repurposed in ways that affect employment, benefits, health access, political confidence, security, or reputation. A scandal that ends in a report but leaves affected individuals to absorb the practical cost alone is not a repaired system. It is an institution learning that public embarrassment can be managed without changing how harm is distributed. Remedy means more than compensation, though compensation may matter. It includes correction of records, reversal of decisions, restoration of access, notice to those affected, clear routes for appeal, and a willingness to reduce the administrative burden placed on victims of the institution's own failure. A state or firm that makes harmed individuals struggle to prove damage from a breach it already knows it caused is not rebuilding trust. It is refining the insult.

This is one reason the Dutch childcare benefits scandal became such a defining case. The public reaction did not turn only on the existence of wrongful flags or data-driven error. It turned on the scale of administrative harm and on the recognition that affected families had been forced to live for years inside a system whose correction mechanisms were too weak, too slow, or too hostile to interrupt the damage. When repair finally came, it could not be credible if it offered only new language about fairness or technical reform. It had to confront the lived cost imposed on those already wronged. That is the difference between governance repair and narrative repair. One changes the institution's relation to harm. The other changes the press release.

Redesign is the third requirement, and it is where institutions most often reveal whether they are serious. Redesign means changing the rules, interfaces, defaults, approval paths, staffing patterns, and incentive structures that made the original failure likely. If a scandal involved overbroad access, redesign may require tighter permissions, better logging, and narrower legal gateways. If the scandal involved profiling harms, redesign may require different data inputs, stronger human review, or the abandonment of a scoring model altogether. If the scandal exposed vendor lock-in or blurred accountability, redesign may require new procurement structures, portability rights, independent audit access, or retention of more internal expertise. The crucial point is that redesign addresses recurrence, not only embarrassment. It asks what must be made harder inside the institution if repetition is to become less likely.

A second named example comes from the aftermath of the Snowden disclosures. Many democratic states responded with some combination of reviews, legal reforms, and more visible reporting about surveillance powers. The quality of those responses varied, and reasonable observers still disagree about how far they altered underlying practice. The relevant lesson lies in the pattern. Where governments treated the scandal as a communications rupture and relied mainly on reassurance, the legitimacy deficit persisted. Where they combined explanation with legal revision, stronger oversight, more regular reporting, and some narrowing or clearer articulation of authority, they did more to stabilise trust even among critics not fully persuaded by the reforms. Repair did not require universal agreement. It required visible changes in the machinery of secrecy and review.

This reveals why one-off reforms so often fail. Institutions under pressure are drawn towards discrete, displayable acts: dismiss a leader, pause a programme, hire an independent adviser, commission an audit, publish a charter, create a new ethics board, announce a training package. Each of these may help. The problem comes when they are used to avoid confronting the incentive structure. A platform whose revenue still depends on extracting and retaining maximum behavioural data will not be transformed by a new integrity committee alone. A public agency rewarded for aggressive fraud detection will not become fair simply because a review recommends "better balance". A ministry judged politically on rapid delivery at low cost will not automatically procure accountable systems because a breach has embarrassed it once. Incentives are patient. They wait for attention to move elsewhere.

This is why sustained oversight is the fourth component of credible repair. Oversight matters not only to detect recurrence, but to prevent reform energy from dissipating once headlines fade. A repaired institution needs someone outside the immediate chain of operational interest to ask, over time, whether the promised changes have actually occurred, whether new workarounds have emerged, whether harms have shifted form rather than disappeared, and whether the organisation's self-description still matches its practice. The visible signs of meaningful oversight are continuity and friction. Reports recur. Metrics remain comparable. Findings are not uniformly flattering. Recommendations return in modified form because the institution is being observed as a moving target rather than congratulated for a single performance of repentance.

A credible limitation should be admitted. Not every scandal reflects deep corruption or permanently rotten incentive structures. Some failures are genuinely contingent. A specific software vulnerability may be patched successfully. A contractor may make an exceptional error. A breach may result from an unusual concatenation of haste, misjudgment, and bad luck. It would be simplistic to assume that every institution emerging from scandal is fundamentally incapable of reform or that every crisis proves systemic vice. Some one-off actions really do solve the problem at hand. Prudence requires leaving room for that possibility.

But that limitation does not change the broader diagnosis. Institutions themselves often claim contingency too quickly because contingency is easier to fix than structure. The question is not whether a discrete error occurred. It is whether the surrounding environment rewarded, tolerated, or failed to catch that error in ways likely to matter again. A breach caused by one poor configuration still raises structural questions if logging was weak, review was under-resourced, vendor accountability was diffuse, or risk warnings had repeatedly been deprioritised. A scandal around data misuse still raises structural questions if purpose limits were easy to bypass, training was performative, and redress depended on the persistence of those least able to navigate bureaucracy. The point of repair is not to dramatise every failure into a grand moral collapse. It is to ask what recurrence would learn from the original event if nothing deeper changed.

Public understanding of reform matters here too. Institutions often believe trust will return if they can show motion. The public is usually asking for something more exacting: not motion, but consequence. Who investigated? What did they find? Who was affected? What changed in the actual system? What powers were narrowed, what access withdrawn, what controls added, what contracts rewritten, what remedies delivered, what external body is still watching? These are practical questions. They arise because trust after scandal no longer rests on broad claims of good faith. It rests on whether the institution can narrate its own reform in ways that connect directly to the original harm. If the narrative drifts into general virtue and future ambition, confidence remains thin.

The media environment sharpens this problem. In a fragmented and polarised ecosystem, repair that is invisible, jargon-heavy, or dependent on quiet internal process will struggle to alter public judgment even when some of it is real. That does not mean reform should become pure spectacle. It means institutions must understand that visible redesign and visible accountability are part of repair, not merely communications accessories. A state or firm cannot expect publics to infer deep change from a new governance structure whose practical effect no outsider can inspect. Trust grows when outsiders can point to something tangible and say: that power is narrower now, that remedy exists now, that oversight body can see more now, that data flow no longer happens, that appeal route really works. The institution must make reform legible enough to become socially believable.

The quiet motif of the scar is useful here. A scar is evidence that injury occurred, but also that tissue changed around the injury. Repair without a scar is often amnesia disguised as renewal. An institution that insists on speaking as though the scandal were a brief misunderstanding rather than a wound to legitimacy usually has not rebuilt much. A credible scar is not endless self-flagellation. It is the visible mark of change: a narrowed system, a standing report, a new redress route, a rule that cannot now be evaded so casually, a culture more alert to its own temptations. Scars are not pretty. They are reassuring precisely because they show that damage was not denied.

This is why trust should be understood as a capacity built over time rather than a sentiment restored by apology. A capable institution stores trust the way it stores resilience: through repeated bounded behaviour, honest accounting, usable remedies, and oversight strong enough to endure beyond the mood of the moment. Scandal depletes that capacity rapidly. Repair rebuilds it slowly because each reform must survive the institution's natural desire to return to comfort, opacity, or extraction once pressure recedes. The public does not need to love the institution. It needs enough evidence that the next failure will be less likely, less hidden, less harmful, and more corrigible than the last.

The harder question, then, is not whether a breach or scandal can be survived. Many can. The harder question is what must become harder inside the institution for survival to count as repair rather than mere endurance. If the same incentives still reward overcollection, weak explanation, blurred responsibility, or politically convenient secrecy, then the scandal has not really been metabolised. It has only been outlasted. At that point the next breach will not arrive as an isolated shock. It will arrive as confirmation of a pattern the public already suspects. That is the moment at which trust ceases to be a renewable resource and starts to look like a capacity the institution has chosen, repeatedly, not to rebuild.

Chapter 13

Resilience in an Age of Permanent Memory

What does it mean for a state to be resilient when forgetting has become harder than remembering? The question sounds philosophical until a system fails, a record is challenged, a court demands proof, or a public inquiry discovers that crucial evidence was copied too widely to erase, stored too carelessly to trust, or concentrated too narrowly to survive disruption. Modern data systems promise continuity through replication, backup, and persistence. They also create a new fragility: too much memory in the wrong places, too little confidence in what memory can prove, and too much dependence on infrastructures whose resilience was assumed rather than tested.

That paradox runs through the politics of digital government and national power. States now preserve more than any earlier bureaucracy could have imagined. They retain logs, metadata, images, transactions, messages, access records, and audit trails across layers of cloud storage, contractor systems, and institutional archives. Yet this abundance does not automatically produce resilience. A backup is not the same thing as recovery. A copied record is not the same thing as an authentic one. Retention is not the same thing as control. A system may remember everything and still fail at the decisive moment because nobody can verify provenance, confirm deletion, restore service quickly, or explain who was meant to govern the lifecycle of the record in the first place.

This is the chapter's central tension. Permanent memory appears to offer security, accountability, and continuity, but it can just as easily generate brittleness, opacity, and false confidence. Institutions keep more because they fear loss, litigation, scandal, and operational disruption. They also keep more because deletion is difficult, backup regimes are layered, and digital accumulation feels prudent until it becomes unmanageable. At the same time, accountability often depends on preserving records well enough that courts, inspectors, and future publics can trust them. The state therefore faces a genuine dilemma. It must remember enough to govern and answer for itself, but forget enough to prevent exposure, overload, and uncontrolled replication from becoming strategic liabilities of their own.

The stakes are unusually high because resilience is tested not in ordinary throughput but in moments of rupture. A cyber incident, legal challenge, public inquiry, regional outage, natural disaster, contractor collapse, or political scandal can suddenly reveal what looked robust and what merely looked busy. If retention rules are vague, deletion unverifiable, archives poorly documented, or dependencies concentrated in a small number of vendors and regions, the system may discover too late that its continuity rested on habit rather than design. What fails then is not only service. It is confidence in the state's capacity to preserve truth, restore function, and distinguish recoverable disruption from institutional unravelling.

This is why resilience cannot be reduced to uptime or storage volume. It depends on governance clarity as much as on infrastructure. Who decides what must be retained, and for how long? Who can authorise deletion, and how is that deletion verified across copies and backups? Which records count as authoritative when versions diverge? What metadata must survive alongside content if authenticity is later contested? Which systems are so concentrated that a single supplier, region, or failure mode would create cascading institutional damage? These are not questions for emergency response alone. They are questions of peacetime design. A state that asks them only after crisis has already confused durability with convenience.

The chapter's path follows that deeper problem. It begins with the politics of retention and deletion, where the supposed permanence of digital memory collides with the practical need to forget and the institutional difficulty of proving that forgetting has really occurred. It then turns to archiving and provenance, where accountability depends not simply on keeping records but on preserving them in forms that can survive challenge, manipulation, and the passage of time. From there it broadens into disaster recovery and concentration risk, asking what it means to build redundancy when cost pressures and platform scale push in the opposite direction, before closing on the harder matter of assessment: how resilience can be judged without mistaking neat dashboards for genuine institutional preparedness.

A useful image for the chapter is the lockbox. States fill lockboxes with things they may need later: evidence, entitlements, decisions, logs, and traces of official action. In the digital age the lockbox multiplies. Copies sit in archives, backups, replicated stores, contractor environments, and cloud regions; keys are distributed across teams and suppliers; inventories drift; contents outlast their original purpose. A larger lockbox may feel safer. It may simply become harder to search, harder to govern, and harder to trust when what matters is not whether something was kept somewhere, but whether the right version can be found, verified, and restored under pressure.

That image matters because resilience has a political dimension as well as a technical one. Public trust depends partly on whether institutions can answer simple but unforgiving questions after failure: what was lost, what survives, what can be restored, what was deleted, what was altered, what can be proven, and who was responsible for the design choices that made the outcome possible. A state that cannot answer those questions clearly may still possess vast stores of data. It will not look resilient. It will look like an institution trapped inside its own memory, unable to convert accumulation into assurance.

The harder question, then, is not whether modern states should keep more records or fewer. Both instincts can be dangerous when pursued without discipline. The harder question is what kind of institutional order can decide what deserves to endure, what must be allowed to disappear, and what forms of concentration are too risky to accept merely because they are efficient in normal times. That question leads directly to the first issue: in a world where copying is easy and storage is cheap, who actually controls forgetting, and how would anyone know if it had truly happened?

Retention, deletion, and the politics of forgetting

In May 2014, the Court of Justice of the European Union decided Google Spain and recognised, under certain conditions, a right for individuals to request the removal of links from name-based search results. The case quickly became shorthand for "the right to be forgotten", though the judgment did not erase the underlying newspaper archive and did not pretend that digital memory could simply be wished away. Its deeper importance lay elsewhere. A court had been forced to confront a problem modern states and platforms now face constantly: what counts as deletion when copying is easy, indexing is persistent, and the practical power of information lies not only in its existence but in how readily it can be found? The file could remain. The public meaning of its retrieval had changed.

That tension sits at the centre of digital retention politics. Modern institutions remember by default. Storage is cheap relative to the perceived costs of losing information; backup regimes multiply copies automatically;

analytics reward accumulation; legal teams fear deletion more than over-retention; administrators assume future utility even when present purpose has expired. Under these conditions, forgetting no longer happens naturally through decay, misfiling, or physical scarcity. It must be designed, authorised, and verified. Forgetting has become an achievement.

This matters because retention is not a neutral administrative choice. It governs what future actions remain possible. A retained record may support accountability, continuity, audit, and legitimate investigation. The same record may also enable mission creep, profiling, reputational harm, coercive discovery, or future uses never contemplated when the data were first collected. Retention therefore distributes power across time. The concept is temporal asymmetry: institutions can preserve optionality by keeping records long after the individual who supplied the data has lost practical control over how those records might later be interpreted or combined. The implication is political. A state or platform that keeps too much for too long quietly acquires future leverage even when no immediate misuse is visible.

This is why deletion rights emerged as more than symbolic gestures. They attempt to reverse the presumption that institutions may hold everything unless forced to let go. Yet deletion is far harder to operationalise than public debate often assumes. The visible act may seem simple enough: delete the file, remove the record, clear the account. In practice the same item may exist in production systems, indexes, logs, snapshots, archives, disaster-recovery backups, vendor environments, data lakes, and analytical derivatives. A person may win deletion in the ordinary interface and still leave traces in systems designed precisely not to forget quickly. The institution has removed the object from one shelf while the copies remain in other rooms.

This is where lifecycle policy becomes decisive. Lifecycle policy answers the basic questions most organisations postpone for too long: what is collected, for what purpose, where it travels, how long each copy persists, when it moves from operational use to archive, what legal holds suspend deletion, and who has authority to override or verify each step. The point is not administrative elegance. It is control. An institution without a clear lifecycle policy does not really know whether it remembers by design or by residue. It accumulates because deletion is harder than storage and because no one wants to own the risk of letting something go. In such an organisation, retention becomes the default theology of caution.

A named example from the United Kingdom helps clarify the stakes. The long controversies over police and intelligence data retention, especially surrounding communications data and bulk powers, have repeatedly turned on the fact that collection is only half the question. How long the data remain available, under what conditions they can be queried again, and whether retention rules are narrow enough to match the original justification determine much of the real political meaning of the power. A dataset retained briefly under clear limits tells one constitutional story. The same dataset retained broadly because future utility is imagined rather than specified tells another. Retention is where exceptional access often settles into ordinary infrastructure.

This is one reason forgetting is an institutional achievement, not merely a technical one. Technical deletion requires system knowledge, dependencies, data mapping, and often expensive redesign. Institutional deletion requires authority, confidence, and willingness to accept that some future convenience or litigation comfort will be sacrificed in exchange for present restraint. Many organisations possess the technical means to delete more than they do. They lack the internal incentives. Legal teams fear discovery obligations. security teams fear losing forensic history. product teams fear reducing future analytical value. officials fear being blamed later for deleting something that might have proven useful. These fears are not imaginary. Left ungoverned, they turn every retention decision into a vote for indefinite memory.

The politics of forgetting therefore involves an uncomfortable fact: deletion competes with several other public goods. Courts, inquiries, historians, journalists, and auditors often need records to survive. Public accountability can depend on preserving evidence long enough that later challenge remains possible. A government that deletes too aggressively may protect privacy while impairing justice or historical truth. A platform that erases operational records too quickly may make discrimination, abuse, or security failure harder to prove. The concept here is evidentiary tension. Forgetting can protect the individual from unnecessary future exposure. It can also protect institutions from future scrutiny if invoked opportunistically or designed badly. Any serious deletion regime must live inside that tension rather than pretending it away.

That is why good retention policy cannot be reduced to a simple moral preference for less data. It requires classification. Some records deserve short lives because their purpose is narrow and their future risk high. Others deserve durable preservation because they are central to legal rights, public inquiry, historical accountability, or institutional continuity. The hard cases sit in between: records useful for fraud detection, service improvement, public health analysis, or security assessment but also capable of being repurposed far beyond the original justification. Here the decisive question is not whether retention is ever justified. It is whether the justification is specific, reviewable, and matched to the actual lifecycle of the data rather than to a vague institutional desire for optionality.

A second named example comes from debates over search de-listing after Google Spain. The case exposed the difference between deletion as literal erasure and deletion as practical obscurity. The underlying publication might remain lawful and historically valuable. What changed was the ease with which a person's past could dominate present identity through a simple name search. This matters because digital memory is often powerful not because information exists somewhere, but because infrastructures of retrieval make it persistently actionable. The politics of forgetting therefore includes ranking, indexing, and discoverability as much as storage. A file buried in an archive does not wield the same force as a file placed instantly before employers, neighbours, journalists, or bureaucrats through routine search.

This broader understanding helps explain why verification matters so much. An institution that claims a record has been deleted must be able to explain what that means. Was the operational copy erased? Were derivative models retrained? Were caches refreshed? Did backups retain the record temporarily under a documented schedule? Were legal holds applied? Which logs remain, and why? Deletion without verification is little more than ceremonial language. The visible user experience may suggest closure. The underlying system may still remember enough to restore, infer, or reproduce what was supposedly gone. Verification is therefore the hinge between rights language and operational truth.

A credible limitation should be acknowledged. Full deletion is not always technically immediate or legally appropriate. Backups exist to enable recovery after failure, and many systems cannot surgically remove individual traces from every replicated layer without introducing new integrity or continuity risks. Some records must be preserved because they bear on contractual rights, criminal processes, safeguarding duties, or public accountability. It would be unserious to promise absolute forgetting in all cases. Such promises would collapse under the first audit or disaster-recovery test.

But that limitation sharpens rather than weakens the main argument. Since perfect forgetting is often impossible, institutions owe the public more precision about what kind of forgetting they can actually deliver. Can data be removed from active use? Can discoverability be reduced? Can identifiers be severed? Can retention in backup be time-bound and inaccessible except under controlled recovery procedures? Can evidentiary archives be kept under separate governance from operational analytics? These distinctions matter because they determine whether "deletion" names a real reduction of institutional power over the record or merely a softer interface for the same continuing memory.

This is also where market structure enters the story. Retention and deletion are increasingly governed through cloud platforms, enterprise software, outsourced support, and layered vendors whose defaults often privilege preservation. A public authority or firm may not fully control how many copies exist, where snapshots are stored, how logs are retained, or how difficult selective deletion becomes once data have moved across contracts and services. The institution still bears political responsibility, but lifecycle control may be scattered across technical and commercial layers it does not fully command. That is why asking "who controls lifecycle policy?" cannot stop at the formal data controller. It must also ask who designed the storage architecture, who configured the retention defaults, who can access the backups, and who can independently verify what has actually been removed.

The quiet motif of the shelf helps hold the problem together. In a paper bureaucracy, to keep a file meant putting it on a shelf and deciding how long the shelf would remain part of the institution's active memory. In digital systems, the shelf proliferates. There is the live shelf, the backup shelf, the vendor shelf, the index shelf, the litigation shelf, the archive shelf, the analytics shelf. Politics enters when institutions talk as though removing a file from one shelf resolves the problem. It does not. Real forgetting means knowing how many shelves exist and which of them still matter.

This has consequences for resilience as well as rights. An institution that cannot delete controllably is not only intrusive. It is brittle. Excess retention enlarges attack surfaces, complicates migration, increases discovery burdens, blurs evidentiary chains, and makes incident response harder because no one can say with confidence where sensitive material resides or which copy is authoritative. Permanent memory sounds like strength until crisis reveals it as cluttered dependency. A state that remembers too indiscriminately may discover that it cannot protect, restore, or explain what it keeps.

The deeper question, then, is not whether societies should remember or forget. They must do both. The real issue is whether retention and deletion are governed by clear purpose, verifiable control, and the courage to limit future convenience in order to preserve present legitimacy. If copying is effortless and backups ubiquitous, forgetting will never again be a passive process. It will be a deliberate institutional act, one that reveals who holds power over the lifecycle of information and whether that power is being used to serve accountability, to hoard optionality, or to keep the past perpetually available for whoever controls the shelves.

Archiving, provenance, and evidentiary integrity

In October 2019, the Court of Session in Edinburgh ruled that the United Kingdom Prime Minister's advice to prorogue Parliament had been unlawful, and one of the many features of the wider constitutional drama was how intensely modern politics now depends on records: messages, memoranda, drafts, calendar entries, email trails, and the metadata that place each item in sequence. The content of a record matters. So does its surrounding frame. Who created it, when, in what system, under what version, with what later alteration, and in relation to which other records can determine whether a document counts as evidence or merely as text detached from authority. The words are not enough.

That is the starting point for understanding archiving in an age of permanent memory. Archiving is often imagined as a passive act of storage, a bureaucratic afterlife in which documents are placed somewhere safe for eventual retrieval. In reality, public archiving is an active system of constitutional defence. It preserves the traces through which states can later be held to account, through which courts and inquiries can reconstruct events, and through which future publics can distinguish record from rumour. A state that archives badly does not merely risk administrative inconvenience. It weakens its own capacity to prove what happened, when it happened, and whether the record in front of it is still the same one that existed at the time.

This is why provenance matters so much. Provenance is not decorative archival detail. It is the chain of identity around a record: origin, custody, context, modification history, and relationships to other records and systems. The concept is simple enough to state and demanding to preserve. A document without reliable provenance may still be interesting. It will struggle to function as authoritative evidence. In digital systems this difficulty intensifies because copying is easy, files travel across platforms, collaborative editing obscures discrete authorship, and routine migration between systems can strip away or degrade the very metadata needed to verify authenticity. Public institutions may think they have preserved the record because the content survives. They may have preserved only a shell.

This has direct consequences for courts. A court does not merely ask whether a record exists. It asks whether the record can be trusted to speak for the event, decision, or communication it is meant to represent. Was the document created at the claimed time, or merely labelled as such later? Was it altered, and if so by whom and under what process? Does it sit within a coherent chain of related records, or has it been detached from the context that gives it evidentiary meaning? The visible item may be an email, a spreadsheet, a draft policy note, a messaging export, or a system log. The legal question is not the literary one of what it says, but the evidentiary one of what it is.

This is one reason metadata can be as important as content. Timestamps, sender and recipient fields, version histories, access logs, file hashes, system identifiers, creation and modification dates, routing information, and retention events often determine whether a record can withstand challenge. A message saying "approved" means very little without confidence about who sent it, through which channel, after what previous exchanges, and whether the record produced in court reflects the message as sent or a later reconstruction. The phrase "metadata" can sound technical and secondary. In practice it often carries the burden of authenticity. Without it, archives become collections of words floating free from institutional time.

A named example from the United States makes this plain. The controversies around presidential records, deleted communications, and the use of unofficial or ephemeral channels across several administrations have repeatedly raised questions not just about what was said, but whether official business was being conducted in forms likely to frustrate archival preservation and later scrutiny. The public debate usually centres on secrecy or evasion, and rightly so. The deeper archival issue is more structural. A constitutional system that depends on records cannot remain healthy if senior officials routinely communicate through channels that weaken capture, provenance, or retrieval. The problem is not merely loss. It is deniability.

Public inquiries reveal the same truth under different pressure. When states investigate disasters, wars, procurement failures, wrongful convictions, or administrative scandals, the quality of the archive often determines the quality of the answer. An inquiry can hear testimony, but testimony alone rarely suffices. It needs records that can anchor memory against hindsight, self-protection, and selective forgetting. A weak archive leaves an inquiry vulnerable to ambiguity and performance. A strong archive does not remove dispute. It narrows the range within which dispute can plausibly operate. The state, in that sense, archives not only for its own continuity but for the possibility that one day it may have to answer to itself in public.

This is why archiving is inseparable from accountability. Yet accountability is not the only value in play. Archives must also resist tampering, accidental loss, degradation, and unauthorised disclosure. Those goals can sit in tension. A system optimised for immutability may frustrate necessary correction of classification errors or accidental inclusion of sensitive personal data. A system optimised for easy access may weaken chain-of-custody assurance. A system spread across many copies may reduce single-point failure while increasing uncertainty about which version remains authoritative. The archival challenge is not to maximise one value at the expense of all others. It is to preserve the conditions under which records can remain both durable and trustworthy.

This is why evidentiary integrity should be understood as a design property rather than an archival afterthought. It depends on decisions made long before a record enters a formal archive. How are records created? Which systems capture them automatically? What counts as an official record when work is done across email, messaging apps, collaborative documents, cloud platforms, and contractor tools? Which metadata fields are mandatory? How are versions preserved? Who can alter classification, redact, export, or delete, and what audit trail is created when they do? An institution that asks these questions only at the moment of inquiry or litigation is already late. The record has been living a life long before it arrives at the archive's door.

A second named example lies in the long-running difficulties many governments have faced in preserving text messages, instant messages, and other forms of informal digital communication when official business migrates into tools built for speed rather than archival discipline. This is not a trivial generational problem about etiquette. It is a constitutional one. Modern decision-making increasingly takes place in channels that feel conversational, iterative, and disposable. Yet those channels may carry instructions, approvals, strategic judgments, and crisis discussions of immense public consequence. If the archival system captures only the polished memo and not the conversation that shaped it, the state preserves a misleading image of its own decision-making. Historical memory becomes sanitised by format.

A credible limitation should be acknowledged. Not every state record can or should be preserved forever in full. Privacy, security, practical cost, and institutional overload all require selection. Archives without selection become hoards rather than usable public memory. Nor is every missing metadata field proof of manipulation. Systems differ, migrations are messy, and older records were often created under weaker technical assumptions than present ones. It would be simplistic to suggest that a state can guarantee perfect provenance for every document across every era and platform. Some loss, ambiguity, and imperfection are inevitable.

But that limitation sharpens the central argument. Precisely because not everything can be preserved equally well, states must become more deliberate about what kinds of records, metadata, and chain-of-custody protections matter most for accountability. They must know which classes of decision require strong evidentiary integrity, which systems create the public record by default, and which forms of communication are too fragile or too opaque to sustain constitutional confidence if allowed to dominate official business. The answer is not to archive everything indiscriminately. It is to archive enough, and well enough, that later scrutiny does not depend on luck.

This is also a market question. Public records increasingly pass through commercial software, cloud storage, document management systems, email platforms, contractor workflows, and collaboration tools not designed primarily for the constitutional needs of public archives. A state may believe it owns the records and still depend on vendor architectures to preserve version histories, maintain metadata fidelity, export data in usable formats, and prove chain of custody after migration or incident. Procurement choices therefore shape evidentiary integrity. A cheap system that loses context in export or obscures audit trails may save money in the short term while weakening the future archive. A platform optimised for convenience may become a slow constitutional liability.

The relationship between archive and disaster recovery must also be understood clearly. They overlap. They are not identical. Disaster recovery aims to restore function after disruption. Archiving aims to preserve authoritative memory. Backups can restore a system after failure, but they do not automatically provide evidentiary integrity. A restored copy may revive content without clarifying which version was authoritative at the relevant time, what happened in the interval, or whether restoration itself altered the metadata environment. Institutions that confuse backup with archive often discover too late that they can recover operations without being able to prove history. Resilience of service and resilience of evidence are related but distinct achievements.

This matters for historical memory as much as for immediate litigation. Archives shape how future societies understand policy, conflict, crisis, reform, scandal, and everyday governance. If the preserved record is partial, context-poor, or dependent on proprietary tools that later become unreadable, the state leaves behind a distorted account of itself. Historians and future publics will still write narratives. They will do so from a damaged evidentiary base. The political significance of archiving is therefore longer than any single court case. A state archives not merely to defend itself in the present, but to constrain how easily its past can be falsified by convenience, ideology, or loss.

The quiet motif of the seal is useful here. A seal does not make a document true. It certifies that a document has travelled through recognised custody and can therefore claim a certain authority. Digital systems complicate the old symbolism of seals because records now change, duplicate, and circulate with extraordinary ease. But the underlying need has not disappeared. Courts, inquiries, and democratic publics still need ways of knowing that a record is what it purports to be. The modern seal may be a log, a hash, a metadata trail, a version history, or an auditable archival workflow. Without some equivalent, the archive becomes a storeroom rather than a public witness.

This is why evidentiary integrity is not a specialist concern for archivists alone. It belongs to everyone who cares whether governments can be held to account through something firmer than selective memory and adversarial storytelling. A record must survive. It must also survive with enough provenance that the institution cannot easily deny, sanitise, or reframe its own past once scrutiny begins. That requirement shapes technical design, procurement, legal process, and political culture all at once.

The harder question, then, is not whether states need better archives. They plainly do. The harder question is whether they are willing to preserve not only the content that flatters continuity but the provenance that makes challenge possible. In a digital order saturated with copies, edits, migrations, and informal channels, authenticity will rarely be self-evident. It will have to be built, preserved, and defended through systems whose quiet success is measured by a severe standard: when the day of dispute arrives, can the state still prove that its own memory deserves to count as evidence rather than as another version of events?

Disaster recovery and systemic concentration

On 7 December 2021, an outage in Amazon Web Services' US-East-1 region disrupted a striking range of services, from internal enterprise tools to public-facing applications and connected devices. The immediate story was technical and operational. The deeper lesson was strategic. Systems that appeared widely distributed turned out to share a hidden centre of gravity. The cloud had looked like dispersion. Under stress, it behaved like concentration.

That episode matters because disaster recovery is often discussed in reassuring language that conceals its political and economic foundations. Institutions speak of backup environments, failover plans, mirrored storage, and continuity procedures as though resilience were something one simply adds once the main system is built. It is not. Disaster recovery is the practical test of whether a system was designed to survive the loss of a platform, region, vendor, network path, or operating assumption that had quietly become indispensable. A recovery plan written after concentration has already hardened usually discovers that the most important dependencies are precisely the ones hardest to escape.

This is why systemic concentration deserves more attention than dramatic sabotage scenarios in many discussions of resilience. States and firms are rightly concerned about cyber attacks, natural disasters, hardware failures, and operator error. Yet concentration often determines whether those events remain local problems or become broad social disruptions. The concept is dependency clustering. A single provider, region, software layer, identity service, or systems integrator may serve so many critical functions that one failure radiates across sectors that otherwise appear separate. Payments, health administration, local government portals, logistics tracking, digital identity checks, and internal civil service tools may all be sitting on variations of the same stack. The architecture looks plural from the outside and singular from underneath.

This is the paradox of digital efficiency. Centralisation can improve baseline security, reduce duplication, simplify maintenance, and lower cost. A large provider may patch faster, staff more specialists, and run more disciplined infrastructure than scattered smaller operators could manage. Those advantages are real. They help explain why concentration happens. The problem emerges when operational rationality at the level of one institution produces strategic fragility at the level of the system as a whole. Each agency saves money by choosing the dominant platform. Each vendor standardises around the same interfaces. Each procurement team narrows to proven suppliers. Eventually the system no longer knows how much of itself depends on the same handful of underlying services.

A named example from the public sector makes the point sharper. In several countries, digital government programmes have migrated large portions of public administration to a small number of cloud and software providers because those providers offer scale, compliance frameworks, and rapid deployment that fragmented legacy estates often lack. The decision is usually justified, and often sensibly. But once tax systems, benefits portals, identity services, internal casework tools, and records platforms converge on related commercial environments, disaster recovery ceases to be a question about any one department. It becomes a question about whether the state has created a new critical infrastructure through procurement without fully acknowledging it as such. The visible service is public. The recovery path may depend on a commercial architecture whose concentration the public never consented to debate.

This is why redundancy matters, and why it is so often underprovided. Redundancy looks wasteful in calm periods because it requires paying for capacity that sits unused or underused much of the time. Duplicate environments, alternate suppliers, cross-region replication, offline fallback procedures, parallel communication channels, and rehearsed manual workarounds all cost money, staff attention, and managerial patience. Budget systems dislike this. Procurement systems often dislike it too. They reward visible delivery and measurable utilisation, not preparedness for rare but consequential disruption. The concept here is the politics of apparent inefficiency. A system that looks financially lean may simply be borrowing resilience from an untroubled future.

This is one reason resilience must be treated as a design property rather than an emergency purchase. An institution cannot wait until crisis to decide that it would like a second provider, a different region, cleaner export formats, or a manual fallback mode for essential services. By then data models are entrenched, staff are trained into one workflow, contracts are signed, interfaces are tuned to one platform's assumptions, and switching risk itself has become a source of paralysis. The visible symptom in crisis is improvisation. Officials say continuity plans existed. In practice, the "plan" often proves to be a mixture of vendor assurances, vaguely remembered tabletop exercises, and heroic work by staff rebuilding ad hoc procedures under pressure. Heroism is not resilience. It is what institutions consume when resilience has been underbought.

A second named example lies in the repeated disruptions caused by ransomware incidents against public bodies and critical services. Such attacks are usually discussed as security failures, which they are. They are also tests of concentration and recovery design. An organisation with segmented systems, verified backups, rehearsed restoration procedures, clear dependency maps, and alternate communication channels can sometimes contain and recover more quickly than one with supposedly stronger perimeter controls but poorer recovery architecture. The issue is not only whether the intrusion occurred. It is whether the system was built to absorb loss in one part without surrendering continuity everywhere else. Attackers exploit technical weakness. They also exploit overcentralised convenience.

This helps explain why "backup" is one of the most misunderstood words in digital governance. A backup is necessary. It is not sufficient. Backups can be corrupted, inaccessible, untested, dependent on the same credentials as live systems, or too slow to restore within the real operational window of the affected service. They may also preserve data while failing to preserve functional continuity if applications, identity layers, vendor integrations, or network dependencies cannot be restored coherently around them. The concept is recovery realism. A backup proves that data were copied. It does not prove that service can resume, that priorities are clear, or that staff know how to operate under degraded conditions.

This is where vendor concentration becomes especially dangerous. Many institutions now rely on a prime supplier whose own resilience depends on subcontractors, third-party software libraries, external identity providers, network carriers, and regional power or cooling infrastructure outside the customer's direct view. The customer thinks it has diversified because it has several applications. Those applications may all share the same hidden dependencies. Accountability blurs at precisely the moment clarity is most needed. One provider blames a third-party component, another cites an upstream cloud issue, a contractor says the failover option was outside scope, and the public institution discovers that its continuity depends on relationships it does not fully map. The chain becomes visible only when it snaps.

A credible limitation should be acknowledged. Not every system can or should maintain full multi-provider or cross-region redundancy. The cost can be prohibitive. Complexity can increase rather than reduce risk if duplicate architectures are poorly governed. Some forms of diversification are more theatrical than real, especially when supposedly distinct services rely on the same standards, chips, software supply chains, or skilled labour pools. It would be simplistic to argue that every concentrated system is reckless or that every organisation must purchase maximal duplication to be responsible. Resilience is not achieved by chanting "more redundancy" without regard to purpose.

But that limitation clarifies the real question. The issue is not whether every component should be duplicated at any price. It is whether institutions know which failures would be socially or politically intolerable, and whether they have designed those specific functions to survive with acceptable degradation. A payments notification system, an internal analytics tool, and a digital identity service do not all require the same recovery posture. Criticality must be mapped honestly, not rhetorically. Which services must continue in real time? Which can pause briefly? Which require a manual fallback? Which depend on one region, one credentialing system, one supplier relationship, or one format that cannot easily be ported? Resilience planning becomes serious at the point where these distinctions are made before crisis, not after.

This has implications for sovereignty as well as continuity. A state heavily concentrated on a few foreign-owned platforms or a small cluster of domestic incumbents may discover that disaster recovery is entangled with jurisdiction, market power, and supply chain exposure. The question in crisis is no longer merely how to restore service. It becomes who has the operational authority, technical access, and practical capability to help restore it; whose priorities govern shared infrastructure under stress; and whether the state has retained enough in-house knowledge to make independent judgments about what its vendors are telling it. Concentration thus converts a technical outage into a political event about dependence.

The labour dimension matters too. Redundant infrastructure is not self-executing. Recovery depends on people who understand system priorities, data flows, vendor obligations, sequencing, and the difference between restoring a database and restoring a service. Institutions that have outsourced too much operational understanding often discover that continuity plans are written in a vocabulary their own staff cannot fully enact under pressure. The vendor knows the environment. The state owns the consequences. This is one more way in which resilience proves to be a governance property rather than a storage feature. The plan lives in architecture, contracts, rehearsals, and institutional memory at once.

The quiet motif of the spare key helps hold the argument together. A spare key is useful only if it opens a genuinely separate path into the house, can be found when needed, and belongs to someone who knows when and how to use it. A key hidden in the same locked room as the original is not redundancy. Neither is a second key cut so poorly that it jams under stress. Many continuity arrangements in public and private systems resemble these failed spare keys: nominal alternatives that depend on the same platform, the same credentials, the same staff, or the same assumptions as the primary system. True redundancy feels expensive because it is meaningfully separate.

This is why resilience should be judged not by the elegance of continuity documents but by the awkward questions an institution is willing to ask itself in advance. What happens if this region fails? If this vendor disappears? If this identity service is unavailable? If these backups are compromised? If these logs cannot be trusted? If staff must run the service manually for a period? If contractual rights exist but practical retrieval does not? These questions are uncomfortable because they expose how much ordinary efficiency rests on extraordinary assumption. Yet they are precisely the questions that distinguish design from hope.

The harder question, then, is not whether redundancy costs money. It does, and often more than finance teams or ministers would like. The harder question is what costs are being hidden when redundancy is omitted in the name of efficiency. An institution may save budget, simplify procurement, and consolidate expertise by concentrating on a few platforms, regions, and vendors. It may also be quietly converting continuity risk into a future political crisis whose price will be paid in public trust, service failure, and emergency improvisation. Resilience begins when organisations stop pretending those are external shocks and admit that many of them are already being purchased, negatively, through the design choices they call efficient.

Measuring resilience without false precision

In March 2011, after the earthquake and tsunami in Japan triggered the Fukushima Daiichi nuclear disaster, one lesson emerged with unusual force: systems can appear tightly measured and still prove institutionally fragile under stress. Technical indicators mattered. So did backup procedures, engineering assumptions, and emergency plans. Yet the deeper failure was not captured by a neat dashboard. It involved governance, communication, hierarchy, and the limits of what institutions were willing to imagine in advance. The gauges were not enough.

That problem extends far beyond nuclear infrastructure. Modern states and large organisations increasingly want resilience to be measurable in the same way they measure throughput, uptime, cost, compliance, or growth. The impulse is understandable. Leaders want something they can compare, track, and report. Auditors want evidence. Procurement teams want thresholds. Regulators want indicators that can distinguish prudent preparedness from vague reassurance. Yet resilience resists easy quantification because it is not merely a property of machines. It is a property of institutions acting through machines under pressure. The score may look precise. The system may still break where nobody had thought to measure.

This is why false precision is so tempting and so dangerous. A dashboard can show backup completion rates, recovery time targets, incident counts, patching intervals, storage replication status, vendor certifications, or compliance against policy baselines. All of these may be useful. None of them captures, by itself, whether an institution understands its real dependencies, whether staff would know what to do if several assumptions failed at once, whether internal authority is clear during disruption, or whether people will surface bad news early enough to matter. The concept here is metric comfort: the sense that because something important is being counted, the thing itself is under control. That comfort often arrives precisely where deeper vulnerability is hardest to see.

A better approach begins by treating resilience as a qualitative condition supported by some quantitative evidence, not the other way round. The important question is not simply how many controls exist or how often a recovery test passed. It is whether the organisation has developed habits, structures, and knowledge that make adaptation under stress more likely. The visible signs are not mysterious. Can people explain who decides what during failure? Do teams know which services matter most and why?

Are dependencies mapped well enough that a regional outage, supplier collapse, or corrupted backup would not come as a conceptual surprise? Has the institution practised degraded operation, or only ideal restoration? These are plain questions. They are not easily reduced to a single score, which is one reason they matter.

Governance clarity is the first major indicator because confusion in authority often magnifies technical failure into organisational paralysis. A resilient institution knows who owns the service, who owns the data, who can declare an incident, who can authorise fallback procedures, who communicates with the public, and who can compel action from vendors or partner agencies. This is not glamorous. It is often more revealing than expensive technology. When governance is unclear, teams spend the opening hours of disruption negotiating their own roles, escalating sideways, and protecting themselves against blame. Recovery slows not because tools are absent, but because decision-making is muddy. In practical terms, governance clarity can be observed through behaviour: named owners, rehearsed decision paths, coherent escalation, and post-incident reviews that identify responsibility without descending into theatre.

This matters especially in public systems, where formal accountability and operational control often diverge. A ministry may be answerable to parliament, a contractor may run the platform, a cloud provider may control infrastructure, and a separate agency may manage identity or security functions. On paper, everyone has a role. Under pressure, that can mean no one has full command. A resilience assessment that measures only technical controls while ignoring governance fragmentation is assessing the wrong object. The system is not only the software stack. It is the chain of authority through which the stack is governed.

Testing culture is the second major indicator, and it is far more revealing than test documentation alone. Many organisations say they test disaster recovery, but the real question is what kind of testing they are willing to tolerate. Do they test only the scenarios most likely to pass? Do they rehearse with vendors present to smooth awkward edges? Do they test restoration from the same assumptions under which the primary system normally operates, or do they deliberately break dependencies, delay access, simulate missing staff, and force teams to operate with degraded information? A testing culture can be recognised by its appetite for embarrassment. Institutions that genuinely value resilience allow tests to reveal weakness before the public does. Institutions that value appearances design tests that generate reassuring evidence.

A named example from cloud operations is useful here. Public and private organisations now commonly speak of failover and recovery testing as marks of maturity. Yet repeated real-world outages have shown that documented failover capability may still fail because the exercise did not resemble the incident that actually occurred. Credentials were unavailable, network assumptions were wrong, staff knowledge had drifted, or the supposedly independent recovery environment shared hidden dependencies with the primary one. The lesson is not that testing is futile. It is that resilience requires adversarial rehearsal, not ceremonial compliance. A passed test can mean several things. It can mean the system is ready. It can also mean the test was kind.

Dependency mapping is the third major indicator, and in many modern systems it may be the most important. Institutions often know their direct suppliers and immediate applications better than they know the hidden layers beneath them. A public service may rely on a specific cloud region, identity provider, software library, API gateway, telecoms carrier, logging platform, and contractor support arrangement without anyone maintaining a live picture of how these dependencies intersect. The visible service can appear self-contained while resting on a concentrated and fragile substrate. Dependency mapping asks a harder question than inventory management. It asks which failures would cascade, which single points of concentration sit outside public rhetoric, and which assumptions about independence are false because supposedly separate services share the same underlying components.

This is where qualitative assessment becomes especially valuable. A neat dashboard may show that backups exist, suppliers are certified, and service-level agreements are in place. A serious interviewer or auditor will ask different questions. Can the team explain which dependencies matter most for the first twenty-four hours of disruption? Which systems cannot function without identity? Which public services rely on the same region or vendor despite being procured separately? Which manual workarounds still exist, and when were they last used? Which data exports remain readable outside the primary platform? Can the organisation operate, even partially, if the main provider is available but trust in its integrity is not? These questions produce uneven, narrative answers. That is a strength, not a weakness. Resilience lives partly in explanation.

A second named example can be drawn from the repeated pressures placed on public services during the COVID-19 pandemic. Many institutions discovered that continuity depended not just on digital infrastructure but on previously unglamorous human and organisational factors: whether remote access had been planned sensibly, whether staff understood fallback procedures, whether records could be accessed without the usual buildings, whether call-centre scripts could adapt, whether procurement teams could move quickly without losing control, whether data-sharing arrangements were intelligible enough to scale under emergency conditions. These were resilience questions. They did not lend themselves neatly to pre-existing dashboards. Institutions that had clearer governance and stronger habits of adaptation often performed better than those with more elaborate but more brittle control frameworks.

A credible limitation should be acknowledged. Quantitative indicators are not useless. They matter for spotting neglect, comparing minimum baselines, and identifying obvious weaknesses. Patch rates, recovery objectives, backup integrity checks, staffing ratios, incident frequency, and audit completion can all contribute meaningfully to resilience assessment. An organisation that refuses all metrics in the name of complexity is usually hiding something or avoiding discipline. The problem is not counting. It is mistaking counted variables for the totality of the problem. Numbers are strongest when they support judgment rather than replacing it.

That limitation clarifies the real research agenda. A serious resilience assessment should combine hard indicators with qualitative inquiry into governance, culture, and dependency structure. It should ask whether staff can explain the system in human terms, whether failures are surfaced candidly, whether testing produces uncomfortable learning, whether review findings recur without consequence, and whether resilience language has drifted into ritual. It should also compare formal documentation with observed practice. Does the organisation describe one model of decision-making and enact another? Do vendors promise separations that engineers quietly know are thinner than the contract suggests? Do leaders celebrate redundancy while funding only the primary path? These gaps are difficult to score but easy to miss if scoring becomes the method.

The political value of this approach is considerable. False precision does not merely produce bad management. It can produce misplaced public confidence. A state that reports strong resilience through tidy indicators may reassure ministers and citizens while leaving deeper fragility untouched. The eventual failure then lands harder because the public has been taught to believe the system was prepared. By contrast, institutions that speak more honestly about uncertainty, dependency, and the limits of current resilience may appear less polished in the short term while building stronger legitimacy for the long term. Candour about preparedness is itself a resilience asset when it is paired with visible learning.

This is why measuring resilience must also involve institutional memory. Does the organisation remember past disruptions in a way that changes future design, or does each incident become a closed episode filed under lessons learned and then quietly forgotten? Do post-incident reviews alter procurement, staffing, architecture, and authority structures, or do they merely recommend better communication and more documentation? A resilient system stores not only data but judgment. It learns where its own dashboards misled it. That is one reason purely external assessment will always be partial. Researchers and auditors need internal narratives of failure as well as external evidence of control.

The quiet motif of the map helps hold the argument together. A dashboard is often treated as though it were the territory of resilience. It is not. It is, at best, one map of selected features. Good maps are useful. Bad maps are dangerous precisely because they create confidence in travellers who no longer look at the ground. Governance clarity, testing culture, and dependency mapping are ways of asking whether the institution understands the terrain beneath its own indicators. Does it know where the bridges really are, which roads share the same hidden tunnel, and which routes disappear in bad weather? A map that cannot answer those questions may still look wonderfully precise.

The harder question, then, is not whether resilience can be measured. It can, partly. The harder question is whether institutions are willing to measure it in ways that expose fragility rather than flatter management. That means accepting indicators that are qualitative, comparative, and sometimes awkwardly narrative. It means valuing explanation alongside scoring, and rehearsal alongside compliance. Above all, it means resisting the comfort of dashboards that reduce resilience to visible numbers while the real weakness remains lodged in authority, culture, and unspoken dependence. A state that wants to assess resilience seriously must decide whether it prefers the clean certainty of a score or the more demanding truth of a map that still contains warning signs.

Chapter 14

Strategic Choices for Data Power

What kind of state becomes stronger by seeing more, and what kind becomes brittle in the act of trying? The question sits behind every dispute in this book. Some governments centralise and compel. Some cultivate markets and hope competition will widen capacity. Some lean heavily on legal safeguards and independent oversight in order to preserve social consent. Others trade openness for speed, or consent for administrative reach, or market dynamism for tighter control. None of these choices is cost-free. Each builds one kind of strength by accepting one kind of exposure.

That is why the final task is not to choose a slogan but to recognise a pattern. States do not wield data power in identical ways, because they do not face identical political bargains. Some can demand compliance more easily because coercive authority runs deep and public challenge is constrained. Some depend on broad legitimacy because contested elections, independent media, and active courts make extraction politically expensive. Some sit atop powerful domestic firms and can govern partly through market structure. Others lack that luxury and must improvise through procurement, regulation, or foreign dependence. The architecture of data power therefore reflects not only technical ambition but constitutional temperament.

This creates the chapter's central tension. It is tempting to sort countries into moral caricatures: open versus closed, democratic versus authoritarian, innovative versus controlling, lawful versus extractive. Those labels may satisfy debate. They obscure analysis. Real regimes mix elements that do not fit neatly together. A state may protect privacy strongly in consumer markets while expanding security powers in the background. Another may build impressive digital public services while leaving weak remedies for those harmed by administrative error. A third may speak the language of sovereignty while depending heavily on foreign platforms. The serious question is not which state belongs to the right camp. It is which combination of control, openness, and legitimacy strategy it is actually pursuing, and what that combination permits or sacrifices over time.

The stakes are high because strategic error in this domain rarely looks like error at first. A model that concentrates power may deliver speed, visibility, and disciplined coordination until legitimacy begins to fray. A model that prizes openness and market dynamism may attract innovation while leaving critical dependencies unresolved. A model that surrounds sensitive systems with dense oversight may appear cumbersome in the short term while quietly building the trust needed for durable adoption. Strategic choices in data governance therefore have a delayed character. They alter what a state can ask of citizens, firms, and institutions years later, often after the original architects have left office. What looks efficient in one political season can harden into fragility in the next.

This is why institutional design deserves to stand beside infrastructure and law as a primary object of judgment. Oversight bodies, courts, regulators, auditors, procurement offices, and public-interest technical teams are often described as restraints on power. Sometimes they are. More importantly, they are devices through which power becomes sustainable. A state that can verify, contest, and correct its own use of data can often deploy that data more effectively over time than one that governs through opacity and intermittent force. Checks and balances are not only moral brakes. They are capacity multipliers when legitimacy is contested. Independent auditing, for example, may slow deployment at the margins while making adoption of sensitive systems politically durable enough to survive scandal or change of government.

That durability is the true theme here. Durable strategy does not mean freezing one model and defending it forever. It means aligning infrastructure, incentives, and legal authority in ways that can survive technical change without relying on permanent emergency. A brittle regime chases each new tool - platform, model, identity scheme, cloud arrangement, surveillance technique - as though novelty itself confers strategic advantage. A durable one asks harder questions. Who controls the stack? Who can contest the decision? Which dependencies are being deepened? What happens when a breach, outage, or scandal arrives? How much social consent is being spent, and what is replenishing it? Strategy begins when those questions become ordinary rather than exceptional.

The path ahead follows that logic. It begins by establishing a comparative typology that can sort national data regimes without flattening them into propaganda, then moves to the institutional machinery through which contested systems are made governable over time, before arriving at the larger synthesis: what it means to build data power that does not consume the legitimacy on which it ultimately depends. The movement is deliberate. Classification without institutions becomes abstraction. Institutions without strategy become administrative detail. Strategy without trust becomes self-cancelling ambition.

A useful image for this closing chapter is the hinge. Much of the book has concerned weight: infrastructures, datasets, legal powers, markets, archives, platforms, and institutions that accumulate mass over time. But strategic choice often turns on the hinge rather than the door. A hinge determines how force moves, how far a system can open without tearing itself loose, and whether repeated use strengthens or weakens the structure around it. Data power works in much the same way. The decisive issue is not only how much a state possesses, but whether its mechanisms of control, oversight, and public justification can bear repeated strain without seizing up or splintering.

That image matters because the most serious mistakes in this field come from treating constraint as weakness and adaptation as indecision. A state that cannot revise its model after scandal, court challenge, procurement failure, or public backlash is not strategically confident. It is strategically trapped. A state that builds institutions able to absorb criticism, expose dependency, and recalibrate authority may look slower, noisier, or less visually commanding. It is often stronger in the only sense that matters over decades: it can keep governing after the first theory of power begins to fail.

The harder question, then, is not which country has more data, more advanced tools, or louder claims about sovereignty. The harder question is which regimes have built a form of data power that can persist without exhausting markets, courts, or the public trust on which continued rule depends. That question leads directly to the first task: how to distinguish the major types of national data regime without mistaking classification for caricature.

A typology of national data regimes

In June 2017, China's Cybersecurity Law came into force and gave clearer legal form to a model of data governance that many outside observers had already begun to recognise: strong state steering over networks, infrastructure, and data localisation, combined with close entanglement between public authority and major domestic technology firms. The law did not by itself create that model. It clarified the terms on which it would operate. For analysts abroad, the temptation was immediate and familiar. Here, surely, was one obvious type: centralised, controlling, security-first. The temptation was also misleading. No national data regime is explained fully by one statute, one ideology, or one headline label.

That is the problem a serious typology must solve. Comparative analysis needs categories, because without categories every case becomes a blur of local detail and rhetorical noise. Yet categories become dangerous when they flatten real regimes into caricatures: open versus closed, democratic versus authoritarian, market-led versus state-led. Those binaries can be politically useful. They are analytically weak. They obscure the fact that most data regimes combine elements that sit uneasily together. A government may champion digital markets while quietly widening security powers. Another may centralise identity and records while still relying heavily on private platforms. A third may advertise privacy and legality while tolerating commercial concentration that leaves citizens exposed in different ways. The door has more than one hinge.

A more useful typology therefore begins from three questions rather than one. How much direct control does the state seek over data flows, infrastructures, and access? How much openness does it permit or encourage in markets, standards, and cross-border exchange? And how does it pursue legitimacy - through coercive authority, through material performance, through legal restraint, through public consent, or through some unstable combination of all four? These questions do not produce perfect boxes. They do something better. They allow comparison without pretending that every case must fit one moral stereotype. The concept here is patterned variation. Regimes differ not only by what they value, but by which trade-offs they are willing to make repeatedly.

The first broad type can be described as the control-heavy regime. In this model, the state prioritises visibility, access, and command over data-bearing infrastructures. It tends to favour central authority, strong localisation impulses, closer alignment between security doctrine and digital governance, and more limited tolerance for organisational opacity beyond state reach. The visible advantages are coherence and speed. The state can often compel data, set standards quickly, and integrate surveillance, administration, and industrial strategy with relatively little overt institutional friction. The sacrifice usually comes in another currency: weaker external checks, narrower space for contestation, higher risks of mission creep, and a thinner distinction between state capacity and state overreach. Such regimes may look strong because they can see more. They may become brittle because fewer institutions can challenge how that sight is used.

China is the most obvious named example, though even here simplification would mislead. The system is not merely a monolith of command. It contains provincial variation, commercial ambition, bureaucratic competition, and real tensions between innovation, security, and political control. But as a regime type, it illustrates the control-heavy strategy well enough: public authority seeks extensive leverage over firms, infrastructure, and data circulation, and legitimacy rests substantially on performance, order, and state capacity rather than on strong adversarial checks. That does not mean the regime is immune to public legitimacy concerns. It means those concerns are managed through different institutions and under different political limits than in liberal constitutional orders.

A second type can be described as the market-coordinated regime. Here the state relies more heavily on private firms, competition, procurement, and regulatory steering than on direct command over the entire data environment. Control is looser, market openness is higher, and national capability often depends on the strength of domestic technology sectors as much as on public administration. The visible advantage is dynamism. Such regimes can produce powerful firms, rapid innovation, and strong global influence through standards, platforms, and cloud infrastructure. The sacrifice is often concentration, uneven public accountability, and a tendency to discover too late that critical functions have drifted into the hands of a small number of firms whose interests do not perfectly align with national resilience or democratic oversight.

The United States illustrates much of this type, though again not in pure form. It combines powerful security institutions, deep alliances, strong corporate data capacity, and a comparatively decentralised political order in which market structure often shapes public capability as much as formal state design does. Its strength lies partly in the scale and global reach of its firms and research base. Its recurring weakness lies in the tension between public dependence on private infrastructures and fragmented legitimacy over how those infrastructures are governed. It is not simply "open". It is a regime in which openness, corporate concentration, and security power coexist uneasily.

A third type might be called the legitimacy-intensive regime. Here the central political problem is not only how to gather and use data, but how to do so in ways compatible with strong rights claims, layered oversight, and sustained public justification. Such regimes often develop dense privacy rules, active courts, visible regulators, and a greater willingness to restrict or discipline data practices that appear economically efficient but politically unsustainable. The visible advantage is trustworthiness, or at least a stronger capacity to claim trustworthiness credibly in domestic and international settings. The sacrifice is often speed, simplicity, and sometimes domestic industrial scale. Systems may be slower to integrate, more procedurally burdened, or less hospitable to some forms of platform expansion because legitimacy is treated as a constitutive design requirement rather than as a secondary corrective.

The European Union, taken as a regulatory bloc rather than a unitary state, offers the clearest example. It does not control data with the direct command capacity associated with more centralised authoritarian systems, nor does it rely as heavily as the United States on giant domestic technology firms to project power. Instead it often governs through law, supervision, adequacy decisions, market access conditions, and a normative language that links data governance to rights and democratic accountability. This strategy confers real influence. It also creates tensions: between privacy and industrial ambition, between national security exceptions and shared legitimacy claims, and between regulatory prestige and operational capacity. A legitimacy-intensive regime may be normatively powerful while remaining infrastructurally dependent.

These types are useful because they reveal what each model tends to sacrifice. Control-heavy regimes often sacrifice contestability. Market-coordinated regimes often sacrifice public direction. Legitimacy-intensive regimes often sacrifice speed and sometimes domestic scale. None of these sacrifices is absolute. None guarantees failure. The point is comparative discipline. When a state claims it can maximise security, innovation, and trust simultaneously with no serious trade-offs, the claim should be treated with suspicion. Typology is valuable precisely because it forces such claims back into visible tension.

A credible limitation should be acknowledged. Real countries do not sit neatly inside these types, and many hybrid cases matter more than the ideal forms. India, for example, combines strong state ambition around digital identity and public infrastructure with democratic contestation, market complexity, and uneven legitimacy across institutions and social groups. Singapore combines administrative sophistication and significant state coordination with a different political bargain around public trust and managed openness. Smaller states may borrow regulatory models, cloud architectures, or procurement patterns from larger powers while stitching them into local constitutional traditions. A typology that pretends these hybrids are merely incomplete versions of the "pure" types would be a poor one.

But that limitation does not weaken the value of classification. It sharpens it. The purpose of a typology is not to trap every case in a fixed box. It is to identify dominant tendencies and recurring trade-offs. A useful typology allows one to say that a regime leans strongly towards control while borrowing legitimacy language, or relies on market dynamism while building targeted sovereignty measures, or foregrounds rights while quietly expanding exemptions in security or migration domains. It creates vocabulary for mixed cases without collapsing into either moralism or relativism. The question becomes not "Which camp does this country belong to?" but "Which combination of control, openness, and legitimacy strategies is doing the real work here?"

This matters because strategic choices in data power are path dependent. A regime that normalises central command over infrastructure and data access may later find it hard to make room for meaningful external oversight. A regime that outsources capability to markets may discover that rebuilding state direction is more difficult than announcing a new industrial policy. A regime that invests heavily in legitimacy through law and review may gain long-term trust but struggle to move quickly in crisis or to sustain indigenous technological scale. These are not temporary policy moods. They shape the institutional reflexes through which later conflicts are handled. Typology is therefore also a way of seeing the future inside the present.

The quiet motif of the hinge is useful here because it captures the difference between possession and movement. Two doors may look equally solid. Their hinges determine how they actually open, how much strain they can absorb, and whether repeated pressure will strengthen or damage the frame. Data regimes are much the same. Their formal structures matter, but the decisive issue is often how control, openness, and legitimacy are hinged together. Where does contestation enter? Where does coercion dominate? Where do markets substitute for public capacity? Where do oversight and rights function as real stabilisers rather than ceremonial adornments? These are hinge questions. They tell us how the regime moves.

This approach also helps distinguish national power from simple technical prowess. A state may possess advanced surveillance systems, large data stores, powerful firms, or admired digital public services and still operate a strategically weak regime if those assets are built on legitimacy deficits, concentrated dependencies, or uncorrectable institutional habits. Another may appear procedurally cumbersome and still prove more durable because its checks and balances preserve public tolerance and adaptive capacity. Typology, at its best, turns attention away from spectacle and towards structure. It asks not which system looks most commanding in a given year, but which can continue governing effectively once crisis, scandal, or geopolitical pressure begins to test the underlying bargain.

The harder question, then, is not whether one regime type is universally best. No such answer survives contact with real political orders. The harder question is what each regime can sustain, what it cannot admit to sacrificing, and how long its chosen balance between control, openness, and legitimacy can hold before the costs begin to surface as strategic weakness. That is the point at which typology stops being an exercise in classification and becomes a method of judgment. It asks of every case the same severe question: what kind of power is this system actually building, and what kind of failure is it quietly preparing for in the process?

Institutional design under contested legitimacy

In July 2020, the Court of Justice of the European Union handed down its judgment in *Schrems II* and invalidated the Privacy Shield framework governing certain transfers of personal data from the European Union to the United States. To many observers, the case looked like a conflict between law and innovation, or between judicial principle and administrative convenience. It was both, and more than either. A court had intervened in the architecture of transatlantic data governance because the institutions meant to reconcile commercial integration, state surveillance powers, and rights protection had not produced a settlement robust enough to command lasting legitimacy. The ruling did not simply disrupt flows. It exposed the political importance of the bodies that decide whether a data regime deserves to endure.

That is the proper place to begin because institutional design is often treated as secondary to the great forces of the digital age: infrastructure, market size, platform power, security doctrine, industrial strategy. Yet over time it is institutions - oversight bodies, courts, regulators, auditors, procurement offices, parliamentary committees, and technically literate public authorities - that decide whether ambitious systems remain governable once enthusiasm fades and contestation begins. They do not merely slow power down. They shape what kind of power can become durable. When legitimacy is contested, their design becomes strategic.

This is the central claim that states often resist for understandable reasons. Checks and balances are frequently described by political leaders as friction, and sometimes they are. Independent review delays deployment. Audit requirements complicate procurement. Judicial scrutiny upsets diplomatic arrangements. Regulators demand documentation, revision, and clearer boundaries than executive agencies or firms would naturally prefer. From the perspective of a ministry eager to deliver quickly, these institutions can feel parasitic on capability. The deeper truth is almost the opposite. In sensitive domains, they are often the mechanism through which capability becomes usable over decades rather than spectacular for a few months. The concept here is authorised endurance. A system that cannot survive scrutiny is not strong. It is merely under-inspected.

This is why contested legitimacy changes the value of institutional design. In low-contestation environments, states may extract, integrate, and deploy new data powers with relatively little visible resistance. In democracies and mixed systems, and increasingly even in more centralised polities facing public distrust, the problem is harder. New tools arrive into a political field already shaped by scandal, litigation, vendor dependence, media polarisation, and unequal administrative experience. Citizens, firms, and civil society actors ask not only what the system does, but who can check it, who can stop it, who can audit it, and what happens when it goes wrong. The visible behaviour is procedural - a hearing, an injunction, an audit, a procurement challenge, a regulatory opinion. The strategic implication is profound. These institutions decide whether disagreement remains governable or turns into recurring crisis.

Courts are the most dramatic of these actors because their interventions are public, authoritative, and sometimes sudden. Yet their deeper role is cumulative rather than theatrical. Courts build expectations about proportionality, legality, due process, redress, and the boundaries of institutional imagination. A single ruling may strike down a programme or narrow a power. More importantly, a line of rulings teaches both states and firms what kinds of justification will no longer suffice. The result is often not paralysis but adaptation. Organisations learn to design with litigation in mind. That can be a burden. It can also be a source of strategic discipline, forcing actors to think harder about the conditions under which their systems will remain politically and legally tenable.

A named example from Germany illustrates this long time horizon. The German Federal Constitutional Court has repeatedly shaped the country's information order through decisions about privacy, census practices, telecommunications, and information self-determination. The significance of those interventions does not lie only in the particular doctrines they established. It lies in the way they altered institutional reflexes. Agencies, legislators, and firms operating in that environment cannot easily treat data power as an unrestricted administrative good. They must anticipate a constitutional language in which dignity, proportionality, and informational control are not decorative ideals but operative constraints. That can frustrate rapid expansion. It can also stabilise legitimacy by making the limits more thinkable before scandal forces them into view.

Regulators matter differently. They inhabit the quieter middle ground between law on the books and systems in operation. A strong data protection authority, competition regulator, telecommunications supervisor, or sector-specific oversight body can force documentation, demand design changes, shape standards, and narrow vague ambitions into reviewable procedures. These are not glamorous functions. They are often decisive. A regulator with expertise and institutional confidence can make an organisation answer questions before a crisis, rather than after one. A weak regulator, by contrast, may create the appearance of control while leaving the real bargaining power with ministries, dominant firms, or security agencies. The issue is not whether regulation exists. It is whether regulation has the staffing, authority, and independence to turn abstract powers into operational friction.

Auditing deserves special emphasis because it often provides the most durable bridge between public trust and technical complexity. Independent auditing can stabilise adoption of sensitive systems precisely because it allows a state or firm to say something more serious than "trust us". An audit does not eliminate disagreement. It does create a recurring, inspectable practice through which claims about model performance, access controls, retention policies, procurement compliance, or lawful use can be checked against evidence. The visible behaviour may be humdrum: logs reviewed, controls tested, samples examined, failures classified, recommendations issued. The strategic value lies in repetition. Trust grows less from one dramatic assurance than from an institutional rhythm in which outsiders can verify that assurance has not become empty.

This is why auditing should not be mistaken for a purely technical ritual. In contested legitimacy, it is part of the political settlement. Consider digital identity, algorithmic decision support, or sensitive data-sharing arrangements inside government. Public resistance often does not arise because citizens demand to inspect every line of code or every operational detail. It arises because they do not know whether anyone independent has the authority, competence, and persistence to do so on their behalf. An audit regime answers that uncertainty. Poorly designed audits, of course, answer it badly. Box-ticking exercises, consultant-managed self-assessment, vague public summaries, and non-comparable findings can deepen cynicism. But serious auditing, especially when tied to remedial power, is one of the clearest examples of checks acting as capability enablers rather than as mere brakes.

Procurement offices belong in this conversation for the same reason, though they are often neglected by political theory. Procurement decides which vendors enter the state, which standards become normal, how much exit becomes possible later, and how much operational knowledge remains public rather than migrating into contractors. A strategically weak procurement office buys speed and loses sovereignty in instalments. A strategically strong one asks awkward questions early enough to matter: who will own the logs, how will portability work, what audit rights exist, what happens if the supplier fails, how can another provider realistically replace this one, and what internal capability must remain in-house for the state to keep governing the system it has bought? These are not clerical concerns. They are long-range constitutional choices expressed through contract structure.

A second named example lies in Estonia's digital state, often praised for coherence and efficiency. What deserves equal attention is not only the technical architecture but the institutional arrangement around it: persistent state capacity, auditing disciplines, legal form, and a political culture more willing than many peers to treat digital infrastructure as a matter of public design rather than procurement improvisation alone. Estonia should not be romanticised. It faces its own vulnerabilities and is not a universally transferable model. Yet it demonstrates something important: sensitive systems become more politically usable when institutions capable of checking, explaining, and revising them are built alongside the infrastructure rather than after controversy arrives.

A credible limitation should be acknowledged. Institutional density does not automatically produce wisdom. Courts can overreach, regulators can become timid or captured, auditors can normalise poor practice through ritualised compliance, and procurement offices can turn caution into stagnation. There are moments when checks genuinely slow necessary action, when fragmented authority produces confusion, and when procedural burdens benefit incumbents more than the public. It would be naive to describe all oversight as inherently enabling. Sometimes it functions exactly as a brake.

But that limitation clarifies the more serious point. The problem is not whether institutions constrain. The problem is how they constrain, and in whose interest. Badly designed checks create delay without trust, compliance without understanding, and fragmentation without accountability. Well-designed checks create review without paralysis, correction without collapse, and contestation without institutional breakdown. That is why institutional design matters more than the abstract existence of oversight. Independence alone is not enough. Competence matters. Access matters. Continuity matters. The authority to demand change matters. So does public legibility. An auditor who sees everything but can tell the public nothing useful may improve internal discipline while doing little for wider legitimacy. An under-resourced regulator may possess noble statutory powers and still leave the real field governed by the actors it was meant to supervise.

This is where long time horizons become crucial. Oversight institutions shape outcomes not mainly by dramatic intervention but by repeated patterning. They influence what ministries dare to propose, what firms anticipate regulators will ask, what procurement teams build into contracts, what technical teams document, and what kinds of shortcuts start to look too risky or too embarrassing to attempt. Over decades, those patterned expectations form a governance culture. Some systems become normal because they can survive being checked. Others remain brittle because their architects hope scrutiny will never become serious enough to test them. Institutional design, then, is not only about dispute resolution. It is about pre-emptive statecraft.

This also explains why contested legitimacy should not be treated as a temporary communications problem. Where public trust is thin, where firms are large, where security powers are expansive, and where administrative harms have accumulated unevenly, the state cannot restore confidence simply by speaking more clearly or promising better ethics. It needs institutions capable of absorbing conflict without converting each controversy into a constitutional rupture. Courts, regulators, auditors, and procurement offices do this in different registers, but the strategic effect is similar. They turn disagreement into governed process. Without that transformation, the same system that appears technically elegant may become politically uninhabitable.

The quiet motif of the hinge is useful here. Infrastructure supplies weight. Law supplies frame. Institutions such as courts, auditors, and procurement offices supply the hinge on which power can move without tearing the structure loose. A door without a hinge is not freer. It is unusable. The same is true of data power. A regime that treats checks as enemies may move quickly for a while, but it risks wrenching its own authority from the frame that makes continued rule possible. A regime that builds hinges too weakly may find that every new strain produces sagging, sticking, and public mistrust. Strategic strength lies not in abolishing the hinge, but in designing it well enough that repeated pressure does not destroy the doorway.

That is why institutional design under contested legitimacy should be judged by a severe but practical standard. Does it make sensitive systems more corrigible, more reviewable, and therefore more adoptable over time? Does it keep expertise public enough that oversight bodies can ask intelligent questions? Does it allow governments to proceed where justified while preserving real routes for challenge and redesign? Does it transform trust from a ministerial demand into an institutional achievement? These questions matter more than the familiar dispute between agility and bureaucracy. Agility without durable legitimacy is often just speed on credit.

The harder question, then, is not whether states can govern effectively while being checked. Many do. The harder question is whether they can build institutions strong enough that checking becomes part of governing rather than an interruption to it. Where legitimacy is contested, that distinction determines everything. A state that understands it can adopt difficult systems and still retain room to revise them when they fail. A state that does not will keep mistaking resistance for obstruction and oversight for weakness, until the very capacities it sought to build become impossible to defend in public at all.

What durable strategy looks like

In May 2017, the WannaCry ransomware attack disrupted parts of the United Kingdom's National Health Service and made an old truth newly visible: a state can possess advanced intelligence agencies, strong legal authority, and vast stores of data, yet still find its practical capacity undone by misaligned systems, neglected maintenance, brittle procurement, and weak institutional coordination. The episode was discussed as a cyber incident, and it was that. It was also a strategic lesson. National power in the information age does not reside in technical assets alone. It depends on whether infrastructure, law, and incentives have been arranged so that data can be used with continuity, legitimacy, and restraint under pressure. The network was there. The alignment was not.

That is the core claim this book has pursued from several directions. Data power is not mainly about scale, nor about the romance of artificial intelligence, nor about the prestige of building larger platforms, nor about the fantasy that sovereignty can be restored by slogan. It is about organised capacity. Organised capacity means a state can collect, verify, share, protect, limit, and justify the use of data in ways that support security, economic coordination, and legitimate governance without destroying the social and institutional conditions that make those gains durable. The adjective matters. Plenty of states and firms can gather information. Fewer can govern the consequences of gathering it.

A durable strategy therefore begins with alignment. Infrastructure must support the purposes law authorises. Law must match the realities of technical systems rather than gesturing vaguely towards them. Incentives must reward restraint, correction, and resilience rather than mere accumulation, speed, or extraction. Public trust must be treated not as decorative sentiment but as a resource that institutions can either cultivate or spend down. The concept is simple enough to state and hard to build: data power lasts when the parts of the system stop pulling against one another. A state that centralises data while fragmenting oversight, promises rights while outsourcing intelligibility, or relies on market dynamism while neglecting dependency will eventually discover that one part of its strategy has been quietly sabotaging another.

This is why durable strategy looks less like technological maximalism and more like disciplined settlement. A government with a durable strategy knows which functions require deep control, which can tolerate market dependence, which legal powers need stronger justification, which infrastructures are too concentrated to remain invisible, and which social bargains cannot be stretched indefinitely without political recoil. The visible behaviour is not dramatic. It appears in procurement choices, retention rules, audit rights, fallback plans, court-tested authorisations, data-sharing limits, and the quality of official explanation when a scandal or outage arrives. These things do not usually win headlines. They decide whether the next headline becomes a crisis.

A named example from Estonia remains useful, not because it offers a universally exportable model, but because it shows what alignment can look like in practice. Estonia's digital public infrastructure has often been admired for convenience and coherence. Its deeper significance lies in the relationship between identity systems, legal design, administrative capacity, and a political willingness to treat digital governance as a matter of institutional architecture rather than isolated modernisation projects. The lesson is not that every state should imitate Estonia's form. The lesson is that systems become durable when technical design, public authority, and accountability mechanisms are built together rather than bolted onto one another after failure.

A second named example points in the opposite direction. The repeated turbulence around transatlantic data transfers, culminating in decisions such as *Schrems II* in 2020, showed what happens when infrastructure, market incentives, security practices, and rights claims remain out of joint. Firms wanted continuity, states wanted intelligence flexibility, regulators and courts demanded stronger rights protection, and the governing arrangements repeatedly proved too thin to carry the political and legal weight placed upon them. This was not a marginal dispute. It revealed a central feature of contemporary power: if legal and institutional design do not match the realities of how data move and how states use access, then no amount of economic necessity will produce a stable settlement. Flow without legitimacy is not durability. It is suspended conflict.

That is why durable strategy must reject two temptations that dominate public argument. The first is techno-optimism: the belief that enough compute, enough data, enough digitisation, or enough machine learning will solve underlying political and organisational weaknesses. It will not. Technical systems can intensify both competence and incompetence. A state with poor correction mechanisms, weak procurement, and thin legitimacy may simply automate its own strategic errors. The second temptation is alarmism: the belief that every new technology creates a wholly new world requiring total conceptual reinvention. That is equally misleading. New tools matter, sometimes enormously, but the recurring questions are surprisingly stable. Who controls access? Who sets standards? Who bears dependency risk? Who can contest misuse? Who verifies deletion, provenance, or audit claims? Which institutions gain optionality, and which populations bear the burden when optionality is exercised against them?

These questions suggest a comparative method more durable than headline-chasing. When a new technology arrives - generative AI in public administration, biometric border systems, digital currencies, privacy-enhancing computation, federated identity, quantum-safe security, or something not yet named - the first task is not to ask whether it is revolutionary. The first task is to locate it inside the same three-part frame that has guided this book: infrastructure, institutions, and incentives. What physical and organisational stack does it depend on? What legal authorities, oversight bodies, procurement choices, and correction mechanisms govern it? What incentives drive adoption, overuse, underuse, concealment, or exaggeration? A system that looks extraordinary in marketing language often becomes more legible once these ordinary questions are applied to it.

A serious research agenda follows from this. It should compare not only technologies but state capacities for governing them. It should ask how countries differ in procurement competence, audit culture, data-sharing discipline, retention control, incident response, judicial scrutiny, and the public narratives that sustain or erode social licence. It should study not only moments of successful rollout but moments of scandal, outage, litigation, and forced redesign, because durability reveals itself most clearly where systems are stressed. It should also compare sectors, not just states. A country may govern health data credibly while handling policing data poorly, or build strong public identity while remaining dangerously dependent in cloud infrastructure. "National strategy" is often less coherent than official documents imply. Comparative work should be severe enough to see this.

This is also where false precision must be resisted. Durable strategy cannot be captured fully by one index, one ranking, or one scorecard. States love such instruments because they condense complexity into clean comparative pictures. Investors, consultants, and commentators love them for the same reason. But a state can score well on digitisation, cloud adoption, AI ambition, or cybersecurity maturity while remaining institutionally fragile. The real indicators of durability are often qualitative and stubbornly contextual: whether officials can explain their own dependencies, whether audits produce consequence, whether deletion is verifiable, whether courts and regulators have enough technical literacy to matter, whether fallback procedures exist beyond paper, whether trust survives the first major scandal, whether procurement preserves future choice instead of purchasing future captivity. Hard things to count. Still decisive.

A credible limitation should be admitted. No state can optimise every dimension at once. Trade-offs are real. Tighter control can improve continuity and weaken openness. Stronger privacy safeguards can complicate some forms of rapid investigation or platform innovation. Competitive markets can widen capability while increasing security and dependency risks. Dense oversight can stabilise legitimacy while slowing deployment. It would be unserious to promise a frictionless synthesis in which security, liberty, innovation, resilience, and public consent all rise together without conflict. Durable strategy does not abolish trade-offs. It organises them more honestly.

That limitation strengthens the argument because honesty about sacrifice is one of the marks of strategic maturity. A durable regime knows what it is choosing and what it is giving up. It does not pretend that coercive visibility is the same as trust, that market dynamism is the same as sovereignty, or that legality is the same as social licence. It understands that some forms of speed destroy the conditions of later stability, and that some forms of restraint are not weakness but investment in future governability. The problem with many contemporary data strategies is not that they choose wrongly in every case. It is that they describe themselves as win-win projects even when their underlying bargains are plainly conflictual. Self-deception is a strategic vulnerability.

The quiet motif of the hinge returns here because it best captures what durable strategy really entails. Infrastructure supplies weight. Law supplies frame. Incentives determine the direction of force. Public trust determines how much strain the system can bear before resistance becomes rupture. The hinge is the arrangement that lets these parts move together rather than tearing apart under repeated use. A state may possess immense informational weight and still fail if the hinge is weak: if oversight is decorative, if procurement sells away comprehension, if rights are declared but hard to use, if concentration is hidden until outage, if correction depends on scandal, if legitimacy is treated as something to be managed after deployment rather than built into it.

What durable strategy looks like, then, is less glamorous than most political speeches and more ambitious than most technical roadmaps. It looks like institutions capable of saying no as well as yes. It looks like data infrastructures that can be audited, migrated, and recovered. It looks like procurement that preserves intelligibility. It looks like deletion and archiving rules that recognise both accountability and forgetting as public goods. It looks like legal authorities narrow enough to be defended and flexible enough to remain useful. It looks like market design that cultivates capability without sleepwalking into dependency. It looks like a state that can explain what it is doing before a leak, a breach, or a court order forces the explanation.

This is not a formula. It is a discipline of questions. Which dependencies are being normalised? Which powers are being routinised? Which rights are usable in practice? Which institutions can expose hidden fragility? Which populations bear the cost of classification and error? Which narratives of necessity are masking unresolved strategic bargains? Which parts of the system would still make sense to an informed outsider after the first serious failure? A durable lens for the information age does not chase novelty. It returns, again and again, to the alignment of infrastructure, law, incentives, and trust.

The harder question, then, is not whether data will matter to national power. That has already been settled. The harder question is whether states can build forms of data power that remain effective after success, after scandal, after vendor concentration, after litigation, after public resistance, and after the next technological fashion has spent its rhetorical energy. Any regime can look powerful while conditions are favourable and scrutiny is thin. Durable strategy begins where favourable conditions end. It asks whether the system that has been built can survive being known fully enough to be challenged - and still govern.

About the Author

Kiran Solvay is a nonfiction writer focused on how states turn information into capacity, and how that same process tests the legitimacy of modern governance. With an academic sensibility and a clear editorial voice, Solvay approaches data not as an abstract "tech" topic but as a practical foundation of institutions: budgets, procurement, oversight, standards, and the slow accumulation of administrative habits. The central interest is structural rather than scandal-driven: why some systems produce resilience and public confidence, while others produce brittle dependence, quiet coercion, or cycles of backlash and reform.

Solvay's work is grounded in close reading of public rules, institutional design choices, and the history of state recordkeeping, with particular attention to the grey zones where commercial platforms, security agencies, and regulators overlap. A recurring thread is the European experience of rebuilding governance after rupture, when memory, documentation, and accountability became political necessities as well as moral commitments. That background sensibility informs a consistent question throughout the book: what kinds of "knowing" help a society govern itself, and what kinds quietly undermine consent?

Across complex debates about surveillance, cloud infrastructure, and privacy, Solvay writes for readers who want frameworks they can test, not slogans they can repeat. The aim is to make the power dynamics of data systems legible, so that students, analysts, and informed citizens can argue about trade-offs with clearer concepts and fewer illusions.

www.ingramcontent.com/pod-product-compliance
Lightning Source LLC
Chambersburg PA
CBHW031320230926
51848CB00001B/24

* 9 7 8 9 3 7 7 9 4 2 3 0 4 *